# Land, Landed Elites & Resource Management: South India

# Land, Landed Elites & Resource Management: South India

Dr. J.C. Dua

Delhi-110052

Published by
**Originals**
A-6, Nimri Commercial Centre,
Near Ashok Vihar Phase-IV, Delhi-110052
Phones: 27302453
e-mail: lpp@nde.vsnl.net.in
visit us at: www.lppindia.com



First Published 2007

ISBN 81-88629-62-6

Printed at
**D K Fine Art Press P. Ltd.**
Delhi-110052



PRINTED IN INDIA

# *Preface*

The state through the ages, has always been the instrument of the ruling classes for the exploitation of the ruled, i.e. the direct producers. At the same time, there has been no state in history, which has not performed public functions through which the ruled would have derived some benefits. Other thing, which has been observed in the study of history of English rule in India that the then rulers never completely understood who the proprietor of land was? It was essential because it was he who would be made responsible for paying land revenue according to the tax theory of political economy. Several 'theories', such as state landownership, joint tenure by the village or private ownership of landed property by peasants, were put forward. None of them was sufficiently supported by historical sources. In the present book, which is incidentally a collection of some of my articles presented at various stages of the career, an attempt has been to highlight some of the above subjects in regard to the history of south India.

The article on 'British Economic Thought and Ideas of Thomas Munro on the Introduction of *Rayatwari* System' is an attempt to assess the ideas of different economic thinkers on the land rights and land systems during the pre-British and the early phase of their rule in the south India. The ideas of Thomas Munro and his contemporary Company's officials have also been given a critical assessment. The ultimate analysis is that the essential distinctions between the various types of revenue systems introduced by the East India Company and the forms of agrarian relations accruing out of them did not alter the basic fact that the agrarian system and methods of exploiting the peasants developed in one and the same direction throughout the country.

Through the paper entitled 'Method of Land Measurement and Assessment in Northern Circars during the Pre-British Era as reflected in the *Chetri Ganitam*', hitherto untapped, an important source on indigenous method of land measurement and assessment has been discussed. The importance of the source lies in the fact that this is perhaps one of the very few sources which have given a detailed list of various types of fields, systems of measurement, and the seed consumption and the yield regarding different crops produced in the area.

The paper on the 'Position of *Patels* and *Karnums* in the 'Ceded Districts' during the first quarter of the nineteenth century' is an attempt on an assessment of the position hereditarily enjoyed by these indispensable officials of the local administration and the changes brought therein by the English administrators during the initial decades of their rule in the area concerned. The research based on the records preserved in the various archives in south India and the National Archives shows that barring the political power that the *patels* and the *karnums* had unlawfully attained because of the political disturbances immediately before the districts were ceded to the East India Company, they continued to enjoy the influential position in the land revenue administration of the villages. Being thc early stages of the establishment of the English administration in the areas under research, it would not be wrong to say that the new administrators had acted rightly by not disturbing the local administration as it could have certainly become difficult for them to maintain the law and order to run the revenue administration on smooth footing.

The paper on 'Drought Management in 'Ceded Districts' during the 19th Century' is a critical appraisal of management of drought situations in the concerned areas during the different phases of 19th century and an analysis of the perception and response of the inhabitants/cultivators. The study based on the contemporary documents/sources shows that the English government certainly took steps to salvage the Ceded Districts from the droughts but continued to suffer greatly from droughts, famines and epidemics because their intentions were altogether different. The British firms were able to exploit hired agricultural labourers and reap monopoly on the world market. No doubt the economic effects of irrigation were significant, India's agriculture became more specialized and more industrial crops were grown.

The two papers on 'Nature of Poligar Revolts in the 'Ceded Districts' during the first half of nineteenth century: A Case Study' and 'Landed Elites in Upheaval-Forms and Contents of Resistance of the Palegars-1800-1846 are attempts to highlight the fact that no doubt there had been a continuous resistance against the English rule right since its inception, whereas the earlier revolts were mostly political in character, in the course of time the revolts had started comprising much larger canvas. In latter cases majority of persons who joined and formed the backbone of these revolts were higher and lower classes of *in'amdars* and the petty village officials.

Several friends and colleagues encouraged and helped me in preparing this volume for press. I am grateful to all of them. Warmly acknowledged are Principal Deepak Malhotra, Professor Dilbhag Singh (JNU), Lala Bhagwan Dass God (former Director Prosecution), Mr. Mohinder Singh (Advocate Supreme Court), Mr. A. K. Singh (Reader in History, Dyal Singh Evening College) for their comments and stimulation during the formulation of this book.

My sincere thanks to the publisher, Shri Pradeep Mittal for sustained help in the preparation and publication of this work.

Mrs. Anita Dua, Silky, and Jimmy provided invaluable assistance in the preparation of this book; it is as much theirs as mine.

**New Delhi, 15th August 2006** **Dr. J.C. Dua**

# *Contents*

# 1

# British Economic Thought and Ideas of Thomas Munro— Introduction of the Rayatwari System

In India the various conditions of man and land have been interlocked since ages. Even today India continues to be basically an agrarian country in which nearly 80 percent of her population live by growing crops. The vastness of the country with its divergent geographical features, social organizations, village communities based on tribal and caste ties, the customary practices and successive governments and their land laws complicated the intricate relationships between man and land to such an extent that one gets boggled at the immensity and complexity of problems relating to land tenure and peasant in the Indian sub-continent. By the end of the eighteenth century, when the East India Company had asserted its sovereignty over sizeable territories in India, the attention of political economists turned to the political and economic implications of alternative types of governing structures, whereas in the first quarter of the nineteenth century, the emphasis changed into the formulation of economic policies appropriate to the circumstances of India.

The concept of proprietary rights in agrarian land and the nature of various types of land tenures in pre-British India has been an extremely vexed problem for the English administrators, jurists

Reivsed version of the Papers–(i) 'Thomas Munro on Land Reforms in the 'Ceded Districts', 1800-1807', *Research Students Seminar, Delhi University,* 1969, and (ii) 'Cambell and Hodgson on the Introduction of Rayatwari System in the Ceded Districts', *Indian History Congress,* 1976.

and economic historians ever since the later half of the eighteenth century.[1] British India of the late eighteenth and the early nineteenth centuries provides a most unique example in the history of ideas in which the link between new ideas, taking shape in the minds of abstract theorists and practical policy can be seen in such clarity. Almost every British institution introduced into India had some effect on landholding. The land revenue being the chief constituent in the revenues of the state, its administration offered the first serious problem to the British administrators in India. As such, the Company's attention was focused on a sound land and land revenue policy, which might lead to an improvement and extension of agriculture.[2] It is generally believed by the historians that the British land revenue policies during this period were, to a considerable measure, influenced by the principles of contemporary classical economists, viz. Adam Smith, T.R. Malthus, David Ricardo and James Mill.

During the period between 1765 and 1793 various expedients were tried by the Company regarding the land revenue administration in India. The main problem before them was to so modify and adapt the existing land-system and revenue administration that it should serve the financial and economic purposes of the Company. A mere continuance of the existing usages and customs of landholding and revenue administration could not serve the financial and economic interests of the Company, and, as such, it was absolutely necessary to introduce a change in them.[3] But the crux of the problem was what such changes should be and what principles should determine its course?

In his famous discussion of property, Sir Henry Maine very apty remarked, "Any intelligent man who will be at pains to ask himself seriously what he knows about its origin or the laws or mode of its historical growth will find that his knowledge is extraordinarily small."[4] As a matter of fact there was hardly any specific British policy in any sphere of activity in India. It was either political expediency or only varieties of policies, or attitudes and influences.

Warren Hastings was the first among the British in India to have conceived and succeeded in working out a unified policy of rural administration. The English had taken over the system of revenue accounting from the Mohammadens. But the native terms, units, calendar and languages used for this purpose were all unfamiliar to them.[5] Hastings believed that the best policy for the Company to follow was to give the lands on lease to the *zamindars* and revenue farmers for a specified amount of revenue determined on the basis of past collections. Warren Hastings was very much sympathetic with and drew inspirations from the Indian institutions. He observed that it would be a 'wanton tyranny' to deprive Indians of their own laws and force them to obey laws of foreign origin of which they were completely ignorant.[6] Hence he attempted to establish a system preserving entirely 'the spirit of the constitution' of olden days and making only minor changes to suit the existing circumstances and make the system more effective.[7] He could, however, be accused of lacking a sense of direction. His system was to auction the estates at the end of each term of settlement and farm them out to the highest bidders for leases. This was known as the 'farming system.' The farmers had no abiding interest in the lands settled with them; their leases were far too short to permit this; and all that was achieved in this process was the expropriation of *zamindars* of long standing. In short, the consequence of revenue farming was the subversion of property and there could be no form of instability more dangerous than this.[8]

Meanwhile another plan was proposed by Philip Francis who was considered to be the original promoter of the permanent settlement of Bengal.[9] He was a great believer in the abstract principles of political economy and considered any detailed enquiry into the land tenures of the country or its other institutions as absolutely unnecessary.[10] Francis proposed to settle the land revenue with hereditary *zamindars,* and confer a right of private property in land to them. The basis of his plan was a belief in certain fixed principles of political economy in support of which he summoned forth the authority of Adam Smith, James Stuart, and Montesquieu and assumed that the *zamindars* of Bengal were in no way different from the landowners of Europe and the universal principles of political economy will apply as much in Bengal as in European countries.[11]

Philip Francis' ideas had made deep impression on the minds of the British Legislature at the time of the Act of 1784, which required the Court of Directors to establish 'permanent rules' for collecting the land revenue 'according to the laws and Constitution of India'. They (Court of Directors) instructed Cornwallis to make the settlement with the *zamindars.* Cornwallis realized that in recognizing the *zamindars* as proprietors of the soil, he was going far beyond the mere recognition of the existing rights or claims acquired by prescription. To what extent the rights given to the *zamindars* were in fact innovations was a question in which, surprisingly, he showed little interest.[12] At the time when the question whether the *zamindar* owned the land, and owed the state only customary revenue, or was in fact only an official acting as revenue farmer for the state which owned the land was being debated by the two most eminent Bengal servants, Sir John Shore and Charles James Grant, Cornwallis wrote: 'It is immaterial to the Government what individual possesses the land, provided he cultivates it, protects the ryot and pays the public revenue'.[13] In fact Cornwallis had no alternative to a settlement with the *zamindars.*[14] Cornwallis' permanent settlement of Bengal (1793) was a frank attempt to apply the English Whig philosophy of the government in which private property, free trade, individual liberty and the reduction of the power of the government to a minimum were the articles of faith.[15]

According to the plan of 1793, the property in the soil had been declared to be vested in the landholders, and the revenue payable to the Government from each estate had been fixed forever. This was an innovation as the property in the soil was never before formally declared to be vested in the landholders, nor were allowed to transfer such rights as they did possess, or raise money upon the credit of their tenures, or without the previous sanction of the Government.[16]

It appears that the tide of British policy in India moved within an orbit of ideas primarily determined in Europe and in the direction set by the development of the British economy. Almost every step, which they (the Government of East India Company in India) took was the result of an "abstract theory" commonly drawn from something in their own country. Moreover, 'the legislators were English aristocrats; and aristocratical prejudices prevailed."'[8] Apart from evoking by Philip Francis of the authority of contemporary economists in support of his plans, when the economic objectives of the Permanent Settlement are examined, a close relationship between the premises of Bengal Permanent Settlement and the principles advocated by Adam Smith for agricultural development can be found.

One of the important theories on the concept of property that the British brought to India was—"All the subjects of the king, rich or poor, free or bond, were tenants with the exception of the proletariat and outcasts of town and country; every one held a tenure of the king or of an intermediary, and, ultimately, everyone held tenure, directly or indirectly, of the king."[19] Moreover, as a result of the Civil War and the Glorious Revolution (1688), and also due to the changing basis of the economic power in the seventeenth and the eighteenth centuries, the theories of property had been much debated in England. The land settlements of the eighteenth and nineteenth centuries were the result of exercises in application of the theory and the examination of the nature of property that went on in England from the third decade of the seventeenth century until the beginning of the nineteenth century.[20]

Amongst the Europeans the French traveler, Francois Bernier, who toured India during the seventeenth century was one of the first who declared, "The Great Mogol is the proprietor of every acre of land in the kingdom." and that there was "no idea of the principle of *meum* and *teum,* related to land or real possessions..."[21] The servants of the East India Company like James Grant also held the same central idea. He, in his 'Political Survey of the Northern Circars', wrote "...that some palpably erroneous and dangerous doctrines, subversive of on of the first, most essential, and the best ascertained principles of eastern legislation, by which the proprietary right of the soil constitutional and solely vested in the sovereign ruler.."[22] The same view was held and advanced by James Mill. Doubtless because of his official position he did not publish his views and our knowledge of them is derived from the evidence he gave to the Select Committee on Indian Affairs from 1830-1832. It has been seen that Mill took-up the startling position that the British power in India should not renounce but maintain the traditional right of an oriental sovereign to the ownership of the soil.[23]

Moreover, Locke's concept of property, that "everyman has a Property in his own Person" and that man had "mixed his Labour with, and joined to it something that is his own and thereby makes it his property"[24] found its way into actual fabric of the law in Great Britain and in India through Sir William Blackstone's *Commentries on Laws of England.*[25]

It was envisaged by the Bengal Permanent Settlement that the establishment of private property in land would help to provide the native moneyed classes with a profitable avenue of investment for their capital.[26] It was hoped that with the progress of society the ownership of the great landed estate of Bengal would pass out of the hands of old *zamindar* type into those of modern Indian entrepreneur class.[27]

On his part Adam Smith declared that 'merchants are commonly, ambitious of becoming country gentlemen, and when they are generally the best of all improves'.[28] As against the feudal lords the penetration of the trader and the merchant created an extensive market in the countryside and gave birth to a new class of farmers with resources to develop agricu1ture.[29]

Moreover, the dictum of Bengal Government to abstain from any infringement on the rights of the landlords in its executive capacity bear very close affinity to the Smith's policy of *laissez-faire* with his strong attacks on the policy of state interference and control. It was also determined on the basis of the policy of *laissez-faire* to abstain from interference in the relations of the *zamindars* with their *rayats.*[30] But though, we may find a close relationship between the principles of the Permanent Settlement and Principles of Adam Smith yet we cannot ignore that Smith was against a permanent settlement of land revenue because in the course of social progress, rents were bound to rise with the result that 'constancy of valuation' would be 'advantageous to the landlord and harmful to the sovereign'.[31]

Almost immediately after the Permanent Settlement was effected it was realized that the state could not divest itself of the right to appropriate to itself the whole of economic rent. The theory of state landlordism was trotted out and put forward, in justification of fixing the revenue rates which for the *rayats* were ruinously high.[32] The Permanent Settlement was indefenisible on grounds of economic theory but its many supporters claimed for its political and administrative advantages.[33] The primary object of the Permanent Settlement was to secure an assured amount of revenue for the state every year and to create a class of *zamindars* which would in time of conflict stand by the British Government. But the creation of property rights and handing these over to a small class of proprietors at the cost of cultivating tenants whose interests in land were completely ignored was against the principles of political economy.[34]

The Bengal authorities, however, gradually began to consider it as the best possible measure for all territories, which came under the British rule in subsequent years.[35] Incidently certain new territories[36] came under the British rule in the Presidency of Madras in which 'all the fields were held by an industrious and numerous yeomanry, or a body of small proprietary cultivators, either in severalty or in joint village communities' and 'paid the public revenue direct into the treasury of the State, without the intervention of the *zamindars* of any kind whatever'.[37] There was, an opportunity to look at the problems of land tenures and settlement from a new angle.

Moreover, in the wake of the Industrial Revolution, the nature of the British economic interests had undergone a change. Instead of being content with merely receiving an increasing surplus revenue from its territories, the East India Company had to undertake, to meet the requirements of the British Industry which after the Industrial Revolution needed an expanded market for its manufactured products, new sources for its increasing requirements or raw materials. The East India Company was now required to come out of its own narrow selfish interests and as such could no longer continue to view the economic interests of Britain and India within the limited context of its own commerce and was supposed to see the requirements of creating a free market in India in place of its monopoly. For, under a free trade India would rise rapidly into prosperity as a market for the British manufacturers and a source of raw materials.[38]

But the French Revolution had overshadowed all other questions in Britain in the last decade and half of the 18th century. It was only in the first decade of the 19th century that the offensive of the British merchants and traders gathered momentum. Since the Charter of the Company was due to be renewed in 1813, the rival interests built up a powerful opposition against the entire corrupt monopolist administration of the East India Company in India and against the continuance of their monopolistic commercial privileges.[39] They alleged that the Company was interested only in extracting tribute and not in finding a market for the British goods in India. If India was to be developed as a market for British manufacturers and a source of raw material for the British, the Company's administration had to be drastically changed. The financial burden of the Company's administration had to be kept as light as possible so that the wealth of the people could fructify in their pockets and promote trade. All obstacles hindering the free flow of the British settlers, capital, skill, and goods had to be destroyed. And if this was done, the prospects of profitable trade with India, which benefited both the British Industry and commerce and India, were limitless and would also take off all the surplus manufactures that the British could produce.[40]

The campaign for abolition of the Company's privileges was only a part of the much larger tide of liberalism, which was sweeping across the British Isles in those years. The liberals were generally against the landlords and their aristocratic privileges. As they consisted largely of farmers, manufacturers and merchants, they were opposed to all those classes, which by their hereditary privileges proved to be obstacle in the free competition for land. The tide of their opinion was, therefore, against the *zamindars* and they tried to expose the evil consequences of *zamindary* settlement in Bengal. Everywhere there was a cry for abolition of the monopolistic privileges, exclusive trade organization and everything that stood in the way of free competition amongst all members of society. The British house of Commons in response to this clamour, before renewing the Charter of the East India Company, which was due to expire in 1813, appointed in 1809 a Select Committee 'to enquire into the present state of the affairs of the East India Company'. Thus, the Company stood before the bar of public opinion and many of the abuses of its revenue administration were exposed to public gaze particularly by the publication of the *Fifth Report of the Select Committee of the House of Commons in 1812*.

The publication of this *Report* might be considered to have formed another epoch (next to the year 1793 when Permanent Settlement was introduced in Bengal) in Indian history. Moreover, for the first time, a mass of highly important information was brought to the notice of the public. Many documents pertaining to the land tenures and the system of land revenue administration were brought together and formed part of the Appendices to the *Fifth Report.*[41]

The *Fifth Report* opined that Lord Cornwallis had the option either of consolidating the British rule on the basis of the Mughal system or of adopting an entirely new and foreign foundation. Arguing the case for preserving the Mughal institutions the *Report* pointed out "...when brought back to their original state of utility, and improved by such regulation as might be superadded by the British Government, (they) would, under a just and vigilant administration, unite the liberal policy of an European state with the strength and energy of an Asiatic monarchy, and altogether be better suited to the genius, experience, and understanding of the natives, than institutions founded on principles, to them wholly new, derived from a state of society with which they were unacquainted...(However, Cornwallis was for) the introduction of a new order of things, which should have for its foundation, the security of individual property, and the administration of justice, criminal and civil, by rules which were to disregard all conditions of persons, and in their operation, be free of influence or control from the government itself".[42]

The *Fifth Report* clearly revealed the extreme insecurity and oppression suffered by the actual cultivators under the *zamindari* system and in contrast pointed out the advantages of the *rayatwari* system. The conclusion arrived at by the *Committee* was that the system of *rayatwari* settlements which had afforded to the British Officers the means 'of reforming abuses, removing oppressions, ascertaining individual rights, and obtaining a real knowledge of the people and the internal affairs of the country' was 'highly expedient' at the same time 'the mode ... for permanently setting the land revenues should be reconsidered in its principles, before it be applied to the provinces into which it has not been introduced, with a view to such modifications and improvements of it, as the more intimate practical knowledge...of the local concerns of the country may render desirable to be adopted'.[43]

During the first two decades of the 19th century, important developments had taken place in England as a result of which theory of economic development implicit in the policy of permanent settlement underwent a considerable change. Though contemporary public opinion in England after 1812 had shifted in favor of the cultivating proprietors and against the aristocracy, it remained for classical political economy to provide a precise and incontrovertible theoretical basis for the new thinking on this subject.[44] This period was rich in new economic ideas which eventually were cast to set ideological moulds.[45]

Along with liberalists the utilitarian thinkers (Jeremy Bentham, James Mill, David Ricardo, T.R. Malthus and John Stuart Mill) also came to have great influence in England as well as in shaping the British policy, especially the land and revenue policy in India. They contributed the main elements of the theoretical foundations of the new land revenue policy. These thinkers had developed a comprehensive body of principles and doctrines, which, in their opinion, were to be applied in the regulation of society, not only in the sphere of the government, education and law but also in the sphere of political economy.[46]

T.R. Malthus, the first Professor of History and Political Economy in British East India Company's Haileybutry College in London[47] in 1805 remained in his position till his death in 1834.[48] James Mill had published his *The History of British India* in 1818 and was subsequently appointed in 1819 as Assistant Examiner of the correspondence in the Revenue Department at the East India House.[49] James Mill, who had already expounded in his *History* the principles on which he would have liked the Government of India to be reformed, proved to be the chief vehicle of all those influences which were destined to change the course of the British land and revenue policies in the post-1819 years.[50] David Ricardo, though never directly associated with the Indian affairs, yet, because of his close friendship with James Mill and T.R. Malthus, was frequently drawn into discussion on Indian affairs. It was his theory of rent, which greatly influenced the contemporary thinking and policy. There were other eminent economists[51] who had turned their attention to a study of Indian land tenures, but since they wrote during later period they do not come under the scope of our study.

The principles of political economy, particularly the law of rent and its relationship with the theories of taxation were the most relevant part of the utilitarian doctrine. Law of rent was 'discovered' by Malthus in 1815 in the course of preparing his lectures for his pupils at Haileybury and published a small pamphlet on rent (in 1815). However, his views were made available to a wider audience with the publication of his *Principles of Political Economy* in 1820.[52] According to this law, the rent was a special portion of wealth, which was quite distinct from profits or wages, and was determined in an exact scientific manner. It originated from the tendency of the population to outgrow food resources and the consequent necessity of resorting to increasingly poorer soils as society progressed in population and wealth. Rent, thus, constituted the differential advantage enjoyed by all soils of a higher quality over the marginal soil brought under cultivation, on which the capital employed merely replaced itself and yielded the ordinary prevailing rate of profits after payment of the wages to the labourers at the prevailing rates. Thus, the element of rent could be exactly determined by subtracting from the total or gross produce of any land the cost of wages and the ordinary rate of profit on the capital employed. Wherever land was under private ownership, the landlord had been able to get his land cultivated by a capitalist tenant-farmer working for the ordinary rate of profit and to take away the element of rent as his own property.[53] Malthus's view of the subject of land rents opened new vistas. Not only had a satisfactory solution to a long-standing intellectual problem seemingly been reached, the form of that solution also suggested a course for administrative action. Now that the fundamental cause of economic stagnation in pre-British India had been identified, it was possible to think constructively about appropriate remedies.[54]

Malthus, by regarding rent as a special bounty of Providence wished to create a leisured i.e., a proprietary class to share the rent property to build a richer human civilization and a better world.[55] But Ricardo, proceeding from the same premises as Malthus, interpreted it differently. He demonstrated rent to be a monopoly value which could be charged because land as an instrument of production was limited in quantity and quality, could be appropriated as a private property. He characterized rent as an unearned income which was paid to the landlord for the use of the original and indestructible powers of the soil.[56] Moreover, unlike Malthus, he showed that the landlord performed no economic service and lived as a parasite on the community. He proved that 'the interest of landlords is always opposed to every other class in the community' since 'all classes...except the landlords will be injured by the increase in the price of corn, and also because he was the beneficiary of land monopoly and scarcity of land'.[57]

In the first instance, Ricardo held, the labourers, capitalists and consumers would enjoy the advantages arising from abundance of agriculture produce and the consequent low level wages of labour and the high level of capital accumulation, but later on with the increase of population these advantages will gradually pass over to the proprietors of the soil.[58] According to Ricardo, all extraordinary profits were in their nature but of limited duration, as the whole produce of the soil, after deducting from it only such moderate profits as are sufficient to encourage accumulation, must finally be appropriated by the landlord.[59]

There is no doubt that the Recardian theory of rent diminished the basis of the theory of agricultural development which had inspired the Bengal Permanent Settlement. Moreover, the French Revolution had already created an atmosphere of hostility against the landed aristocracy and its privileges. The new theory of rent, the rigorous logic of which was irrefutable, belied all the assumption that by limiting the assessment on land in Bengal in perpetuity, the portion of land revenue given up to the landlords would contribute to the progress of Bengal. The current belief then was 'that the creation of an artificial class of intermediate proprietors between the government and the cultivators of the soil would be highly inexpedient', and was asserted that the 'removal of intermediate landholders or middlemen has been considered as an advancement' in cultivation.[60]

On the other hand, James Mill in his *History* had most forcefully put forward the belief that the immediate cultivator of the soil would be a far better instrument of agricultural improvement than the large landed proprietors who had no direct interest in cultivation. While condemning the theory of the Bengal Permanent Settlement he wrote, "When our countrymen draw theories from England, it would be good if they understood England. It is not because in England we have a landed aristocracy that our agriculture has improved, but because laws of England offered to the cultivators who have increased so wonderfully the produce of the land in England, not only without assistance from the proprietors but often inspite of them.[61]

James Mill further maintained that 'no principle is more thoroughly established and indeed more universally admitted than that the grant of leases and leases of a long duration to the immediate cultivators of the soil are essential to all spirited and large improvement.[62] He was of opinion that if any portion of the land revenue was given up, it should be given up in favour of the cultivating peasant instead of sacrificing it to those of the *Zamindars* (by fixing their land revenue in perpetuity and making them the proprietors of the land). These rights 'might have been bestowed upon those upon whom they would have operated with force incomparably greater than that with which they could operate upon any other class of men... upon those from whom alone, in every country, the principal improvements in agriculture must be derived, the immediate cultivators of the soil.[63]

Jeremy Bentham's political philosophy and ideas were imperfectly publicized in his lifetime as only a small part of his *Constitutional Code* had appeared before his death and full works were edited and published only in 1843.[64] He seems to have much greater influence on Indian administrative structure than Blackstone and there has been a tendency to overlook the latter's *Commentaries* as a source of ideas. The nineteenth century administration of India is a clear evidence of the fulfillment of Bentham's prediction that after he was dead he would be the despot who ruled India.[65] About James Mill he observed, 'Mill will be the living executive—I shall be the dead legislative of British India.[66]

Among British economic analysts in the first half the nineteenth century, Richard Jones was the one significant thinker who directly challenged the conceptual adequacy of Ricardian reasoning to Indian conditions. He, in fact, was among the highly select group of 'bourgeois' economists whose works were treated charitably by Marx. Jones was of the view that Ricardian analysis might apply reasonably well to contemporary England and, as such, had been mistakenly appropriated in India. Wrapping up James Mill also along with Ricardo, Jones asserted that the official notion of rent was adequate 'only in a country of capitalists' and not 'so in a country where no classes of capitalists are found, as India'. For Jones, there was no escape from the fact that the general condition of India was miserable and that an important job needed to be done. India's difficulties, however, would not be relieved by strategies inspired by theories alien to the Indian environment. In Indian agriculture, conducted primarily for subsistence purposes with unpaid family labour, the income shares written about in classical theory could not be readily distinguished.[67]

John Stuart Mill also agreed with the views expressed by Richard Jones that the Indian *rayat* was a type of cottier-tenant, by and large, similar to the Irish peasant. He was neither a capitalist farmer nor a wage labourer, but one earning his subsistence from the soil by his own labour and stock. As against the position in the classical political economy in which the rent of a capitalist farmar was determined by the competition of capital, the size of the population, and the varying fertility of the soil, Mill expressly acknowledged that cottier-rent was not determined in that way. It, as a matter of fact, was decided directly by the proportion between population and land, instead of between population and capital, the regulating factor being the competition of tenants for land rather than competition of capitals. In other words, the cottier-tenant cultivated the land as the only means of livelihood and paid as rent almost all the produce except the bare amount necessary for his subsistence. The remedy suggested by J.S. Mill was 'to bring the principle of population to act directly on the land'.[68]

However, it would not be proper to concede that it was only the utilitarian philosophy propounded by the above thinkers, which paved the way for the introduction of the *kulwar* or *rayatwari* settlement in many parts of India. Most of the decisions regarding principles and policy in both the revenue and judicial spheres had been reached before 1819, and the motive force behind those decisions was not utilitarian philosophy,[69] rather the influence of the native tradition was manifest in them.

Above all, Read, Thomas Munro and Thackeray had already taken an opposite stand vis-à-vis the Permanent Settlement in Bengal. Read and Munro had already developed a *rayatwar* system of revenue in some parts of the Madras Presidency in which they had settled for the payment of land revenue directly with the cultivating ryots. In their methods of assessment of land revenue they followed the practices of the preceding Indian rulers. We do concede that they did not have a clear-cut theory for the determination of the 'full economic rent' of each field, and which was made largely in a pragmatic manner on the basis of records of past collections and an arbitrary estimate of what the land could yield. The Philosophers supplied them with a scientific basis for the assessment of rent for an individual farm. James Mill, accepting the Munro's plan of revenue settlement, introduced into it a clear-cut theory which had logical rigour and was based on the unquestionable principles of political economy.

Thus an alternative mode of revenue settlement, known as the *rayatwari* system had already been developed by the officers of the Madras Presidency before the utilitarian philosophy came into lime light.

In contrast to the Bengal mode of Permanent Settlement, the *rayatwari* mode appeared to be more sound in theory, expedient and beneficial in practice, and more in accordance with the native institutions, customs and manners of the people. Its guiding principles as enunciated by the chief exponents, viz., Alexander Read, Thomas Munro and W.M. Thackeray, in their elaborate and able *Reports*, tended to prove that it was far superior to the Bengal system from the point of view of the fiscal interests of the British Government, the economic interest of the *rayat* and of the promotion and development of agriculture.[70]

As early as year 1792 A.D. the districts of Salem and Baramahal were placed under the charge of Alexander Read, with Thomas Munro, Graham and Macleod as his assistants. In these areas, there was, for the most part, no *zamindars* or middle-men, and there were numerous chieftains called, Poligars both as semi-independent revenue collectors and as police in aid of the revenue collector. In both cases they did not hold out much prospect of their proving suitable landlords to hold the settlement.[71] As such, they were instructed to make the revenue assessments on the basis of the records of the preceding governments, as corrected by a comparison with the accounts of actual cultivation. But, the class of persons with whom they were to make revenue contracts, was not specified.[72] However, Read had been instructed by the Board of Revenue to make a settlement with the cultivators for three to five years; and they further intimated that if the headmen of villages should oppose these measures the land might be let out in small proportions to strangers.[73]

Read had no preconceived plan of a *rayatwari* settlement nor was it the result of a sudden brain wave. Rather in the first instance he concluded at least for five years and thought this would provide sufficient time in which 'every necessary information ought to be obtained relative to the value and state of the country.[74] As such, Read and his assistants began an exhaustive enquiry into the 'nature and progress of agriculture'—this being the 'surest of means of ascertaining an equitable mode of assessment and collection of land rent.[75] It was only after the survey of the land that he came to the conclusion that as there was no intermediate agency for revenue collection available, and such as was available had to be eliminated for political reasons, he came to the conclusion that the direct settlement with the cultivators was the best course. Thus, a vast amount of data had to be collected before the amount of revenue assessment for a particular field could be fixed. Separate assessments for different fields were aggregated, to arrive at the revenue of any given area, which again was corrected with reference to past collections from that area.[76] Lands were in rent to the first and second class of *rayats* below the *patels.* Those *rayats* now held land immediately from the Government.[77] This system, as such, came to Read's mind by the logic of the facts only. And though this came to be known by the name of the *rayatwar* system, yet it was hardly mentioned as such in the voluminous Baramahal records.

According to this plan the settlement was to be made with every cultivator directly who was supposed to pay rent to the Government, without joint responsibility and without the intervention of a *zamindar*, a village headman, or any other intermediary.

Thomas Munro, during the early years of his stay at Baramahal, did not appreciate the ideas of *rayatwari* settlement and produced anti-arguments,[78] but we find in the later years he fully endorsed the ideas of Read and subsequently became the strongest champion of the ideas of *rayatwari* system in Madras.[79]

In 1800, when Munro was appointed Principal Collector of Ceded Districts,[80] though the first revenue settlement, *i.e.*, for 1800-1801 (*Fasli* 1210) that he introduced was a village settlement,[81] regarding the settlements of *fasli* 1211 and onwards, Munro believed in introducing *kulwar* or *rayatwar* settlement, that is to say, with every cultivator directly who paid rent to the Government. The cultivators were to be severally responsible for their rent, and they and the *patel* jointly for the rent of whole village.[82]

The question arises why Munro thought it expedient to make settlement with the cultivators *i.e.*, why was he interested in concluding *rayatwari* settlement only and no other? Whether it was because of the influence of any political philosopher or the influence of 'native tradition' that was manifest in that?

He believed that 'when a country falls under the dominion of a foreign power, the wisest plan is to leave it in possession of its own laws and customs, and to endeavour rather to ameliorate than to abolish them and substitute others in their room. Moreover, more ancient and civilized the subjected nation is, the more requisite is to pursue this course, for the institutions of such a people are not only in themselves perhaps better adapted than any that could receive from strangers to their own circumstances and habits, but they have also over their minds the strong influence which is derived from respect for antiquity.[83]

Munro clearly stated that if the system of landlord property and tenures which had always prevailed in India be examined it would appear that the 'sovereign' had at all times, been regarded as the sole landlord'. To him the land seemed at all times to have been regarded as the property of the state, and no traces could be discovered of its ever having been that of the cultivators or renters. The country had been divided into an immense number of small farms held immediately under the Ruler by their respective cultivators. That great mass of tenants were all tenants at will. That the numerous classes of '*Enamdars*', who might be mistaken for landlords, were in fact only landed pensioners whose lands were resumably at pleasure, and that the private property in land was altogether unknown.[84]

The people usually termed *zamindars* were not more land owners than the '*Enamdars*'. The appellation of *zamindars* among the natives of India, Munro felt, comprehended every person who held land and discharged the duties of a civil officer down to the village *talliari*, and also the *Poligars* and hereditary Rajas. The higher classes of *zamindars*, the *Deshmukh*, *Deskpandi*, *Desai* were all revenue servants holding *in'am* lands or villages, and receiving a percentage on the collection as an allowance performing the duties of their employment. They differed in no respect from the common *patels* and *karnams* of the villages, but in holding a more extensive jurisdiction which was in one respect inferior to theirs (*patels* and *karnams*) by being only during pleasure, while theirs was hereditary. Even the class of *zamindars* denominated *Rajas* and *Poligars* had certainly seized their respective districts because of the weakness of the Government and had become petty sovereigns and, as such, proprietors of the soil, but still they were not properly landlords.[85] He was firm on this point that 'in India there has been a body of private landlords that has always been composed, as at present, of *rayats* holding petty farms. The *Zamindars* and *Poligars* who possessed great estates were not private individuals, but tributary and sometimes independent princes'.[86]

They did not buy or sell land, or they disposed of it by gift, it was an *inam* and resumably at will. If they were subdued by a neighboring state, they did not, like the feudal vassals in Europe, retain possession of their lands after losing their power but all their rights in them of every kind passed to the new Sovereign, as such if, therefore, the settlement, Munro urged, was concluded directly with the cultivators, it was only following the system which had always prevailed in these districts, but improving it by limiting the demand of the Government instead of letting continue arbitrary and uncertain.[87] As such, it would cause 'no innovation' but would continue the system to which the inhabitants have always been accustomed. Moreover, it would be the most agreeable to the inhabitants, because it could hardly be doubted that they would prefer the system to which they had always been accustomed, to any other.[88] It would be an innovation if large estates and new description of land holders, hitherto unknown to the inhabitants, were created.[89]

'The complete abolition of an ancient Revenue System', Munro believed, could 'never be advisable' until it had been 'fully proved that which was 'intended to supplant' that was 'better'. In order to decide whether the new was preferable to the old, it should be first ascertained whether it was practicable, whether it would be linked by the inhabitants, and whether it would ultimately augment the wealth of the country and the resources of the Government.[90]

Munro also tried to relate the *rayatwari* system to the socio-economic conditions of the Ceded Districts. In his opinion the economic conditions and habits of the people ruled out the chances of success of any other system except the *rayatwari.* The Ceded Districts were thinly inhabited in proportion to their extent. They had only few large towns, and the merchants who resided in them, being seldom rich, carried on but little trade.[91] Many of the middling class of *rayats* often failed from the most trifling accidents. The loss of cow or bullock or a bad crop were evils, each of them sufficient to force an ordinary *rayat* to throw up a part of his farm and poor one, to relinquish that entirely and became a common labourer.[92] The lands closed to the village were well cultivated, those at a little distance hardly yielded any rent and beyond them lied waste. As such, large tracts of land were waste. The rich cultivators usually remained fixed in their native villages, though they did not always occupy the same. But the poorer classes of cultivators would go from village to village wherever they could get land on most favourable terms.[93]

Moreover, prevailing civil institutions and manners of the people according to Munro, were hostile to the continuance of extensive landed property in the hands of few families. Early marriages and the religious obligations under which there would be the equal division of land among all the sons, and the general practice of adoption where there was none,[94] all would continue to break up and distribute the land among a multitude of owners. Thus, the division would perpetually accelerate by the above causes.[95] On the other hand, the *rayatwary* system did not require any artificial restraints contrary to customs and the laws of inheritance to prevent the division of estates.[96] At the same time the distinction of caste also prevented the accumulation of the land, for the husbandman never abandoned his own occupation or sold his land in order to engage in manufactures or trade, and hence estates could hardly even be augmented by purchase unless where lands were sold for arrears of rent. But that very operation of selling would frequently diminish than enlarge estates, for, Munro believed, purchases would often be made by under tenants than by neighbouring landlords. In that case, the establishment of the system of large estates would, therefore, be only forcing for a time the landed property from the form in which it had always been, and to which it must again, sooner or later, inevitably return, namely small farms or estates cultivated by their owners.[97]

To Munro a settlement with the cultivators was the best course taking into consideration 'the manners and prejudices of the inhabitant'. He though that was well suited to the narrowness of their circumstances as it did not insist on the same amount of revenue being paid every year, rather regulated it by the extent of cultivation which increased or diminished according to the seasons. Moreover, the *kulwar* settlement would seldom injure the revenue by any considerable failure, for the failures were only those of individual *rayats,* who would recover their losses by cultivating smaller farms, and by being allowed to hold them for 2 or 3 years below the standard rent. Whereas when a great landholder failed, he had previously exhausted a great part of the resources of the whole estate, for he must, in the first place, have made away with the whole of the remission of rent granted by Government at the time of forming the estate and he would, besides, often have borrowed and applied the money of his tenants to discharge his own arrears. The *rayat* would be more apt than the greater proprietor to employ his savings in the improvement of his land for he would have no cause to doubt the permanence of his tenure as long as he paid the rent. In this way, Munro argued, the Districts would yield not only more revenue but more produce of every kind, in the hands of small farmers than in those of great landowners. If this was admitted, then they *(Rayats)* would also make the land more saleable and the realization of revenue more secure.[98]

Munro argued that the *rayatwar* system would render the *rayats* more independent as proprietors holding directly of the Company, than as the tenants of the great landholders and they would enjoy more freedom in the management of their lands than the *mootadar* who was restrained from demanding a higher rent than what might have been fixed by survey, for they would be at liberty to take whatever rent they could get for any part of their farm.[99]

He was of the view that *rayatwar* settlement would diffuse more widely, than any other system, the benefit of private property in land, for it would extend to the great body of *rayats* instead of confirming it to a few great land-holders. At the same time, Munro believed that this system was well adapted to the narrow circumstances of the *rayats,* for by not requiring the same rent every year from each individual would enable them to increase or diminish their farms according to their means of cultivating them.[100] *Rayatwari* system admitted of all gradations of large and small farms, as there were *rayats* who paid from one to one thousand *Pagodas.*[101]

Moreover, Munro felt that the authority of the Government and the Courts of justice would be more respected under *rayatwar* than any other settlement,[102] for the *rayats* as proprietors of their several farms would have no armed followers, and could form no combination to disturb the public tranquility. They would on the contrary, rather be disposed to assist in maintaining it, for as those among them, who acquired property, would be indebted for it, chiefly to the exertions of their own industry, favoured by internal quiet, they would employ their influence, in supporting that order of things, under which they had improved their fortunes.[103]

To Thomas Munro, thus, *Rayatwari* system was better calculated to promote industry and to augment the produce of the country for it made more proprietors and farmers, and fewer common labourers than in the *zamindary* or *mootadary* schemes. *Rayats* as proprietors were more likely to improve their lands than as the tenants of the *zamindars.* Moreover, they would be more able to do it as they would be enjoying the whole remission instead of a small part. They would be better managers and farmers and would be more immediately interested than the great ones in the cultivation of lands. They would bestow more price upon it and make it yield more abundant crops. Supposing the amount of property to be the same, 'it would be better that it should be in the hands forty or fifty thousand small proprietors, than four or five hundred great ones'. And by the remission going at once to the *rayats,* the circumstances of the class of men, from whom the revenue was principally drawn, would be improved and would enable them to raise a greater quantity of food, and thus would favour the increase of population. By allowing the revenue to increase or diminish according to the extent of land in cultivation, would cause the farmers, without occasioning, on average years, any loss to the Government. Lastly, the *rayatwar* system, by retaining *in* the hands of government all unoccupied land, would give her the power of gradually augmenting the revenue without imposing any fresh burden upon the *rayats,* as long as there was an acre of waste in the country.[104]

He admitted that there were certain difficulties in the way of a *rayatwar* settlement but he had ready arguments to support his case. For instance, he agreed that the expenses of management and collection, which was always somewhat greater than where estates consisted of one or more villages, was supposed to be a serious obstacle. But he argued that a part of that extra expense would still have been incurred in great estates by the owners who would defray that from the remission of rent or profit, whereas in a settlement with the *rayats* the whole of that was made up by the additional revenue and by the rent waste lands brought into cultivation. Moreover, it would be, in a great measure, done away, whenever the lands became saleable. That the great detail of account was another argument against the *kulwar* settlement, but Munro felt that it was only from such accounts, that any information could be obtained of the state of the country. The possession of such detailed accounts was also desirable in case of any emergency, which might compel the Government to make a temporary increase of the land rent which, without such information, could not be done upon any sure foundation. So this objection was perhaps counterbalanced by exhibiting a complete view of the state of the cultivation and of the resources of the country.[105] Moreover, when a country was surveyed, and the rent of every field fixed the accounts would become perfectly simple. They were nothing more than a list of *rayats* and fields. If the *rayats* in subsequent year did not take new or throw up old land, the same register would serve again. It 'was easier to get an account of a hundred *rayats* from a *karnam* than of a *mootahder,*[106] if it might be argued that the same information could be obtained from the records of the *karnam* under the system of great estates, Munro replied that no man acquainted with Indian accounts would believe that the records of a *karnam* appointed by a land holder, would tell within thirty or forty percent of the actual produce of the estate.[107] The best way of getting proper rate of assessment was either by reference to the accounts of former years, or by comparison with the rent of lands of the same quality, which had long been nearly stationary. The condition of the poorer *rayats* was learned from the concurring testimony of their neighbours, who at the same time would not exaggerate their poverty, lest the remission, which might in consequence be granted, should fall upon themselves. A short explanation of what took place in the *kulwar* settlement of a single district, or *tehsildari,* would apply to the whole number of districts forming a Collectorate.[108] To Munro the objection to the collection of land rent immediately from the *rayats* did not seem to be justified by experience. He argued that the Government had always done so in India; and it certainly could not be said that the agriculture had not been carried to high degree of perfection in every part of it.[109] Another objection urged against the *rayatwar* system was the excessive interference of revenue servants. In this connection Thomas Munro opined that in order to prevent private collection and the decrease of cultivation such interference was necessary. Comparing the areas under study with England, he stated that in case of the latter the interference was greater and more vexatious than in the former. Land-rent was Indian, what the excise and customs were to English revenue. Hence it became necessary to give particular attention to it, and to employ a large establishment of servants, to secure every part of it, that was justly due to the Government.[110] If such a remission was granted as would leave the *rayats* a private rent, after discharging the public one, the interference of revenue servants would be unnecessary. Their own interest would stimulate them to cultivate; as in Canara, where no revenue officer even thought of calling upon the owner to plough or sow his field. Moreover, after the lands became saleable, as has already been observed, every kind of interference would become superfluous, because their produce would ensure their cultivation.[111]

To the objection that *rayatwari* system left no person between the cultivator and the revenue officer, Munro argued that the objection was made, from not understanding the condition of the Indian husbandmen. He was of the opinion that in India, the landlord and cultivator could never be permanently separated, as in England. The minute division of property would always render them the same person, with very few exceptions. The landlord must always cultivate his own fields; and hence the collections must always be made directly from cultivator in his capacity of landlord. In the areas under study there could be no person between the cultivator and the revenue officer, without a creation of *zamindars.*[112]

Another difficulty or disadvantage to the introduction of the *rayatwar* settlement was regarding the repairing of great tanks. Trifling repairings were often made by the *rayats* themselves, by each individual furnishing a quantity of grain in proportion to his land towards the expense of the work. But whenever the charges were so heavy that neither a share nor even the whole of the crop would defray them, they were borne by the Government, as they were often equal to the whole produce of the tank for three or four years. The *rayats* would never agree to assess themselves to such an extent, and even if a remission of rent adequate to the making good of all expenses were granted, the sums which would be wanted for repairs could neither be collected nor disbursed by the *rayats* as a body. This inconvenience might perhaps be gradually remedied by making all tanks, what is called, *dasabandham.*[113]

As regards the necessity of issuing *taqavi*[114] to the poor *rayats,* Munro emphasized that no reduction of rent that could be granted under a permanent settlement would, for a long time, have any sensible effect in diminishing their demand for that, for the proportions which they required, was seldom more than half their rent.[115]

The annual fluctuation in the amount of revenue, had also been brought as an argument, against, the *rayatwar* system. But for that too, Munro had a ready answer, who stated that the fluctuation would never be so great, as to cause any serious inconvenience. He was of the opinion that it would, in the initial stages, never exceed ten percent in one year. As the *rayats* became proprietors, it would also gradually diminish and in ten or twelve years, it would scarcely be above five percent.[116] If it were thought an indispensible object that the amount of the land rent should be the same every year, it might be attained without any great difficulty by imposing an extra assessment upon villages or districts for the deficiencies of bad years, and relinquishing to them the increased produce of good ones.[117]

But while advocating the advantages of the *rayatwar* settlement, Thomas Munro did not completely rule out the advantages of the *Zamindari* or *mootadari* settlement in the Ceded Districts. The most important advantage that might follow, he wrote, was the immediate encouragement of agriculture. He felt that as the *mootadar* would have a deeper interest, than the revenue officer or even than the *rayat,* in the cultivation of the country, he would be more anxious to promote that. The revenue officers who superintended cultivation derived no benefit by its improvement and lost nothing by its decline. They had, as such, no interest in giving any more attention to that than what might be sufficient to prevent their removal from neglect. Nor had the *rayat,* in a *rayatwar* settlement, so immediate or so great an interest, as compared to a *mootadar* in the *mootadari* settlement, in the improvement of his land. The *rayat* would have no particular interest in the improvement of waste land, because if he had broken it up himself

he would be obliged to pay the rent of that, too. Similarly, if it were broken up by another person he could draw no other advantages from that than simply a small remission of rent proportioned to the excess above its fixed rent which the village might yield from the cultivation of waste. He would, in the first case, not consider his land as his own property. At the same time he would be uncertain whether some trifling loss might not force him next year to relinquish a great part of it. It would probably be some years before he could ascertain what he would be able to keep permanently, and before that he would not venture to employ his whole means in improving it as a private estate. The *mootadar* or *zamindar* on the other hand would perceive at once that he was a land-owner, he would therefore, exert himself to keep up cultivation to its present level in order to prevent the decrease of his income. Moreover, as all additional cultivation would be clear profit, he would have the strongest inducement to cultivate it.[118]
Another advantage of the *mootadari* system, visualized by Thomas Munro, was that it might apportion the rent to the circumstances of the *rayats* better than under the *rayatwar* system. In case of the latter system the rent was necessarily to be fixed upon the land. Though the rent might be occasionally lowered by the revenue officer in case of the poor *rayats* or those who had met with accidental losses, yet as compared to the *mootadar,* a revenue officer, could neither know so well the state of their affairs, nor the amount of the remission that ought to be granted. He would, from this ignorance, often remit where it was unnecessary, and collect rigidly, where payment could not be made without distress or perhaps ruin. The *mootodor,* who was supposed to have been previously, either a *patel* or head farmer, would rarely commit such errors.[119] He would be perfectly acquainted with the circumstances of the *rayats,* and at the same time his own interest would refrain him from exacting rent where it could not be paid without the subsequent failure of the individual and would also induce him to grant leases at a reduced rent whenever that was necessary.[120]

The introduction of the *mootadari* system might bring indulgence to the *rayats* in general and particularly to the poorer *rayats.* The advantage which every *mootadar* derived from the arrival of the desertion of an old one, would, Munro felt, urge him to show every reasonable indulgence, not only to their real wants, but to their prejudices. A *zamindar,* in order to prevent his tenants from going off to another estates, was often obliged to grant a great reduction of rent than was absolutely necessary. And the additional rent, which he obtained from the cultivation of the waste, would enable him to meet the expenses without failing himself. In a *rayatwar* settlement, on the other hand, there was no particular motive for such indulgence, for the Government lost nothing by the *rayats* moving to another estate, as wherever they would do so, they must cultivate land and pay rent.[121]

Another benefit to be achieved by the introduction of the *mootadars* was that it would help speedy establishment of private property. The ownership would become universally and instantly established by the *zamindari* settlement, for every *zamindar* understood at once that village or villages, composing his estates, were his own property. But, under the *rayatwar* system, private ownership could neither be immediate, nor general until the lapse of many years. Even the substantial *rayats* would take many years to determine what lands they would permanently retain as their estates, and the poorer *rayats* would take many years to relinquish old, and take new lands.[122]

The question of tank repairs, and the issue of *taqavi* would also be transferred from the Government to individuals. The tank repairs, in which a branch of revenue charges were quite liable to abuse, could be kept in better order and be repaired at much less expense by individuals than by the Government. The transfer of this work from the Government to individuals would be an advantage to both parties. Secondly, the *mootrdars* would, for the sake of their own interest, issue *taqavi* wherever it was requisite. They were much better judges of the necessity than any public servant.[123]

Last of all, the introduction of the *zamindari* system would also reduce the number of revenue servants and the expense of collection. As the cultivation was to be supervised by the *mootadar,* and the Government was not required to keep any accounts of the lands, and rents of the *rayats,* the pays of the extra servants, employed for those purposes, would be saved.[114]

But in spite of the possible advantages of the *zamindary* settlement mentioned by Munro, his trend of arguments makes it clear that he believed that the practical disadvantages of the *zamindary* settlement would outweigh the possible advantages.[125] He argued that it would alter the established order of things, and that *rayatwar* system had 'always prevailed in India'.[126] Every village was a kind of republic under the management of the *patel* or head farmer, assisted by the *karnum,* the *taliari* etc.[127] The *patel* enjoyed an *in'am* land, usually equal to about 5% of the rent of the village. Of course, his post and the *in'am* were hereditary, but with regard to all other land, which he might cultivate, he had no better advantage or right than the other common *rayats* in the village. If, therefore, the *patel* became the *mootadar,* the right, which was common to all the *rayats,* would become exclusively his, the *rayats* in that case would hold the fields upon the terms which he might choose to prescribe, a change which could not possibly be agreeable to them. At the same time if a person other than the *patel* became the *mootadar,* the change would be still greater, for the latter himself would lose his ancient rights. He might retain the *in'am,* but he would lose his office. He would be degraded from the rank of hereditary chief of a village to that of a pensioner. Under the change from the established to the *mootadari* system, according to Munro, it was quite probable that the whole establishment of village servants, which was so well adapted to the convenience of the inhabitants, to the preservation of order and to the maintenance of the authority of the Government, would be greatly done away by the *mootadars.*[128]

It would concentrate the landed property in few hands. The result would be that the great body of *rayats* would never become wealthy and would remain in a state of dependence on the *mootadar.* The *rayats* would get only short leases, just sufficient to encourage them to cultivate the land, but at same time the chief share of the profit of all the improvement, would remain secured for the *mootadar.* The *mootadars* would definitely become richer individuals, but the aggregate wealth of the country would be less than under the *rayatwar* system. The *rayats* would not cultivate their farms so well or draw so great a produce from them as tenants, as they would, as owners. Moreover, the authority of the

Government and of the court of judicature would also be less respected.[129] Whereas the *rayatwar* system would facilitate the establishment of the authority of the court of justice.[130] It would be more easy for great land-owners, than for petty ones, to form combinations to oppose an increase of rent, or any other unpopular measure, and also to acquire such an influence over their tenants as might deter them from complaining of acts of oppression.[131]

The introductions of the *mootadari* system, would automatically give the *mootadars* the power of raising, at their own will, the rents of the *rayats,* as without this power their position would be more of contractors, or farmers of revenue, than of a landowners. As a result, the *rayats* would not be so comfortable, or independent, as they would be, with their rents fixed, and reaping themselves the whole benefit of every improvement, as tenants of the Government.[132]

The economic condition of most of the *patels* and head farmers, who were likely to become *mootadars,* was also very bad. Many of them were not in a position to cultivate their own farms without *taqvi,* and only a very few had the means of advancing it to others, if the Government had ceased issuing it. Thus, the *rayats* would seldom be able to obtain it from their new landlords. Undoubtedly, a great part of the profit of their labour would go to the *mootadar,* while they would be able to obtain from him little or no help in advancing the improvement of their farms. It would, as such, result in the division of the country amongst a few poor landholders, who would hardly afford any aid towards promoting its cultivation, and who would depend, almost entirely, on the stock of industry of their tenants for discharge of their own rent to the government.[133]

Thus, according to Munro, the system of great estates would raise less produce from the soil than that of small farms; that it was more liable to failure and afford less security to the revenue; that it would be less agreeable to the inhabitants, because they would rather prefer to hold their lands under government than under private individuals; and that it could not be permanent because their laws and customs continually urged upon the rapid division of landed property. Therefore, be was induced to recommend the *rayatwar* system or settlement with the cultivators not only as a temporary, but as a permanent arrangement for the Ceded Districts.[134]

Nor was Munro in favor of the Village Settlement. Though a settlement very much akin to it was prevalent in quite a few villages of the Ceded Districts, known as the *visabadi* villages,[135] especially in the Cuddapah District. As a matter of fact, Munro was against the principle of joint responsibility. As early as 1794 in a letter to Read he observed that though this system was good and effective for the full collection of revenue under the normal circumstances yet during the war and famine this would not work. He rather preferred to forego the revenue if necessary but would not recommend this system. This system, to him, might tend to encourage idleness because many lazy *rayats* would become less anxious to pay off their dues in full, for they knew whatever might be their deficiencies would be collected from others. This might also encourage the *rayats* to come forward every now and then with false statements of losses, involving the collection in endless discussions to know whether they were real or imaginary. It might also enable the *patels* and *karnams* to collect more from the *rayats* than the real loss.[136]

Munro believed that though the *kulwar* settlement might appear tedious when compared to the village one, it was, however, not only better calculated to realize that revenue, but was on the whole a saving of time. When it was once made, there was no other trouble, but in the village settlement there was so much room for malversations and so many disputes between the *patels* and *rayats* about the extra collections, on the one hand, and the withholding of rents on the other; that more time was consumed, in inquiring into those matters, than in the original settlement.[137]

It was on September 30, 1802 that Munro for the first time got an opportunity of giving a description of the methods of conducting a *rayatwar* settlement.

He explained that there were three methods of conducting annual *rayatwar* settlement;

(i) to make *mauzawar,* or village settlement with all the villages in a district at once, and then to proceed to the *kulwar,* or individual *rayatwar* settlement with every *rayat* of each village;

(ii) to make the village settlement of one village, and then the individual settlement of it, before beginning with another; and

(iii) to begin by settling with each individual of one village separately, and then by adding their rents together to make the village settlement.[138]

Munro himself was in favour of the first alternative as he thought that to be advantageous and comparatively expeditious. He felt that by assembling all the *patels* and *karnams* of a district in one place the variety of opinion and information was likely to produce a more accurate estimate of the value of each village, and the joint responsibility of the *patels* for the district revenue would make it difficult for any one conceal resources and in this manner, the total actual produce of the districts would soon be known. After the gross amount of the assessment was once fixed, should that still fall so heavy on any particular village that would be easily equalized by the *patels* themselves with the assistance of *kachahri.* Once the country had been surveyed, the individual would supersede both the village and district settlements, 'because it is then no longer necessary to waste time, in endeavouring to persuade the cultivators to accede to the assessment. The rent of every field being fixed, each cultivator takes, or rejects, what he pleases, and the rents of all the fields occupied in the course of the year in any one village from what is called the settlement of that village.'[139]

The whole discussion about the ideas and convictions of Thomas Munro shows that he had some preconceived notions about the type of land settlement that he wanted to introduce in the 'Ceded District'. He had perhaps more anti *zamindary* settlement feelings than pro preserving of the existing landed institutions feelings. Moreover, he, too, had both economic and political motives behind the introduction of the *rayatwar* system and as such the needs of the new ruling power were foremost in his mind.

Thomas Munro along with like-minded fellow administrators and all the utilitarian thinkers believed in the idea of state or royal ownership of land. Also, the success of his ideas depended solely upon land becoming a saleable commodity. J.H. Nelson, giving his own assessment on the subject, has opined that in South India ordinary people had no idea of *meun* and *tuum* and spoke always in terms of "ours" and mine. A thing of value was regarded as being part of an aggregate, rather than belonging to a single person.

The feelings of group possession, rather than the absence of the sense of private ownership, were so deeply rooted that Nelson even claimed that the idea of selling an estate never entered the minds of the South Indians until after the establishment of English rule.[140] The view upheld by the European visitors in India in the 16th and 17th centuries that all the land was owned by the state[141] was based on their gross ignorance of the working of the *Jagir* system. Moreover, though both in theory and practice, the state was the proprietor of all the waste lands which included hills, jungles and unclaimed plain areas for agrarian purposes, it did not possess any proprietary rights in absolute sense over the vast cultivable lands already in hereditary possession of various classes of *riaya.* Any fresh transfer of a jungle land or any unclaimed *banjar* land to the *riaya* was always accompanied by a *defacto* possession embodying with it a clear title to proprietorship so long as the land remained under cultivation.[142] Besides, there were royal villages or *bhandara qramas* or the *khas* lands (in other words the *khalsa* land) the income of which was used by the king "for his personal use, and benefit as distinct from lands held under him by others, the revenue of which ought to go to the public purse."[143] At the most the land on which state could have its claim could be classified under two heads viz. (i) the *bhandara* villages and (ii) lands alienated either on beneficiary tenures like, *brahmadeya, devadaya, mathapura srotryam, bhattavritti* and *adhyayanavritti* or, in consideration of service rendered or expected of the one in whose favour the alienation was made.[144]

Moreover, the right of the people for the proprietorship of the soil was fully recognized. The state claimed a share in the produce of the land rather than title to its proprietorship. This fact is also borne out by the frequent purchases of land by the kings and their feudatories for providing for festivals and services in the temples by making endowments of the same. If a king wanted to make to a person or an institution, a grant of land or a village which was already in the possession of private individuals, then he had to purchase from the person concerned and then make a grant of the same.[145] The cultivators in a village could be divided into two main categories, viz. (i) *ulkudi* (*i.e.*, *khudkashta),* who was a peasant-proprietor and had his holding and residential house situated in the same village. His holding was hereditary and he had full rights in land for the purposes of its transfer, mortgage and sale, which, of course, was extremely rare: (ii) *pirakkudi (pahi-kashtkar);* was also 'a peasant proprietor but his holding was in a different village from that of his residence. He had a permanent and inalienable right *(kudikkani)* to cultivate the land.'[46] There were, of course, other types of cultivators viz. (i) those under the *kuttagai* or lease system who were required to raise a particular kind of crop on land for a specified number of years: and (ii) *kadamai uliyars* or the forced labourers.[147]

But despite the proprietorship and ceremonial purchases of lands by the kings, the idea of absolute ownership of land did not exist, and especially during the eighteenth century, due to lack of political security, land possessed no market value. All the classes of cultivators connected with the land possessed absolute rights of certain kind. It was basically the question of "interests" that different groups had in land. Moreover, during the nineteenth century, owing mainly to the introduction of order and security, land had gradually attained a market value and, thus, became a saleable commodity.[148]

Thomas Munro's statements enumerating the benefits of the *rayatwari* settlement *viz.,* "it will ultimately augment the wealth of the country and the resources of the Government"; "the *ryots* as proprietors of their several farms will have no armed followers, and can form no combination to disturb the public tranquillity", and the statements against the *zamindar* settlement *viz.,* (under it) "the authority of the Government and of the Court of Judicature will be less respected"; and "It will be more easy for great land-owners, than for petty ones, to form combinations to oppose an increase of rent, or any other unpopular measure," and also against the village settlement, *viz.*, (under it) "during the war and famine this (full collection of revenue) would not work" clearly prove the fact that apart from other factors he had economic and political motives as well.[149]

The success of the *rayatwar* settlement, as is clear from the writings of Thomas Munro, also depended upon the proper survey of the land. In this regard also certain grievances and objections put forth of the members of the Madras Native Association, the spokesmen for the residents of Madras, show that it was not properly done. They asserted that it had been "commenced without the aid of a single surveying instrument, except a chain of 33 feet, or a glimpse of scientific knowledge beyond that of their native *cutcherry gomastahs* or clerks, who, as a part of their duty, were to instruct others in the art of mensuration, an art in which being completely untaught themselves, they had to acquire from no better education than the progress of their own survey."[150] Moreover, even if plots had been accurately measured, the problem of classifying land by its fertility would remain. The Association petitioned that this task was undertaken 'by sending two assessors to classify the space measured by ten surveyors; their business was to arrange it under the principal divisions of wet, dry, and garden land, subdividing these again into various classes according to the presumed quality by a process so perfectly arbitrary, that in some districts the wet land had 12 classes, the dry 20, and the garden land as many... As might have been expected, there assessors, partly from ignorance, and partly from the persuation of bribery, made a great many erroneous classifications..."[151] In view of the objections raised by the petitioners the accuracy of survey and assessments could not be justified.

As such, one can conclude, what Thomas Munro, like other administrators else where in India, achieved was neither a synthesis of the alien nor that of the indigenous. Instead, distortions took place that, strictly speaking, were not the product of the new institutions, but were alterations in the old structure.[152] Moreover, the essential distinctions between the various types of revenue systems introduced by the East India Company and the forms of agrarian relations accruing out of them did not alter the basic fact that the agrarian system and the methods of exploiting the peasants developed in one and the same direction throughout the country.

## References

It is a revised version of two papers (i) "Thomas Munro on Land Reforms in the 'Ceded Districts', 1800-1807" (Paper read at the *Research Students Seminar, Dept. of History, Delhi University, 1969)* and (ii) "Campbell and Hodgson on the Introduction of Rayatwari System in the Ceded District" (Contributed at the *Indian History Congress,* 1976 session).

1. For a detailed discussion on pre-British position see, B.R. Grover, "Nature of Land-Rights in Mughal India", paper read at the *Indian Economic History Seminar, Delhi,* April, 1961, *Indian Economic and Social History Review,* i, (1963), pp. 1-23; and "Elements of Continuity and Change in Land Ownership and Rights from the Mughal Age to the Early British Administration in India", *Presidential Address,* Medieval India Section, *Indian History Congress,* 37th Session, Calicut, 1976.
2. Sulekh Chandra Gupta, "The Influences of Classical Political Economy on British Agrarian Policy in the Bengal Presidency in the late 18th and early 19th centuries" in Bisheshwar Prasad (ed), *Ideas of History,* (Delhi, 1968), pp. 246-63.
3. *Ibid.*
4. Sir Henry Maine, *Village Communities in the East and West* (London, 1890), p. 221.
5. Ranajit Guha, *A Rule of Property for Bengal: An Essay on the Idea of Permanent Settlement,* (New Delhi, 1982) p. 154.
6. Letter from Warren Hastings to Lord Mansfield, 25 Aug. 1774, Gleig, G.R., *Memories of the Life of Warren Hastings, first Governor General of Bengal,* (London, 1841), i, p. 400.
7. Letter from Warren Hastings to Hon'ble Josias Dupre, *ibid.,* p. 272.
8. Ranajit Guha, *op. cit.,* pp. 16-17.
9. W.K. Firminger, *Historical Introduction to the Bengal Portion of the Fifth Report,* (Indian Studies, Calcutta reprint) (pp. ccciv-cccvi) pp. 302-304.
10. *Ibid.;* Holt Mackenzie's Letter to the Select Committee of 1832, *Report of the Select Committee on East India Affairs 1832* (London, 1853), iii—Revenue, p. 298; S. Gopal, *The Permanent Settlement in Bengal and Its Results* (London, 1949), pp. 13-14, and E.D. Ascoli, *Early Revenue History of Bengal and the Fifth Report, 1812* (Oxford 1917), p. 34.
11. Minute of Philip Francis dated 5 Nov. 1776, *Selection of Papers front the Records at the East India House,* (London 1826), iii, p. 439. In the above Minute he states, "I am sensible that my opinion, on this or any other great political question, is no authority; I desire therefore to support it by those of men already in possession of' the public respect and esteem. I fear no condemnation which may involve me with Doctor Smith, Sir James Stuart, and Montesquieu."
12. T.H. Beaglehole, *Thomas Munro and the Development of Administrative Policy in Madras, 1792-1818: The Origins of The Munro System,* (Cambridge, 1966) pp. 4-5.

13. Minute of Cornwallis, 18 Sep. 1789, Charles Ross (ed.), *Correspondence of Charles, First Morquis Cornwallis,* (Second edition, London, 1859), i. p. 562; also W.K. Firminger, *The Fifth Report of the Select Committee on the Affairs of the East India Company 1812* (Calcutta, 1917), ii, p. 512.
14. H.R.C. Wright, 'Some Aspects of the Permanent Settlement in Bengal', *Economic History Review,* second series, Vol. VII, No. 2, p. 212.
15. Eric Stokes, *The English Utilitarians and India,* (O.U.P., 1969 edition), pp. 4-6.
16. Preamble to Regulation II in the Code of Permanent Settlement Regulations, Richard Clarke (ed.), *The Regulations of the Government of Fort William in Bengal,* (London, 1854), i. p. 10.
17. Eric Stokes, *op. cit.,* p. xii.
18. James Mill, *The History of British India,* v, (Fourth Edition, London, 1840), pp. 488-89.
19. C. Petit—Dutaillis, *The Feudal Monarchy in France and England,* (London, 1949), p. 27.
20. Ainslie T. Embree, "Landholding in India and British Institution", Robert Eric Frykenberg (ed.) *Land Control and Social Structure in Indian History,* (New Delhi, 1979), p. 38,
21. Archibald Constable (trans.), Francois Bernier's *Travel in the Mogul Empire* 1656-68, (London, 1914), p. 204; also Ranajit Gupta, *op. cit.,* pp. 99-100.
22. *The Fifth Report of the Select Committee on the Affairs of the East India Company, Madras Presidency,* (London, 1812) (Madras, 1883), p. 151.
23. Eric Stokes, *op. cit.,* p. 90.
24. Ainslie T. Embree, *op. cit.,* pp. 39-40.
25. Edward Christian (ed.), Sir William Blackstone's *Commeararies on the Laws of England,* (London, 1818), p. *138; Fifth Report, Madras Presidency, op. cit.,* p. 301; and *Historical Introduction op. cit.,* (p. ccxiii) p. 311.
26. Amles Tripathi, *Trade and Finance in the Bengal Presidency, 1793-1833,* (Calcutta, 1956), p. 18.
27. Eric Stokes, *op. cit.,* p. 61.
28. Adam Smith, *An Inquiry into the Nature and Cause of the Wealth* of *Nation,* (Modern Library Edition, New York) p. 384.
29. *Ibid.*
30. *Ibid.,* p. 651.
31. *Ibid.,* p. 781.
32. 'Land System of India', *Calcutta Review,* 1873, p. 114.
33. Shelvankar, *The Problems of India,* (London, 1940), p. 105.
34. B.M. Bhatia, *Famines in India: Study in Some Aspects of the Economic History of British India (1860-1945),* (Bombay, 1963) p. 269; "An Enquiry into the condition of the Agricultural classes in India, 1888" *Contributions to Indian Economic History,* Vol. 1. 1960.

35. Sulekh Chandra Gupta, *op. cit.,* p. 255.

36. The East India Company acquired Salem, Dindigul and Malabar after the third Mysore War in 1972; Canara, Coimbatore and Soonda after the final defeat of Tipu Sultan in the fourth Mysore War in 1799; Tanjore from the Maratha Raja Serfogi in 1799; in 1800 got (what came be known as 'Ceded Districts)' the territories south of river Krishna and Tungabhadra, comprising the districts of Cuddapab, Anantapur, part of Kurnool, two talooks (Madanapally and Vyalpad) in Chittor District (in the modern Andhra Pradesh) and Bellary (in the modern Karnataka) from the Nizam of Hyderabad, and finally in 1801 compelled the Nawab of Arcot to Cede the districts of Nellore, North and South Arcot, Trichinopally, Madura and Tinnevelly.

37. 'A Paper on the Land Revenue of India, prepared at the request of the Committee' by A.D. Cambell, Esq., of the Madras Civil Service, *Fifth Report, Madras Presidency, op. cit.,* Appendix No. 6, p. 785.

38. R. Palme Dutt, *India Today,* (Bombay, 1949), pp. 104-120; Eric Stockes, *op. cit,,* p. 38; and Thomas Daniel, *Investment in Empire,* (Philadelphia, 1950), pp. 1-2.

39. Amles Tripathi. *op. cit.,* pp. 123-32.

40. Eric Stokes, *op. cit.,* pp. 38-39.

41. John Sullivan's 'Observations on the Revenue Systems of India', *Affairs of the East India Company: Report from Select Committee 1832.* Appendix, p. 50; also *Fifth Report, Madras Presidency, op. cit.,* Appendix 8, pp. 819-849.

42. *Fifth Report op. cit.,* p. 18; also Eric Stokes, *op. cit.,* p. 4.

43. *Ibid.,* pp. 236, 320-21.

44. Sulekh Chandra Gupta, *Agrarian Relations and Early British Rule in India: a case study of Ceded and Conquered Provinces, (1801-33),* (Bombay, 1963), p. 159.

45. B.N. Ganguli, 'Foreward', *Ibid.,* pp. viii-ix.

46. William J. Barber, *Economic British Thought and India 1600-1858: A Study in the History of Development Economics,* (Oxford, 1975), Chapters 9 and 10; also Eric Stokes, *op. cit.,* Chapters I & II.

47. Haileybury College was a residential establishment started by the East India Company to train their Officers in the European branches of learning and other oriental subjects before they embarked on their duties in India.

48. A.K. Ghoshal, *Civil Service in India under the East Indian Company: A Study in the Administrative Development,* (Calcutta, 1944), pp. 298-99; also Eric Stokes, *op. cit.,* p. 87.

49. William Foster, *The East India House, Its History and Associations* (London, 1924), p. 197. In 1830, James Mill succeeded to the office of Chief Executive (i.e. that of Examiner) and worked in the East India House until his death in 1936.

50. Eric Stokes, *op. cit.,* p. 48.

51. Viz. John Stuart Mill *(Principles of Political Economy,* (London, 1886), 9th Edition, Book II, Chapter VIII, pp. 399-404); (ii) J.R. McCulloch *(Taxation and Funding System,* (London 1852), Appendix II, 'Indian Revenue System; pp.

485-93); (iii) Rev. Richard Jones *(An Essay on the Distribution of Wealth and on the Sources of Taxation* (London, 1831), Chapter IV, Sec. 11, 'On Ryot Rents in India', pp. 109-84; Rev. William Whewell (ed.), *Literary Remains of Richard Jones,* (London, 1859), pp. 211-15 and 271).

52. T.R. Malthus, *An Inquiry in to The Nature and Progress of Rent,* (London, 1815), Preface. He acknowledged the stimulus it had provided to his thinking; "The following Tract contains the substance of some Notes on Rent, which, with others on different subjects relating to political economy, I have collected in the course of my professional duties at the East India College".

53. The writings of Malthus revealed that rent was a special portion of wealth, distinct from profit or wages, and determined in an exact scientific manner. Moreover, he, along with Ricardo and West, believed that rent originated in the natural fertility of the soil and that vents as a proportion of the national income could be expected to swell with growth in the economy and in the size of the population. Eric Stokes, *op. cit.*, pp. 87-88; William J. Barber, *op. cit.*, p. 150.

54. William J. Barber, *op. cit.*, p. 155.

55. T.R. Malthus, *Principles of Political Economy, Considered with a View to Their Practical Application,* (London, 1820, second edition, London, 1836), pp. 194-217.

56. David Ricardo, *Principles of Political Economy and Taxation,* (Everymen's Library Edition, London 1949), p. 33.

57. *Ibid.*, p. 225.

58. *Ibid.*

59. *Ibid.*, pp. 224-25, Karl Marx, *On Colonialism,* (Moscow, 1959), p. 54.

60. George Canning, President of the Board of Control to the Chairman and Deputy Chairman of the East Indian Company, 17th August, 1817, cited in John Sullivan's 'Observations', *op. cit.*, p. 56 and pp. 830-833 respectively.

61. James Mill, *op. cit.*, pp. 489-90.

62. *Ibid.*

63. *Ibid.*

64. J. Bowring (ed.), *The Works of Jeremy Bentham,* 11 vols., (London, 1843).

65. *Ibid.*, vol. X, p. 577.

66. *Ibid.*, p. 490.

67. Richard Jones, *An Essay on the Distribution of Wealth and on the Sources of Taxation* (Combridge, 1831), pp. xv, xxiii, xxv, 189, 193, 205-6, 282, 286-87, 290; William Whewell (ed.), *Literary Remains, Consisting of Lectures and Tracts on Political Economy of Late Rev. Richard Jones,* (London, 1859), pp. 273-74, 288-89, 598, 600; William J. Barber, *op. cit.*, pp. 194-201.

68. John Stuart Mill, *Principles of Political Economy,* (London, 1848), pp. 319, 324-28; Eric Stokes, *op. cit.*, pp. 135-36.

69. However, Eric Stokes has opined that the Utilitarian ideas influenced various British policies in India, including the land revenue question. He has also

emphasized that the administrators like Thomas Munro were largely in agreement with certain aspects of the Utilitarian viewpoint, 'The union of judicial and executive powers in the collector; the simplification of the chaotic jungles of the law to a compact intelligible code which respected Indian custom; the prejudice for a *ryotwar* form of land settlement; and an accurate survey and record of land rights—in all these reforms they were in agreement with the radical authoritarian strain in Utilitarian thought'. But for the most part, his discussion begins only around the year 1820, whereas vital decisions regarding land revenue policy had been taken quite earlier than that year. Eric Stokes, *op. cit.*, pp. 23, 75 & c.; Also Imtiaz Husain, *Land Revenue Policy in North India the Ceded and Conquered Provinces, 1801-33,* (New Delhi, 1967), p. 2.

70. *A further Inquiry into the Expediency of Applying the Principles of Colonial Policy to the Government of India and of Effecting an Essential Change in Its Landed Tenures and in the character of its Inhabitants,* Anonymous, (London, 1828), p. 98.
71. J.C. Dua, 'Poligars: Their Rise in the Ceded Districts', *Indian History Congress,* thirty third session, Muzaffarpur, 1972, pp. 467-474; Nature of the Poligar Revolt in the Ceded Districts during the first half of the Nineteenth Century: A Case Study', *Indian History Congress,* thirty fifth session, Jadavpur, 1974, pp. 235-45; B.H. Baden-Powell, *The Land Systems of British India,* 3 vols., (iii), (Oxford, 1892, reprint, Delhi, 1974, pp. 15, 34-38.
72. *Baramahal Records,* Section 1, p. 177, Lt. Col Barry Close to Capt. Reed, 31st March, 1792; *Fifth Report, Madras Presidency, op. cit.*, p. 66; B.H. Baden Powell, *op. cit.*, iii, p. 16.
73. J.B.B. Dykes, *Salem, an Indian Collectorate,* (London, 1853) p. 24.
74. *Madras Board of Revenue Consultations and Proceedings of the Board of Revenue at Fort St. George, 25th* March 1793, Minute of C.N. White, Member of the Board of Revenue dated 25th March, 1793; *Fifth Report, Madras Presidency, op. cit.*, pp. 273-90.
75. *Baramahal Records,* Vol. 6, p. 1. Read to Board of Revenue, June 1793.
76. 'Paper on Land Revenue' by A.D. Campbell, *op. cit.*
77. *Baramahal Records,* Vol. 1, pp. 203-04, Read to David Haliburton, dated August 10, 1794.
78. Letter of Thomas Munro, dated Nov. 15, 1796, A.J. Arbuthnot, *Sir Thomas Munro: Selections from his Minutes and other Official Writings,* 2 Vol., (London, 1881), i, pp. 3-11.
79. Letter of Thomas Munro, dated Sept. 5, 1797, A.J. Arbuthnot, *op. cit.*, i, pp. 23-24; J.B.B. Dykes, *op. cit.*, p. 142.
80. J. Webbe, Chief Secretary to Govt. of Fort St. George to Major Thomas Munro, dated 24th Oct/Ist Nov., 1800, *Selections from the Records of Bellary District—Political, Revenue and Agriculture matters,* 1800-1856, (TNSA) ASO (D) Vol. 73; *Revenue Despatches to England,* Vol. 7A, p. 136.
81. *General Reports of the Board of Revenue,* January 31, 1803, Vol. 7-9, p. 123.

82. T.N.S.A., *Bellary District Records, 397/79*, Thomas Munro to Board to Revenue, dated, 3rd Nov. 1802; Circular issued by Thomas Munro, dated 10th Aug. 1801, *Selections...Bellary...1800-1856, op. cit.*

83. T.N.S.A., *Madras Board of Revenue Consultations 26 Sept.* 1805 *and Selections from the Old Records of Bellary District 1800-1807, ASO (D)* Vol. 72, Thomas Munro to William Petrie, President of the Board of Revenue, 25 Aug. 1805.

84. *Ibid., Munro's Report regarding the Poligars in the Ceded Districts, 1801-1802,* RSO (D) Vol. 62 (21), Letter from Thomas Munro to the President and Members of the Board of Revenue, dated 12 Aug. 1801; *Selections Bellary...1800-1856, op. cit.*, Munro to the President and Members of the Board of Revenue, dated 30 Nov. 1806.

85. Thomas Munro to Board to Revenue, 25th Aug. 1805, *op. cit.*

86. T.N.S.A., *Selections from the Records of Bellary District,* ASO (D) Vol. 72 and K.N.V. Sastri, *The Munro System of British Statesmanship in India,* (Mysore, 1939), pp. 22-46, Letter from Thomas Munro to Archibald Obins, Esquire, Private Secretary to the R.H. the Governor of Madras (Answers to question regarding Ryotwari Settlement) dated 20th June 1806 (hence forth *Munro's Answers to Questions).*

87. Munro to Board of Revenue dated 25th Aug. 1805, *op. cit.*

88. *Munro's Answer to Questions, op. cit.*

89. Munro to Board of Revenue dated 25th Aug. 1805, *op. cit.*

90. *Ibid.*

91. *Ibid.*

92. *Munro's Answers to Questions, op. cit.*

93. Munro to Board of Revenue, dated 25th Aug. 1805, *op. cit.*

94. *Ibid., Madras Board of Revenue Consultations, 4th Feb. 1808; Selection of Papers from the Records at East India House Relating to the Revenue Police aid Civil and Criminal Justice tender the Company's Governments in India* (London, 1820-26), i, pp. 94-98; *Fifth Report, Madras Presidency, op. cit.*, pp. 646-663; *Col. Munro's Correspondence regarding the Survey and Ryotwari Settlement of the Ceded Districts 1802-1807,* ASO (D) Vol. 79, Report of Thomas Munro, dated 15th Aug. 1807 (hence forth *Report of Thomas Munro dated 15th Aug. 1807).*

95. Thomas Munro to Board of Revenue dated 25th Aug. 1805, *op. cit.*

96. *Report of Thomas Munro, dated 15th Aug. 1807, op. cit.*

97. *Ibid.*, Thomas Munro to Board of Revenue dated 25th Aug. 1805, *op. cit.*

98. *Ibid., Munro's Answers to Questions dated 20 June 1806, op. cit.*

99. *Ibid.*

100. *Munro's Answers to Questions, dated 20 June 1806, op. cit.*

101. *Report of Thomas Munro dated 15 Aug. 1807, op. cit.*

102. *Ibid.;* also *Munro's Answers to Questions, dated 20 June 1806, op. cit.*

103. *Ibid.*

104. *Report of Thomas Munro, dated 15 Aug. 1807, op. cit.*

105. *Munro's Answers to Questions dated 20th June 1806, op. cit.;* Munro to Board of Revenue, dated 25th Aug. 1805, *op. cit.*

106. *Report of Thomas Muuro, dated 15th August 1807, op. cit.*

107. Munro to Board of Revenue, dated 25th Aug. 1805, *op. cit.* Munro to the Board of Revenue, dated 30th Nov. 1806, *op, cit.; Madras Board of Revenue Consultations 5th Jan. 1807.*

108. Letter from Munro to the Board of Revenue, dated 30th Nov. 1806 *op. cit.* N.B. Munro here meant a district in its ordinary state of prosperity, not of one that had been reduced below it by war or any other calamity.

109. *Ibid.*

110. *Report of Thomas Munro, dated 15th August 1807, op. cit.; Fifth Report, Madras Presidency, op. cit.*, p. 650.

111. *Ibid.*

112. *Ibid.*

113. *Munro's Answers to Questions, dated 20th June 1806, Dasbandham* means, grants of land free of revenue for the construction, maintenance, and repair of irrigation works, Mauro intended to grant such lands to heads of the villages or to substantial *rayats* which would answer all the expenses of the *rayats.*

114. An advance or loan made to the agriculturists to make improvements on the land, buy seeds, cattle etc.

115. *Munro's Answers to Questions, dated 20th June 1806, op. cit.*

116. *Report of Thomas Munro, dated 15th Aug. 1807 op. cit.; Fifth Report, Madras Presidency, op. cit.*, p. 650.

117. *Munro's Answers to Questions, dated 20th June 1806, op. cit*

118. *Ibid.*

119. But this, according to Munro, was possible if the person of the same village was made *mootadar.*

120. *Munro's Answers to Questions, dated 20th June 1806, op. cit.*

121. *Ibid.*

122. *Ibid.*

123. *Ibid.*

124. *Ibid.*

125. *Ibid.;* Munro to the Board of Revenue, dated 25th Aug. 1805, *op. cit.*

126. *Report of Thmas Munro, dated 15th August 1807, op. cit.*

127. Munro to Board of Revenue, dated 30th Nov. 1806, *op. cit.; Madras Board of Revenue Consultations, 5th Jan. 1807, Bellary District Records,* 397/79, Munro to the Board of Revenue, dated 3rd Nov. 1802, *Public Sundries,* Vol. 123A, p. 31, Munro to Sub-Collectors, dated 30th Sep. 1802, *Madras Board of Revenue Consultations 19th May 1803* and ASO (D) Vol. 79, Munro to Board

of Revenue, dated 2 May 1803, Munro to Board of Revenue dated 25th Aug. 1805, *op. cit., Munro's Answers to Questions, dated 20th June, 1806, op. cit.*

128. *Munro's Answers to Questions dated 20th June 1806, op. cit.*, Munro to Board of Revenue, dated 25th Aug. 1805, *op. cit.*

129. *Ibid.*, Munro to Board of Revenue dated 30th Nov., 1806, *op. cit.*

130. *Report of Thomas Munro, dated 15th Aug. 1807, op. cit.*

131. *Munro's Answers to Questions dated 20th June 1806, op. cit.*, Munro to Board of Revenue, dated 30th Nov. 1806, *op. cit.*

132. *Ibid.*

133. *Ibid.*

134. *Ibid.*

135. *Visabadi* village was that village where a fixed sum was assessed on the whole village, and a number of *rayats* agreed to be responsible in a fixed fractional shares. The revenue was divided into sixteen shares. The *rayats* exchanged holdings periodically so that each might have his turn at the good and bad land. It is believed that if a *rayat* thought his holding over-assessed, and that his neighbour under-assessed, he offered to exchange on paying for the latter an increased sum which he named. If his neighbour agreed that was just, his holding was raised to the amount named, and the objector obtained a reduction on his land. The village was under the management of *patel* or head farmer, who was, from long habit, perfectly capable of making the settlement of his village, and the *rayats,* from having been long accustomed to be guided by him, would readily agree to what he fixed or proposed, as it was usually what they, themselves knew, to be the proper revenue. In all such villages, the *rayats* were in habit of meeting, and debating upon the subject of revenue, but there were many villages, in which they settled among themselves the exact proportion of the whole revenue that each individual was to pay. See for reference, Munro to the Board of Revenue dated 30th Nov. 1806, *op. cit.*, Baden-powell, iii, *op. cit.*, pp. 46, 125.

136. *Baramahal Records,* section I, p. 218, Munro to Read, dated 31st July 1794.

137. Munro to the Board of Revenue, dated 30th Nov. 1806, *op. cit.*

138. *op. cit.*, f.n. 127.

139. *Ibid.*

140. J.H. Nelson, *A Prospectus of the Scientific Study of the Hindu Law,* (London, 1881), p. 189.

141. 'Eulogy of Father Jerme Xavier, S.J.A. Missionary in Mogor', tr. from Spanish by Rec. H. Hoston, S.J. in *Journal and Proceedings of the Asiatic Society of Bengal,* New Series, Vol. XXIII, p. 121, *Bernier's Travels, op. cit.*, pp. 211-12, 220-226.

142. B.R. Grover, *op. cit.*, B.H. Baden-Powell, 'Is the State, the Owner of all Land in India? *A.Q.R.*, July-October, 1894, pp. 4-8.

143. Foreign Chroniclers, like Nuniz, have referred about the existence of royal estates or demesnes during the Vijayanagar empire. Robert Sewell, *A Forgotten Empire (Vijayanagar),* (1900), p. 384 and f.n; *Madras Epigraphical Report of 1920,* para 390.

144. *Epigraphia Carnatica,* vii, Sh. 71; *Madras Epigraphical Report of 1890,* para 21; *South Indian Inscriptions,* iv, No. 344.

145. *Epigraphia Carnatica,* viii. Ng. *5; x,* Mb; iii, My, 81; *Madras Epigraphical Report of 1929-30,* para 538.

146. B.R. Grover, *op. cit.;* K.R. Venkatarama Ayyar, *A Manual of the Pudukkottai State,* i, p. 138; T.V. Mahalingam, *Administration and Social Life under Vijayanagar: Part II Social Life,* (Madras, 1975), p. 94.

147. Madras Epigraphical Report of 1913, para 409; 1914, para 30; T.V. Mahalingam, *op. cit.,* pp. 96-97.

148. Vera Anstey, *The Economic Development of India,* (London, 1939), pp. 97-99.

149. Refer f.n. 90; 103; 131.

150. The Humble Petition of the Madras Native Association, and others, Native Inhabitants of the Presidency of Madras, *Parliamentary Papers, 18S2-53,* Vol. 27, p. 443.

151. *Ibid.,* p. 440.

152. Ainslie T. Embree, 'Landholding in India and British Institution', in Rebert Eric Frykenberg (ed.), *Land Control and Social Structure in Indian History,* (New Delhi, 1979), p. 47.

[illegible] ... Thompson and [illegible] ... "Introduction" ...

143. Though [illegible] earlier scholars have [illegible] about the existence of [illegible] during the Vijayanagara empire. Robert Sewell, *A Forgotten Empire* [illegible] (1900), p. 384 and [illegible] *Imperial Gazetteer* [illegible] p. 193.

144. *Imperial Gazetteer*, vol. [illegible] ... (1906) [illegible] ... *Gazetteer* ...

145. *Epigraphia* [illegible] ... *Annual Report* 1929-30, para 48.

146. B.R. [illegible] op.cit., K.V. Venkatarama Ayyar, *A Manual of the Pudukottai State*, [illegible] ... [illegible] ... Madras, 19[illegible], p. [illegible]

147. Madras Epigraphical Report of 1917, para 109; 1918, para [illegible]; Malabar Gazetteer, op.cit., pp. 16[illegible]

148. [illegible] Ayyar, [illegible] ... (London, 1934), p. [illegible]

149. Report on [illegible] 1894 [illegible]

150. The Humble Petition of the Madras Native Association and other Native Inhabitants of the Presidency of Madras, *Parliamentary Papers*, 1852-53, vol. [illegible], p. 45.

151. *Ibid.*, p. 40.

152. Amiya [illegible] ... in India and [illegible] ... [illegible] ... *Land* ... in *India*, New Delhi, 19[illegible]

# *Appendix I*

# Sketch History of Land Revenue in the Madras Presidency

## (A) Ancient History

*Growth of landed institutions*—No conjecture can be made as to when the races of Southern India passed from a pastoral to an agricultural state. The oldest portion however of the Tamul language shows agriculture as being practised. The first step in the transition between the two states is wandering or shifting cultivation, such as still remains among the hill-tribes. The next step is the formation of stationary villages. In the earliest villages of the south the community was governed by a headman, there was a concentrated system for regulating common affairs, and the division of labor was carried out in the practice of the different trades and professions by individuals receiving a regulated remuneration. Local taxes also for common purposes were levied rateably. The ownership by the individual however in the soil itself was at first weak, for the land being abundant was the property of him who liked to take it, and, there being more in reserve, occupation alone could give to the land but a slight marketable value. Ownership gradually grew stronger as occupants closed in on the first settlers. The Government, as soon as any arose, limited its operations to taking from each individual cultivator a share of the produce. This primitive form of village corporation remains more of less intact in many places to this day, the only difference being that the lower orders have been to a considerable extent emancipated and that the Government have assumed the additional duty of assigning waste lands to new occupants. In the village system here described there was no joint claim to the whole village area, including waste; and there was no

Based on Government of India, Revenue and Agricultural Department: *Agricultural Statistics of British India*, Vol. I, (British India) for 1884-85 to 1901-02; and Government of India: *Report of Royal Commission on Agriculture*, 1928.

combination to exclude strangers. Another form of village community sprung up at a more recent date. This form was the result of occupation by a body democratic among themselves, but forming an exclusive oligarchy as regards others whom they found before them. The distinctive features of this system of village corporation were that the dominant race claimed a strong proprietary right in the whole of the village area whether, cultivated or uncultivated; that they gave no franchise to strangers; and that in their own internal administration they had a tendency to communism, and adopted...were the same as in the more ancient form. The details of their land administration will be mentioned in this note hereafter. The Government had no concern with the distinction of lands, and it is believed that they settled, not with the individual cultivator singly, but jointly with the village authorities. These communities also exist to this day, but their special characteristics have been much curtailed. The punchayets are of less importance than they were, and have generally given place to headmen. The rents to the dominant body survive in a few cases only of what are called Swatantrams in the Chingleput district; and the rights to the waste, though still asserted by Mirassidars and kareikarar in the southern districts, are recognized by Government only as a preferential claim, to be indulged under certain conditions and in common with other inhabitants of the village. It has been stated by some that this form of community is due to Aryan influence. It may be so, but it is equally possible that it represents the system of the more civilized Dravidians when in contact with an earlier and weaker race.

(2) *Ancient Proprietary Rights*—In the times of the early village communities proprietary rights, as defined by powers to alienate, existed to a very trifling extent. In the more ancient form of community, as has been said, tenures had no market-value; and in the later and more democratic communities where rights were more decided, the land was not an individual but a common property, and one man could not without the consent of the others sell to a stranger. Still transactions occurred in the latter case among the members of the community themselves, which showed an individual ownership within that limit. Sales were not common, and mortgages were usually not foreclosable for a very long period;

but the latter existed in abundance, showing a certain value in individual ownership of landed property. Individual property in land sprung up earlier than elsewhere in the districts on the western coast, probably owing to the political circumstances, which rendered the Government authority weak and the State demands light. The attitude of the Dravidian or Hindoo rulers with regard to the soil has been much discussed. It probably varied entirely with the circumstances or times and places. The object of Government in this connection is to obtain revenues for Government purposes. If it found communities so organized as to be able to farm the villages properly and to render the proper State dues, the Government would not interfere in the direction of the disposal of the lands claimed by the community. If it found an imperfect organization it would be forced to interfere in the disposal of the lands especially of the waste lands, with a view to the proper development of the country and realization of the revenue. The tendency probably was for the villagers to lean more and more on the Government in these matters, and hence in many parts of the country the State interference became a regular institution. Still there is no evidence that any Hindoo government ever took the step of ejecting an occupier; even if they failed to obtain their dues from him they limited their reprisals to personal torture or sale of movable property. The land sale law is not a native institution. As indicated in the text, the discussion whether the Indian governments are "proprietors" of the soil or not seems to be little more than a dispute about woods.

(3) *Slavery*—By far the greater part of the laboring classes of the people must have been, during the early historical periods, in a state of acknowledged slavery. In Malabar and Canara, where the land became gradually the subject of distinct properties, the laborer was the personal slave of the occupier of the soil and was liable to be sold and mortgaged by him independently of his lands. In Tamul country the slave was considered rather as attached to the soil. In the Teloogoo country only does slavery seem to have been weak. It must be noticed, however, that South Indian slavery was always domestic, and never the subject of foreign traffic. It even appears that in the Tamul country the Pariahs or Pullars, slaves attached to the Vellalars and the Pullies, slaves attached to the

Brahmins, used to claim hereditary landed property as the incident of their rights(?). Slavery did not survive the Hindoo peroid, except to a very limited extent. As long as the Government land tax was moderately light, as it is believed to have been in the Hindoo period, the proprietor could afford to maintain slaves and servants to cultivate for him. The Mahomedans are believed to have raised the land-tax and rendered it necessary for the landlord to work at the plough in his own person or with the help of his family. This is the explanation usually given, and there is probably some truth in it, is by some, however, denied that the land-dues of the Mahomedans were higher than those which obtained before their time. It is at any rate certain that slavery has gradually died out.

(4) ***Early System of Government Land Revenue***—In the earliest times the land-revenue was the sole Government impost, and the revenue system of the country may be said to have been founded on the absence of taxation properly so called. This principle has been brought down to the present day with no very great modification, and has met with opponents. The oriental theory, as now interpreted, is that the portion of the produce of the land which is given by nature, as opposed to which is produced as the interest of invested capital, is the proper source from which to draw revenue; and that if this be not alienated to individuals, or appropriated by them by prescription, the necessity of taxing labor or capital is obviated. This state of things is not inconsistent with the creation of private properly in the occupation of land, in capital sunk in it, and in that portion of the rent which is allowed to individuals to give them an interest in the soil. The land-revenue was levied by all Hindoo governments in the shape of a proportion of the gross produce fixed according to the capacity of different soils and the value of different products, or the commuted money-value of that proportion. There was no settlement for a succession of years or seasons, but each crop was divided as it was produced. The Metayer system of Italy and some other modern continental countries is but a repetition of this plan. The Government share was usually taken in kind under what is now called the Amauny system. In those times when the boundaries of fields were ill-defined and the holdings very small and intermixed, and where it

was the practice to thresh out grain at once after reaping, it was easier, and gave less opportunity for abuse, to divide the grain so threshed out than to calculate annual money-payments according to the quantity and quality of land actually cultivated. In certain cases, however, the value of the crop was estimated after reaping, and a portion of this value was paid in money to the State. The communication system would naturally take the place of the other where joint settlements were made with villages. It was also considered more applicable to dry-land crops than to wet-land crops. The amount of the Government share in Hindoo times was very fluctuating. The institutes of Menoo would have it that the State should take of grain only "an eighth part, a tenth, or a twelfth, according to the difference of the soil, and the labor necessary to cultivate it". But it is quite certain that the average share under Hindoo governments considerably exceeded these theoretical limits. The Hindoo share was, as first mentioned, probably less than the Mahomedan share, but it must have been very much above the share of Menoo or it will be impossible to account for the slow development of individual landed property. It is probable that in times of war the land demand was increased.

(5) **Modern Premahomedan Period**—*Division of the Country*—Certain characteristics have been mentioned which are believed to have been broadly true of the whole of Southern India in ancient Hindoo times. If a step forward is taken, and the approximately modern pre-Mahomedan period is considered, considerable variations are found in different parts of the country. For convenience sake the country as existing at that period may be roughly divided into three principal tracts, the Tamul Country, the West Coast, and the Teloogoo Country.

(6) ***The Tamul Country***—The Tamul country lies between Nellore on the north and the most southern extremity of the East Coast, skirting the Mysore plateau on the eastern side. It was the scene of the three old Hindoo dynasties of Pandya, Chola and Chera. The exact limits of these kingdoms cannot now be traced, and without doubt were in a state of constant charge. It is only known with certainty that they met near Caroor, about 40 miles west of Trichinopoly, a town which alternately passed into the hands of each of the rivals. Pandya is generally identified with

Madura, Chola with Tanjore, and Chera with Salem. In the Tamul country the republican form of village community above mentioned was especially prevalent. On the first establishment of a Tamul village the rights of occupancy of the whole land were divided into a number of equal shares or "ploughs", and apportioned to the different members of the settling community. At the earliest stage it is probable that there was common cultivation, and that the net produce after payment of taxes was divided accordings to the seeds. Subsequently individual cultivation seems to have been carried on, but the land to be cultivated by each was reapportioned by lot in the original proportions either annually or at every five, six, or ten years. In Tanjore, Tinnevelly, Madura, Dindigul, and the other Tamul provinces south of the Coleroon, individual occupancy seems to have arisen at an early date. The division of lands was then considered permanent, and as far as occupation and cultivation went, the ancient collective tenure was converted into one of severalty. For all other purposes, however, the communistic principle still prevailed. A sharer cold not sell his land without the consent of the community and on the other hand the possession of a share, whether inherited or acquired by sale or mortgage, gave a proportionate claim to all incidents common to the village, as for instance the advantage arising out of mines or quarries, fisheries, forests, taking up of new waste pasturage, &c. Gradually the shares became subdivided; but in the accounts of the village the original partition always remained, the small holdings being represented in terms fractional of the original shares, and the possessor of a reduced share possessing a corresponding share of the communistic rights and duties. The name given to these communistic rights and duties was Caniauchy among the Vellalars. When the property fell into the hands of the Brahmins it was called Swastiam. The same property when found in the possession of Mahomedans or native Christians was called Mirassy, the name now most usually employed in all cases; Mirass is an Arabic word, meaning inheritance or patrimony. Pasangkaray in Tamul and Sarwadayam in Sanscrit are also terms for the same thing. In some instances, principally in Tanjore, the whole Mirassy of a village was vested, either by purchase or otherwise, in the hands of one individual; it was then called Yecabhogam. The duties of the individual

Mirassidars, as such, consisted of paying certain small taxes or "Meray" to the community for purposes of internal village administration. The following list taken from old accounts is illustrative of the nature of these taxes:—To feeding Brahmins on particular festivals; to lighting the village temples and gates; to expenses incurred on certain anniversaries; to feeding travellers and strangers, one meal to each; to repairing the village wall; to repairing the chief temple; to constructing a new gate for the village; paid to certain men for killing a tiger, &c. The rights of the Mirassidars were more numerous than their duties, the institution being one for the assertion rather of the former than of the latter. Against the Government the Mirassidars asserted freedom from all interference in the apportionment of land within the village boundary, or in the management of village affairs; claiming the exclusive right to a hereditary possession and usufruct of the former and a hereditary authority in the latter. In Tondeimandalam lying between the south of Nellore and the Coleroon, or the country now comprising Chingleput and North and South Arcot, the Mirassidars claimed also as a perquisite a portion of arable land called gramamanyam, free of all Government demands. Against non-Mirassidars the claims of the Mirassidars were the same as those of any owner of landed property against strangers, the latter having no part in the corporation and being admitted to cultivate only on sufferance. Non-Mirassidars paid village taxes to the Mirassy corporation, and these contributions eventually no doubt removed the necessity for the Mirassidars themselves making any contributions at all; at the present day we find the Mirassidars in some localities claiming such contributions from non-Mirassidars, in the form of a proportionate deduction from the gross produce of lands paying tax to Government, and this merely as a perquisite and without making any return for it. The village government was carried on by a punchayet, or body of five, and the headman was only president in a sort of council. The management of all internal details and the realization of the Government dues from the individual cultivator vested with this body or their delegates, and public opinion was no doubt the check on injustice. The collection of the revenue cost the Government nothing. The demand was a maximum demand liable to remissions on the report of the village authorities. In early times each village was composed of a number of families cliaming to be the same brotherhood or class, and generally the villages in the same part of the country were of one tribe or sub-division of a tribe. The principal caste was that of the Vellalar, the professional cultivator. Non-Mirassidars were nearly always tenants of the Mirassidars collectively or severally, and in that capacity they were called Poyacarries. Besides the village merays, they paid an ordinary rent. The profit of the Mirassidar owner after paying Government dues was called Swamibhogam or landlord's profit. In many cases one family of tenants rented the same farm at a stipulated amount of share of produce for several generations, and thus gradually acquired a prescriptive right to remain and not to have their rents raised. They also gradually acquired rights of alienation. This class of tenants was called oolcoody or inside cultivator. Tenants who had not attained to such a position were called paracoody or foreign cultivator. These tenancies resembled very closely those of the 'coloni' and 'aratores' of the Roman empire. That the Mirassidars enjoyed a clear landlord's rent, and that individual property gradually arose, may be seen from deeds of sale belonging to the period. The Mirassy system flourished as long as the Government demand was not excessive. The Mahomedan rulers are generally supposed to have augmented the land-tax to such a point as to have absorbed all landlords' rents, and to have reduced the Mirassidars to much the same position as an oolcoody. Tanjore retained the Mirassy system the longest, and at the begining of this century the landlord's rent was still about 25 per cent. of the crop. At the same period the Tinnevelly rent had sunk to 15½ per cent. It should be mentioned, to render the description of the Tamul system complete, that Manyams or alienations of State demands on certain lands were already prevalent in the Hindoo period. In these cases the alienation was either in favor of a village servant in accordance with custom and under the authority of the village register, when it was classed as Tarapady; or in favor of some independent person under special grant from the ruling power, when it was called Sunnud or Dumbarla. The Mirassidars paid the Government tax on Manyam lands to the persons to whom the rights of Government were under these arrangements transferred. Occasionally the payee would himself get possession of the land, and pay the Government dues to himself; whether this was done with the consent of the Government, or only by accident and encroachment, is a point much debated.

(7) ***The West Coast***—The tract of country known to ancient Hindoo geographers as Kerala comprised the whole of the tract lying along the Western Coast and under the mountains as far as Gocarna in North Canara. Travancore and Cochin were from the first under rajahs belonging to the land-owning class. Malabar was similarly ruled, but broke up in the ninth century into a number of petty principalities, among the chief of which was that of the Zamorins at Calicut found still in authority by Vasxo da Gama at the end of the fifteenth century. Tooloova, or Canara as it has erroneously been called by the British, was established as a separate Hindoo dynasty held by the land-owing class; but in the twelfth century this dynasty made way for that of the Pandyans, and a century later for that of the Teloogoo-speaking kings of Vijianugger, the representatives of the old Carnatic or Canara empire. The characteristic of the whole of the Kerala country was the presence of a strongly developed personal and individual land-property, the absence of a Government tax on land, the absence of a concentrated village system such as obtained in the Carnatic, and the existence of a military tenure similar to the feudal system of Europe. The country was originally sub-divided between a race of Brahmins or priests called Mumboories, and a military tribe called Nayars; these two holding in subjection the agriculturalists of the country, consisting of persons called Teeyars and others. The Nayars paid no land-tax, but attended the kings to the field with their retainers. The Numboories also paid no land-tax, but furnished the expenses for the support of the temples. In the ninth century a Zamorin of Calicut became a convert to Mahomedanism, and about this time a large colony of Mahomedan settlers of Arabian descent were allowed to occupy lands in Malabar. These Mahomedans, called Moplahs, were mostly merchants, and were equally exempted from payment of direct land-tax. In the absence of land-tax the kings of the country had considerable domains assigned to them, which were cultivated by slaves and yielded a sufficient revenue for household expenses. The subordinate chiefs maintained their own

internal police arrangements, and, excepting in time of war, the personal expenses of the rajah's were not large. But they were not without other branches or revenue. A succession duty equal to 25 per cent. on the value of estate was levied on Mahomedan being landholders. There were also import and export duties, mint duties, fines, escheats, confiscations, protection money received from persons of other States who claimed asylum, benevolences in the shape of offerings made to the Crown at great festivals or on an occasion, and fees on marriages of important persons. There were also license-taxes and royalties on gold ore, elephants, ivory, teak-trees, bamboos, and vessels wrecked on the coast. The inhabitants of the West Coast did not congregate together in villages, but resided in scattered habitations on their farms and in their gardens. For fiscal arrangements there were authorities in charge of defined tracts of country. The proprietary right in the land differed from Mirassy right in being individual and not communistic. Whether enjoyed by the original Nayars and Numboories, or by the more recent Moplahs, it was equally called Jenm or birth-right. The owners seldom cultivated their own lands, but let them out on limited leases to tenants called Pauttomcars. The Crown ceased to recognize the immunity from land-tax if an original Jenmdar once parted by sale with his right. Hence mortgage was the rule of the country, and sales scarcely ever occurred. The mortgagee again could not acquire the Jenm right by simply foreclosing; the landlord never losing the power of subsequently reclaiming his property by paying the principal, and being always entitled to some recognition of his ownership even if it were only given in the shape of a sheaf of corn or a pound of butter. The Malabar mortgages possessed another peculiarity in the principle of self-redemption. On the death of the owner of mortgaged lands, it was usual for the heir to furnish a new instrument recognizing the act of his predecessor, but on this occasion he was entitled to deduct 13 per cent. from the principal of the debt. Thus in a few generations the lands reverted to the ancient family proprietors. These were the primitive tenures of the West Coast, and as long as they were recognized by the Governments, there can be little surprise that landed property so carefully protected should be strongly asserted by the holders. There is no trace that up to the time of the

Mahomedan invasions there was any land-tax south of Tooloova, and in the southernmost part of Tooloova, it must have been even then a very light one. The Tooloova country began to change its land-revenue features in the thirteenth century when invaded by the Pandyan king. On that occasion the original Nayars seemed to have been dispossessed in favor of a race of cultivators called Hullers, and in making the transfer of property the land tax, such as it was, suffered an increase. It is reported that the new government required the grain to be husked before being delivered into the public stores, thus adding 10 per cent. to the impost. In A.D. 1336 when Tooloova came under the Rajah of Vijianugger, the system was still further adapted to that prevailing in the north.

(8) *The Teloogoo Country*—Regarding the Teloogoo country as it existed in the pre-Mahomedan period there is much less to say than regarding the two other main divisions of the Presidency; partly because it had less characteristic features, and partly because such special features as it possessed have been almost entirely obliterated by the subsequent Mahomedan and British occupations, and information on the subject is therefore very meagre. As far as can be ascertained, the village system in the Teloogoo country was more of the ancient not republican form than in the more southern parts of the country. There are traces, however, in certain parts, of a right akin to Mirassy right right in the ancient landholders whom the Mahomedans called Kadeem. It is known that a large proportion of the cultivators, if not all of them, possessed under the old rajahs the privilege of hereditary occupancy,, and that the assessment was light. Hence the land must have saleable. Traces of landed proprietorship are however by no means so clear as on the West Coast, or even as in Tondeimandalam. The hilly portions of the country seem to have been from time immemorial parcelled out among chieftains of the military class, who held hereditarily, exercised uncontrolled territorial jurisdiction within their limits, and appropriated the entire revenues subject to the condition of performing military service or other offices at the Court of their superior rajah, at Cuttack or Vijianugger for instance. In the plains were found a number of petty non-military Hindoo rajahs, forming an ordinary landed aristocracy. These petty chieftainships obtain more or less all over the Presidency, but are the more noteworthy

in the Teloogoo country, because it is there, that they have been principally supported and incorporated into the revenue system by subsequent governments. The origin of these chieftainships was no doubt various, and while some represented old families, others were at the time of the Mahomedan invasions little more than Government officers for the collection of revenue in large tracts.

**(9) The Mahomedan period.** ***Mahomedan Invasions***—India has twice been subject to Mahomedan rule, once under the Turks after the invasion of Mahmood of Ghuznee in the eleventh century, and once under the Moghuls after the invasion of Baber in the sixteenth century. On each of these occasions the southern part of the peninsla was overrun by the conquerors, though not to the same extent as more northern provinces. About the year 1300 Allah-ood-deen formally completed the conquest of the Deccan; and in the year 1347 we find direct Mahomedan authority extending as far south as the Kistna river. There is no accurate account of the mode in which the Turks raised supplies, but it was probably through the local Hindoo chiefs. The occupation was strictly a military one, and the police and revenue administration still remained for the most part in the hands of the local chiefs. There is no distinct trace of any changes of the land revenue system. The Mahomedans were well content to leave such institutions as they found them, and indeed the only information now available as to the rates of taxation peculiar to the Hindoos is that given by the Mahomedan historian Ferishta. It is asserted that the Turkish invasion had the indirect effect on landed property of forcing up the land demand exacted by the Hindoo chiefs, and so of weakening private property. In the interval between the Turkish and Moghul dynasties a number of the Hindoo kingdoms of the south were absorbed by Mahomedan kingdoms, the result of incessant petty wars. This period saw the rise of the farming system, mere outside speculators taking the place in many cases of the old native rajahs. Where the Mahomedans found it inconvenient to deal with village communities and native rajahs were not at hand, they appointed farmers of the land revenue. Such men undertook the farm as a mere temporary speculation, without acquiring any local rights claims or ties of any kind and without interfering in any way with the existing rights of the cultivators. By the time that Acbar succeeded to the throne in 1556, the conquest of the country was sufficiently confirmed to enable him to inaugurate measures of a more detailed nature for regulating the revenue system. Acbar perfected the land settlement of his predecessor Sher Khan; and Malik Amber, an Abyssinian under the Mahomedan princes of the south, and Sivajee among the Mahrattas, carried out Acbar's principles in a large portion of the south. The farming system had naturally led to abuses on the part of the farmers and to resistance on the part of the cultivators, and Acbar was desirous of superseding it. He endeavoured to settle in all cases with village communities. With this object he surveyed and classified the lands in the villages, took the average produce of each class of land, ascertained the average price of produce for ten years past, and took one-third of the average gross produce paid in cash as the Government demand. In this way was calculated the amount to be paid by each village. At the same time a detailed statement was drawn up of the amount payable by each cultivator, for the guidance of the village authorities. The close similarity between these assessment arrangements and the assessment arrangements of the present day will be observed and at the same time this important distinction, that village settlements have been abandoned. The assessment obtained under Acbar's system was less than former assessments, but it was anticipated that the difference would be made up by increased punctuality of payment, for the joint responsibility of the community was the condition on which the reduced rates and other advantages were accorded to the villagers. The community managed their own affairs and disposed of their own waste. Under this settlement lands exempted from revenue were registered and inquired into, and those that were improperly held were resumed. Remissions were given on the occurrence of great calamities, but not otherwise. Payment was enforced by a personal restraint and seizure of goods, but not by sale of lands. On the other hand the Government reserved the right to take land from those who would not cultivate and give it to others. The Mahomedan arrangements of this period were probably in many respects rather theoretical than practical, for a very short time afterwards the former farming system is found again re-established all over the country.

**(10) British Period.** *Early Measures of the British Government*—When the administration of Southern India fell into the hands of the British the state of things was briefly as follows. Large farms were held by large renters called Zemindars, or in a few cases by native chiefs dating from the pre-Mahomedan period; certain single villages were farmed by the headmen; and in other villages the more perfect democratic communities made joint bargains for lump payments. The part of the country first acquired, and where the first administrative steps had to be taken, was the Northern Circars, or the tract lying on the northern extremity of the present Madras Presidency between the sea-board and the Orissa hills. As little was known by the Company's servants about the tenures or settlements of the country the detailed administration was at first left entirely in the hands of the natives, the European officials merely keeping the books. The farming system was carried out even further than before. This administration was not successful. The Circars were divided into Zemindarry lands, or land found in the hands of middlemen, and Havelly lands or lands not so found. At the outset the British put renters even into the Havelly lands. The zemindars invariably sub-rented the lands to another middleman, and the speculators or renters put in by the British into the non-Zemindary lands had little regard for the welfare of the cultivators. In either case the actual cultivator retained a very small share of produce. This state of things lasted but a few years however, and in 1769 the Fort St. George Government took the detailed administration into its own hands and set about making improved settlements. The first step was to appoint Provincial Councils. They found the work too great, and did not effect much. The next step was the appointment by the Court of Directors of a Special Commission, or Committee of Circuit as it was called, consisting of certain members of the Madras Council, with instructions to make tours in the districts and institute inquiries into rights and interests. The instructions of the Court of Directors were conceived in a liberal and enlightened spirit, and were clearly and emphatically expressed. But this committee was also a failure. The Provincial Courts did not sufficiently support its operations, and the middlemen did their best to create impediments. No fixed system was introduced. Annual leases were granted in the first instance, then settlements for three and five years. The Havelly lands were let in some cases on the village joint-settlement system, but the settlements were imperfectly made. In 1786 a Board of Revenue was established at Madras, on the pattern of the Board already existing in Bengal, and about the same time individual Collectors took the place of the Provincial Councils in the Circars.

(11) ***Contemporary Measures in Bengal***—In the same year that the Madras Government entered on the management of the Northern Circars, the Bengal Government assumed that of Bengal, Behar, and Orissa; and experiments were conducted in the latter case in very much the same way as in the former. The Bengal Government however came earlier to a decision, and when Lord Cornwallis came to India as Governor-General in 1786 the plain of the permanent settlement with the Bengal Zemindars had already been arranged. An experimental settlement of the whole of Bengal for a ten-year period was announced in 1789, and in 1792 the experiment of a permanent settlement was declared to be confirmed.

(12) ***Permanent Settlement in Northern Circars***—The permanent alienation of the land revenue thus made to the Bengal middlemen had some supporters in Madras, and pressure was brought to bear on Madras by the Bengal Government to adopt the same policy in this Presidency. The Court of Directors wrote out to the same effect in 1795. The Madras Board of Revenue however reported that they were hardly prepared to recommend the perpetuation of the settlement, and that they required time for the collection of further information. In 1799 positive orders were brought out from England that Lord Cornwallis' permanent system was to be adopted throughout the Madras Presidency. On this occasion the Governor-General proclaimed his resolution to remove from office any public servant who evinced a want of zeal in fulfilling the intentions of Government. Eventually the Madras Government reported to the Supreme Government that they were possessed of materials for a permanent Zemindarry settlement in certain parts of the country. Lord Wellesley, who had by this time succeeded to the Governor-Generalship, directed the commencement of operations in the lands on the East Coast. A Special Commission was accordingly appointed, and between the

year 1802 and 1804 the northern districts of Madras were permanently assessed. The lands already in the hands of Zemindars were confirmed to them in perpetuity, the assessment being fixed according to local circumstances. The Havelly lands were parcelled out into estates of a convenient size, yielding from 3,500 to 17,500 rupees annual rent or in some cases more, and were sold as Mootahs or perpetually-settled revenue farms, to the highest auction bidder. Regulation XXV of 1802 constituted both those descriptions of landholders "proprietors", and detailed the terms on which they held their property.

**(13)** ***Settlement in the Jagheer***—The country round Madras known as the Jagheer had been obtained from the Nawab of Arcot, partly in 1750 and partly in 1763, in return for services rendered to that State. The history of its settlement at the period now under notice is of special interest, inasmuch as it shows joint village settlements made as late as the end of the last century, and only superseded by the forcible imposition of the permanent settlement. The Jagheer was placed in 1794 in the hands of Mr. Lionel Place, and it is to this gentleman that we are indebted for the first correct information as to landed tenures in Southern India. The villages in the Jagheer were discovered by Mr. Place to be of the class already described as democratic or Mirassy. The villages, that is to say, were corporate bodies, with an internal municipal constitution, and with the land the property of the corporation. The land was sub-divided into shares which were saleable, and still retained all the value of real property. In each village there were besides the corporate members, cultivators holding as tenants of the corporation and having on their side prescriptive rights according to ancient agreements. Again there was a third class cultivating from year to year without other privileges than that of doing so. The distinction between the shareholder and the tenant consisted in the fact that the latter could not sell his rights of occupancy, nor enjoy any of the various immunities and advantages belonging to the former as a member of the corporation. Mr. Place in making his settlements, dealt with the whole communities and not with any particular individual, and left it to the villagers to assess themselves individually. Each village chose its own representative or representatives. There is every reason to suppose that the joint village settlements of Mr. Place would have proved successful. They were not allowed however even a few years' trial. Under the orders of the Court of Directors the Jagheer was permanently settled in 1802, the lands being divided into sixty-one estates bearing an assessment of from 7,000 to 17,500 rupees, and put up to public auction as Mootahs or proprietary estates.

(14) *Acquisition of other Territories*—Whilst these measures for the settlement of the more ancient territories of the Company were in progress, new territories were being added to the Presidency, and the question of land-assessment came up again for discussion in connection with the parts of the country ceded to the English in the south. In 1792 the first war with Tippoo placed a considerable tract of country, comprising the Baramahaul, or Salem as it is now called, Dindigul and Malabar, in the hands of the English. The second war with Tippoo added Canara and Coimbatore. According to a treaty made with the Nizam of Hyderabad in 1800 the whole territory lying south of the Toongabudra and of the Kistna river after its junction with the former, was ceded in perpetuity, constituting what are now called the Ceded Districts. In 1801 all the possessions of the Nawab of Arcot in the Carnatic were made over to the British, thus carrying their possessions down to Cape Comorin.

(15) ***Dealings with the Poligars***—In the land thus newly acquired the same distinction was found in the Northern Circars. That is to say, there were lands holding direct from Government and lands holding through intermediary chiefs. The latter went in the south by the name of Poligars. They may be classed under three heads, as—1st descendants of the royal families of Vijianugger, Conjeevaram, and Madura; 2nd, the military feudal chieftains of those sovereignties who had resisted the conquest of the Mahomedans and had either retained by force or through indulgence and tolerance, the estates which they had enjoyed under their ancient governments; 3rd, district collectors who had contrived to elude the immediate control of the Mahomedans and who had gradually usurped the sovereignty of the districts. These distinctions were not recognized by the Mahomedans. All the Poligars were made to pay tribute and not according to any fixed principle, but according to the power of the government to enforce

it. The management of their chiefships, and the control of their subjects, were left entirely to the Poligars; but they were almost always at war with their neighbours or in revolt against the State. Whenever the exactions of the Mahomedans were considered exorbitant they were resisted, and even if the dues were eventually paid, the Poligar took the earliest opportunity of reimbursing himself and of taking revenge by an attack on the villages holding direct of the Government. In many cases the Government ryots were obliged to compromise with the invaders by agreeing to pay stipulated amount, denominated cauval or protection money. This was, in fact, a sum paid to one Poligar to induce him to give protection against the encroachment of others. Under the systematic control of the British Government it was highly necessary to check the unbridled conduct of the Poligars, but having no knowledge of their true rights the Government were not always successful in dealing with them. Permanent settlements, which left about two-thirds or more of their estimated revenue, were made in the Chittore, Calastry, Vencatagherry and Bomrauz Pollams; and most of those chieftains or their descendants still retain their hereditary estates. In the southern part of the Tamul country there were thirty-three Poligars, for the realization of whose tribute it was found necessary to appoint a separate European Collector. These Poligars fought desperately for what they conceived to be their rights, and their reduction forms a noteworthy incident in the military history of the Presidency. Of those chiefs who had held then patrimonial estates for several generations, we find in the year 1803 thirteen only still in possession; the lands of fourteen others were under charge of the European Collector, and six were forfeited, given away, or sold. In the districts ceded by the Nizam in 1800 there were eighty Poligars. These also resisted the Government, and had to be reduced to subjection by force of arms. In 1807 they were found to have been thus disposed of: Pensioned 2, holding a Jagheer 1, residing on their estates deprived of authority 23, managing their own estates 40, expelled by force 6, in confinement 8, total 80.

(16) *Settlement of Baramahaul*—Turning to the settlement of the lands held by Poligars, the first case calling for special notice is that of the operations in Baramahaul, showing the rise of the

ryotwarry system. In 1792 a commission was appointed to take charge of the baramahaul, with Captain Read at its head. Captain Read was assisted by three junior Military officers, Macleod, Graham, and Munro, and by Mr. Hurdis, a Civilian. The military exactions of Tippoo are supposed to have disorganized the natural institutions of the country and to have impaired the efficiency of the village corporations. However this may be, it is certain that the new commission directed their attention rather to individuals than to communities. In the Tahsildars of the periods they found mere receivers of the revenue, and as the idea of dealing with village communities was not favored, there was no alternative but to deal with the individual cultivator. A system of individual settlements involved a detailed survey of fields, and this work was at once undertaken. The settlement also aimed at making moderate assessments and at guaranteeing them for a short period of years. Though the assessment was to be fixed for a period, every man was to be able to add to or throw up his lands annually. No increases were to be made in the assessment on account of improvements made by the ryot, such as digging of wells, building tanks, or converting dry land into garden or rice-fields. By 1798 the commission had completely surveyed the Baramahaul and determined the rents which should be paid or the ryot-warry system. The average assessment per acre was on the dry lands in the southern division 2 rupees, in the centre 1½ rupees, and in the northern division 1 rupee. On wet lands, it was in the southern divisions 11 rupees, in the centre 6½ and in the northern division 5½. The average rent was little more than 8 shillings an acre on the common soils, and the average contribution of each cultivator was about 70 shillings a year. The ryotwar system, as thus propounded, was approved in theory by the Directors in England, but it was treated as an experimental measure and no practical steps were taken for confirming it. In 1799 orders were received, as already mentioned, for a permanent Zemindarry or Mootahdarry settlement throughout Madras. In pursuance of this decree the Baramahaul was divided in the years 1803, 1804, and 1805 into 228 revenue farms, which were sold by auction to the highest bidders. The numerous bankruptcies which occurred showed that there was some flaw in the system. A great many of the farmers failed in the second year after having pillaged the villages placed under them. The system could not be carried out, and a return was almost immediately made to ryotwarry. The supporters of the Zemindarry system asserted that it failed in Baramahaul only because the assessments had already been fixed too high by Read's Commission. In the side of the village-settlement system it is said that no trial was made of it. The practical result however was that ryotwarry prevailed. What is said here of the Baramahaul applies for the most part to the history of adjacent parts during the same period, for instance of Dindigul and Coimbatore. The Ceded Districts were brought under the ryotwar system by Colonel Munro a few years later.

(17) ***Settlements in Malabar***—The remainder of the Madras provinces consisted of Malabar and Canara. The ancient feudal system which existed in Malabar has already been mentioned. The country was in the hands of a race of rajahs or military leaders and their retainers the Nayars, holding in subjection the Teeyars, and other labourers, the ancient inhabitants of the country. Instead of the districts in Malabar being assessed at so many thousand pagodas, they were rated at so many men liable to be called to the field. At the peace of 1792 Malabar was ceded to the British Government by Tippoo Sultan. It had been first invaded by the Mahomedans under Hyder Ally thirty-four years previously; its invasion being invited in the first place by the Palghaut Rajah to enable him to repel the attack of the Zamorin of Calicut. The landlords of Malabar did not yield readily, and in the struggles which ensued between them and the Mysore Government most of the ancient landed proprietors were either killed or expelled. In the year 1783 Ashed Beg Khan was put in by Hyder as Governor of Malabar, and his administration appears to have been more lenient and equitable than that of any of his predecessors. The principles of his assessment are said to have been as follows:—to the cultivator 5½ tenths, to the proprietor 1½ tenths, to the Government 3 tenths. Shortly after the cession to the British a committee, consisting of two Bengal and to two Bombay servants, were deputed to make a settlement of the country; and their report, issued in 1793, consisting of several volumes, furnishes a full account of the district. In this province, where the landholders

maintained that not only were they the proprietors of their estates, but that under the Native princes they had never paid a land-tax at all, the doctrine of State proprietary right to the land then prevailing and a claim to half the produce assumed in other places, were not likely to be acceptable. The Bengal and Bombay commissioners found that in Malabar no such claims could be enforced, and they proposed to regulate the future demand by the assessment of Ashed Beg Khan. The first settlement, or rather realization of revenue, fell short of that amount by about 25 per cent., and an attempt to raise the rates caused an open rebellion, which lasted for some years and cost a heavy expenditure of lives and money. In 1800 the province was transferred from the Bombay to the Madras Government, and its management was made over to Major Munro, the advocate of ryotwarry, who in effect introduced the ryotwarry system there. One of the earliest of this officer's measures was a survey and assessment. These led to urgent complaints, which were unattended to, and which ended in another rebellion more violent than the former. The second rebellion was suppressed, more by conciliation than coercion, and the result was the recognition on the part of Government of the proprietary right of the landholders to their estates. Peace being restored, the chief Brahmins and landed proprietors assembled at the Collector's invitation at his office, where they selected a committee from among themselves, to arrange matters for the future administration of the province. On this occasion the landholders agreed, after allowing 50 per cent. of the produce to the cultivator, to pay to Government a sum of money estimated at 20 per cent. of the gross produce themselves, retaining 80 per cent. is rent. It was decided that the assessment should be founded on the survey and assessment of 1800. Affairs remained thus for several years, but meanwhile many complaints were made as to the inequality of the assessment, the people not being satisfied with the arrangement of 1800. In 1817 Colonel Munro, who had been the principal agent in suppressing the last rebellion and in making the last settlement, was deputed to visit and report on the condition of the province; the chief result of the visit was a reduction in the assessment. It should be mentioned that there are no compact villages in Malabar similar to those in the Carnatic. The talooks in

Malabar are divided, into Amshom, which are again subdivided into Deshoms. Over each Amshom is a headman called Adigary, associated with an accountant called Menon. These officials are paid by fixed salaries. The Deshoms are presided over by honorary headmen called Mookhyastans. The houses are scattered, and there is therefore no village-site.

(18) *Settlement in Canara*—In Canara individual landed property was not so demonstrable a fact as in Malabar. The primitive constitution of the district had been changed at its conquest in the thirteenth country by the Pandyan kings, and subsequently by the kings of Vijianugger. In later times it had been partially subdued by Hyder, whose exactions continued and augmented by his successor Tippoo, are said to have impoverished the landlord class. When the British Government obtained possession, the saleable lands were few in number and limited in extent, and many of the landlords were reduced to the situation of laborers on their own estates. Still there could be no doubt with whom the Government should settle; proprietary rights were strong enough to render the question of employing middlemen or of making joint-rent village settlements quite unnecessary. Major Munro entered this district for settlement in 1800, and at once established a ryotwarry system which was not subsequently modified. The extent of land in Canara for purposes of assessment has always been measured by the amount of seed it takes to sow it. The settlement for a share of the produce has always been in the name of an individual holder, against whose name in the public accounts is entered every charge to which he is liable. This is the holder's "wurg" or account, a word which has come to mean "holding" in the revenue system. Major Munro found this method of settlement obtaining, and continued it without change. No alteration was allowed in any man's wurg except on good cause being shown. No general survey of the district was introduced, but partial surveys were instituted for the purpose of obtaining general data for assessment. A complete register, called the Beejwary register, was formed of the extent, calculated by the seed, of each holder's wurg. The only difficulty was with the amount of the assessments. The settlement of Hurry Hur Roy, Rajah of Vijayanugger, made in the fourteenth century, was for a long time

the standard assessment. Hurry Hur Roy took 2½ katties of seed as the basis of the calculation, and assuming the proportion between seed and gross produce to be that of 1 to 12, he apportioned the gross produce thus—to the landlord 7½ katties, to the cultivator 15 katties, to the Government 7½ katties. The Bednore Government left this assessment as they found it till 1618, when the Government share was increased by 50 per cent. The total jummah of Canara at the close of the Bednore Government amounted to pagodas 320,827. Hyder increased this to pagodas 533,202. Colonel Munro's settlement in 1800 amounted to pagodas 465,148; of this pagodas 284,603 was composed of the ancient land-tax or Shist, and pagodas 180,545 stood for extra assessments imposed by the Bednore and Mysore Governments, the extra imposts of the latter being called Shaumil. The inequalities caused by the new British assessment were found in the course of a few years to be intolerable, and in 1817 a thorough investigation was instituted, ending eventually in the so-called Tharow assessment in 1819. The Tharow was a maximum assessment which the Collector could not exceed of his own authority, and was based on a detailed investigation of the collections on particular estates. The Tharow assessment was considered a moderate one when it was made, but it was a considerable time before the country attained even that standard and constant remissions were necessary. The total amount of the Tharow assessment for the entire province of Canara was Rupees 15,24,879 on 34,216 ryots as against Rupees 16,72,607 of the ancient Beriz comprising both Shist and Shaumil. Canara has since been divided into two separate divisions, the southern division only remaining with Madras, the northern division going to Bombay. The village arrangements in South Canara are somewhat similar to those in Malabar, each wurg having its house situated upon it. The headmen of villages are called Potails, and the curnums, of whom there is one for each group of villages termed Magnny or Taraf, are called Shanbogues.

(19) *Trial of Village-rent System*—In the various experiments which were made during the first twenty years of the century in the mode of settlement for the land-revenue, the Zemindarry and Ryotwarry systems played the most important. The village joint-rent system was not, however, entirely overlooked. In 1808 this

method was given a general trial in several districts on the authority of the Court of Directors. The Madras Board of Revenue were distinctly in favor of the system, and had not Colonel Munro been so much opposed to it, it is possible that it might have had a different fate. The plan was tried at first for a term of three years. The result was not entirely satisfactory. In many parts the head inhabitants, conceiving the assessment excessive and finding themselves obliged to ask for remissions annually, refused to rent their villages. Speculators then came forward and out-bid each other, so that the villages were rented at a sum beyond what they could yield, and the contractors failed. Still the Government were satisfied on the whole and in many cases made a further ten-year settlement on the same principle. It was even proposed by some to make a perpetual village settlement. The ten-years' settlement was not approved by the Court of Directors, but their objections arrived too late to be acted on. A visit to England, however, made by Colonel Munro had probably not been without its effect upon the opinions of the Court of Directors, and the Board of Control; and towards the close of 1817 instructions were received at Madras for the abolition of the village system, and the confirmation in all practicable cases of the plan of ryotwar settlement with individual holders. It was alleged that the village system had been tried and had failed. The revenue authorities declared that it had not been subjected to a fair trial, and that it had not failed. They alleged too that the Home authorities had decided hastily on insufficient evidence. "The judgement", the Board of Revenue wrote, "which has been pronounced in England against the village system, is founded on a very partial and unfavourable view of its results; for it does not appear that authorities at home had, at the time when that judgement was passed, any information before them respecting any other portion of it than its commencement, the triennial settlement". And they urged that the result of that settlement was no test of the success or failure of the system, inasmuch as the lands had been subjected to an over-assessment, "founded upon the fallacious data of the Ryotwar collections".

(20) *Final Establishment of ryotwarry*—The Ryotwar system was, however by this time in favor at home, and orders were sent out for its reintroduction, in all possible cases, under certain

modifications, prescribed by the Court. At this period, in Ganjam, Vizagapatam, Rajahmundry, Masulipatam, Goontoor, Salem, Chinghleput, the Cuddalore district, and the Western, Southern, and Chittore Polliems, the Permanent Zemindarry system prevailed; in the Ceded Districts, Nellore, the two divisions of Arcot, Pulnaud, Trichinopoly, Tinnevelly, and Tanjore the village system had been introduced; and the ryotwar system was fully established only in Malabar, Canara, Coimbatore, Madura, and Dindigul. The orders were carried out, and all the necessary preliminaries having been gone through, the village leases having expired, many of the new Zemindarries or Mootahs having lapsed or been bought in, the improved ryotwar system was declared to be established in Madras. Colonel Munro himself, who had been appointed to the chief place in the Government, took his seat in time to preside over the act of final establishment in the spring of 1820. Since 1820 there has been a periodic revision of the rates of assessment in ryotwarry lands; a Special Commission has dealt with the whole question of inam of rent-free lands; and various legal enactments have been passed for the protection of various landed interests or for the realization of the Government dues. In the broad policy of Government however as to tenures and settlements there has been no change.

# *Appendix 2*

# Principles of Ryotwari System

## *I*

## A Brief Account of the Old Revenue Systems

In the *ryotwari* system, the ryot pays his fixed assessment in money direct to the Government, and the assessment is not liable to arbitrary fluctuations from year to year except for water-rate for water taken from a Government source in cases where this has not been included in the assessment. The ryot cannot be evicted from his land so long as he continues to pay the assessment, and he can transfer his rights in the land to others by sale, gift, partition etc. He can, moreover, relinquish his land when he finds that its cultivation is no longer profitable, and in that case he would not be liable to pay the assessment, once his reliqusihment has been accepted. In favourable seasons, remission are granted on liberal principles. In short, under the *ryotwari* system, a ryot enjoys all the advantages of a perpetual lease without its disadvantages and responsibilities.

This may be contrasted with the state of affairs that prevailed in the case of the other systems of settlement which preceded the *ryotwari* system. A brief account of these earlier systems is given below:—

***1. The renting System:***—Villages were let on lease either to the highest bidder or on a rental based on the average collections of past years. Under this system, individual distribution would be iniquitous and arbitrary and there would be scope for illegal exactions.

---

C.A. Ramakrishnan, ICS, Government of Madras, Revenue Department. Printed by the Superintendent, Government Press, Madras, 1952.

2. *The Asara:*—Conversion into money of the Government share of the crop as ascertained by estimate or actual measurement at the threshing floor. Under this system, the ryot would be the victim of inquisitorial visits and extortionate demand of a host of petty officials. The public revenue would be at the mercy of ill-paid and unscrupulous subordinates to whom the system would afford a most easy opportunity for embezzlement. The cost of collection would be great.

3. *Visabadi*—Distribution with the sanction of the Collector of the total demand of the village on the lands of each ryot.

4. *Joint rent System*—The whole body of the villages were jointly and severally responsible for the rent, which was revisable. Adjustment of individual responsibilities was left to the ryots.

5. *Mucta System*—Rent was fixed on the village as a whole on a consideration of its resources. Details were left to the ryots. The demand was fixed so long as the system continued.

6. *The Ooloongoo System*—Confined to the districts of Tanjore, etc. Grain rent commutable into money every year at the current market price.

7. *The Motha Fysal System*—This prevailed only in Tanjore. It superseded the Ooloongu. A lump money assessment not liable to variation according to current prices was fixed over each village. The main feature of the Motha fysal system was the removal of the variable element in the fixing of the commutation rate.

8. *Tharao or Sarasari*—This obtained only in South Kanara. The demand was based on the average collections realized from each estate for the preceding 16 or 17 years.

## II

# Basic Principles of the Ryotwari Settlement

*1. Main Principles*—The main principles laid down, from time to time, by the Govenment, for the settlement of assessment of ryotwari lands, are given below:—

(1) The assessment shall be on the land and shall not depend upon the description of produce, or upon the religion or profession of the landholder.

(2) The classification of soils is to be as simple as possible, and is to be alike everywhere instead of each village having its own.

(3) The assessment is to be fixed so as not to exceed half the net produce after deducting the expenses of cultivation, etc.

(4) No tax is to be imposed for a second crop on dry land, but wet lands which in all ordinary seasons have an unfailing supply of water for two crops are to be registered as double crop, the charge for the second crop being generally half the first crop assessment. Remissions may be given when the supply of water fails. Some abatement is allowed in cases where water is raised by baling.

(5) The Tahsildar, or in the course of a resettlement the Special Settlement Officer or Special Assistant Settlement Officer, may allow the charge for second crop to be compounded in respect of all irrigated lands of which the supply of water is not ordinarily unfailing. The rates of composition will generally be as follows:—

For wet land irrigated from a second-class irrigation source—one-third.

For wet land irrigated from a third-class irrigation source—one-fourth.

For wet land irrigated from a fourth-class irrigation source—one-fifth.

For wet land irrigated form a fifth-class irrigation source—one-sixth.

Where the irrigation is precarious and the supply is supplemented by wells, the divisional officer, or in the course of a resettlement the Special Settlement Officer or Special Assistant Settlement Officer, may allow the charge for second crop to be compounded at one-half of the rates referred to above, except under sources grouped in class 1 or 2 for settlement purposes. Composition at such favourable rates may be allowed to lands for which the charge for second crop has already been compounded at the ordinary rates. If the wells, however, fall into disrepair, the land should be transferred from compounded double crop to single crop wet. Ryots may be permitted to compound at any time and to any extent even after the settlement. It is immaterial whether the well, from which the supplementary supply is received, lies within the wet land or not, but before granting composition at the special rate, the divisional or settlement officer must satisfy himself that the well water is actually used to supplement, the supply from the irrigation source. It will also be necessary to ascertain by annual inspection that the well is properly maintained and that it is used to supplement the supply from the irrigation source.

(6) Collectors may sanction transfers of registered and compounded double-crop wet lands to single crop on the application of the holders of such lands in cases where the supply of water from the registered source is sufficient for raising only one wet crop.

(7) As a rule, all lands are classed under the two general heads "wet and dry". In some districts, however, another class of lands called "*manavari*" has been recognized by Government. These are lands upon which wet crops are grown with the aid of rain water impounded on the land or with the water of swamps, small ponds or the like, or in some cases tank-bed lands. Manavari lands are usually assessed at special rates which are intermediate between the dry and the wet rates otherwise applicable.

Collectors are authorized to sanction with the consent of the registered holder during the term of a settlement, transfers of ryotwari lands from "dry" to "wet" and *vice versa* and from manavari to "dry" or "wet" and *vice versa.*

(8) Lands forming the aycut of doruvu wells should be charged with water-cess at one-fourth or one-eighth of the water-cess that would be leviable for irrigation by direct flow of a first wet crop on dry lands irrigated from the sources on the banks of which the doruvu wells are situated, according as the water is raised by single or double lift.

When different rates have been prescribed for a first wet paddy crop and any other first wet crop, the rate applicable to a first wet crop of paddy should be adopted for the purpose of this rule.

No water-cess shall be levied for the irrigation of a second or third crop with water from *doruvu* wells.

Notes:—

(1) *Doruvu* wells comprise wells of the following descriptions, constructed on the banks of rivers, *vankas, vagus* or *odais*:—

(a) Brick or stone wells connected with rivers, *vankas, vagus* or *odais* by tunnels or open channels.

(b) Wells which consist of an excavation on the face of the banks of rivers, *vankas, vagus* or *odais* reveted with stone.

(2)The above rule will apply equally whether water is lifted from *doruvu* wells by engine-power or other means.

(3) For the purpose of the above rule, Collectors of districts in which there are *doruvu* wells should have lists of *doruvu* wells in those districts prepared and their ayacuts fixed. As regards future constructions, the concession in this rule will apply only to *doruvu* wells constructed in the districts of Bellary, Anantapur, Kurnool and Cuddapah and in the taluks of Madanapalle and Vayalpad in the Chittoor district and recognized by the Collectors. In other tracts the ordinary concession for lift irrigation will alone be given.

***2. Government demand how arrived at***—In carrying out the settlement with the reference to the foregoing principles, the Settlement Department divides the soils into certain classes with reference to their mechanical composition, subdivides them into sorts or grades with reference to there chemical and physical properties and other circumstances affecting their fertility, and attaches a separate grain value to each grade after numerous examinations of the actual outturn of the staple produces in each class and sort of soil. The grain value is then converted into money at the commutation price based generally on the average of the 20 non-famine years immediately preceding the settlement, for the whole district, with some abatement for traders profits and for the distance the grain has usually to be carried to the market. From the value of the gross produce thus determined, the cost of cultivation and a certain percentage on account of vicissitudes of season and unprofitable areas is deducted, and one-half of the ramainder is the maximum taken as assessment or the Government demand on the land. After this, soils of similar grain values, irrespective of their classification, are bracketed together in orders called *tarams*, each with its own rate of assessment. These rates are further adjusted with refernce to the position of the villages in which the lands are situated and the nature of the sources of irrigation. For this purpose, villages are formed into groups, in the case of dry lands, with reference to their proximity to roads and markets, and, in the case of wet lands, with reference to the nature and quality of the water-supply. This accounts for different rates of assessment being imposed on lands of similar soils, but situated in different groups or under different classes of irrigation.

*3. What the Government demand represents*—The assessment thus fixed represents the commuted value of the Government share of the surface cultivation, but if minerals are discovered and worked in the lands a separate assessment will be levied therefore. This rule does not apply to lands sold under the waste land rules subsequent to the issue of G.O. No. 2029, dated 7th October, 1879, by which full minerals rights in such lands have been reserved to Government.

*4. Period of Settlement*—At each settlement or resettlement of a district, Government fix at their discretion the period for which such settlement or resettlement shall be in force. The collector has then to notify the period in the district gazette, and explain to the ryots that the new rates will not be liable to alteration during the currency of the settlement period; but that, on the expiry of the said period, Government reserve to themselves the right to revise the assessment with references to a rise or fall in prices. It should be further explained that Government will refrain from enhancing the assessment in respect of any additional value which may have been given to land by improvements effected by the ryots, even if carried out by means of money borrowed from Government. A partial exception to this rule probably be necessary in the districts of Malabar and South Kanara where the Government reserve the right to introduce at the end of the settlement period, such changes in the classification and assessment of "wet" "dry" and "garden" land as may then seem proper.

*5. **Present policy of Government in regard to resettlement in ryotwari areas***—In G.O. No. 1067 [12 (S)], Revenue, dated 21st May, 1937, the Government directed in pursuance of the policy of the Ministry then in power, that no resettlement operations should be taken in future. These orders continue to be in force at present.

# III

# Classification of Soils

## Section I—The Surface Soils

*1. The five great series of soils*—An intelligible and systematic classification of soils is an essential preliminary in forming an assessment of the land, based on its productive powers, and such classification, to be correct and generally useful, must be founded upon a consideration of the nature, composition and properties of the several soils.

The ordinary terms applied to soils in the country, such as *regar, musub, lal* or red earth, etc., though useful in representing certain characteristic features connected with the origin of the soils, do not convey so definite an idea of their constituent parts and properties as is needed for the purpose; for instance, *regar* may, sometimes be a stiff clayey soil, at others a light loam; *lal* or red earth may be either a sandy soil, a clayey soil or a light loam; and all these may have different productive powers.

In the course of 1858, Mr. Newill, who was then Director of Revenue Settlement, prepared a Manual of Classification for his department, and arranged for giving the productive powers for the soil in terms of grain. He divided the soils into five great series, which have different origins or bases for their formation—

I. *The alluvial and exceptional*, which comprise the rich island and delta soils of extraordinary fertility.

II. The *regar* or black-cotton series, with all its varieties.

III. The red ferruginous series, originating from sandstone, laterite etc.

IV. The calcareous series, originating from underlying strata of *chalk* or lime.

V. The arenaceous series.

In Madras Presidency, the soils most commonly met with will fall either in the "*regar*" (i.e., black) series or in the "red" series. Alluvial soils are met with in the delta areas of the Godavari, Krishna and Cauvery rivers. Arenaceous soils are met in coastal tracts. Calacareous soils are very rare.

Mr. Newill said: "The origin or characters of the soils, are particularized in the above series, have a very decided influence upon their fertility; but as the soil of each series varies in quality, it is necessary, next, to consider what other circumstances mainly affect that productive powers. These may be resolved into, first their mechnical composition of clay, sand, lime and organic matter; and secondly, their chemical composition, in which is to be taken into account the minute quality of salts, acids and other mineral ingredients, the presence of which is essential to the nourishment of plants. To these might be added the physical properties of the soils, but these again depended, mostly, upon the mechanical composition. The mechnical composition is easily resolved and brought under arbitrary rules, but the resolution of the chemical composition is a difficult task beyond the comprehension of ordinary agency, and is only attainable at best, on a limited scale. The determination of the mechnical composition of clay, sand, etc., is found of great practical use, as it often distinguishes the soils according to the particular texture suited for the several crops, and also according to the relative cost of cultivation. For instance, as stiff clay *regar* is found to grow *cholam* well, and is unfit for *cumbu* and some other grains, while a mixed or sandy *regar* will grow *cholam* only scantily but produce good crops of *cumbu*, *ragi* and *varagu*, while the expenses of cultivation differ in the stiff clay and the light loose soils. Some of the loamy soils also will grow groundnut, indigo and other choice products, which cannot be obtained in the clay lands. These are very important considerations in arriving at the proper assessment and are thus in the system pursued; placed in a tangible form".

It follows, then, that with the agency at command, soils may be advantageously classified under arbitrary rules, according to their mechanical composition, and that chemical and physical properties must be taken into account, discretionally, with other circumstances affecting their fertility. This plan, obviously, affords the means of an important check by re-examination, which would be wanting were the whole left to the discretion of the classifier.

The principles laid down by Mr. Newill are further elaborated below:—

***The alluvial and exceptional series:***—This takes in the rich *lanka*, or island soils, deposited from rivers, and also provides for the lands met with in the delta areas of the perennial rivers like the Godavari, Krishna and Cauvery. At some remote period the great plains in the delta tracts (e.g. the Godavari) which are now covered with alluvial soils, must have been occupied by the sea, and gradually raised above tidal level by the deltaic deposits of the rivers. The delta lands are of exceptional fertility, and are easily the best lands for agricultural purposes.

***The regar series:***—Some consider this soil to be decomposition of volcanic rock, others the fluviatile deposit of a former period, whilst another suggestion is that it may be divluvium consisting of the same matter as the sedimentary rocks, but deposited mechanically without induration.

Whatever may be the origin of this soil, the character of it is such that it may be easily distinguished from other series, even when mixed with large proportions of sand, as in the "*musub* or *masaka*", which is included in this general head of *regar*. The great fertility of the *regar* is ascribed to its containing, besides a large proportion of organic matter to which it probably owes its colour, much mineral matter in such a finely mixed state, as to be easily available for the supply of nourishment to vegetation by the ordinary processes of chemical affinity and mechanical action, which are constantly going on.

***The red ferruginous series:***—This is also easily distinguished, and has its origin, mostly, from ferruginous sandstone, laterite or other rocks. The red colour is, generally, the result of iron, and is easily distinguished from the reddish brown belonging to some of the *regar* soils, with which this series forms a great contrast in its want of natural fertility, arising probably, from the smaller proportion of organic matter and the other rich constituent elements, and its general dryness.

***The white and grey calcareous series:***—This derives its character from a substratum of lime, the properties of which, in the surface soil, may sometimes be partly or wholly removed by influences to which it is exposed from the air, moisture, etc. The colour is chiefly dependent on the chalk, or lime in the soil, and, sometimes, verges into a dark shade.

***The arenaceous series:***—The characteristic of this is the seashore, or flinthy sand, which forms the basis of the soil in littoral tracts of country. Vegetation and cultivation have contributed much, in places, to the improvement of the composition of these sandy soils, by introducing some fertile elements, but still the original character is easily discernible.

***2. The division of the series into classes:***—After determining the general classes to which the soils belong, the component parts of the same are to be considered. The principal ingredients of all soils are clay, sand, lime and vegetable, or other organic matter. Organic matter is what enters into the fabric of animals and all kinds of trees and plants that grow out of the soil. Thus the dung and ramains of animals and insects, decayed leaves, roots and stems of trees, bushes and plants form organic matter.

The chief ingredients of soils are derived from minerals and rocks, which are gradually dissolved, or rather reduced to powder, or grains, by potash and other small, but powerful ingredients such as above described, as well as by the action of the air and moisture. In some cases, also, decayed vegetable deposit forms, or combines with the earth; a portion of the soil is thus in a state of fine impalpable powder, whilst the remainder is hard and insoluble as in the case of sand, pebbles, etc.

It is only from the fine portion, or powder, that the crops derive their nourishment, and, as a rule, the greater proportion of it, generally speaking that a soil contains, the greater will be its fertility. Some of the richest regar soils are almost entirely, composed of this impalpable powder.

For settlement purposes, this impalpable powder is called clay, though it includes vegetable matter, and the remainder is termed sand.

It is upon the proportion of sand and clay that a general classification is based, for settlement purposes, as this can be easily determined by simple experiments, if not by merely looking at the soil and examining it with hands.

The presence of smaller, but not less important ingredients, such as potash, soda, magnesia, phosphoric acid, oxide or iron, sulphuric acid, chlorine, etc., and their actual quantities can be determined only by elaborate chemical analysis by experts in laboratories. From a settlement point of view, such chemical analysis will not generally be necessary.

Each of the five great series of soils can be split up into classes, with reference to the proportion of clay and sand. Three kinds of such proportions are recognized in settlement, as given below:—

(1) Clayey—containing more than two-thirds of clay.

(2) Mixed, or loamy—containing from one-third to two-thirds of clay.

(3) Sandy, or gravelly—containing not more than one-third of clay.

The five great series of soils are divided into the following fourteen settlement classes, with reference to their being clayey, loamy, or sandy.

In the case of arenaceous soils, the classes adopted are loamy (one-third to two-thirds clay), sandy (one-third to one-tenth clay), and heavy sand (under one-tenth clay).

I. Alluvial clay

II. Alluvial loam

(Note: Alluvial lands containing less than one-third clay, i.e., more than two-third sand are not met with and have not been recognized for settlement purposes.)

III. Regar clay

IV. Regar loam

V. Regar sand

VI. Red clay

VII. Red loam

VIII. Red sand

IX. Calcareous clay

X. Calcareous loam

XI. Calcareous sand

XII. Arenaceous loam

XIII. Arenaceous sand

XIV. Arenaceous heavy sand

Classification should, as a rule, depend upon the upper soil, but where necessary, the sub-soil also should be considered. If the soil is of the depth of nine inches which is the minimum limit, it may, generally, be considered sufficient for the root of plants, but where it is less, it may be inferred that vegetation derives its nourishment from the sub-soil, and this, therefore, should guide the classifiers.

River sand should come under "Regar sand" (Class V), or "Red Sand" (Class VIII) and not under the arenaceous series.

The classes of soils, for each village should not be more numerous than necessary.

It is an established fact, as shown in text-books on "Agricultural Chemistry", that, where two soils of different constituents meet, the fertility is greatly increased and often is greater than that of either soil, taken individually. Where two series intermingle, it, therefore, requires the exercise of some discretion in determining the class to which the fields in which this occurs should be assigned. The nature of the substratum, its depth and that of the upper soil, as well as the character of the vegetation, should be considered when classifying. Should doubt still exist, the grain values should guide the decision.

*3. The division of classes into sorts—*

*(a) "Sorting" explained*

(i) the main purpose of "sorting" in settlement work is to allow for various local peculiarities and other factors that may exist in respect of lands falling in the same settlement class in a village, in order that some discretion may be exercised in deciding the rate of assessment to be adopted for individual fields. The settlement "class" of a land is determined merely by the proportions of sand and clay in the soil, but various other factors besides the mere proportion of sand and clay affect the fertility of the soil, and the general value of the land to the ryot. To quote an instance, suppose it is found that all the dry lands in a village fall in only one settlement classification—say class VII, it is a matter of common experience that all these lands will not be of the same fertility, nor posses the same advantages in regard to facilities for cultivation, manuring, watching the crops, etc. Enquiries of the ryots will generally show that certain blocks of land are considered to be more fertile, while other blocks may not be so fertile, owing to reasons such as salinity, existence of stones, liability to submersion or erosion by rivers and channels, etc. It will accordingly be quite unreasonable to levy the same rate of assessment on all the lands in a village, even though they may lie in the same settlement classification. Allowance has necessarily got to be made for factors such as those mentioned above, and hence the need for sorting.

(ii) In modern settlement, a maximum of five sorts are recognized for each settlement "class" of land. These sorts will roughly correspond to what may, in regard to the aggregate of the factors affecting the value and fertility of the land, be called respectively, "best", "good", "ordinary", "inferior" and "worst" lands. It must however be pointed out that in certain previous settlements, only two or three sorts were recognized, and this was not interfered with during resettlement except in special cases.

(iii) The money rates for the higher sorts will be higher than those for the lower sorts, a difference of one sort in general implying a difference of one *taram*. This will be clear from the following concrete examples relating to Kurnool and Bellary districts:—

| **Class of soil** | **Sort** | **Money Rate** | | **Taram** |
|---|---|---|---|---|
| | | **Rs.** | **A.** | |
| | **(Kurnool distirct—Wet lands)** | | | |
| IV | 1 | 10 | 0 | 1 |
| IV | 2 | 9 | 0 | 2 |
| IV | 3 | 8 | 0 | 3 |
| IV | 4 | 7 | 0 | 4 |
| IV | 5 | 6 | 0 | 5 |

**(Bellary District—Dry lands—Black soil—Taluks—I Group)**

| | | | | |
|---|---|---|---|---|
| III | 1 | 2 | 13 | 1 |
| III | 2 | 2 | 4 | 2 |
| III | 3 | 1 | 11 | 3 |
| III | 4 | 1 | 2 | 4 |
| III | 5 | 0 | 14 | 5 |

The principles of sorting are not the same for dry and wet lands, but some of them are common to both. The more important principles are set out below:—

***(b) Principles common to dry and wet lands—***

(i) *Intrinsic fertility of the land*—Enquiries of ryots and observation of crops on ground will show that certain lands are considered by the ryots to be more fertile than other lands. Ordinarily, fertility varies with the differing proportions of clay and sand in the soil; and a general principle in assigning sorts is "the larger the percentage of sand, the lower the sort". The superior fertility may also be due to various other factors, e.g., greater percentage of organic matter, advantageous level of the land, etc. On the other hand, the existence of harmful ingredients like saline substances, nodules of lime or stone, etc., and disadvantageous level of the land will generally result in poor yields. Such exceptional fertility or exceptional handicap may be allowed for by putting the lands one sort higher or lower as the case may be than what would be assigned to them but for the special factors.

(ii) ***Liability to submersion, erosion, etc.***—Lands situated by the side of rivers, supply and drainage channels, etc., may be liable to become sand cast, and also to erosion. If they are so liable, such lands will not only yield less than other lands, but their sale value also will be less. Lands of this type may be put one or two sorts lower than other lands with similar constitution of soil in the village.

(iii) ***Distance from Village-site***—In the case of fairly small villages, there will not be much difference in yield and in cost of cultivation between lands situated close to the village-site, and lands situated at the extremity of the village boundary. But in the case of large villages—say, with a radius of over 1 or 2 miles—it will often be found that lands situated close to the village-site, sell at higher prices than those farther away. The cost of cultivation and manuring, the trouble of watching the crops and of bringing in the produce, the liability to damage by wild beasts, etc., will be more in the case of lands which are farther away from the village-site. To allow for this factor, the more distant lands may be placed one or two sorts lower than the other lands. It has however to be mentioned that there may be cases where though a particular land may be at the extremity of the boundary, it is situated close to the village-site of another village, in which case there may not be any need to lower the sort.

(iv) ***Necessity to adopt only a minimum number of sorts in a village***—It should be remembered that as far as possible the number of sorts assigned to the lands in any one village should be kept down to the minimum possible. In a village of average site, it should not be necessary to have more than, say, two or at the most three sorts. It should seldom be found necessary to have resort to as many as five sorts in one village.

(v) ***Sorting to apply only to fairly large blocks***—The question of sorting should be considered only with reference to fairly extensive blocks in a village and not with reference to individual fields. The various factors mentioned above should be evaluated and examined for such fairly extensive blocks. It is quite possible that within one block, there are slight variations in fertility, etc., as between one field and another, but these should be ignored in deciding the sort. Except in very special cases, the sorting will not vary from one field to another within a fairly extensive block.

(vi) ***Special responsibility of Settlement Officers and Assistant Settlement Officers***—The questions whether more than one "sort" is necessary, and if so the number of sorts and the principles to be applied in any particular area, are to be decided by the Settlement Officer or the Assistant Settlement Officer concerned. The matter should not be left to Settlement Deputy Tahsildars, much less to Settlement Inspectors. Within the broad principles to be laid down by the Settlement Officer or the Assistant Settlement Officer, on the basis of the local peculiarities and circumstances, the work of field-to-field sorting may be left to the subordinate staff, subject, of course, to close supervision by the higher officers.

(c) ***Principles specially applicable to dry lands—Anomalies due to dry grouping***—For the purpose of dry grouping, generally only two or three groups are recognized for vast areas covering the whole or portion of a district, with the result that hundreds of villages may fall in the same dry group, though, as among these villages, there will be difference in the matter of accessibility to roads, nearness to market, etc. It may often happen that one village is only a mile from a main road and a market, and another village is over 10 miles from these, but that both have been put in the same dry group. No doubt it is not possible to have more than a few dry groups from the settlement point of view, but at the same time it will be unreasonable to levy the same assessment on the lands in the two villages of the nature mentioned above. Equity requires that the more distant villages should get some reduction of assessment. Where distance from a road or market is not already sufficiently allowed for in the group assigned to the village, resort may be had to "sorting", to allow for the factor. The sorting of lands in the more distant villagers may commence one sort lower than those in the nearer villages, even though the lands are generally of the same degree of fertility. Thus, the village very near to the road and the market may have—say, sorts 1 to 3, whereas the more distant village may have sorts from 2 to 4 even though the lands in the two villages are identical in other respects.

(d) ***Principles specially applicable for wet lands***—

(i) The principles of sorting to be adopted in the case of wet lands are slightly different from those adopted in regard to dry lands. Wet lands will have to be sorted mainly with reference to their irrigation.

(ii) *Level of sluices*—Where a tank has got more than one sluice, it will be often found that some of the sluices are situated in a much higher level than others. The low level sluices will begin to function a few days ahead of high level sluices; and, likewise, water can be drawn off through them even when the level of water in the tank is so low that it cannot flow through the high level sluices. As a consequence, the lands irrigated by a low level sluice will be found to be more valuable and also will yield a better outturn than the other lands. In cases, therefore, where a distinct advantage is enjoyed by lands under the low level sluices as compared to those under a high level sluices, the latter should be placed one or more sorts lower than the former.

(iii) *Distance from the irrigation source*—Another factor that will be met with in the case of wet lands is that the lands at the tail end of the ayacut do not get such a copious and assured supply of water as the lands which are situated nearer the irrigation sources. If an ayacut is fairly small, this circumstance will not be met with. But, in the case of large ayacuts, especially in unfavourable seasons, it is quite a common feature to find that wet crops are successfully raised in the lands lying nearer the irrigation sources, while it is not possible to raise a wet crop successfully in the tail-end lands. To allow for such a factor, the tail-end lands may be placed one sort lower than the other lands. However, only in exceptional cases will it be found necessary to have more than two sorts under the same irrigation source.

(iv) *Level of the lands*—The intrinsic level of the fields also has to be taken into account in the matter of sorting of wet lands, even though the lands may lie under the same sluice. If a land lies at a higher level and can be irrigated only with difficulty, e.g., by cross-bunding a channel, it will be justifiable to show some concession to such lands by lowering the sort suitably.

(v) *Other factors*—The principle of nearness to village may also be allowed for in regard to wet lands where this is found absolutely necessary. Likewise, factors such as liability to submersion, inadequate drainage, distance from thrashing floors, and liability to ravages by wild beasts may also be taken into account when deciding the sort to be assigned to wet lands.

It is quite possible that several other factors also may be met with which affect the intrinsic value and outturn of a land for the better or for the worse. Such factors may be allowed for, by suitable alterations of the sorting.

(e) *Conversion of dry lands to wet*—From what has been said above, it can be seen that when a dry land is converted into wet, the sorting previously given to the dry land may have to be altered with reference to the conditions prevailing under the irrigation source under which the dry land is proposed to be registered as wet. The sorting already assigned to the dry land cannot always be adopted for the purpose of fixing the wet assessment on it. The converse proposition will also hold good, when wet lands are transferred to dry.

(f) ***General***—It will not require much training, or 'experience', for a classifier, first of all, to determine to which series a soil belongs, and then to judge, by the eye and the use of his fingers, of the relative proportions of clay and sand. This will enable the 'class' to be fixed. A little further experience will also enable him to readily determine whether a soil has much vegetable, or other fertilizing matter, or whether it contains injurious ingredients, but in doing this, recent manuring is not to be taken into account. Based on this and other relevant considerations, the 'sort' can be fixed.

For a time, the idea existed that field classification might be altogether abandoned and that classification by tracts, to be made by the Settlement Officers at the head of field parties, might be substituted for it. This course, it was thought, would be both more expeditious and more equitable than that under which the classifiers, besides distinguishing black soil from red, and clay from sand, were required to assign each individual field to one of the five sorts under each soil and to do this without any reference to surrounding circumstances and existing rates of assessment. The proposed change having, after due consideration, been held to be impracticable, the Government resolved to continue the existing method of classification and then to block the fields according to the following system.

The class and sort of each field should first be noted on the survey maps, and then, adjoining fields of the same soil should be blocked together by drawing a boundary line around them. If isolated fields of different soils be found in a block, they should be merged with the major fields of that block as regards class and sort unless the area of the detached fields is large enough to form a separate block. This arrangement admits of an explanation in the "Descriptive Memoirs", of the mode in which the classification of the villages was conducted.

The following table of classification results from what has been said above, and, although it has been framed on a scale sufficiently comprehensive to take in a large tract of country, and to afford the means of comparative values being assigned for numerous varieties of soils, the classes and sorts for each village will be few, and, as some of these will have similar grain values, the resulting money rates will be within as small a limit as could be desired for simplicity of account.

**Table of Soil Classification**

| | **Class and description of soils** | **Sort** | **Unirrigated** | | | | **Irrigated** |
|---|---|---|---|---|---|---|---|
| | | | **Grain value in Madras measures** | | | | |
| **Series** | **Class and description** | **Number and quality** | Cholam | Cumby | Ragi | Vatagu | Paddy |
| 1 | 2 | 3 | 4 | 5 | 6 | 7 | 8 |
| | | | Rs. | Rs. | Rs. | Rs. | Rs. |
| Alluvial and exceptional series | I. Alluvial clay | 1. Best.. | | | | | |
| | | 2. Good.. | | | | | |
| | | 3. Ordinary.. | | | | | |
| | | 4. Inferior.. | | | | | |
| | | 5. Worst.. | | | | | |
| | II. Aluvial loam | 1. Best.. | | | | | |
| | | 2. Good.. | | | | | |
| | | 3. Ordinary.. | | | | | |
| | | 4. Inferior.. | | | | | |
| | | 5. Worst.. | | | | | |
| Regar series.. | III. Regar clay containing | 1. Best.. | | | | | |
| | | 2. Good.. | | | | | |

| | | |
|---|---|---|
| | upwards of | 3. Ordinary.. |
| | 2/3 of clay | 4. Inferior.. |
| | | 5. Worst.. |
| | IV. Regar loam | 1. Best.. |
| | containing from | 2. Good.. |
| | 1/3 to 2/3 | 3. Ordinary.. |
| | of clay | 4. Inferior.. |
| | | 5. Worst.. |
| | V. Regar sand | 1. Best.. |
| | containing not | 2. Good.. |
| | more than | 3. Ordinary.. |
| | 1/3 clay | 4. Inferior.. |
| | | 5. Worst.. |
| Red ferruginous | VI. Red clay | |
| series | containing | 1. Best.. |
| | upwards of | 2. Good.. |
| | 2/3 clay | 3. Ordinary.. |
| | | 4. Inferior.. |
| | | 5. Worst.. |
| | VII. Red loam | 1. Best.. |
| | containing from | 2. Good.. |
| | 1/3 to 2/3 | 3. Ordinary.. |
| | of clay | 4. Inferior.. |
| | | 5. Worst.. |
| | VIII. Red sand, | 1. Best.. |
| | or gravel, | 2. Good.. |
| | containing not | 3. Ordinary.. |
| | more than 1/3 | 4. Inferior.. |
| | clay | 5. Worst.. |
| White and grey | IX. Clay, | 1. Best.. |
| calcareous series | upwards | 2. Good.. |
| | of 2/3 clay | 3. Ordinary.. |

| | | |
|---|---|---|
| | | 4. Inferior.. |
| | | 5. Worst.. |
| | X. Mixed or loamy 1/3 to 2/3 | 1. Best.. |
| | | 2. Good.. |
| | | 3. Ordinary.. |
| | | 4. Inferior.. |
| | | 5. Worst.. |
| | XI. Sandy, or gravelly under 1/3 clay | 1. Best.. |
| | | 2. Good.. |
| | | 3. Ordinary.. |
| | | 4. Inferior.. |
| | | 5. Worst.. |
| Arenaceous series | XII. Loamy, or mixed 1/3 to 2/3 clay | 1. Best.. |
| | | 2. Good.. |
| | | 3. Ordinary.. |
| | | 4. Inferior.. |
| | | 5. Worst.. |
| | XIII. Sandy, from 1/3 to 1/10 clay | 1. Best.. |
| | | 2. Good.. |
| | | 3. Ordinary.. |
| | | 4. Inferior.. |
| | | 5. Worst.. |
| | XIV. Heavy sand under 1/10 clay | 1. Best.. |
| | | 2. Good.. |
| | | 3. Ordinary.. |
| | | 4. Inferior.. |
| | | 5. Worst.. |

The following statement shows that the nature and percentage of the different kinds of soils in the *ryotwari* areas of each district in the Province, and will give an indication of the kind of soils likely to be met with in the zamindari areas,, when they are taken up for ryotwari settlement :—

| **Districts** | **Nature of Soil** | | | |
|---|---|---|---|---|
| | **Regar** | **Red-ferrugi-nous** | **Aluvial** | **Arena-ceous** |
| | (2) | (3) | (4) | (5) |
| | % | % | % | % |
| Visakhapatanam (plains) | 21.0 | 79.0 | .. | .. |
| (Agency) | .. | .. | | |
| East Godavari (Plains) | 8.7 | 32.0 | 52.7 | 6.7 |
| (Agency) | .. | .. | .. | .. |
| West Godavari | 31.72 | 28.91 | 35.53 | 3.65 |
| Krishna | 65.89 | 5.88 | 18.41 | 9.70 |
| Guntur | 90-10 | 6.60 | .. | 3.30 |
| Kurnool | 59.7 | 40.3 | .. | .. |
| Bellary* | 39.7 | 22.00 | .. | .. |
| Anantapur | 20.5 | 79.5 | .. | .. |
| Cuddapah | 46.2 | 53.4 | .. | .. |
| Nellore† | 22.38 | 31.40 | .. | ‡0.19 |
| Chingleput | 30.22 | 63.02 | .. | 6.76 |
| South Arcot | 35.00 | 61.00 | .. | 3.00 |
| North Arcot | 15.00 | 84.00 | .. | .. |
| Chittoor | 10.92 | 89.08 | .. | .. |
| Salem | 16.00 | 83.00 | .. | .. |
| Coimbatore | 9.12 | 89.70 | .. | .. |
| Tiruchirappalli | 32.90 | 60.70 | 6.40 | .. |
| Tanjore | 42.83 | 27.45 | 21.58 | 8.14 |
| Ramanathapuram | 67.44 | 32.56 | .. | .. |
| Madurai | 15.00 | 85.00 | .. | .. |

| | | | | |
|---|---|---|---|---|
| Tirunelveli | 21.5 | 78.5 | .. | .. |
| Malabar | .. | 99.22 | .. | 0.78 |
| South Kanara | .. | 97.9 | .. | 2.1 |

* Black and red mixed 38.

† Mixed 32.6; Sandy 13.27.

‡ Special rate.

## Section II

### Sub-soils

The sub-soil is that which immediately underlies the culturable surface soil. For our purpose, about one yard in depth will be considered as the proper surface soil. This is ample for the roots of all kinds of crops; below this will be the sub-soil.

The sub-soil may consist of the same earthy substance as the soil itself, or it may be of similar character, differing only in degree or in kind, or it may be of quite an opposite character, or may consist of hard rock. Soils and sub-soils do sometimes, but not invariably, take their character from the underlying rocks of the country.

The red soils are sometimes extensively met with over ferruginous sandstone and laterite, and partake of the same elements as these. The *regar* soil may be found sometimes over large tracts of country of which the volcanic, the gneiss, and other primaeval rocks are the characteristic basis; at other it is found overlying large tracts of limestone, chalk, and other rocks of different characters.

The sub-soil has, generally, a great influence on the condition and agriculture of the soil above it. If it is clay, it is impervious to water, and tends to keep the upper soil wet or moist; on the other hand, a sandy, gravelly, or a calcareous sub-soil will, rarely, suffer from excess of water except during a period of long submergence. A tenacious soil, such as clay, upon a similar sub-soil, will, generally, suffer comparatively much from inundation, and the injurious effects of excess of moisture will be of longer continuance.

The tenacious, or retentive character of soils and sub-soils is an important consideration in irrigation, as some soils, from their difference in this respect, require very much more water than others. Rock may be either a retentive or a porous sub-soil according as it is a solid structure, or will admit of water percolating through it.

The soil will not, always, be of one kind to the depth of the one yard prescribed for the surface soil: gravel, sand, rock, or other substances may be found at the depth of a few inches below a more fertile surface. In classing the surface soil according to its constituent parts and quality, its depth, also, should be noted, when it is less than one yard.

The sub-soils may consist of the same substance as the soils above described, but to complete their classification, some further particulars are required, such as those added in the following lists :—

**Sub–soils**

1. River alluvium
2. *Regar* soil
3. *Lal* or red ferruginous earth
4. Calcareous earth or beds
5. Sand
6. Clay beds
7. Laterite rock
8. Limestone rock
9. Limestone in large nodules
10. Sandstone rock
11. Slate rock
12. Granite rock, etc.

An examination of the sub-soil will be facilitated by looking at the sides of channels and canals, and the excavations for wells in the neighborhood. Where these are absent, pits 1½ yards deep should be dug in several places in a village.

# IV

# Other Matters Incidental to Ryotwari Settlement

## Section I

### Determination of grain values

There are two points involved in this operation—

(1) To determine the products to be taken as the standard for each district, or tract of land, under consideration.

(2) To estimate the quantity of such standard crop which each description of soil may yield.

The principles which should be given the former of these processes are—

First—Limitation of standards, or in other words, the subordination of merely local production to general distribution, when this can be done without injustice, as for example, when a product, generally grown throughout the tract under examination, is substituted for one of a more local character, because their prices are the same, or nearly so.

Second—The preference of ordinary to special products and of food products to those which are not:—

This is founded on the following reasons:—

(1) The soil produces both indifferently.

(2) Food products are the ultimate standards of value; and other products must, themselves, be finally commuted into them.

(3) It is often, as in the case of cotton, for example, difficult, or rather impossible, to ascertain, by actual experiment, the

produce of a given extent of land. In cotton, actual experiments by the officers of Government are simply impracticable. There are said to be three great pickings, but the fact is that the cotton is picked as it ripens. All the information available is supplied by the ryot, whose interests or ignorance are sufficient to throw doubts upon its accuracy.

From these two principles follows, as a corollary—

Third—The elimination of products, not taken as standards, the areas under them being added to the areas under the standard crops.

To arrive at an accurate estimate of the quantity of grain of each of the standards of communication, the following conditions are necessary, viz. :—

(1) Numerous examinations of the actual outturn of each of the staple product should be made in irrigated and unirrigated lands, the extent tested being about ¼ acre, selected so as fairly to represent the whole field.

(2) The quantity of a full, ordinary and indifferent crop should be ascertained.

(3) The opinion of experienced officials, non-officials and agriculturists, as regards the outturn of each standard, in each description of soil, should invariably be obtained.

The arrangement of the table into *Tarams* (classes), by putting together soils of similar grain values, is a matter of some difficulty, owing to the soils possessing relatively different productive powers, when irrigated and dry, thus rendering essential to accuracy, two scales of tarams (classes), one for dry lands, and another for wet lands. Moreover, all soils is similar value, falling udner one taram of the dry scale, cannot always, if minute accuracy is required, be placed in any one taram of irrigated scale, but without such adjustment it is not easy to convert, without risk of confusion, the dry taram to a wet one, when dry land is irrigated.

The difficulty is avoided by adopting an "irrigated" scale of tarams for wet lands and an unirrigated scale of tarams for dry.

The chief object of the arrangement under tarams is to render the classification more intelligible to the ryots than it would be if it was exhibited in the more complicated forms of 'series' 'classes' and 'sorts'.

The table of tarams thus prepared is subject to revision with reference to actual experiments as to outturn.

## Section II

### Commutation rates

The principles laid down for guidance in converting the Government share of the produce into money are—

(1) That the commutation rate shall be fixed upon an average struck on the prices of a long series of years, so as to ensure that the advantages of good and the losses of bad years may be balanced, and to preclude all risk of the Government share of the produce being sold to the ryots at a price which he cannot always command.

(2) That the averages of prices shall be considered for the years and for the months in which the ryots sell their grains, the latter being, as a rule, adopted for settlement purposes.

(3) That a percentage allowance shall be made for cartage of grain to recognized markets.

(4) That the averages thus arrived at need not necessarily be adopted, but may be modified under other general considerations, such as—

(a) The high prices of famine years.

(b) The state of internal communications as affecting prices.

The Government, in their proceedings, Revenue Department, No. 881, dated 30th July 1885, passed the following orders. The period to be adopted, in all settlements, for the determination of the commutation price, shall be the 20 non-famine years immediately preceding such settlement. The commutation rate will be the average price for that period, less whatever allowance may be considered necessary for the difference between the ryots' and market prices. With the progress of the country and the improvement of communications, this allowance must always grow less and less. If, however, the commutation price thus arrived at should be greater than the lowest rate touched by prices during the standard period, then such lowest rate or some convenient round number slightly less than it, should be accepted as the commutation rate, without further deduction.

## Section III

### Vicissitudes of season

From the decision that the share of the State, or in other words, the land revenue demand, should be based on a percentage of the net produce, follows the consideration of allowances to be made from the gross produce on account of—

(1) Vicissitudes of season and unprofitable areas; and

(2) Expenses of cultivation

As regards the allowances to be made on account of vicissitudes of season and unprofitable areas, the principles to be borne in mind are—

(1) the general run of seasons, good and bad;

(2) the extent of land left follow; and

(3) the unproductive portions of fields, such as ridges, channels, small rocks, etc.

The allowance to be made may, as a rule, be from 10 to 25 percent, according to circumstances.

## Section IV

### Cultivation expenses

The actual cost of cultivation is a matter very difficult to determine, and it is impossible to attempt calculation in respect of any particular sort of soil, other than the first of a series, the gradations to be allowed to each if the numerous divisions being merely empirical. The points to be considered in the matter of cultivation expenses, therefore, are to ascertain—

(1) The extent of land that can be cultivated by a ryot with a plough and a pair of oxen.

(2) The number of years for which the cattle and plough and other agricultural implements will last.

(3) The other items of expense, as such as cost of ploughing, weeding, transplanting in wet lands, manuring, reaping, threshing, etc. on the whole holding.

(4) The amount of labour requisite for the several soils, since some are more easily worked than others.

This done, the next step is to reduce the total expenses of the holding to terms of an acre commuting grain payments, if any, into money, at the commutation price to be determined. The straw is usually taken as a set-odd against the item "feed of bullocks" in the cultivation expenses, and no separate provision is, therefore, made for it, nor does it find place in the matter of ryot's assets. Where, however, the cattle are fed on grain and the allowance of straw is not considered sufficient to meet the charge, the item may be specially provided for.

## Section V

## Grouping of villages for dry lands

The dry lands in all villages have not the same advantages, and, to correct inequalities which the adoption of unvarying standards for a whole tract might involve, the expedient of classifying them in groups is adopted. It will be obvious that under a restricted and inelastic soil classification table, a larger number of groups will be required than under an elastic classification table. At the early settlements, when they had only two or three sorts in the soil classification, extra groups had to be formed owing to similarity of soils, etc. Under the five sorts system of soil classification now in force, only two groups are allowed; but if a third group is found necessary, the special orders of the Board of Revenue should be obtained.

The considerations that weigh in the matter of grouping are—

(1) Proximity to markets and ports, which facilitate the sale and export of the grain to others areas.

(2) Means of communication—Road, railways, canals, etc., which facilitate the transport of the grain to the markets and ports.

(3) Healthiness of the tract, e.g., malarial areas have to be placed in a lower group.

(4) Immunity from damages to crops by wild animals, e.g,, villages in remote areas adjoining dense forests have to be placed in a lower group.

In touring in the area, and exhaustive enquiries of the leading ryots and non-officials are necessary to enable the Settlement Officer to formulate his proposals relating to grouping of villages.

## Section VI

### Classification of sources of irrigation

The classification of irrigation sources is decided on other principles than those prescribed for the grouping of villages, the sole criterion being the capacity of the source of water-supply. By capacity is meant the period for which water can be supplied by the irrigation source to its *ayacut* lands in the course of the year, with such repeated fillings as the source usually receives as a result of periodical rains in its catchment area, flow in the supply channels, surplus from the sources higher up, etc. Five classes of irrigation sources are recognized for settlement purpose.

*First class*—Exceptionally good sources, based on ancient or reservoirs across perennial rivers like the Godavari, Krishna and Cauvery. The *anicuts* across the two former rivers, and the Stanley reservoir across the last river, supply water unfailingly to extensive channel system dependent on them, for practically the whole year.

*Second class*—Irrigation sources affording a supply for eight months and over. Examples are the Red Hills tank and Chembarambakkam tank in Chingleput district.

*Third class*—Irrigation sources affording a supply for five months and above, but less than eight months.

*Fourth class*—Irrigation sources affording a supply for three months and above, but less than five months.

*Fifth class*—All minor sources affording supply for less than three months.

In some districts, irrigation sources affording a supply for more than five months have been placed in a lower class on account of labour and expense to the ryot in digging and keeping the channels clear, e.g., the Pennar and the Hagari channels in Bellary and Anantapur districts.

It may be urged that wet grain, grown at a distance from markets and roads, is in no better position, as regards facilities for sale, than dry grains would be. But the mode of grouping described above is virtually a concession, and it is found that wet lands do not need any such grouping. As a matter of fact, large irrigated areas attract markets.

## Section VII

## Money Rates

The calculations of the net value, half the net, and the money rates, is merely a mechanical process. The gross produce of the several descriptions of soil having been carefully scrutinized and tested by numerous experiments is converted into money at the communication price arrived at in the manner previously indicated. From this are deducted the expenses of cultivation and a certain percentage on account of vicissitudes of season and unprofitable areas, and the remainder is the net produce. The Government demand should not exceed half of this net produce. The difference of gradations as between different *tarams* may be a rupee in the lower *tarams*, and the rates for the lower groups should invariably commence one rate below the highest of the previous group, the object of this being to maintain an uniform difference all through.

List of money rates thus fixed for each district or portion of a district should then be made out and the assessment calculated on the fields accordingly.

## Section VIII

## Increment Remission

When the resettlement results in the assessment payable on any individual *patta* being increased by more than 25 percent, the increased assessment will be imposed gradually, i.e., by increases spread over a series of years in accordance with the rules given below. The temporary abatement of the full resettlement assessment is called, "**increment remission**". In estimating the increase which will give a claim to "increment remission", enhancements due to—

(a) increases in area by re-survey,

(b) increases due to transfer of land from "dry" to "wet" and

(c) increases due to transfer from "single crop" to "double crop"

will not be taken into account.

Increases due to reclassification of soil or sources of irrigation or to revision of grouping will, however, be taken into account, and in these cases minor increases in area will not be deducted and the increment remission admissible will be calculated on the total enhancements of the new assessment on the holding over the old assessment. If the increase of assessment in the individual cases exceeds 25 percent of the old assessment, an amount equal to the old assessment plus 25 percent thereof will be levied at once and the remainder by annual increments equal to 12½ percent, of the old assessment. Increment remission will not be granted when the total increase does not exceed Rs. 3 (three). It is, however, clearly to be understood that if the whole or a portion of the land held by a *pattadar* at the resettlement is relinquished or transferred, the full assessment will be charged for the lands remaining in his *patta* and for those which have passed to other hands. This rule, however, will not apply to cases in which the change in the holding may be due to causes beyond the ryots' control, i.e., where a portion of his land is washed away by a river or he is obliged to relinquish it or where a piece of land is taken up for public purposes. In the latter class of cases the excess assessment upon what remains of the holding will be levied in the same number of installments as those fixed for the entire holding. Similarly, when one of the joint holders of *patta* transfers his interest therein either to co-*pattadar* or to a stranger, increment remission will be granted.

# V

# Preparation of Settlement Schemes

The general principles upon which the revision of the land assessment of the Madras Presidency should be conducted having been detailed in the preceding pages, the method of procedure that was usually adopted by the department will now be alluded to.

The first step on taking up a new district is the determination, in consultation with the Collector of the portion of the district in which operations should be commenced, the chief consideration influencing this being the question as to where revision of the assessment is first and most needed.

This done, a printed notice to the villagers calling upon them to render all needful assistance in the work of classification, etc., is issued through the *Tahsildar* of the area selected, he having to supply the officers of the Settlement Department with the *ayacut* account, showing the area and assessment of occupied lands, distinguished under the heads of irrigated and unirrigated, as well as unoccupied, *poramboke* and *inam* lands, and also a list of the *karnams* showing the villages managed by each. Survey has necessarily to precede settlement. The following records will be supplied by the Survey Party to the Settlement Party before the latter commence their field work:—

(1) Land Register,

(2) Location sketches,

(3) Duplicate F. M. Book,

(4) Area lists, and

(5) Encroachment lists and sketches.

With these accounts and records and a skeleton map of the *taluk* showing the villages as demarcated and survey, the villages are allotted to the classifiers by the Supervisor under the orders of the Assistant Settlement Officer and the field of operations arranged so as to conveniently admit of supervision.

The classifier deputed to each village is supplied with the following registers and accounts:—

(1) Classification Register, with printed headings and lines uniformly ruled in pencil, and bearing on each page the seal of the Settlement Officer.

(2) Location sketches.

(3) Area Lists.

(4) F. M. Books.

(5) Encroachment lists and sketches.

(6) Other miscellaneous inspection registers.

Besides these, the *Inam Register* and the *Revenue chitta* of the village are made available to the classifier. He is further provided with a certificate, printed in the regional language, authorizing him to summon the villages with the necessary accounts and to require of them assistance in conducting his operations.

Furnished with these, he visits the village, and, with the aid of the survey map and the *karnam*, who accompanies him, as do, if possible, the ryots, makes, in the classification statement already alluded to, a complete registry of the fields.

In doing this, he first classes the fields into one or other of the 14 classes of soils already mentioned, according to the nature and composition of the soil. These classes are to be divided into five sort, viz., "best", "good", "ordinary", "inferior" and "worst". This classification and sorting is marked in pencil on the survey map in denoting figures, thus forming a detailed map of the soils of the village.

As each village is inspected by the classifier, the extent of land supplied by each source of irrigation has to be correctly ascertained, and the changes from dry to wet and *vice versa* and from single to double crop and *vice versa* have to be duly recorded in the classification register, in which have also to be shown the reasons for the entries.

In the survey map, symbols are inserted to show—

(1) The fields already registered as wet and allowed to stand as such.

(2) The fields registered as wet, but transferred to dry during 0the revision.

(3) The fields registered as dry, but, during the revision, transferred to wet.

(4) The fields registered as double crop and retained under this head.

(5) The fields registered as double crop, but, on revision, transferred to single crop.

(6) The fields registered as single crop, but transferred to double crop during the revision.

As each field is classified and registered, a *patta* book, showing the individual holdings contained in each survey number, is prepared in volumes of uniform size.

Information regarding concealed cultivation, evasion of water-rate on dry lands irrigated by Government water, evasion charge for second-crop lands situated in tank-beds, those irrigated by *itifak* and *doravu* wells, as well as all other particulars regarding each individual field has, during the progress of classification, to be carefully ascertained and recorded in the register, against each field, and, in addition to these, separate returns, giving information regarding each of the above-mentioned items have to be prepared for the information of the Collector. The encroachments should be inspected and full remarks made about their age, nature, i.e., whether objectionable or not, etc.

As each page of the classification register is written up, it is totalled, and, when the whole village is completed, a grand total for the whole should be struck.

If the harvest of standard crops is in progress during the period when classification is in hand, experiments as to the outturn are made by the classifier, and a return, in the prescribed form, is submitted by him.

During the time that the classification is in progress, the Supervision, as well as the Settlement and Assistant Settlement Officers, visit the village in order to ensure that the work is being carried on as it should be and that errors do not occur.

Where any doubt regarding the class to which any soil should be assigned occurs, the soil and sub-soil should be sampled and tested. For this purpose the surface and sub-soils to a depth of about nine inches should be taken in equal parts. The quantity selected for test and the proportion of sand, etc., found in the same is recorded against the several numbers in the classification register. Specimens of the soils, with the survey numbers noted on them, are forwarded to the higher authorities for orders.

As each village is completed by the classifiers, the records are forwarded to the supervisor, who, on the survey map, in which the class and sort of every field has already been marked in pencil, draws a line around all fields of similar value of class. To guard against fraud and errors of classification on the part of the classifiers and to ensure that the line between "best" and "good", "good" and "ordinary", "ordinary" and "inferior", and "inferior" and "worst" soils is drawn, as evenly as possible, the supervisor walks over the boundary of each block, tests the correctness of the classification, and revises, where necessary, by transferring fields of a different class and sort, found in the block, with the class and sort of the block in which they are situated, the only exception to this being where the extent of such scattered fields is sufficiently large to make a separate block of itself.

The supervisor should inspect all encroachments and record his opinion as to their disposal.

Opportunity is, at the same time, taken to check the proposals of the classifier to effect transfer of various kinds, e.g., from dry to wet, etc., and to test the entries of lands, irrigated by the different descriptions of wells, in view of their being properly dealt with under the new settlement. He further makes experiments as regards outturn and reports the results of these in the form prescribed for the purpose. The various returns prepared by the classifier are also examined, and, on them, the supervisor carefully notes all the changes he proposes in what has been recommended by the classifier. The supervisor should collect full particulars regarding cultivation expenses, and fix the groups of villages and classify irrigation sources. He also records, in a statement in a form prescribed, the repairs which each source of irrigation needs.

All the accounts are then transmitted to the Assistant Settlement Officer.

The Assistant Settlement Officer examines a certain number of blocks in each village, excepting where the errors discovered are so frequent as to call for a complete examination of the whole area.

When the series of examination, detailed above, is concluded, the classification and other accounts, which have been prepared in the field, are passed into the office of the Assistant Settlement Officer. The Assistant Settlement Officer in the meantime sets about obtaining a general view of the characteristics of the district or the parts of it in which operations are in progress, and he sees to collecting the data necessary to enable him to draw up his proposals for the revision of the assessment.

This accomplished, the next point to which he turns is the ascertaining and assignment of grain values to the several classes and sorts of soils. To effect this, the staple products of the districts are first fixed with reference to the following consideration:—

The percentage area of each crop, raised in each *taluk*, is examined; those foodgrains which show a higher percentage are taken to be the standards; then the prices of these standards are compared with those of the other crops occupying a subordinate position; the area of those of equal or approximate value is distributed under each of the standards; and lastly the percentages of areas of the staples thus arrived at will be the proportion of each standard, the outturn of which is calculated on an area of land, as illustrated below:—

| | ACS | Percentage | Respresented by |
|---|---|---|---|
| *Ragi* | 11,614 | 13½ | *Ragi* |
| *Paddy* | 17,839 | 20 ¾ | *Ragi* |
| *Indigo* | 11,743 | 13 ¾ | *Ragi* |
| | | ----- | |
| | | 48 | |
| | | ----- | |

| | | | |
|---|---|---|---|
| *Varagu* | 11,631 | 13½ | *Varagu* |
| *Cumbu* | 7,561 | 8¾ | *Varagu* |
| *Cholam* | 3,242 | 3¾ | *Varagu* |
| *Gram* | 1, 951 | 2¼ | *Varagu* |
| *Topes* | 13,546 | 15¾ | *Varagu* |
| Oil-seeds plantations and vegetables | 6,475 | 8 | Varagu |
| | --------- | | ---- |
| Total | 44,406 | | 52 |
| | --------- | | ---- |

Having thus obtained the standards wherewith to work out the money rates, the estimated outturn of each soil is assigned thereto, half in *ragi* and half in *varagu*, thereby equalizing the value of the crop by taking the mean of the two grains most extensively grown. The following will explain the course pursued:—

| Class | Sort | Crops | Extent | Outturn | Value at Rs. 142 for *ragi* and Rs. 89 for *varagu* | | |
|---|---|---|---|---|---|---|---|
| | | | ACS | M.M. | Rs. | A. | P. |
| 4 | 2 | *Ragi* | 0.50 | 160 | 7 | 1 | 7 |
| 4 | 2 | *Varagu* | 0.50 | 220 | 6 | 1 | 11 |
| Total value of gross outturn | | | | | 13 | 3 | 6 |

*Paddy* being the only standard for wet, *ragi* and *varagu* can be taken as the standards determined for dry lands upon the foregoing considerations.

Sometimes, the areas of special products of higher value may need to be added to the area of the standard of a lower value in order to equalize the burden of assessment on all kinds of soils. To arrive at the grain values, much consideration is given, and every precaution is taken to obtain as fair results as possible.

The Settlement Officer and his subordinates make numerous experiments for the purpose of ascertaining the actual outturn, or yield of land, sown with staple product, taking full, ordinary, indifferent crops; and, with the aid of intelligent and respectable ryots, an *average outturn per acre,* such as will apply to a series of years, good and bad, and to ordinary tillags, is eventually fixed for each kind of soil for one class of land as specified below by way of example:—

***Regar* loam, Class IV, wet-outturn per acre in sort 1**

| | *Best* (1) | *Good* (2) | *Ordinary* (3) | *Inferior* (4) | *Worst* (5) |
|---|---|---|---|---|---|
| 1. As per opinion of villages | 516 | 464 | 414 | 359 | 307 |
| 2. As per opinion of *Tahsildars* | 528 | 504 | 465 | 439 | 372 |
| 3. As per experiments in procedure | 528 | 504 | 465 | 439 | 372 |
| (a) Good— | | | | | |
| (1) By Revenue Department | 953 | 790 | 760 | 682 | 547 |
| (2) By Settlement Department | 1,076 | 936 | 773 | 689 | 567 |
| (b) Middling— | | | | | |
| (1) By Revenue Department | 688 | 595 | 408 | 524 | 298 |
| (2) By Settlement Department | 704 | 643 | 527 | 455 | 382 |
| (c) Bad— | | | | | |
| (1) By Revenue Department | 533 | 511 | 438 | 301 | 292 |
| (2) By Settlement Department | 581 | 480 | 402 | 318 | 283 |

| | | | | | |
|---|---|---|---|---|---|
| (d) Average— | | | | | |
| (1) By Revenue Department | 775 | 681 | 529 | 522 | 331 |
| (2) By Settlement Department | 853 | 701 | 581 | 491 | 422 |
| 4. Proposed grain value for wet. | 840 | 720 | 600 | 530 | 460 |
| 5. Proposed grain value for dry | 444 | 380 | 316 | 286 | 246 |

The same process is repeated for all classes of soils of wet, as well as of dry lands.

The yield thus arrived at is converted into money at the commutation price, to be determined according to the average prevailing during the series of twenty years preceding the settlement. The averages are, say, Rs. 120½ for white paddy, Rs. 161 for *ragi* and Rs. 97 for *varagu.*

These quotations, however, represent the merchants' selling prices, and if applied to the transactions of the *ryots*, would, obviously, tend to over-assessment, but in order to obtain the wholesale, or *ryots'* prices, a percentage deduction, ranging from 8 to 20 percent, according to the local circumstances of the district, is usually made from the market prices. This not only meets the cost of cartage and the merchants' profits, but fixes for the ryots, with a liberal margin, the approximate wholesale price he really obtains. Supposing it to be 12½ percent, the commutation prices resolve themselves into—

Rs. 105 for white paddy,

Rs. 142 for *ragi*, and

Rs. 80 for *varagu.*

From the results thus obtained, a deduction of from one-sixth to one-fourth is usually made in order to compensate for vicissitudes of seasons, as well as to allow for such portions of fields, as being occupied by *bunds*, pathways, water-courses, etc., are unproductive, but which are nevertheless, included in the area of the "survey field".

The fields having been classified, according to their physical and mechanical composition, their productive powers having been ascertained by experiment, etc., and these results having been converted into a money equivalent based on the average selling prices of a series of twenty years, and a percentage deduction having been made on account of carriage and merchants' profits, the next operation is the estimation of the cultivation expenses, which used to be one of the most difficult and most conjectural of the various steps in connexion with a settlement.

The mode in which this was done was to ascertain, separately, what extent of wet land and what of dry could be, under the ordinary conditions of the district, cultivated by one plough and one pair of bullocks.

The result was, to a certain extent, checked by the average acreage per plough. The results were reduced to acres and decimals. The items of cost usually included in the estimate were—

(1) Cost of ploughing cattle.

(2) Cost of agricultural implements.

(3) Seed.

(4) Manure.

(5) Wages of labor required for sowing, transplanting in wet, reaping, threshing, etc.

The method of calculation varied according to the description of crops grown and of culture, as well as according to the practice of making the various payments in each district. In some, these are made in grain, in others in money and in some in both grain and money. The payments made in grain were converted into money at the commutation price adopted for the settlement.

The cost of bullocks and of the implements of husbandry was distributed over the number of years during which they were estimated to be serviceable and the other items were calculated for each year.

It must be remembered that, as already stated, these calculations were made for the area which one plough cultivate and then reduced to terms of an acre.

The usual practice was to work out the expenses for the best soil and then to proportionately diminish this standard, as the quality of soil descends.

The cost of feeding cattle was not provided for in the estimate of cultivation expenses, as the straw was taken as a set-off against this item. If, however, in any district or tract, the feeding charges were known to be specially higher, owing to grain being given to ploughing cattle, this was taken into account.

The cultivation expenses were calculated, say, at Rs. 11 for class 4, sort 1. They would run something as under :—

| **Wet land** | **Cost per acre** | | |
|---|---|---|---|
| | Rs. | A. | P. |
| Plouging cattle | 1 | 12 | 0 |
| Agricultural implements | 1 | 0 | 1 |
| Seed | 1 | 2 | 5 |
| Manure | 1 | 10 | 8 |
| Wages | 5 | 6 | 1 |
| Cost of cultivation per acre of wet land | 10 | 15 | 3 of Rs. 11 roundly |
| Cost of cultivation per acre of dry land (one half of the above) | 5 | 8 | 0 |

These expenses being deducted from the gross assets, i.e., the value of the total outturn, the result will be the approximate net produce of the land under examination. The Government demand shall not exceed half of this net produce.

When this system is applied to each description of soil, we get what is termed the "**money rate**" or future assessment for wet and dry lands, respectively.

The following figures will illustrate in a concrete manner how these money rates are arrived at:—

The grain values assigned to the wet and dry lands or *regar* loam are in the third-class, irrigated, and first group, dry, respectively, as follows :—

| | Wet third class source Madras measures | Dry first group | |
|---|---|---|---|
| Best | 840 | 444 | *varague* and *ragi* |
| Good | 720 | 380 | *varague* and *ragi* |
| Ordinary | 600 | 316 | *varague* and *ragi* |
| Inferior | 530 | 286 | *varague* and *ragi* |
| Worst | 460 | 246 | varague and ragi |

The commutation price is Rs. 105 for paddy and Rs. 89 and Rs. 142 *varagu* and *ragi*, respectively, these being the market prices on a series of twenty years, less 12½ percent, deducted as being the difference between the market and *ryots'* selling prices, and as allowance for cartage.

The commuted value of the gross produce per acre stands as follows :—

| | Wet | | | Dry | | |
|---|---|---|---|---|---|---|
| | Rs. | A. | P. | Rs. | A. | P. |
| Best | 27 | 9 | 0 | 15 | 8 | 6 |
| Good | 23 | 10 | 0 | 15 | 3 | 6 |
| Ordinary | 19 | 11 | 0 | 10 | 14 | 7 |
| Inferior | 17 | 6 | 3 | 9 | 13 | 3 |
| Worst | 15 | 1 | 6 | 8 | 6 | 1 |

From these values are deducted a sixth for wet lands and a fourth for dry lands, the corresponding amounts being—

| | Wet | | | Dry | | |
|---|---|---|---|---|---|---|
| | Rs. | A. | P. | Rs. | A. | P. |
| Best | 4 | 9 | 6 | 3 | 14 | 1 |
| Good | 3 | 15 | 0 | 3 | 4 | 10 |
| Ordinary | 3 | 4 | 6 | 2 | 11 | 8 |
| Inferior | 2 | 14 | 4 | 2 | 7 | 4 |
| Worst | 2 | 8 | 3 | 2 | 1 | 6 |

After deduction, we are left with the following figures :—

| | Wet | | | Dry | | |
|---|---|---|---|---|---|---|
| | Rs. | A. | P. | Rs. | A. | P. |
| Best | 22 | 15 | 6 | 11 | 0 | 5 |
| Good | 19 | 11 | 0 | 9 | 14 | 8 |
| Ordinary | 16 | 6 | 6 | 8 | 2 | 11 |
| Inferior | 14 | 7 | 11 | 7 | 5 | 11 |
| Worst | 12 | 9 | 3 | 6 | 4 | 7 |

From these are again deducted cultivation expenses of the following amounts :—

| | Wet | | | Dry | | |
|---|---|---|---|---|---|---|
| | Rs. | A. | P. | Rs. | A. | P. |
| Best | 11 | 0 | 0 | 5 | 8 | 0 |
| Good | 9 | 12 | 0 | 5 | 0 | 0 |
| Ordinary | 8 | 8 | 0 | 4 | 10 | 0 |
| Inferior | 7 | 8 | 0 | 4 | 6 | 0 |
| Worst | 6 | 8 | 0 | 4 | 2 | 0 |

The net values left are :—

| | Wet | | | Dry | | |
|---|---|---|---|---|---|---|
| | Rs. | A. | P. | Rs. | A. | P. |
| Best | 11 | 15 | 6 | 6 | 2 | 5 |
| Good | 9 | 15 | 0 | 4 | 14 | 8 |
| Ordinary | 7 | 14 | 6 | 3 | 8 | 11 |
| Inferior | 6 | 15 | 11 | 2 | 15 | 11 |
| Worst | 6 | 1 | 3 | 2 | 2 | 7 |

Half these amounts, i.e., the share which is the maximum that can be taken by Government, are shown below :—

| | Wet | | | Dry | | |
|---|---|---|---|---|---|---|
| | Rs. | A. | P. | Rs. | A. | P. |
| Best | 5 | 15 | 9 | 3 | 1 | 2 |
| Good | 4 | 15 | 6 | 2 | 7 | 4 |
| Ordinary | 3 | 15 | 3 | 1 | 2 | 5 |
| Inferior | 3 | 8 | 0 | 1 | 7 | 11 |
| Worst | 3 | 0 | 7 | 1 | 1 | 3 |

The above amounts are rounded off to the following rates, which are those finally fixed as the assessment :—

| | Wet | | | Dry | | |
|---|---|---|---|---|---|---|
| | Rs. | A. | P. | Rs. | A. | P. |
| Best | 6 | 0 | 0 | 3 | 0 | 0 |
| Good | 5 | 0 | 0 | 2 | 8 | 0 |
| Ordinary | 4 | 0 | 0 | 1 | 12 | 0 |
| Inferior | 3 | 8 | 0 | 1 | 8 | 0 |
| Worst | 3 | 0 | 0 | 1 | 0 | 0 |

Next, the villages in the tract are "grouped" for dry lands and the sources of irrigation are classified. The rates appertaining to each group, or class, are next determined. In the illustration already given, the rates arrived at are for the third class of wet and for the first class of dry, which were taken as being normal groups. The rates of the second and fourth classes in wet are respectively obtained by raising or lowering one grade. For the first, is affixed a set of rates, one gradation higher throughout, than those of the second. In the same manner, the rates for the second and third groups in dry are worked out from the first-class rates given above. The highest rate of a lower group village is, for the same class and sort of soil, a rate lower than the assessment for the group immediately above it.

The following table shows the rates of the normal groups for wet and dry in the case for which figures were worked out above as example :—

| | | | Wet | | | | | | | | |
|---|---|---|---|---|---|---|---|---|---|---|---|
| Class | Sort | Primary *taram* | First class source | | | Second class source | | | Third class source | | |
| | | | Rs. | A. | P. | Rs. | A. | P. | Rs. | A. | P. |
| IV | 1 | 1 | 7 | 8 | 0 | 6 | 0 | 0 | 5 | 0 | 0 |
| III | 1 | 2 | 6 | 4 | 0 | 5 | 0 | 0 | 4 | 0 | 0 |
| IV | 2 | 2 | 6 | 4 | 0 | 5 | 0 | 0 | 4 | 0 | 0 |
| VII | 1 | 2 | 6 | 4 | 0 | 5 | 0 | 0 | 4 | 0 | 0 |

| | | | | | | | | | | | |
|---|---|---|---|---|---|---|---|---|---|---|---|
| III | 2 | 3 | 5 | 0 | 0 | 4 | 0 | 0 | 3 | 8 | 0 |
| IV | 3 | 3 | 5 | 0 | 0 | 4 | 0 | 0 | 3 | 8 | 0 |
| V | 1 | 3 | 5 | 0 | 0 | 4 | 0 | 0 | 3 | 8 | 0 |
| VI | 1 | 3 | 5 | 0 | 0 | 4 | 0 | 0 | 3 | 8 | 0 |
| VII | 2 | 3 | 5 | 0 | 0 | 4 | 0 | 0 | 3 | 8 | 0 |
| VIII | 1 | 3 | 5 | 0 | 0 | 4 | 0 | 0 | 3 | 8 | 0 |
| XII | 1 | 3 | 5 | 0 | 0 | 4 | 0 | 0 | 3 | 8 | 0 |

| | | | | | | | | | | | |
|---|---|---|---|---|---|---|---|---|---|---|---|
| III | 3 | 4 | 4 | 0 | 0 | 3 | 8 | 0 | 3 | 0 | 0 |
| IV | 4 | 4 | 4 | 0 | 0 | 3 | 8 | 0 | 3 | 0 | 0 |
| V | 2 | 4 | 4 | 0 | 0 | 3 | 8 | 0 | 3 | 0 | 0 |
| VI | 2 | 4 | 4 | 0 | 0 | 3 | 8 | 0 | 3 | 0 | 0 |
| VII | 3 | 4 | 4 | 0 | 0 | 3 | 8 | 0 | 3 | 0 | 0 |
| VIII | 2 | 4 | 4 | 0 | 0 | 3 | 8 | 0 | 3 | 0 | 0 |
| XII | 2 | 4 | 4 | 0 | 0 | 3 | 8 | 0 | 3 | 0 | 0 |
| XIII | 1 | 4 | 4 | 0 | 0 | 3 | 8 | 0 | 3 | 0 | 0 |

| | | | | | | | | | | | |
|---|---|---|---|---|---|---|---|---|---|---|---|
| III | 4 | 5 | 3 | 8 | 0 | 3 | 0 | 0 | 2 | 8 | 0 |
| IV | 5 | 5 | 3 | 8 | 0 | 3 | 0 | 0 | 2 | 8 | 0 |
| V | 3 | 5 | 3 | 8 | 0 | 3 | 0 | 0 | 2 | 8 | 0 |
| VI | 3 | 5 | 3 | 8 | 0 | 3 | 0 | 0 | 2 | 8 | 0 |
| VII | 4 | 5 | 3 | 8 | 0 | 3 | 0 | 0 | 2 | 8 | 0 |
| VIII | 3 | 5 | 3 | 8 | 0 | 3 | 0 | 0 | 2 | 8 | 0 |
| XIII | 2 | 5 | 3 | 8 | 0 | 3 | 0 | 0 | 2 | 8 | 0 |
| XIV | 1 | 5 | 3 | 8 | 0 | 3 | 0 | 0 | 2 | 8 | 0 |

| | | | | | | | | | | | |
|---|---|---|---|---|---|---|---|---|---|---|---|
| III | 5 | 6 | 3 | 0 | 0 | 2 | 8 | 0 | 2 | 0 | 0 |
| V | 4 | 6 | 3 | 0 | 0 | 2 | 8 | 0 | 2 | 0 | 0 |
| VI | 4 | 6 | 3 | 0 | 0 | 2 | 8 | 0 | 2 | 0 | 0 |
| VII | 5 | 6 | 3 | 0 | 0 | 2 | 8 | 0 | 2 | 0 | 0 |
| VIII | 4 | 6 | 3 | 0 | 0 | 2 | 8 | 0 | 2 | 0 | 0 |

| | | | | | | | | | | | |
|---|---|---|---|---|---|---|---|---|---|---|---|
| XII | 3 | 6 | 3 | 0 | 0 | 2 | 8 | 0 | 2 | 0 | 0 |
| XIV | 2 | 6 | 3 | 0 | 0 | 2 | 8 | 0 | 2 | 0 | 0 |
| | | | | | | | | | | | |
| V | 5 | 7 | 2 | 8 | 0 | 2 | 0 | 0 | 2 | 0 | 0 |
| VI | 5 | 7 | 2 | 8 | 0 | 2 | 0 | 0 | 2 | 0 | 0 |
| VII | 5 | 7 | 2 | 8 | 0 | 2 | 0 | 0 | 2 | 0 | 0 |
| XII | 3 | 7 | 2 | 8 | 0 | 2 | 0 | 0 | 2 | 0 | 0 |
| XIV | 2 | 7 | 2 | 8 | 0 | 2 | 0 | 0 | 2 | 0 | 0 |
| | | | **Dry** | | | | | | | | |
| II | 1 | 1 | 4 | 0 | 0 | 3 | 0 | 0 | 2 | 8 | 0 |
| | | | | | | | | | | | |
| II | 2 | 2 | 3 | 0 | 0 | 2 | 8 | 0 | 2 | 0 | 0 |
| IV | 1 | 2 | 3 | 0 | 0 | 2 | 8 | 0 | 2 | 0 | 0 |
| | | | | | | | | | | | |
| III | 1 | 3 | 2 | 8 | 0 | 2 | 0 | 0 | 1 | 12 | 0 |
| IV | 2 | 3 | 2 | 8 | 0 | 2 | 0 | 0 | 1 | 12 | 0 |
| VII | 1 | 3 | 2 | 8 | 0 | 2 | 0 | 0 | 1 | 12 | 0 |
| | | | | | | | | | | | |
| III | 2 | 4 | 1 | 12 | 0 | 1 | 8 | 0 | 1 | 4 | 0 |
| IV | 3 | 4 | 1 | 12 | 0 | 1 | 8 | 0 | 1 | 4 | 0 |
| V | 1 | 4 | 1 | 12 | 0 | 1 | 8 | 0 | 1 | 4 | 0 |
| VI | 1 | 4 | 1 | 12 | 0 | 1 | 8 | 0 | 1 | 4 | 0 |
| VII | 2 | 4 | 1 | 12 | 0 | 1 | 8 | 0 | 1 | 4 | 0 |
| VIII | 1 | 4 | 1 | 12 | 0 | 1 | 8 | 0 | 1 | 4 | 0 |
| XII | 1 | 4 | 1 | 12 | 0 | 1 | 8 | 0 | 1 | 4 | 0 |
| | | | | | | | | | | | |
| III | 3 | 5 | 1 | 8 | 0 | 1 | 4 | 0 | 1 | 0 | 0 |
| IV | 4 | 5 | 1 | 8 | 0 | 1 | 4 | 0 | 1 | 0 | 0 |
| V | 2 | 5 | 1 | 8 | 0 | 1 | 4 | 0 | 1 | 0 | 0 |
| VI | 2 | 5 | 1 | 8 | 0 | 1 | 4 | 0 | 1 | 0 | 0 |
| VII | 3 | 5 | 1 | 8 | 0 | 1 | 4 | 0 | 1 | 0 | 0 |

| | | | | | | | | | | |
|---|---|---|---|---|---|---|---|---|---|---|
| VIII | 2 | 5 | 1 | 8 | 0 | 1 | 4 | 0 | 1 | 0 | 0 |
| XII | 2 | 5 | 1 | 8 | 0 | 1 | 4 | 0 | 1 | 0 | 0 |
| XIII | 1 | 5 | 1 | 8 | 0 | 1 | 4 | 0 | 1 | 0 | 0 |
| III | 4 | 6 | 1 | 0 | 0 | 0 | 12 | 0 | 0 | 8 | 0 |
| IV | 5 | 6 | 1 | 0 | 0 | 0 | 12 | 0 | 0 | 8 | 0 |
| V | 3 | 6 | 1 | 0 | 0 | 0 | 12 | 0 | 0 | 8 | 0 |
| VI | 3 | 6 | 1 | 0 | 0 | 0 | 12 | 0 | 0 | 8 | 0 |
| VII | 4 | 6 | 1 | 0 | 0 | 0 | 12 | 0 | 0 | 8 | 0 |
| VIII | 3 | 6 | 1 | 0 | 0 | 0 | 12 | 0 | 0 | 8 | 0 |
| XIII | 2 | 6 | 1 | 0 | 0 | 0 | 12 | 0 | 0 | 8 | 0 |
| XIV | 1 | 6 | 1 | 0 | 0 | 0 | 12 | 0 | 0 | 8 | 0 |
| III | 5 | 7 | 0 | 12 | 0 | 0 | 8 | 0 | 0 | 6 | 0 |
| V | 4 | 7 | 0 | 12 | 0 | 0 | 8 | 0 | 0 | 6 | 0 |
| VI | 4 | 7 | 0 | 12 | 0 | 0 | 8 | 0 | 0 | 6 | 0 |
| VII | 5 | 7 | 0 | 12 | 0 | 0 | 8 | 0 | 0 | 6 | 0 |
| VIII | 4 | 7 | 0 | 12 | 0 | 0 | 8 | 0 | 0 | 6 | 0 |
| XII | 3 | 7 | 0 | 12 | 0 | 0 | 8 | 0 | 0 | 6 | 0 |
| XIII | 3 | 7 | 0 | 12 | 0 | 0 | 8 | 0 | 0 | 6 | 0 |
| XIV | 2 | 7 | 0 | 12 | 0 | 0 | 8 | 0 | 0 | 6 | 0 |
| V | 5 | 8 | 0 | 8 | 0 | 0 | 6 | 0 | 0 | 4 | 0 |
| VI | 5 | 8 | 0 | 8 | 0 | 0 | 6 | 0 | 0 | 4 | 0 |
| VIII | 5 | 8 | 0 | 8 | 0 | 0 | 6 | 0 | 0 | 4 | 0 |
| XIV | 3 | 8 | 0 | 8 | 0 | 0 | 6 | 0 | 0 | 4 | 0 |

These rates, applied to the survey areas placed under each class and sort of soil give what are called the financial results of the new settlement for a village, *taluk* or district.

Upon these data, a report called the "**scheme report**" is drawn up by the Settlement Officer, in which he enters into full particulars of the political and revenue history of the district under report gives details of the physical features of the country; goes into statistics and resources; and discusses the several processes worked out by him in arriving at the results, indicated above. Statements must next be prepared showing the financial results of the new assessment, as compared with the revenue of the year, on the basis of accounts of which the classification was conducted, and in these should be embodied the area of cultivation, the demand, remissions, gross collections, average rate of assessment and also the available resources of revenue derivable from the assessment of the whole of the arable land of the district settled.

The fluctuations of the demand and cultivated area must be carefully compared, in order to see how far any increase in the former may have led to decrease in the latter, or *vice versa,* and also, how far the new assessment appears to accommodate itself to these circumstances. Any striking contrasts between the old and new rates must be carefully examined and any explanation that may be necessary should be given. The Settlement Officer should discuss in detail the question of the fairness of the revision of assessment proposed by him, and explain the causes which influenced the enhancement or diminution in assessment, in any locality or localities, as the case may be.

These proposals are reviewed and revised, if necessary, by the Board of Revenue, and finally submitted for the sanction of Government.

## VI

# Introduction of Settlement Rates

When a settlement scheme has received sanction of the Government, a notification giving a brief summary of the principles on which the new money rates were worked out is prepared by the Settlement Officer and with the approval of the Board of Revenue, published in the District Gazette.

The following steps are then taken :—

1. The area under each source of irrigation is finally revised and extended, or curtailed, as the state of the water-supply renders it necessary.

2. Subdivisions of holdings are measured up and entered in the register.

3. The whole of the holdings, shown in the classification registers, are then checked, and corrections are made with reference to the adangal accounts of the *fasli* on which the introduction of the settlement is based.

4. The miscellaneous accounts, already partly prepared in the field, are finally completed.

5. Comparative statements of the assessment are prepared on the basis of the occupied lands of the year in which the settlement is to be introduced.

6. Transfers of registry are made.

7. The *samudayam* or common lands are divided where this is practicable.

8. Grazing-grounds, threshing floors, building sites, burial grounds, etc., are allotted.

9. *Pattas*, wrongly entered in the names of deceased *ryots*, vendors, donors are transferred to the rightful holders, where the consent of the parties concerned can be obtained.

10. *Chittahs* are prepared.

11. The composition of second-crop cultivation is carried out.

With the exception of compounding for second-crop cultivation, none of the above named operations call for remark.

The method of composition usually adopted, with reference to the principles already described, is to grade the charge according to the quality of the irrigation upon which the land concerned is dependent. This having been attended to in classing the sources of irrigation, it is once for all decided under what class of sources land should be registered as double crop, and under what class of sources the composition for second crop should be permitted. The rate of composition beginning from one-third, descends to one-fifth; say, one-third, for second-class sources, one-fourth for third-class sources and one-fifth for fourth-class sources; the lands under the first-class sources having been registered as permanent double crop, half of the first-class charge is entered in the accounts. Remissions are granted when the water-supply fails in the case of double-crop wet lands, but in regard to land compounded for, the charge is invariably paid.

Sometimes, variation of rate may be allowed under one and the same source. For instances, under a particular tank, a portion of the area may be favourably located and in a position to be supplied with water for second crop, with much greater certainty than the more distant lands or than those on a higher level. These variations may be recognized and treated by the officer introducing the settlement, where he finds a sufficiently large area requiring special considerations.

Such instances, however, will be rare, because they may, as a rule, be equally inconveniently situated as regards irrigation of the first crop, and these cases are adjusted in the classification of soils.

Another method of fixing the charge for second crop was adopted for Tirunelveli, i.e., the charge was graduated according to the *taram* or assessment, as shown below, but this was treated as a special case, and it was ordered that the usual method should be the rule of the department:—

| Rate of assessment or *taram* | Rate per compound |
|---|---|
| I and II | 2/3 |
| III | ½ |
| IV | 1/3 |
| V | ¼ |

After the completion of the preliminaries alluded to above, provisional *pattas*, called "***rough pattas***", are prepared and sent to the villages for distribution to the ryots. A notice is affixed to each village naming the time and place for the hearing of all objections to new entries and rates. A description of the method of assessment, together with a sketch map, showing the different blocks of land, is furnished to the village authorities for the use of the villagers. On the day named in the notice, those who have cause for complaint appear with their village officers before the settling officer, and their complaints, as redressed, or rejected, are entered in the settlement diary. This enquiry is called "***Rough Patta Objection Hearing***".

The accounts are then corrected with reference to his final settlement. The "**diglott**" registers of each village are thereupon prepared and forwarded to the Board's Office to be printed.

This register, called the **Settlement Register**, is the foundation on which the whole revenue administration rests. It forms a complete **Domesday Book**, recording accurate information regarding every separate holding, whether large or small. The area of each field is given in acres and rents, and the assessment thereon and other particulars relating to the field are shown in parallel divided amongst twenty *ryots*. In such a case, there will be twenty sub-letters and each *ryot* will have a separate line in the register, giving full particulars of his holding, even though the extent of it (as sometimes happens) is no more than one-hundredth part of an acre. From the register is prepared a ledger known as the ***chittah***, which gives each *ryot's* personal account with Government. Every field, or fraction of a field, held by the same *ryot*, is picked out from the settlement register and entered in this ledger, under his name, with particulars of area, assessment and other details. The total of the area shows the extent of his different holdings in the village, and the total of the assessment, is the amount due thereon by him to Government. A copy of this, his personal account, is given to each *ryot* with a note as to the date on which each installment falls due and is known as his "*patta*".

An English descriptive memoir giving full details touching each village and its settlement and an account of all lands held tax-free, or on favourable tenure, is prefixed to each "***Diglott***" ***Register***. A sketch map of the village, showing the tanks and channels, and all similarly assessed fields, laid out into blocks is also attached to it.

Sufficient number of copied of the "Diglott" Register are printed for use of Government Departments, for sale to *ryots*, and for purpose of reserve.

## 2

# Method of Land Measurement and Assessment in Northern Circars During the Pre-British Era as Reflected in the *Chetri Ganitam*

The *Chetri Ganitam*[1] is one of very few works on the indigenous method of assessment, which has, somehow, escaped the attention of the scholars who have worked on the different aspects of pre-British agrarian system of the Deccan, especially the Northern Circars. They have mainly banked upon the information derived from the inscriptions or from the travellers' accounts or from the Mackenzie Manuscripts or some of the Persian works or the relevant English records. It is, by no means, the intention of the present writer to minimize the importance of the above sources. It is, however, difficult to understand how exactly the system internally worked, which has been duly reflected in the source under study. It is quite well know that the system of land measures and assessment varied not only in every group of villages and often in every village, but also according to the nature of soil and sometimes even in respect of the same soil and also according to local usages and customs, As such, however perfect the system of assessment established by the Vijayanagar rulers, the Golconda sultans, the Mughals and the Nizam of Hyderabad might have been, it could hardly introduce any kind of uniformity, and regional and local agrarian order had practically remained intact.[2]

The *Chetri Ganitam* was originally a Sanskrit work on field mathematics and it seems that its Telugu version was found, translated into English and edited by Dr. B. Heyne during 1797-

---

Paper presented at *Indian History Congress*, 49th Session, Dharwad, 1988.

99 while on tour from 'Bejwada to Temmeri Cottah'.[3] Heyne has neither given the name of the original author nor the probable period when this work was written. He has, however, given the name of the Telugu translator as 'Pavaluru Mallaia, a Brahmin'[4] and names of other known books of the 'Ganitam'.[5] Heyne happened to tour various parts of the peninsula and subsequently published his results along with source under study in 1814.[6] The present writer had the opportunity of going through the manuscript of the source and also comparing it with the published version and has thereby found some difference between the two.

The published version has nowhere mentioned the year in which it was found and translated. But it makes lot of differences whether a particular method of assessment was in vogue during the eighteenth century or it was there in the first quarter of nineteenth century as well. Whereas the names of books, persons and places in the manuscript have been spelled more the way eighteenth century Englishmen used to spell and in the later version they are very much modified and are more or less on the modern lines.[7] The name of the work was earlier translated as 'a Sanskrit work on land measurement' and later as 'Field measuring of the Hindoos'.[8] In the manuscript it is not clear whether Heyne had found the translated version or had got it translated into Telugu. The printed one clearly states, "Translated into Telinga by Pavaluru Mallaja, Brahmin, who lived, it is said some centuries ago, at Rajamundry".[9] As against the conversion of different land measures into Sq. Poles in the manuscript, the printed version has given feet and sq. feet instead.[10] Apart from comparing the land measures in vogue in the Masulipatnam Circar with certain neighboring areas viz., Kondavid, Venikonda and Bellamkonda districts of Guntur Circar, Kondapalle (also called Mustafanagar) and on the islands of Godavari, the published version has also compared it with Ellore and Rajamundry.[11] The conversions of measures of weight into *seers,* Ibs. and *maund* given in the later version saves us from lot of botherations as they varied much in different places.[12] The areas for which the yield has been given have been described in the earlier version as 'most productive in the Circars', while the later version says, 'except the Delta of the Godavery, the areas are the most productive'.[13] Lastly in one of the two lists of the produce and yield the manuscript does not mention the name of the area to which it concerned while the printed version has also given that name.[14]

The *Chetri Ganitam* is a work on traditional method of assessment relevant not only to the areas concerned but in principle to different parts of India which seems to have remained in vogue along with the official methods introduced from time to time. It touches almost all the aspects of assessment. It deals with the different types of land measures in vogue; possible shapes of the fields; method of measuring them; and seeds and yield ratio of the different commodities sown. For the earlier portion the centre of discussion is Masulipatnam Circar, though it also includes Heyne's own observations and comparison with some of the neighboring areas. The last portion has concentrated mainly on the different areas of Rajahmundry and, of course, the editor's own comments and observations. In any case it gives a fair amount of idea about the possible yield of the different commodities during the eighteenth century, though in a specific region.

The fundamental theory of measures of length, according to *Chetri Ganitam,* was the same in the area under study as in other parts of India. It was primarily based upon such natural tests as finger-bredths, spans, cubits and seed arbitraments of local metrologies though the names of' different measures were local".[15]

In the Masulipatnam Circar the land was measured in *tana* (span or foot), *mura* (cubit), *ghada* (bamboo), *kunta* and *pooty* etc. While a *pooty* of this area according to Heyne, was in theory equal to approximately 10 acres, 100 *kuntas* formed one *pooty,* 4 *ghadas* formed one *kunta,* 32 *muras* formed one *ghada* and 2 *tanas* formed one *mura.*[16] The land was measured in terms of *Kuntas* with the help of a *ghada* of 32 *muras* (cubits) made of a rope which was equal to 64' in length. The measurement was generally done by a local *kesary,* i.e., a chuckler, tanner or a shoe maker and *kesary tana* and *kesary kunta* were considered standard measures.[17] The editor in his comments on the subject pointed out that despite in theory one *pooty* was equal to about 10 acres, because of the fact that measuring was normally done 'with hand of a middle sized man', a span 'seldom exceeded nine inches', 'a cubit eighteen' and hence a *pooty* approximately 7½ acres. He would also disagree with the common notion that a *kesary kunta* was larger than a common one, as though his span was three inches longer than his *ghada* (bamboo) and *kunta* were considerably less.[18]

As is also clear from the editorial remarks made in the source under study and elsewhere by Heyne that the Brahmins who, by nature quite clamorous for charity were provided with the *maniams* by the chiefs and share from the produce with great reluctance. Even the measurement of the land granted to them was rarely done properly which would cause complaints by the grantees.[19] But having different land measures for such and even other purposes, was perhaps not a unique thing for the area under study and was rather the continuation of the earlier practices. It appears from the *Arthasastra* also that in measuring pasture lands, the ground for the encampment of the army, timber forests and *brahmadeya* land different measuring rods were used.[20] The above two reasons would account for the eagerness on the part of the Brahmins to get employed in the revenue service so that they could get double payment.[21] Moreover, *'Chetrie Ganietam'* has given only one set of land measures for the areas under study which tends us to believe that the same measures were used in the whole circar and also for the wet, dry and garden lands.

The comparative study of the land measures in a few neighboring areas made by Dr. Heyne shows though the lengths of inch, *tana* (span) and *mura* (cubit) were identical, the *ghada* (bamboo) and *kunta* differed considerably. Whereas in Masulipatnam a *ghada* was of 64' and had 32 *muras,* in the districts of Guntur Circar it had 120' and 86 *muras,* in Kondapalle it was of 48' and had 32 *muras* and in Godawary islands it was of 120' and had 80 *muras* respectively. Moreover, in all the above areas 4 *ghadas* formed a *kunta* but its length naturally varied. Because of the varied length of a *kunta,* its conversion into the acres was different in the above areas. Whereas, as discussed above, 100 *kuntas* were equal to one *pooty* which was around 10 acres in the Masulipatnam Circar, in the districts of Guntur 64 *kuntas* were equal to 1 *koohara* the length of which was more than 20 acres and in Godavary island 60 *kuntas* formed one *pooty* equal to more than 19 acres.[22] In Ellore 16 *Barus* formed one *kunta;* 35 *kuntas* were equal to one *kutty* which was equal to 3,22,560 sq. ft. While in Rajahamundry 8 *Barus* formed one *kunta* and 32 *kuntas* were equal to one *kutty.*[23]

As compared to the above circar areas the contemporary land measures in the Rayalsema areas also varied. For instance in Kurnool, Penugonda and Kodikonda the available sources lead us to the possible conclusion that for the wet-land the *ghada* was equal to 18 cubits and 18 cubits square formed one *kunta* of land. For the dry land the *ghada* was equal to 22 cubits and 22 cubits square formed one *kunta* of land.[24]

B. Heyne's views on basic issues also correspond with the situations prevailing in the Vijayanagar empire. The study based upon the inscriptions of that period shows that not only there was no uniformity in the prevailing system of land measures hardly any serious attempt appears to have been made to standardize them either, During the Vijayanagar period also the length of a span and a cubit could never be the same as has been shown in the *Chetrie Ganitam,* i.e., 12"and 24" respectively. There is, of course, slight difference, that whereas according to Heyne the length of a cubit could never exceed 18" a rough study about Vijayanagar period put it at 19.68 inches?[25] The length of a cubit *(hasta),* according to *Arthasastra* also, was equal to 18".[26]

One thing, which has missed the attention of the writers, including Heyne, commenting on land measures, is that the prevailing traditional system had made it almost impossible to have any uniformity. Traditionally land was not measured with any standard *ghada, kunta, cunchum, toom* or *pooty* but was measured according to the capacity of seed required by a particular land e.g. a *toom* or a *pooty* land would mean the land which had the sowing capacity of one *toom* or one *pooty* seed respectively.[27] The land measures were however, accordingly standardized for a particular area. They could, of course, be identical in certain areas where the capacity of seed required was the same. As a matter of fact, the names of above measures were not only applicable to the measurement of the land but were also the cubic measures used for measuring the capacity/weight of a particular thing. For example, a *pooty* was equal to 500 lbs.; and a *cunchum* equal to 320 *tolas* or 8 1/3 lbs?[28] Sometimes due to the local usages or due to the influence of a particular language the names of the measures could be different but the idea or the principal was the same.

Since the measurement of land was done in the form of *kuntas, Chetri Ganitam* has given the subdivisions of a *kunta*[29] and has also provided a Table by which to find out the area of a piece of ground in terms of *kuntas* and sub-divisions thereof. Moreover, the method of finding the area of a field has also been mentioned in it. However, in the Table only square and rectangular fields have been taken into consideration. The maximum length and breadth taken in the Table ranges from half a bamboo or *ghada* (32') to 1/64 of a bamboo or *ghada* (l).[30]

The second part of the *Chetri Ganitam* is purely mathematical and deals with different types of fields (including their nomenclature and figures) that could possibly be found in a village and also the methods of measuring them. The translator/editor has also used his discretion in omitting some of the figures of the fields considering them to have existed "only in the fancy of the author". Moreover, Heyne did not find the existence of the use of compass in the measurement work.[31]

The third and rather most important part of *Chetri Ganitam,* namely, *Biejah Pramanum* has dealt with the period in which different crops were sown; quantity of seed required for one *pooty* (or 7½ acres of land) of ground; and yield expected out of that. As a matter of fact, the information given is a mixture of the information available in the text and the observations and conclusions drawn by Dr. Heyne, making it difficult to mark a line of demarcation between the two. The above information relates to only two sets of the 'most productive' districts of the area namely, Peddapuram, Pithapur and Etacottah, Tatipaka all in the Rajahmundry Circar, which had 'throughout the year a supply of water'.[82]

The importance of the source lies in the fact that this is perhaps one of the very few sources which, though only for a few districts, gives the detailed list of the seed consumption and the yield regarding different crops produced in the area. Due to the diversity of conditions prevailing in different areas and on account of the paucity of evidence on the subject, it has generally been difficult to give even a rough idea of the general yield of lands especially in the Deccan and South India during the pre-British period?[33]

**table in chapter no. 4 original page no. 74-75, to be pasted on page 130**

**The Table Provides that if a field is:**

| Long | Broad | Area |
|---|---|---|
| ½ Ghada or ½ Bamboo or 32 feet | ½ Ghada or ½ Bamboo or 32 feet | One *Patika Kunta* or ¼ *Kunta* |
| ½ Ghada or ½ Bamboo or 32 feet | ¼ Ghada or ¼ Bamboo or 16 feet | One *Panaka Kunta* or 1/8 *Kunta* |
| ½ Ghada or ½ Bamboo or 32 feet | 1/8 Ghada or 1/8 Bamboo or 8 feet | One *Veessum Kunta* or 1/16 *Kunta* |
| ½ Ghada or ½ Bamboo or 32 feet | 3/16 Ghada or 3/16 Bamboo or 12 feet | One *Veessum & Ara Veessum Kunta* or 3/32 *Kunta* |
| ½ Ghada or ½ Bamboo or 32 feet | 1/16 Ghada or 1/6 Bamboo or 4 feet | One *Ara Veessum Kunta or* 1/32 *Kunta* |
| ¼ Ghada or ¼ Bamboo or 16 feet | ¼ Ghada or ¼ Bamboo or 16 feet | One *Veessum Kunta or* 1/16 *Kunta* |
| ¼ Ghada or ¼ Bamboo or 16 feet | 1/16 Ghada or 1/16 Bamboo or 4 feet | One *Kaney Kunta or* 1/64 *Kunta* |
| ¼ Ghada or ¼ Bamboo or 16 feet | 1/64 Ghada or 1/64 Bamboo or 1 feet | One *Peerakaney Kunta* or 1/256 *Kunta* |
| ¾ Ghada or ¾ Bamboo or 48 feet | ¾ Ghada or ¾ Bamboo or 48 feet | Nine *Veessum Kunta or* 9/16 *Kunta* |
| ¾ Ghada or ¾ Bamboo or 48 feet | 3/16 Ghada or 3/16 Bamboo or 12 feet | Two *Veessum & One Kaney Kunta* or 9/64 *Kunta* |
| ¾ Ghada or ¾ Bamboo or 48 feet | 1/8 Ghada or 1/8 Bamboo or 8 feet | One *Veessum & Two Kaney Kunta* or 6/64 *Kunta* |
| ¾ Ghada or ¾ Bamboo or 48 feet | 3/64 Ghada or 3/64 Bamboo or 3 feet | Two *Veessum & one Peera Kaney Kunta* or 9/256 *Kunta* |
| ¾ Ghada or ¾ Bamboo or 48 feet | 1/32 Ghada or 1/32 Bamboo or 2 feet | Six *Peera Kaney Kunta* or 3/128 *Kunta* |

| | | |
|---|---|---|
| ¾ Ghada or ¾ Bamboo or 48 feet | 1/64 Ghada or 1/64 Bâmboo or 1 feet | Three *Peera Kaney Kunta* or 3/256 *Kunta* |
| ¾ Ghada or ¾ Bamboo or 48 feet | 1/128 Ghada or 1/128 Bamboo or ½ feet | 1½ *Peera Kaney Kunta* or 6/256 *Kunta* |
| 3/16 Ghada or 3/16 Bamboo or 12 feet | 3/16 Ghada or 3/16 Bamboo or 12 feet | Nine *Peera Kaney Kunta* or 9/256 *Kunta* |
| 1/8 Ghada or 1/8 Bamboo or 8 feet | 1/8 Ghada or 1/8 Bamboo or 8 feet | One *Kaney Kunta* or 1/64 *Kunta* |
| 1/16 Ghada or 1/16 Bamboo or 4 feet | 1/16 Ghada or 1/16 Bamboo or 4 feet | One *Peera Kaney Kunta* or 1/256 *kunta* |
| 1/64 Ghada or 1/64 Bamboo or 1 feet | 1/64 Ghada or 1/64 Bamboo or 1 feet | One *Gokara Kaney Kunta* or 1/1026 *Kunta* |

As it is/was not possible to have fields of such dimensions, it must have been a type of ready-reckoner containing answers to calculations of smaller fractions of measures commonly needed in finding the exact area of a piece of land.

Heyne's account is practically the only contemporary eighteenth century source on the subject for the Northern Circars and South India. No doubt there are other sources like the *Baramahal Records* (Section IV) 1799, Dr. R. Wight's *Report on the Resources of the Presidency*, 23rd Nov., 1837, Pharoah & Co's *Gazetteer*, and *Report of tile Agricultural Commission,* 1888.[34] But they are either nineteenth century sources or they do not deal with the Northern Circars. Though *Chetri Ganitam* as well as the method of assessment given in that related to a period much before the eighteenth century, the seed-yield given by Heyne was contemporary.

The following table, based upon the information given in the *Chetri Ganitam* and observations made by Heyne, gives a detailed account on the subject

| *Name of the Produce* | **Seer** *in 1 acre in K.G.s.* | *Produce in 1 acre in K.G.s* |
|---|---|---|
| **Paddapuram and Pithapur districts of Rajahmundry** | | |
| Sugar *(Jaggery)* | 574.55996 | 1511.9999 |
| Chilly,Papsicum, Turmerick, Sweet Potato | 30.239999 | 907.2 |
| Paddy | 30.239999 | 907.2 |
| *Jonna,Cholam* (Sorghum Vulgare) Millet *(juari)*, Maize. Also grown as fodder crop | 2.5199999 | 453.6 |
| *Ragi* (Pleusive carracana) *Natcheny* | 2.5199999 | 604.79998 |
| Gingelly, Sesamum indicum (called *til* in North India) | 2.5199999 | 453.6 |
| Red Cotton (Dry. cultivation) | 6.0479998 | 907.2 |

| | | |
|---|---|---|
| *Chamulu, Samai* Panicum miliare, Miliaceum (A variety of millet) | 2.5199999 | 453.6 |
| *Ganta* (stub of corn stalks fodder) | 2.5199999 | 604.79998 |
| *Nalla* or Black *Pesara,* Phaseolus Radiotus (Pulse; *Nalla Pesalu)* | 6.0479998 | 302.39999 |
| *Minapa, Phaseolus minimus* (Black gram) | 8.0639996 | 302.39996 |
| Geen Pesare, Phaseolus, *Mungo* | 6.047998 | 181.44 |
| *Anapa* (Gram) Lamp Oil (Castor) Ricinus | 5.039994 | 151.19999 |
| Communis | 5.039994 | 241.92 |
| *Sanaga, Channa* Bengal Gram, ChickPea | 5.039994 | 181.44 |
| Horse Gram *Ulavalu* | 6.048 | 241.92 |
| Bobbaralu (Beams) Dolichos Catiang | 5.0399998 | 151.19999 |
| **Etacottah and Tatipaka Districts of Rajahmundry Circar** | | |
| Paddy | 30.24 | 604.8 |
| Red gram Cytisees Cajan | 0.503999 | 151.2 |
| Cotton | 1.512 | 302.4 |
| *Korra* (Panicum Italicum) Italian Millet *(Tenai* in Tamil) | 2.5199998 | 302.4 |
| Natcheny, *Ragi* | 2.5199998 | 453.6 |
| *Jonna* (Dzomma) | 2.5199998 | 453.6 |
| *Ganti* (spiked millet) | 2.5199998 | 302.4 |

| | | |
|---|---|---|
| *Alloo* | 2.5199998 | 453.6 |
| Varagu (Varagalu) Wild Kidney Beams | 2.5199998 | 302.4 |
| *Minapa* (Black gram) | 5.0399998 | 151.19999 |
| *Anapa* (gram) | 5,0399998 | 241.92 |
| Lamp oil (Castor) | 5.0399998 | 241.92 |

Tobacco Plants in one acre—160

Coconut Trees in one acre—54

Mango Trees in one acre—27

Though Heyne, due to obvious reasons, was not very much convinced about the method of measurement and assessment he seemed quite satisfied with his results and remarked that ".. if acceptable I could render more complete *(sic.)* and extend it to all districts in Masulipatam and Guntoor Circars".[36]

The sources pertaining to the Northern Circars and parts of South India show an all round decline in the yield of different areas within eight to ten years of their acquisition by the English.[37] This fact was duly accepted by some of the English administrators also. Writing about Chinglaput, one of the earliest settlements of the English in the Madras Presidency; W.W. Place, its collector, gave very interesting explanation for this decline. He was of the opinion that due to vast influx of Europeans and more so since the British Government acquired stability the consumption of sheep and cattle had increased enormously. It had started adversely affecting the supply of the manure of sheep and cattle, which was the natural vigour of the soil in India. He suggested that decline could be overcome by improving the state of tanks on which agriculture chiefly depended and by stopping the excessive use of cattle for "supplying the accumulation wants of Madras."[38]

## References

* The grand divisions of the Northern Circars, were naturally and properly five; being so many portions of its length, principally marked by rivers running across from the hills on the west to the sea. But besides these, a sixth district had been formed from the maritime border of the four southerly circars or provinces, to serve as an appendage to, and to secure the salt made, or customs collected at the ports of Nizampatam, on a southern outlet of Krishna, and of Machilipatnam one of its northern branches, as welt as at their respective dependencies along the Coast. Before ultimately coming under the East India Company, the different areas of the Northern Circars, during the past roughly three centuries, had been under the different Governments, viz., the Bahminis, Vijayanagar Empire, Qutubshahi dynasty of Golconda, the Mughals, the Nizam or Hyderabad and the French etc. In, 1765 Lord Clive, got a *farman* from the Mughal Emperor Shah Alam ceding all the Northern Circars (Kondapalle, Rajahmundry, Ellore, Machilipatnam Chicacole and Guntur), which the Nizam refused to accept. In 1766 Nizam agreed to lease the five Northern Circars to the English but Guntur was surrendered only in 1788.

1. National Archives of India, *Survey of India Memoirs,* 16 OM, pp. 53-65, Cursory Observations made on a tour from Bez Wade to Temmeri Cottah. *"The translation of the 'Chetrie Ganietam" a Sanskrit work on land measurement",* by Dr. B. Heyne, 1797-1799.
2. See for example, Das, Dipakranjan, *Economic History of the Deccan,* Delhi, 1969, pp. 43-41; Mahalingam, T.V., *Administration and Social Life Under Vijayanagar, ii, Social Life,* Madras, 1975, pp. 168-169; Richards, J.F., *Mughal Administration in Golconda,* Oxford, 1975, pp. 306-316. Guha, Nikhiles, *Pre-British State System in South India,* Calcutta, 1985, pp. 7-36.
3. For B. Heyne's role as a surveyor see, Phillimore, Col. R.H., *Historical Records of the Survey of India,* Vol. II, Debra Dun, 1950, pp. 113-14.
4. *Chetrie Ganietam, op. cit.,* p. 53 n.
5. Other books of the *Ganitam* mentioned by Heyne are: *Pavaluru, Begarah, Suvarnah, Mistreta, Beena, Geta, Chayah, Sutra* and *Prakirna, Ibid.*
6. The book is: Heyne, Benjamin, *Tracts, Historical and Statistical, on India; with Journals of Several Tours Through Various Parts of the Peninsula. Also, An Account of Sumatra, in a Series of Letters.* London, 1814, pp. 172-180. Surprisingly authors like A. Sarda Raju, Nilmani Mukherjee and Nikhiles Guha who have used the above book have neither mentioned about *Chetrie Ganitam* nor have they anywhere given correct/complete name of the book.
7. For example *Chetrie Ganietam (Chetri Ganitam),* Pavalooroo Malliah (Pavaluru Mallaia), Soovarnah (Suvarnah), Mestreetah (Mistreta), Sootra (Sutra), Prakeemah (Prakdmah) etc.
8. *Chetrie Ganietam, op. cit.,* p. 53 and Tracts, *op. cit.,* p. 172.
9. *Tracts, op. cit.,* p.172 i.
10. *Chetrie Ganietam, op. cit.,* p. 56; *Tracts, op. cit.,* p. 174.

11. *Tracts, op. cit.,* p. 175 n.

12. *Ibid.*, p. 179 n.

13. *Ibid.,* p. 178 n. For the description about he nature of the soil in this area also see *The Fifth Report from the Select Committee on the Affairs of the East India Company (Madras Presidency)* Vol. II, (London 1812), Madras, 1883, p. 137.

14. *Tracts, op. cit.,* p. 130.

15. *Chetrie Ganietam, op. cit.,* pp.54-55: *Tracts, op. cit.,* p. 174. Also see Thomas Edward, *Ancient India, Weights,* (Varanasi, 1910 edition), p. 29. Heyne pointed out that the fundamental measure was that of an Inch which was determined in three different ways:

I. By placing three rice corns in a line length ways—the place they occupied was called an Inch.

II. By measuring the circumference of the second joint of the Thumb, a half of the length of which was an Inch.

III. By measuring the second joint of the middle finger, the half of which was called an Inch.

12 of these Inches were one *Tana*

32 *Tanas* were **one** *Ghada* or Bamboo

4 *Ghadas* or one Square Bamboo was one *Kunta*

16. Different measures mentioned are:

12 inches—1 *Tana*=1 foot.

2 *Tanas*—1 *Mura*=1 cubit.

32 *Muras*—1 Bamboo=64 feet=3 7/8 sq. poles

4 Bamboos, i.e.

One square

Bombay—1 Kunta=4096 sq. ft.=**sq. poles.**

1¼ *Kuntas*—1 *Cuncham*=5120 sq. feet=18 7/8 sq. poles.

2 *Cunchums*—1 *Virasa*=10,246 sq. ft.=37¾ sq. poles.

2 *Virasa*—1 *Tum*=20480 sq. ft.=75½ sq. poles.

5 *Tums*—1 *Yedum*=1,02,400 sq. ft.=377½ sq. poles.

4 *Yedums*—1 *Putty*=4,09,600 sq. ft.=1510 sq. poles

=9·5/8 acres.

The printed version has given the following conversions of the above measures into feet and sq. feet:

| | | |
|---|---|---|
| 1 *Tana* | = | 1 foot |
| 1 *Mura* | = | 1 Cubit |
| 1 Bamboo | = | 64 feet |
| 1 *Kunta* | = | 4,096 sq. feet. |
| 1 *Cunchum* | = | 5,120 sq. feet. |

| | | |
|---|---|---|
| 1 *Virasa* | = | 10,246 sq. feet. |
| 1 Tam | = | 20.480 sq. feet. |
| 1 Yedum | = | 1,02,400 sq. feet |
| 1 Putty | = | 4,09,600 sq. feet. |

*Chetrie Ganietam, op. cit.*, p. 56 and *Tracts, op. cit.*, p. 174.

17. *Ibid.*
18. *Chetrie Ganietam, op. cit.*, p. 56 n; *Tracts, op. cit.*, p. 175.
19. *Ibid.*, p. 54 n and pp. 67-68 respectively.
20. *Arthasastra* (Kautilya), tr. R . Shamasastry, Fifth Edition, Mysore 1956, II, p. 20.
21. *Tracts, op. cit.*, pp. 67-68.
22. *Chetrie Ganietam, op. cit.*, p. 56 n, Tracts, *op. cit.*, p. 175 n.
23. *Tracts*, p. 175n.
24. Mahalingam, T.V. (ed.) *Mackenzie Manuscripts: Summaries of the Historical Manuscripts in the Mackenzie Collection*, Madras 1976, ii, pp. 57, 94, 334 and 339.
25. Mahalingam, T.V., *Administration and Social Life under Vijayanagar, ii, Social Life*, Madras, 1975, pp. 168-169.
26. *Arthasastra, op. cit.*
27. *Mackenzie Manuscript., op. cit.*, p. 325.
28. Slater, Gilbert, *Economic Studies, Vol. I, Some South Indian Villages* (University of Madras) O.U.P. 1918, p. 254; Thomas, P.J. and Ramakrishnan, K.C. (ed.), *Some South Indian Villages: A Resurvey*, University of Madras, 1940, p. 449.
29. Subdivisions of *Kuntas* mentioned are

    One *Kunta*=2 *Ara Kuntas*=15-1/5 Poles sq.

    1 *Ara Kunta*=2 *Palikas Kuntas*=7-7/10 Poles sq.

    1 *Patikas Kunta*=2 *Panaka Kuntas*=3-17/20 Poles sq.

    1 *Panaka Kunta*=2 *Vessum Kuntas*=1 Pole 28.1/4 yards sq.

    1 *Veessum Kunta*=2 *Ara Vessum Kuntas*=29-1/8 yards sq.

    1 *Ara Veesum Kunta*=*Kaney Kuntas*=14-7/8 yards sq.

    1 *Kaney Kunta*=2 *Ara Kaney Kuntas*=7-7/16 yards sq.

    1 *Ara Kaney Kunta*=2 *Peera Kaney Kuntas*=3 yards 4-11/16 feet sq.

    1 *Peera Kaney Kunta*=1 yard 6-7/8 feet sq.

    *Chetrie Ganietam, op. cit.*, p. 56, *Tracts, op. cit.*, p. 176.
30. *Ibid.*, p. 58 and 177 respectively.
31. *Ibid.*, p. 63 n and 178 n respectively.
32. *Ibid.*, p. 64 n and 178 n respectively.
33. The type of information that we get is, for example, Madhavacharya while writing commentry on Parasara assumed that average turnout from land was

twelve, times the seed sown. Wilks, Mark, *Historical Sketches of the South India in an attempt to trace the History of Mysore* (1810), Mysore, 1930, I, p. 169.

34. *Baramahal Records* (Section IV) (Printed), pp. 2-3; *Bellary District Records*, Printed **Sections**, Vol. 19, *Dr. R. Wight's Report on the Resources of the Presidency*, 23 Nov. 1837; *Report of the Agricultural Commission, 1888*, Appendix C, p. 62, Pharoah & Co., *A Gazetteer of Southern India with the Tensserium Provinces and Singapore*, Madras 1855, pp. 28-36.
35. Heyne has mentioned seed put in one *pooty* i.e. 7½ acres. The measure used for seed was *Kuncham* which was equal to 8-1/3 lbs=3.7799999 Kg. For yield the measure used was candy=500 lbs=226.8 Kg.
36. *Chetrie Ganietam, op. cit.*, p. 64 n and *Tracts, op. cit.*, p. 179 n.
37. For example cotton yield per Acre in Rajahumundry in 1837 was 500 lbs. (see Dr. Wight's *Report, op. cit.*, f.n. 34; For Chingleput, North Arcot, South Arcot, Tanjore, Tinnevelly and Coimbatore, see Ratnam, R., *Agricultural Development in Madras State prior to 1900*, Madras, 1966, pp. 7-88.
38. Extracts from Report of Mr. Place, respecting the Land Tenures in the Jaghire, 6th June 1799, *Fifth Report, op. cit.*, pp. 298-315; also see Ratnam, R. *op. cit.*, pp. 9-10.

# 3

# Position of Patels and Karnums in the 'Ceded Districts' (i.e., the Present Districts of Cuddapah, Kurnool, Anantpur and Bellary) During the First Quarter of the 19th Century

The offices of the *patel*[1] (the village headmen) and the *karnum*[2] (the village accountant) have been very old and hereditary institutions indispensable for the local administration. They discharged multifarious duties and enjoyed considerable power and position. Every village had within itself, a complete establishment of hereditary revenue servants, a *patel* to direct the cultivation, realize the rent, maintain peace and order and manage its affairs in general; a *karnum* to keep the accounts and the land records of the village. He looked after the revenue administration of the village.[3]

The office of the *patel* was anciently bestowed on the founder of a village in return for the benefits which the state derived from his exertions and ever since became hereditary[4] and as such its being hereditary is distinctly an original feature. It seems that when the plan of taking the revenues by means of a share of the produce was introduced, and some kind of public administration was organized, the State felt the necessity of a literate person who could keep accounts.[5] This accounts for the existence of the office of the *karnum.* Of the two, as the *patel* continued to possess some 'magisterial powers and various duties of police and protection', he remained, at least nominally, superior to *karnum.*[6]

---

Paper read at the *Indian History Congress*, Chandigarh Session, 1974 and also published in Bhattacharya, Sabyasachi (ed.), *Essays in Modern Indian Economic History, Indian History Congress Golden Jubilee Year Publication Series: Volume Four*, Delhi 1987, pp. 25-40.

As such, the main duty of the *patel* was to collect and remit the State's share of the produce. He also acted as the head of village police, the *munsif* and the magistrate of the village. Every village had one *patel.* But there were cases when some villages had more than one *patel,* while at times one or more villages shared one *patel.* Normally a *patel* was a landed person of wealth and his position was more or less of an honour. Both the offices of *patel* and *karnum* were remunerated by lands on very favorable terms, other privileges and gratuitous services from the villages notwithstanding. The lands attached to their office were, like their offices, hereditary.[7] The powers, functions and the economic position of the *patels* and *karnums* very often varied according to the political and economic condition of the district.

At the time when the districts under study were ceded to the East India Company (1800), Thomas Munro, the first Principle Collector of the Districts found most of the *patels* and *karnums* acting like Chiefs in their respective villages. The description as taking up the Government of his 'little Republic' may be justified because of the anarchy prevailing in the Districts due to the rapid change of the government during the past many years.[8] There was hardly and *patel* who could not muster a party of armed persons at a few hours notice. The *inam* land attached to the offices of *patel* which had given rise to the endless feuds,[9] had also rendered necessary for him to maintain armed persons. He was not only given the privilege and encouraged by the late government on the payment of a *nazranah* to plunder and extort money from the inhabitants but also to carry on predatory warfare against one another for political gains,[10] which had resulted into the impoverishment, if not almost depopulation, of the villages.[11] This was a unique feature in the Ceded Districts that the persons like the *patels* and *karnums,* who were very peaceful in other provinces, should have acted like the captains of the banditri garrisoning independent castles.[12] Particularly in Gurramcondah, almost every head of a village favoured by political anarchy had become a *poligar,*[13] and in spite of his income being not more than two or three hundred *pagodas,* was regularly installed with all the form of a Chief of an extensive territory and his nominal officers of state subsisting on small portions of land. Many a time even a *karnum* was compelled to make over to him large tracts of the state land and to enter them in his accounts as waste.[14]

It was not only in the political field that the *patels* and *karnums* had attained unduly unique position, but they had managed to improve considerably their economic status. The survey of the Ceded Districts conducted by Thomas Munro revealed that the amount of the *inams* of *patels* and *karnums* was seldom in any uniform proportion to the rent of their respective villages and that in some places it was as low as one percent and in others as high as fifty—and that in many villages there was no *inam* at all.[15] But at the same time this was found that no native government had ever allowed more than 10% of the revenue as the total *inam* to both the *patel* and *karnum* in a village whose rent had exceeded five hundred *Pagodas.*[16]

It is not clear from the information available whether this variation was actually not seriously looked into by the previous rulers or there were some other factors conducive to this variation. It seems that it was mainly because of the frequent changes of the Government, and the loss or rather concealment of accounts[17] which had brought about the variations. No doubt at the same time, we cannot completely rule out the previous proposition. Thomas Munro was of the opinion that probably the previous rulers paid little attention on the limiting of *inam* as whenever the *inam* was greater than usual, it was made answerable to complete the deficiencies in the village collections.[18] Even after 1800, Munro himself admitted that there were many villages, in which, the *patel* and even the *karnum,* were liable for deficiencies as far as the equivalent of their *inam* lands.[19] Moreover, even the assessment of those *inam* lands for deficiencies did not seem to have been regulated by any fixed principle. In some villages it was assessed only when accidental losses occurred, whereas in others it was a regular annual feature. In the latter villages the settlement was always fixed so high to make its realization impossible, without, of course, taking the *patels'* and *karnums' inams* at one-half or two-thirds of their produce.[20] A research in the Mughal age has also revealed such types of variations in the *inam* of the *patels* and *karnums.* The *inam* during that period 'depended on the customary practices and would vary from region to region and at times from village to village...In any particular region, the rate during the Mughal age could not have exceeded the one prevalent (even) in the mid-19th century...'[21] So, such a variation in the Ceded Districts was not a new phenomenon during the period preceding their cession nor in the region under review alone. But at the same time, it cannot be completely ignored that the political disturbances and frequent changes of government during the period prior to 1800 did play a significant role in creating variations in the *inams* of the *patels* and *karnums.* As already stated the *inam* land attached to their offices especially in the case of *patels* had given rise to endless feuds. It was not only an attraction for a *patel* to attack his counterpart in the neighbouring village and dispossess him from his *inam* land but would even attract him to drive his relations, if they possessed any *inam* land, from their land and seize their possessions.[22] At the same time even *poligars* used to give land to the *patels* on their helping them with the parties of armed persons. Normally the *patels* who had parties of ten, fifty and hundred were given a piece of land worth 9 to 24 *Pagodas.*[23] Those *patels* and *karnums* who refused to accede to the demand of the *poligar,* either of armed persons or of money, were treated very harshly and were even kidnapped, beaten and put into the confinement, till the required demand was met.[24] There are cases when a *karnum* was even compelled by threats to make over to the *patel* large tracts of the state land, and was to enter that in his accounts as waste.[25] The same land was later on declared as *inam* land attached to his office by the *patel.* At the same time, we cannot rule out the possibility of Thomas Munro being given the false accounts by the *patels* and the *karnums.* He himself felt that they were in habit of doing so in a general measure in the consequence of the change of government.[26] Thus, all these factors account for the variations in the *inam* lands attached to their offices. It has been computed that in all there was an average of above 5% of the total *inam* land which could be regarded as unauthorized *inam* attached to their office.[27]

Apart from this, for Thomas Munro, there were few other things, which were quite peculiar in the character of the *patels* and the *karnums* in the Ceded Districts. He agreed that the *patels* and *karnums* would everywhere make small private collections by forwarding wrong accounts but it was an extraordinary feature in the Ceded Districts that many a time they would abscond with public revenue. They would not return unless they were granted permission to make up the deficiency by a new assessment upon the inhabitants.[28] In this way, a considerable amount of revenue was embezzled by the *patels* and the *karnums*. This affected the punctuality of the *tahsildars* to remit the revenues and at times resulted in loss to the government.

Another thing peculiar about the *patels* and *karnums* in the Ceded Districts was that they used great highhandedness in regard to the grant of *taqavi* to the *rayats*. It was the custom that the *patels* and *karnums* would appear as sureties at the *cutcherry* for a body of *rayats* to get them *taqavi*.[29] They often got the whole of the amount from the *rayats* the moment they would quit the presence of the *tahsildars*. Normally it used to be previously concerted and the *rayats* were brought before the *tahsildar* merely as a deception to obtain a sum of money for themselves. But the tragedy was that they would not stop there. Sometimes, the money thus obtained was called a loan which was to be paid whenever found convenient. But often the practice was that when the payment of *taqavi* back to the *cutcherry* would become due, the *patels* and the *karnums* would exact the amount from the *rayats* in whose name it was originally disbursed.[30] Above all the accounts maintained by the *karnums*, the purpose for which they were holding that office, were always false and would amount to 30% to 40% of the actual revenues of the village concerned.[31]

Thomas Munro was of the view that the jurisdiction and power of the *patels* and *karnums* had been in no way inferior to that of any higher officer in the village. Though any one holding land, whether he was discharging the functions of a high civil office or was merely a village *taliari* was called a *zamindar*, yet the actual position of the *patels* and *karnums* was far more superior to that of higher classes of *zamindars*, *deshmukhs* and *deshpandyas* etc. The latter categories were all revenue officials, holding *inam* land or villages, and received a percentage on the collection as an allowance for performing the duties of their employment. But they held their office and land only during pleasure of the state, whereas in the case of the *patels* and *karnums* both the office and the *inam* were hereditary. As such, technically the position of the *deshmukhs* and *deshpandyas* was inferior to that of the *patels* and *karnums.* And in actual practice, at the time of the cession of the districts, these were the persons who were all powerful and there were no *zamindars* excepting them.[32] But Munro is not correct in holding this view. He had exaggerated the position of the *patels* and *karnums* vis-à-vis the *deshmukhs* and *deshpandyas.* Actually the latter also held hereditary offices and worked in co-ordination rather their being inferior to the former. It is possible that because of the chaotic conditions immediately preceding the cession of the districts this development might have taken place temporarily. But in theory it is not correct.

Now the problem before Thomas Munro was that in spite of the flaws in the character and working of the office of the *patels* and *karnums,* it was not possible for him to do without them. It had been an ancient practice to entrust management of the village to the *patels* and *karnums* and the inhabitants were used to that. The Collector had merely to confirm what the *pàtels* and *karnums* had already done.[33] Moreover, they enjoyed considerable influence over the *rayats.* The *rayats* could be instigated by them to throw up their land for obtaining a reduction in the assessement.[34] They would be encouraged to do so for in case they obtained any reduction, the *patels* and *karnums,* would be induced to raise equal amount of objections.[35] At the same time they used to make better use also of their influence. It was only with their influence that the *rayats* could be persuaded to take up extra land, without which as much as ¼th of the total land would be a waste land.[36] They continued to enjoy the same amount of influence even in the later period,[37] and the Collector had to seek legal authority to punish the *patels* and *karnums* whenever the extra ordinary influence used by them was detected.[38] Munro did not want to entrust the *patels* and *karnums* with the power of fixing the revenue as there was a danger of their being partial to their relations and friends and biased towards their enemies. Above all they themselves too, were cultivators.[39] At the same time, he did not want any landowner holding the appointment of the *Karnum.*[40] But in spite of these difficulties, Munro was confident that they were the persons most capable of making the settlement correctly,[41] only if certain checks were imposed upon them. As such their position and functions were kept precisely on the same footing as in theory they were meant for.[42] Those *patels* and *karnums* who had acquired political power and had attained the title of the *poligar* were reduced to the normal position. It was both administrative and agrarian necessity. It was an administrative necessity because unless the peace was restored, efficient running of administration would not be possible. These two officials exercised a considerable influence on the agrarian life of the villages. The *rayats* were under their command and the records of the villages were under their supervision and possession. The settlement of the districts was not possible if full co-operation was not forth-coming from them. Though it might be difficult to reduce them to the most honest village officials, it was at least certainly within the hands of administrators to finish completely the political power that they had attained because of political disturbances. That was done, even though at times military actions had to be taken against them.

In the beginning, since it was not possible to go into the details of revenue aspects, a *mauzawar* or village settlement was introduced. In this type of settlement the *patels* were made severally answerable for the rent of their own villages, and jointly for that of the whole of the district.[43] But this was not the final arrangement and the details had yet to be worked out. Later on, when the *kulwar* settlement was introduced, the *patel* was to manage the whole village and was made answerable for the rent only of the lands which he occupied and every *rayat* was answerable for his own rent, and jointly they were made responsible for the rent of the whole village.[44] Apart from the other reasons for not introducing a permanent *mauzawar* or village settlement in the Ceded Districts, one important reason was that it would give much room for malversation to the *patels.* It would also have created many disputes between the *patels* and *rayats,* and would have become easier for *patels* to withhold the revenue.[45]

By the introduction of the village lease system in the Ceded Districts (roughly between 1808-1820) the settlement of village was made with the *patel* of that village. One of the chief reasons of its failure seems to be the type of responsibility conferred on the *patels.*[46] No doubt the *karnums* were not considered to be fit for that purpose and it was thought expedient to avoid forming the settlement with them. This was decided nor because the Board of Revenue had any apprehension of the preponderance of the *karnums,* but because it was thought to be 'improper that the office of village Registrar should be united with the proprietary right in the village'. In case of emergency when there was no other person in the village able or willing to undertake the rent, the settlement could be concluded with the person holding the office of *karnum* but only after the office in question was taken away from him and conferred on some other person.[47]

Thus the *patels* and *karnums* kept on enjoining the respective position given to them in accordance with the practice of region. The *patels* were entrusted to manage the village. They had always held that office and were better qualified than any other person for that, and, as such, could not be removed without great inconvenience and probably loss of revenues.[48] The collector was only to confirm what the *patels* had already done,[49] and except in the case of misconduct and incapacity the collector could not remove them from the office, nor could interfere in their appoinment.[50] As regards the *karnums,* according to the Regulation II of 1802 (Section I & II), the collectors were prohibited from dismissing them from their office without the authority of Board of Revenue.[51] Apart from regular duties assigned, *pattah* and *muchilkas* stating the amount of land with every *rayat* and the revenue to be paid by him, was to be countersigned by the collector incharge of the district, because it was felt that the inhabitants had more confidence in the collector than in that of the *patel,* and that they (the inhabitants) knew that it was intended to guard them against extra demands, and would be essentially guided by the *patels.*[52] Regarding the accounts maintained by the *karnums,* though it was known that they never gave perfectly true statement, yet they could give tolerably accurate accounts on account of fear of removal, or suspension.[53] At the same time the collectors were given authority to call the *karnums* for explanation about the accounts without assigning any reason because Munro felt that unless the *karnums'* accounts were constantly opened to the collector without any form of requisition it would be impossible to obtain within the year the necessary information for ascertaining the amount of revenue.[54]

Now the most important problem before the British administrators was to deal with the remunerations to the *patels* and *karnums,* which traditionally were paid in the form of hereditary *inam* lands. As already stated that these officials had managed to get, apart from the legal *inam* land assigned to them, a considerable amount of illegally acquired land as well. Thomas Munro, the man on the spot, made up his mind not to settle anything unless the survey of the districts had been done, no matter how much time and money that might consume. He felt that the survey would bring to light the extent of unauthorized *inam* being retained by the *patels* and *karnums* in their own hands and as a result were enjoying the greatest part of the produce. There was no other means to detect the real value of those lands and their comparative value with the land held by the ordinary *rayats.*[55] Thus survey was essential to regulate a sort of semi-fedual class, which at the cost of the common *rayats* and state revenues had emerged to be a fairly dominant class.

The survey revealed that all authorized and unauthorized *inam* land with the *patels* and the *karnums* amounted to acres 4,02,011-21-33.[56] Of this only 4/5th was cultivated. The whole of the State and *inam* land capable of cultivation amounted to acres, 1,20,66,923 of which the rent, as fixed by the survey, was *Star Pagoda* 39,54,417.[57] This means that about 5.36% of the total estimated rent was in the shape of *inam* with the *patels* and *karnums.*

The immediate action that Munro took as a result of survey was the fixation of the maximum percentage of the *inam* land to be allotted to the *patels* and *karnums* in the Ceded Districts. He decided that in this respect the customs prevailing since the previous regimes should be adopted. Keeping in view the past practices as has been shown in the table belwo.[58] The table depicts that the percentage of *inam* was based upon the value of the land *i.e.,* according to the survey rent fixed upon it. The range of the value of land taken into account is between C. Pagodas 50 to 6000. Accordingly the corresponding percentage of *inam* allowed to the *patel* ranges from 8% to .97% and to the *karnums* from 12% to 1.52%. Thus if the survey rent was C. Pagodas 50, the *patel* got 8% and *karnum* got 12% worth of *inam* land in the village, in case it was C. Pagodas 100, they would get 6% and 9%; on C.

Pagodas 300, 4% and 6%; on C. Pagodas 800, 3% and 4%; on C. Pagodas 1000, 2.8% and 3.7%; on C. Pagodas 2000, 1.9% and 2.55%; on C. Pagodas 3000, 1.43% and 1.9%; on Pagodas 4000, 1.2% and 1.57%; on C. Pagodas 5000, 1.06% and 1.38%; and on C. Pagodas 6000, .97% and 1.25% respectively. The total percentage of *inam* allowed to the *patels* and *karnums* in a village worth of C. Pagodas 50 survey rent would be 20%. In case the survey rent was C. Pagodas 100, the *inam* to the *patel* and *karnum* would come down to 15%; on C. Pagodas 300, 10%; on C. Pagodas 800, 7%; on C. Pagodas 1000, 6.5%; on 2000, 4.45%; on C. Pagodas 5000, 2.44%; and on C. Pagodas 6000, 2.22%. The share of the *patel* in the total *inam* allowed in a village was always between 39% to 43.44%. This shows that the major portion of the *inam* went to the *karnum.* Munro has not given any explanation for this variation. It seems that this was because of the other legal and illegal means by which *patel* could manage to earn extra money. The excess of the above percentage of *inam* land if any, with the *patels* and *karnums* should be assessed according to the survey rent.[59] Thus, there was no fixed percentage of the *inam* attached to the office of the *patel* and *karnums.* At the same time the table also depicts that as the survey rent increased the percentage of the *inam* attached to their office decreased.

Table

| Survey rent in C. Pagodas | % of *inam* allowed to the *patel* | % of *inam* allowed to the *karnum* | Share of the *patel* in the maximum *inam* allowed in a village (in %) | Total % of *inam* allowed in a village to the *patel* and *karnum* |
|---|---|---|---|---|
| 50 | 8 | 12 | 40 | 20 |
| 100 | 6 | 9 | 40 | 15 |
| 150 | 4.67 | 7.33 | 39 | 12 |
| 200 | 4.50 | 6.75 | 40 | 11.25 |
| 250 | 4 | 6.40 | 39.02 | 10.25 |
| 300 | 4 | 6 | 40 | 10 |
| 400 | 4 | 5.63 | 41.54 | 9.63 |

| 500 | 3.60 | 4.80 | 42.86 | 8.40 |
|---|---|---|---|---|
| 600 | 3.33 | 4.42 | 42.97 | 7.75 |
| 700 | 3.14 | 4.14 | 43.13 | 7.28 |
| 800 | 3 | 4 | 42.86 | 7 |
| 900 | 2.89 | 3.89 | 42.63 | 6.78 |
| 1000 | 2.80 | 3.70 | 43.08 | 6.50 |
| 1500 | 2.20 | 2.93 | 42.88 | 5.13 |
| 2000 | 1.90 | 2.55 | 42.70 | 4.45 |
| 2500 | 1.62 | 2.16 | 42.85 | 3.78 |
| 3000 | 1.42 | 1.90 | 42.94 | 3.33 |
| 3500 | 1.30 | 1.71 | 43.19 | 3.01 |
| 4000 | 1.20 | 1.57 | 43.32 | 2.77 |
| 4500 | 1.12 | 1.47 | 43.24 | 2.59 |
| 5000 | 1.06 | 1.38 | 43.44 | 2.44 |
| 5500 | 1.01 | 1.31 | 43.1 | 2.32 |
| 6000 | .97 | 1.25 | 43.24 | 2.22 |

Of course, in report, immediately before his departure, Thomas Munro, while recommending the reduction of 25% of the survey rent; suggested another formula for the fixation of the total *inam* to be allotted to the *patels* and *karnums* in a village. It was suggested that in the villages with not exceeding 250 pagodas rent, the total *inam* would be to the extent of 10% of the total village revenue; in the village with 250 to 500 pagodas rent, the *inam* would be to the extent of 7½; and that in the village with more than 500 pagodas rent, the *inam* would be to the maximum of 5%.[60]

The percentage of the *inam* to the *patels* and *karnums* also comprised the *Marah Wurtana*,[61] *i.e.,* the perquisites from the crops. Wherever the amount of *inam* together with the *Marah Wurtana* was less than the rate shown in the table, the difference was made up. In case the *inam* exceeded the approved percentage, both the *patels* and *karnums* were permitted to enjoy the whole as due to the unavailability of the official accounts of the previous government, there was hardly any means left of ascertaining the fact. But, as stated earlier, the excess was to be charged according to the survey rent.[62] This certainly did not prohibit them from taking any amount of state land on the usual survey rent. Taken on the face value of the *inam* recommended for the *patels* and *karnums,* their position was certainly given a great set back and it was considerably lowered.

A Sarda Raju[63] has pointed that with the introduction of the new judicial system, all the offices connected with revenue collection were abolished except that the *karnums,* and it was only in 1816 that the office of village headman was revived with very much curtailed power.[64] But is does not seem to be correct in regard to the Ceded Districts. Upto 1807 the office was very much in existence as it was only in 1807 that Munro had recommended the scale of *inam* to be granted to the *patels* and *karnums.* After his departure when the village lease system was introduced in the Ceded Districts, even Sarda Raju has accepted the reinstatement of the office of *patels.*[65] Thereafter it remained in existence.

As regards the office of the *karnum,* there are no two views that it remained as powerful as it was. His services remained indispensable under any mode of revenue collection. During the survey, both the *patels* and *karnums* had managed to get their land, *inam* as well as other, assessed very low.[66] Moreover, they could take any amount of waste land in their own names directly from the *amildar* on the fixed *cowle,* and were permitted to give that for their own advantage at a higher rate to the *rayats,* granting them *pattahs* specifying the quantity of the land and the rent. The government would not demand anything extra except the rates specified in the *kaulnamah* (agreement deed). So this was not only an extra source of income, but it proved to be a great boost to their position.[67]

With the introduction of the village lease system in the Ceded Districts, the position of especially the *patels* had become more important and they had become more indispensible. They were found to be the persons most qualified and best adapted to their village with respect to the interests of the government, and the *rayats.* As such the government wanted that they should rent their village. It was expressed that under the native Governments, it was generally the *patels* who used to rent their villages. Even during the first year (1800-1) of the Company's Government, it was found expedient to rent the village in the Ceded Districts to the *patels.*

Of course, the Government accepted that since the introduction of the *rayatwari* system (1801-1807) their duties had been to superintend the general administration of the village and to see that the cultivation was carried on the full extent, whereas collection of the revenue was done directly by the state. With the introduction of the Village Lease System, they were expected to perform other duties as well.[68] But contrary to the expectations of the Government it proved to be an uphill task to bring the *patels* round to accept the terms and conditions of the Government. In spite of the several restriction imposed upon them, they had been enjoying a considerable position and influence in the village.

They had thrown up the land and wanted the *bariz* (*Jamma* or Rent) to be considerably reduced. They could not only influence the *rayats* to restrain from accepting the land, but would create lot of problems for an outsider if he had accepted to rent the village. They could influence the *rayats* to restrain accepting the land thereby making it impossible for the renter to fulfill his commitments to the Government.[69] The Government was not in favour of renting the villages to the *karnums* due to reasons already explained.

In this way the Government had to adopt a little harsh policy towards the *patels*. They were told that it was a part of their duty to direct and promote the cultivation of the State land, and to collect and pay the rent of the village to the Government.[70] No doubt the *inam* was hereditary, but continued to be conditional and was a remuneration for their services. The only useful service that the *patels* could render under the existing circumstances was to rent the village. The Board of Revenue was of the opinion that in case they refused to accede to that or interfered in the operations of other renters, the collector was at liberty to dispense with their services and resume their *inam*.[71] In case the *patels* were allowed to refuse to rent the village and at the same time retain their service *maniyam*,[72] it was feared, that the refusal might become general, which would lead to a great loss to the government. At the same time, the persons who would undertake to rent the village, would certainly demand some abatement equivalent to the value of *maniyam* which would, of course, involve a double expense to the Government.[73]

At the same time, the Government did not want to be very harsh either and wanted to induce the *patels* only to undertake the rent of their respective villages. As such, the Government had to moderate the rent to make it acceptable to the *patels.* This scheme certainly worked and it was not found necessary to deprive any *patel* of his office. Rather the Board recommended that they should not be removed unless there was a clear proof of embezzlement, tyranny, or contumacy on the part of the *patels.*[74]

Thus barring the political power that the *patels* and *karnums* had unlawfully attained because of the political disturbances immediately before the districts were ceded to the company they continued enjoying the influential position in the land revenue administration of the villages. Though with the introduction of the *rayatwari* system of land tenure, (again after 1820) in the Districts, theoretically the position of especially the *patels* was once again given a set back, they continued to be as strong, influential and indispensable part of the village society as ever. Of course, the position of *karnums* remained unchecked. The British Government had acted rightly by not disturbing the local administration otherwise it would have certainly become very difficult for it to maintain the law and order to run revenue adminsitration on smooth footing.

## References

1. Also known as—*Reddi, Naidu, Nattamkar, Peddacapu, Manikkaren, Monigar* etc.
2. Also known as—*Kulkarni, Patwari, Shenabogue, Menon,* etc.
3. Madras Records Office, *Board's Consultations, 5 Jan. 1807; Selections from the Records of the Bellary District. Political Revenue and Agricultural matters, 1800-1856,* ASO (D) 73, Letter from Thomas Munro to the President and Members of the Board of Revenue, 30 Nov. 1806
4. MRO, *Bellary Records,* 382/4, Letter from the Collector of Bellary District to the Board of Revenue, 22 Aug. 1817.
5. Since a literate person was required and in the then South Indian society and it were only the Brahmins who were educated, a Brahmin was chosen for that job. In South India and the Deccan, Brahmins kept on holding this position. (see for reference MRO, *The Proceedings of the Board of Revenue on the introduction of the Village Lease in the Ceded Districts, 1811,* ASO (D) 31 and 32, Minute of the Board of Revenue, 9 May 1811). Whereas in Punjab and other parts of North India this does not seem to be the practice.

6. Baden-Powell, *The Indian Village Community,* pp. 13-14.
7. MRO *Bellary Records,* 382/14, Letter from the Collector of Bellary to the Board of Revenue, 22 Aug. 1817.
8. MRO, *William Thackeray's Report on Malabar, Canara and the Ceded Districts,* Sept. 1807, ASO (D) 66; also see *Fifth Report,* 1812 (Madras, 1883), II, 709-45.
9. MRO, *Madras Board of Revenue Consultations, 31 Aug. 1801; Col. Munro's Report regarding Poligars in the Ceded Districts with a memorandum of Poligars,* 1801-1802, RSO (D) 66 (21), Letter from Thomas Munro to the President and Members of the Board of Revenue, 12 Aug. 1801.
10. MRO, *Selections from the old Records of the Bellary District, 1800-1807.* ASO (D) 72, Instructions issued by Thomas Munro, the Principal Collector to the Subordinate Collectors, 31 Dec. 1800; also see—*William Thackeray's Report.....,*ASO (D) 66.
11. MRO, *William Thackeray's Report....,*ASO (D) 66.
12. *Ibid.*
13. For details about Poligars, J.C. Dua, 'Poligars: Their Rise in the Ceded Districts,' *IHC,* XXXIII, 1972, pp. 467-74.
14. MRO, *Col. Munro's Report Regarding the Poligars....,* RSO, (D) 62 (21), Letter from Thomas Munro to William Petrie, President and members of the Board of Revenue, 20 March 1802.
15. In case no *inam* was attached to the office of the *patel* and *karnum,* this does not imply that they served without any proper and adequate compensation, rather they continued to hold State land at a very low rent and the income thus derived by them was greater than the income derived by others from the *inam* lands.
16. MRO, *Bellary Records,* 384/54, Thomas Munro to the Collector Adoni Division, 14 April 1807; also—*Board's Consultations, 24 Aug. 1807, and Col. Munro's correspondence regarding the survey and rayatwari settlement of the Ceded Districts, 1802-1807,* ASO (D), 79, Thomas Munro to the Board of Revenue, 26 July 1807.
17. MRO, *Board's Consultations,* 24 Aug. 1807; and *Col. Munro's Correspondence regarding the survey...,* ASO (D) 79, Thomas Munro to the Board of Revenue, 26 July 1807.
18. MRO, *Bellary Records,* 384/54, Thomas Munro to the Collector of Adoni Division, 13 April 1807.
19. MRO, *Selections from the Records....,* ASO (D)72, Thomas Munro to Archibald Obins, Private Secretary to the Governor, F.S.G. 20 June 1805.
20. *Op. cit.,* fn. 28.
21. B.R. Grover, 'Nature of *Dehat-i-Talluqa* (*Zamindari* Village) and the Evolution of the *Talluqdari* System during the Mughal Age,' *IESHR,* II, 3 (July 1965), p. 259.

22. *Op. cit.*, fn. 9.
23. *Ibid.*
24. MRO, *Col. Munro's Report regarding the Poligars...*, RSO (D) 62 (21), Munro to the Board of Revenue, 20 March 1802.
25. *Ibid.*
26. *Op. cit.*, fn. 17.
27. MRO, *Settlement from the Old Records...*, ASO (D) 72, Instructions issued by Munro to his subordinate collectors, 31 Dec. 1800.
28. MRO, *Bellary Records* (1802) 396/346, Munro to the Board of Revenue, 26 June 1802; also *Selections from the Records of Bellary...*, ASO (D) 73, Circular issued by Thomas Munro, 10 Aug. 1801.
29. MRO, *Bellary Records* (1802) 396/346, Thomas Munro to the Board of Revenue, 26 June 1802
30. MRO, *Selections from the Records of Bellary...*, ASO (D) 73, Circular issued by Thomas Munro, 16 June 1801.
31. MRO, *Public Sundries,* 123 A, *MBRC,* 19 May 1803; Col. Munro to his subordinate Collectors regarding the modes of conducting the Rayatwar settlement, 30 Sept. 1802; also—*Bellary Records,* (1805) 391/30, Munro to William Bentinck, Governor of FSG, 8 May 1806; also...*MBRC,* 26 Sect. 1805; *Selection from the Records...*, ASO (D) 72, Munro to the Board of Revenue, 25 Aug, 1805.
32. MRO, *MBRC*, 26 Sep. 1805, and *Selections from the Records...*, ASO (D) 72, Munro to the Board of Revenue, 25 Aug. 1805.
33. *Op. cit.*, fn. 3.
34. *Op. cit.*, fn. 28.
35. MRO, *Public Sundries,* 123A, 31, *MBRC,* 19 May 1803, and *Col. Munro's Correspondence regarding the survey...*, ASO (D) 79, Thomas Munro to his subordinate Collectors, 30 Sept. 1802.
36. *Op. cit.*, fn. 32.
37. APSA, *Cuddapah Records* (F. 1219), 419/348, Chaplin to the Board of Revenue, 2 Nov. 1809; also...MRO, *The Proceedings of the Board of Revenue on the Introduction of Village Lease in the Ceded Districts*...1811, ASO (D) 31 & 32, Minute of the Board of Revenue, 1 July 1811.
38. MRO, *Bellary Records,* F 1230, 388/42 Campbell to the Board of Revenue, 2 Nov. 1820.
39. *Op. cit.*, fn. 3 & 35.
40. *Op. cit.*, fn. 32.
41. *Op. cit.*, fn. 3.
42. *Op. cit.*, fn. 32.
43. *Op. cit.*, fn. 27.

44. MRO, *Bellary Records,* 1806, 391/30, Thomas Munro to William Bentick, Governor, FSG, 8 May 1806; also—*Selection from the Records of Bellary*...ASO (D) 73 and 76, Circular issued by Thomas Munro, 10 Aug. 1801.

45. *Op. cit.,* fn. 3.

46. MRO, *The Proceedings of the Board of Revenue on the Introduction of Village Lease*...ASO (D) 31 & 32, Minute of the Board of Revenue, 9 May 1811.

47. *Op. cit.,* fn. 32.

48. *Op. cit.,* fn. 3.

49. *Op. cit.,* fn. 4.

50. MRO, *Bellary Records,* (1806) 403/154; 410/27, Circular—Collectors—Ceded Districts, 16 Aug. 1806; Also—*Bellary Records,* (1806), 408/215, Thomas Munro to Frederick Gahagan Collector of Adoni division, 16 Aug. 1806.

51. *Op. cit.,* fn. 35.

52. MRG, *Public Sundries,* 123A, 31, Munro to his subordinate Collectors, 30 Sept. 1802.

53. *Op. cit.,* fn. 3.

54. *Op. cit.,* fn. 32.

55. MRO, *Bellary Records,* (1802), 397/73, Thomas Munro to the Board of Revenue, 29 Oct. 1802.

56. The total *inam* land in the Ceded Districts was acres 25,747 which was worth Star Pagodas 12,34,458. This shows that the *inam* land with the *patels* and *karnums* was about 24.89% of the total *inam* acreage in the Ceded Districts and was worth 25.39% of the value of the total *inam* land.

57. *Op. cit.,* fn. 17; also...APSA *Cundapah Records,* (1809), 625/245, W. Wayte, Secretary, Board of Revenue, to the Collector of Cuddapah, 14 Dec. 1809.

58. I am very much grateful to the Director and Mr. Jha of the Computer Centre, University of Delhi, for preparing this table for me.

59. MRO, *Bellary Records,* 384/54; and *Selections from the Records*...ASO (D) 72, Circular issued by Thomas Munro, 14 April 1807.

60. MRO, *Boards' Consultations,* 5 Feb. 1808; *Col. Munro Correspondence regarding the survey*...ASO (D) 79; *Selection of Papers from the Records at East India House relating to the Revenue, Police, and Civil and Criminal Justice under the Company's government in India, London, 1820-26, I, 94-98; Fifth Report,* II 646-663, Report of Principal Collector of the Ceded Districts, 15 Aug. 1807.

61. *Marah Wurtanah* were not collected in all villages. The rates also differed from place to place and item to item. For example on sugarcane and betel plantations, it was much higher than even the government rent.

62. *Op. cit.,* fn. 59.

63. Raju, A. Sarda, *Economic Conditions in the Madras Presidency 1800-1850,* Madras, 1941.

64. *Ibid.,* p. 20.

65. *Ibid.*, p. 21.
66. *Op. cit.*, fn. 17.
67. MRO, *Selections from the Records of Bellary*, ASO (D) 73, Circular issued by Thomas Munro (Undated) but issued sometime in 1801-02 (Fusly 1211).
68. APSA, *Cuddapah Records*, (1809) 636/245, letter from W. Wayre, Secretary, Board of Revenue to the Collector of Cuddapah, 14 Dec. 1809; also MRO, *The Proceedings of the Board of Revenue...*, 1811, ASO (D) 31 & 32, Minute of the Board of Revenue, 9 May 1811.
69. MRO, *Bellary Records*, (F. 1219), 417/348, Letters from Chaplin, Collector to the Board of Revenue, 2 Nov. 1809.
70. *Ibid.*
71. *Op. cit.*, fn. 68.
72. A grant of land, or assignment of the government share of the produce there from, to the revenue officers, and the public servants of the villages.
73. *Op. cit.*, fn. 68.
74. *Ibid.*

# 4

# Drought Management in 'Ceded Districts' During 19th Century: A Critical Appraisal

## Ceded Districts

Draught/famine/scarcity are some of the important subjects of modern India, which have attracted very voluminous and rapidly growing literature. In south India, the inland belt from Tirunelveli district in Tamil Nadu to Krishna River in Andhra Pradesh has been most vulnerable to frequent draught and famine, with the Ceded Districts, due to their remoteness from south-west monsoon of the summer months and north-east monsoon of winter months, being driest and thus more exposed to such conditions. Many a writer would describe the 'Ceded Districts' as "Dry" districts. Since the cultivation in these districts was entirely dependent on rains, agriculture was at the "mercy of deficient monsoon". Moreover, being made up of barren and poor soils, the area could not withstand continuous cropping. It was, as such, more fallow than under cultivation giving "a poverty stricken appearance" to the region.[1] The basic soil types of the Ceded Districts are black regar and red ferruginous.[2] Whereas the black regur soils being "very fertile and highly retentive of moisture" are suited to the cultivation of cotton and *jowar,* the red soils are generally poor in fertility. It was 'dry cultivation' which was practiced in the Ceded Districts and the population growth was not very great and consequently the density was low.[3]

In this paper an attempt has been made to make a critical assessment of management of drought situations in the Ceded Districts during the different phases of nineteenth century and to analyze the perception and response of the inhabitants/cultivators.

## Nineteenth Century

Each phase has its particular significance for the peasantry, agriculture related problems, and general well being of the people. Nineteenth century not only witnessed transition from pre colonial to early East India Company's agrarian understanding and policies but also to industrial, scientific and administrative advancements. Railways, telegraph and steamships had started lowering transport costs, managerial and print technologies had lowered information and processing cost, agricultural expertise had started developing rapidly, thriving on standardization and above all Christian missionaries had become more serious in their task.

The nineteenth century separates South India, like other parts of the country, from medieval times. It saw migrations and technological changes transforming linguistic, social and agricultural geography as well as political economy in South India. Approximately the first quarter of the nineteenth century was a formative period during which the new regime, practically under the overall leadership of Thomas Munro, not only had somewhat sympathetic attitude towards the problems of the agriculturists but also tried to educate itself about the nature of land rights and the agrarian system prevailing in the areas under present study. The new regime tried to settle into already functioning networks of village power and authority. Thomas Munro was of the opinion that "when a country falls under the dominion of a foreign power, the wisest plan is to leave in possession of its own laws and customs, and to endeavor rather to ameliorate than to abolish them and substitute others in their room".[4] Moreover, Company officials made efforts to adjust that system, as much as possible, to their needs. However, in the process they successfully created an Anglo-Indian language of official discourse, which had come into being by the early 1820s. By the middle of the nineteenth century the English government had attained vast administrative experience, political authority, military power and better position to suppress any armed and recalcitrant opposition, if present, rather more easily and effectively. They would not hesitate in deviating from the position and privileges enjoyed by the cultivators/inhabitants earlier and policy adopted by earlier rulers/English administrators in a bigger way.[5]

Similar to various objects of knowledge, the British colonial bureaucracy codified agriculture as well. The handwritten manuscripts gave way to printed reports. Modern formation of agricultural power/knowledge began to engage agrarian life in India. With the wide introduction of print technologies, information transaction and processing costs got lowered. This helped in converting the cities of the empire into data processing centre for different world-wide markets. By the last quarter of the nineteenth century, a modern information apparatus had been fully developed by the British government. This led to rapid development of agricultural expertise thriving on standardization. Moreover, the 'state personnel imported industrial technologies, both material and organizational, during four decades of profound economic and imperial expansion from 1840 to l880.'[6] The government officials started working under what was called 'rule by manual'.[7] With the publication of an *Agricultural Class-Book* in 1880 and holding of an Agricultural Exhibition in 1883, the Madras government would no longer tell Europeans about farming in India rather had transformed itself as an expert on Indian agriculture. In doing so it also defined the style and substance of modem agricultural expertise.[8] The Madras Agriculture Department in order to encourage and advance 'knowledge of the agriculture of the country, encouraged the collection and publication of 'sayings and proverbs' on agriculture. In this context C. Benson, the Collector of Kurnool did a pioneering job. While writing *An Account of Kurnool District* (Madras, 1889), he became aware of 'proverbs and sayings…as illustrative of agricultural life and practice there', compiled Telugu sayings for the whole Presidency and published them.[9] Further examples in this context were the publications of the Madras *Manual of Administration*[10] and glossaries by H.H. Wilson[11] and H. Yule and A.C. Burnell.[12] English records from the early 1800s evidence agrarian conditions in the early 19th century, 'and despite their European interests and cultural background these texts embody consistent early-modern view's of agriculture as of concern only for state revenue.' Moreover, by '1900, the colonial state's discursive domination of agrarian India was complete and its attitude towards farmers set in modern mould.'[13]

The Indian economy and subsistence of the poor had (and have) largely extreme dependence upon agriculture, which would depend upon the arrival of adequate monsoon rains. The history of agriculture is inextricably interwoven with the progress of civilization because it was taking tip of agriculture that made it possible for primitive man to live in selected spots, forming a society, and growing a significant portion of his food nearby.[14] Agriculture has been defined as 'cultivation of the soil'; 'the science or practice of Large-scale soil cultivation'; 'the cultivation of crops and the keeping of domesticated animals for food fibre, or power'. The English words *culture* and *agriculture* became nouns to denote crop cultivation in the seventeenth century as did *cultivate*—'to bestow labour and attention upon (land) in order to (raise) crops'.[15] As far as discovery of agriculture is concerned, it is believed that Ali Kosh, Jericho. Jarmo and other ecologically similar localities witnessed the first attempts at agriculture.[16] There are 21 references to agriculture ploughing in the *RigVeda,* the bulk of which are in books I and IX.[17] There are important literary sources on agriculture and allied subjects in South India. One is *'Erelupadu,* a poem composed by Kambar (10th or 12th century A.D.). The poem is ostensibly in praise of the plough—'Seventy stanzas on the plough'. The poet has described the function of each part of the plough and incidentally the process of agriculture.[18] The other works—*Ksetra Ganita* and V*yavhara Ganita* by Rajaditya, are works on field mathematics, weights and measure.[19]

**Rainfall**

Agriculture is the source of perpetual creation on which cultivation depends. It is a way of life, unique and irreplaceable in human values. Agriculture has different meanings for those involved in it in different roles—for cultivators, for labour, and in regard to markets or socio-political structures. It has different social implications in its various forms and modes. It provides food, employment and commodities.

The agriculture would mainly depend on the rainfall. If the rains were scanty or untimely, the crops would be lost and the area would suffer from a shortage of food and the money wherewith to buy it. If the rains failed for two seasons in succession there would be a famine and unless government stepped in to help by providing work for those who could work and relief for those who could not, many would die of starvation. The two rain-bearing currents are (1) the south-west monsoon, commonly called the monsoon or the rain, is from May to October, and (2) the so-called north-east monsoon or 'the winter rains'. The region, the average rainfall of which is between 25 and 35 inches, is probably that which suffers most from drought. The annual rainfall in the Ceded Districts is liable to extraordinary variations. This is one of those parts, which, with an average rainfall of about 30 inches or less, is most liable to drought or famine and is recognized as famine zone in the plateau of Peninsular India. Here, although on the average the supply of rain is sufficient to support an agricultural population, the fluctuations which reduce the fall below which is essential are so frequent, as to lead to repeated seasons of scarcity of greater or less severity.[20] It is true that importance of fall of rain, for general purposes of agriculture, will be determined by the requirements of the principal crops, and particularly on those crops on which the food supply of the people depends.

Life generally passes in a continued struggle between the forces that it tends to preserve and to destroy it. Amongst the most active of these forces are the conditions of local climate, and notably those of atmospheric heat and moisture. It has generally been observed that the areas where the productive powers of nature are the greatest, the opposite influences are also commonly the most active. The warmer parts of the earth, where the gifts of nature are most profuse, one has to encounter in ones extreme form the devastating forces of tempest, drought, food, and disease. The frequent recurrence of scarcities, droughts and famines render the permanent improvement and well being of the inhabitants/area hopeless.[21]

### *Scarcity, Drought, Famine*

What then is a 'scarcity' or 'drought' or 'famine'? Erroneously there is tendency to use these words interchangeably. *Scarcity* is dearth of food, state of being scarce, and a limited or insufficient supply due the absence of rainfall for a short period. The English administrators were of the view 'that seasons alone, however adverse, can never in one year occasion a famine'.[22] Otherwise a large percentage of the population not only of the Ceded Districts or the Madras Presidency but of whole India could be said to be almost permanently in a state of famine. As a matter of fact, famine would not come entirely without warning, as might an earthquake or tidal wave. *Drought* ('dryness, lack of moisture, prolonged/ continuous period of dry weather, and lack of rain') is an extended period of dry weather, or excessively dry climatic conditions. These conditions are generally due to absence of rainfall that is associated with blocking anticyclone in which evapotranspiration exceeds precipitation, causing soil moisture deficits. A region is classed as arid or drought-stricken when the annual precipitation is below 10 in (25.4 cm.). Under such conditions, farming becomes extremely difficult. Some regions, especially arid and semi-arid areas, are particularly prone to droughts, which can result in food shortages and human suffering.[23] *Famine* is a state of extreme scarcity of food; starvation, hunger; acute food shortage resulting in widespread hunger and death. It is usually caused by natural disasters such as drought, floods, or plant diseases cropping crop failure. Drought could be more, or less fatal, 'according as it follows a season of bad or good rain fall; and it has commonly happened that severe famines have been caused by a severe drought following one or two years of indifferent rain. The stocks of food become exhausted, and the cattle and the population enfeebled, and thus less able to resist the pressure put on them.'[24] According to the *Indian Famine Commission Report 1880,* famines were 'in all eases to be traced directly to the occurrence of seasons of unusual drought, the failure of customary rainfall leading to the failure of the food crops on which the subsistence of the population depends'.[25] Moreover, 'the price of grain which is in all countries the best ground on which a judgment may be formed of the probability of a dearth or famine must be peculiarly so in them for it is more easy for the grain dealers to calculate the stock in a country which can draw no supply from any other and to regulate their prices accordingly'.[26] These could be attempts made by the traders to fix prices of grains beyond the paying capacity of the customers. This has been termed as 'man-made' or 'price famines'.[27] Though the situations of drought and scarcity did prevail for many a time during the 19th century the famines occurred only on a few occasions.

### *Causes of Drought Situations*

Droughts and famines have been a disease of all agricultural countries. There has not only been extreme dependence on agriculture but also on the arrival of adequate and timely rains. Even a few weeks' delay or a partial failure of the monsoon could create drought conditions. The Ceded Districts during the satisfactory rainfall would produce commercial cash crops like cotton, as well as the millets *ragi, cholam* and *cambu* that formed the staple food grains of the area. But the requirements of agriculture in the matter of rain and the precise manner in which it was required during the critical times had to be distinguished. Even though the average fall in any year might be fully enough to carry on the ordinary process of growth, the failure of rain even for a few days at one of the critical periods might lead to complete loss,[28]

There was almost complete dependence on a direct supply of rain. No government could control the rainfall and at the same time if the rains failed for two consecutive seasons there would be a famine. There would always be a danger of losing lives owing to starvation. There was absence of proper roads and railways to bring grain quickly to distressed areas. There were irrigation works—wells, tanks, canals—but not that of enormous scale or large irrigation works to keep the drought stricken areas under constant cultivation. Above all there was no one to take measures to prevent disease breaking out in the affected areas. Under the circumstances there was always a likelihood of deterioration in the conditions.

The cultivators practically had no capital and depended on organized credit, which was likely to shrink further when harvests failed. There was a large population of agricultural labourers, the vast majority of whom had only casual employment and were invariably thrown out when the harvests failed. As such, masses of agriculturists and other inhabitants depended upon harvests, and these depended upon a periodic, but by no means regular, rainfall.[29]

Right since the ancient period droughts and famines have been very frequent, and frightful when they came. The period practically from the last quarter of the 17th century to the first quarter of the 19th century was a period of chaos when the whole area was harried by the armies of various chiefs including those whose kingdoms were there one day and gone the next day. There was an obvious complete neglect of' the maintenance of irrigation works.

The food habits of the inhabitants had also very significant role to play in making after effects of the failure of rains more serious. A very vast majority would subsist on vegetable food, cereal grains, pulses, rice, and vegetables, with milk and butter. Other animal food was comparatively little eaten. The grain crops therefore, were of usually great importance. As such, the importance of fall of rain in India would be determined by the requirements of the crops on which the food supply of the people depended.[30]

Apart from the general causes of drought and famine, discussed above, there was a very a strong belief that human skill or endeavour had nothing to do as far as adequate and timely monsoon or sufficient harvest were concerned. The unpredictability of the seasons and perpetual dependence on sufficient rains had made their belief on divine and super natural power in this respect even more forceful. All these things, i.e., drought and famine, or cholera, smallpox, and even crop blight were attributed to the correct or incorrect way of performing the rites and celebrations. It could also be due to the sinful activities of either the whole villages or some individuals. Some archival records have also corroborated this contention, For instance, a letter written by the Deputy Collector to the Collector, Bellary mentions that some peasants had attributed the drought of 1876-7 in their region to the failure of pilgrims in Hampi to pull the main temple car or to draw even the smaller one more than half-way round its customary circuits at the annual celebration in March 1876.[31] It was also noted that in the Ceded Districts all agriculturists, irrespective of their caste (right from the *Kapus,* the leading peasant caste, down to the *Malas,* the untouchable labourers), participated in rain-making rituals. In this ceremony, a female frog tied to a winnowing-fan was taken in procession by women and children singing 'Mother Frog should have her bath. The tanks are full (ironic in view of the drought). Give water. O Rain God!'[32] Religion being an essential and integral part of the everyday life of the peasants and other inhabitants interpreting drought and famine in religious terms would make it easier for them to understand. It would not only deviate their attention from reality to myths but would also provide them an option of cultural responses to get riddance from their sufferings.

On many an occasion, the drought, famine, and even cyclones have got frequent reference in the Hindu myths and legends.[33] A severe famine (1396 A.D.) was long remembered as the result of the destructive power of the Goddess Durga and was distinguished from all others by name 'Durgadevi' as 'whole districts were entirely depopulated and the people suffered much'.[34] Some sayings in vernacular languages, like Telugu, make predictions about the rainfall, season, and the crop. For example—'If there is rain in *Aruda* (the Telugu astral period 23 June to 4 July), there will be no scarcity'; 'If there is no rain in *Chitra* (the Telugu astral 9-22 October), even an ant will suffer from the heat'; if the sky fails, the earth will fail'; if Jupiter sets at the rising of Venus, there will be rain', & co.[35] The sayings were/are the result of observations made by several generations, obviously the success rate of predicting the weather by the cultivators was/is remarkable.[36]

## Pre-Colonial Period

During the pre-colonial period droughts and famines visited the areas at periodical intervals causing much suffering to the people. However, there was difference between the natures of such calamities during the pre-colonial, early colonial and later half of the nineteenth century. During the earlier period the hardship that resulted was great and heartrending. The calamities were more or less local in character and relief measures would reach at the very slow pace. People had to be allowed largely to drift for themselves in spite of the efforts of the government to give them relief. Many of them had to abandon their lands and forced migration would occur on a large scale. However, such migrations were often only temporary, the people returning to their original homes after a certain period of time.[37] The only flourishing economic activity would be the slave trade. The Dutch and other European trading companies bought and shipped large numbers of people trying to save themselves from starvation.

Though famines were frequent, there is hardly any evidence of the existence of well-shaped famine code or 'famine policy'. However, the available evidence points to the fact that kings were anxious as any one else to afford relief to the suffering people during the times of droughts and famines. There was realization on the part of the kings that irrigation facilities must be improved. The grain was brought and sold at low rates. Public stores of grain were opened for the use of the poor. Tolls on grain and land revenue were remitted, partially or completely. Among the private bodies and agencies that undertook relief work during such times mention could be made of the temples.[39] *Tuqavi* (lit. strength-giving) loans were provided for agricultural purposes, mainly for sinking and repairing wells, and purchase of food grains, seed grains, fodder and bullocks. These loans were, as a rule, advanced through the *patels,* who distributed them among the individual peasants and stood surety for their payment.[40] However, it would be difficult to draw a useful generalization regarding the part played by the state during the pre-colonial rule in relieving the drought and famine distress. In brief what can be said is that there was little thought for and no effective means of remedial action. Occasionally a large relief work was started and spasmodic attempts were made to send food to the affected areas.

**Early Nineteenth Century**

After the areas under discussion had been ceded to the East India Company in 1800, no doubt the English power had emerged to be the strongest in the region, its energies were confined to consolidating its position. The Company fought against the local chiefs like the palegars in order to defend its newly acquired territories.[41] It was not so easy for the Company to protect the people from the terrible results of the droughts in the Ceded Districts. It tried to devote its attention in trying to understand the problem of the droughts in the region, its reasons, attitude of the people, and control the price of grain. It also tried to see that as far as possible the stocks of grain that existed were brought into the market. In brief it tried to continue the policies adopted by the earlier rulers ruling over various places before the occupation by the East India Company.

Before 1800, elsewhere in the Madras Presidency, a charitable fund was opened which proved to be the origin of the Monegar Choultry where in during many subsequent droughts and famines thousands of destitute people were fed. It would temporarily suspend the duties that were then imposed on the import of grain. During 1790-92 famine in the Northern Circars, the government employed as many as 2,000 people in public works and fed them on grain from government granaries. This was followed in 1807 when there was a severe famine in the districts of Nellore, North Arcot and Chingleput. During this period though many people died of scarcities, starvation and disease, a large number of them flocked into Madras and were fed in the Monegar Choultry. In some places grains were brought to the starving districts in large quantities and relief depots were opened. To encourage merchants to import grain by sea, government would sometime give them a return cargo of salt at reduced rates. At times when the price of principal food stuff rose very high the Company would provide employment to the able-bodied on road works.[42]

The early policies of the East India Company were mainly directed towards meeting the situations created by the droughts rather than thinking or initiating any long term solutions. Thomas Munro was of the opinion that distress created by the drought could be mitigated by a four-fold policy—by encouraging importation; prohibiting exportation; by reducing the rents of the lower classes of rayats; and by giving employment to the poor in public work. These views were expressed keeping in mind the extreme drought situations being experienced in 1807. The suggestions given by him were endorsed by the Board of Revenue.

He was very particular about the maintenance of the irrigation means. 'The public ought to be employed in repairing of tanks, nallas, wells and in general all such works as these tend to increase the produce of the country'. He wanted that more and more people in distress be provided employment for repairing the irrigation means so that they were ready by next sowing season.

If either a portion or whole of the revenue was to be remitted, employment was to be provided 'to poor of all classes in tank repairs as the means of furnishing them subsistence, and of compensating for the extra expense by the more speedy completion of the work'.

He was not very much in favor providing relief in the form of distribution of grain either free or at reduced price. It would encourage them to 'abandon themselves to the protection of the public and to neglect the salutary means of preserving themselves by their own exertions.' Moreover, distribution of charity by government would always increase the number of the poor. 'Were grain in this country to be issued to the poor at any particular station, the report would soon reach the remotest corner . . . poor who now procure a livelihood by their labour would crowd in from all sides in the hopes of procuring it upon easier terms ... cultivation of the ensuing season would suffer from the want of hands.'[43]

While classifying the sources of irrigation in the Ceded Districts even though the sources afforded a supply for more than five months had been placed in the lower class on account of labour and expense to the rayat in digging and keeping the channels clear and also keeping in mind the perennial drought conditions there.[44]

Moreover, honouring the expectations of the rayats, the Collectors of the Ceded Districts also contributed in the collective action of the villagers for the rain compelling ceremonies being regularly performed there. For example, in December 1811 the Collector of Cuddapah paid 150 Star Pagodas for rain making ceremonies 'with a view of satisfying the ryots and convincing them that the Sirkar is not an indifferent spectator of the present calamity' .[45]

No doubt, East India Company had developed a policy for the management of droughts in the Ceded Districts, conditions scarcely changed in the early years of its rule. However, attempts were being made to draw by degrees a scheme of systematic relief for the drought affected cultivators. The modern view of the responsibility of the state was not reached until India had passed under the Crown.

### *Mid-Nineteenth Century and Onwards*

The middle of the nineteenth century not only saw English success in establishing complete political domination on India but also saw arrogance in their attitude and at the same time serious realizations in respect of controlling/ avoiding deaths due to droughts and famines. Moreover, certain new phenomenon had also started emerging, which had a very serious bearing on the British policies *vis a vis* response/attitude of the cultivators and other inhabitants. In this respect mention may be made of the impact of the *rayatwari* system on the peasants, rural indebtedness and agrarian relations: the uprisings of 1857; introduction of the railways; the Christian missionaries; and, not the least, the rise of Indian nationalism.

High land revenue demand, its fixity and rigidity, and new legal and administrative systems were leading to the expropriation of the peasant proprietors. The peasants in the *rayatwari* areas were not able to get adequate livelihood from their lands and consequently were compelled to borrow at exorbitant rates of interest in order to pay the land revenue, feed themselves and their families. For the peasants the choice would often lay between starvation and the moneylender. All this resulted into an alarming increase in rural indebtedness and transfer of agricultural land into the hands of non-agricultural and non-cultivating classes. The cultivators were practically reduced to agricultural laborers in their own lands.[46]

The British and Western life, civilization, culture and even their political institutions, including their imperialism and colonialism, were based on their religious (Christian) spirit. Also without safeguarding the supremacy of British rule in India, which alone in the ultimate analysis stood as the best guarantee for missionary free enterprise, Christian mission could not hope to have India as the mission outpost.[47] No wonder the British policies even towards the drought management would directly or indirectly support the Christian missionary activities.

Moreover, there was a change in the attitude of the higher authorities towards the recommendations made by the Collector of a district. When the Collector of Nellore had suggested the Board of Revenue's intervention by setting aside 'theories of political economy which will lead only to starvation and riot', the former was not only rebuked but was also told that violation of free trade in grain could not 'for a moment be entertained'.[48] Contrary to their earlier practice of contribution for the rain-making ceremonies, it is observed that by 1870s they had abandoned such responsibilities. The neglect of an ancient and important duty by the English was not appreciated by especially the Hindu inhabitants.[49]

The severity and the devastations caused by the famine of 1876—78, covering practically the whole southern India, made the English government realize the need of introducing some permanent measures to manage the drought and famine situations more effectively. In 1878, the whole question of relief protection, management and future course of action was referred to first Famine Commission under the presidency of Sir Richard Strachey. 'The Famine Commissioners insisted that relief should be so administered as not to check the growth of thrift and self-reliance among the people, or to impair the structure of society which, resting in India upon the moral obligation of mutual assistance, is admirably adapted by common effort against a common misfortune'. These views and further recommendations were embodied in a Provisional Famine Code, which was circulated in 1883. In this the government laid down the fundamental principle of the famine wage, which was 'the lowest amount sufficient to maintain health under given circumstances'.[50]

The British government realized that there were some practical difficulties which came on their way in dealing with the serious impacts caused by the drought situations. For instance, there was no poor law. While private charity would support the poor in ordinary times, in times of droughts the charities dried up, and the recipients of it were thrown upon the state together with large numbers of the agricultural population. The peoples of India had very strong habits, customs and caste leanings. Thousands would die sooner than resort to relief camps than touch food, which they thought was unclean, either in itself or reason of the agency employed in its preparations. One caste would not feed with another. Skilled weavers would not go to ordinary relief works for fear of losing their delicacy of touch. There was also low standard of intelligence and integrity'.[51]

It is of still more essential importance, said the Secretary of State in 1878, 'to ascertain how far it is possible for Government by its action to diminish the severity of famines or to place the people in a better condition for enduring them.' It was realized that there should be an elaborate system of agricultural intelligence and that standing preparations had to be made on a large scale in ordinary times. The government should be kept informed daily of meteorological conditions, weekly of crops, and monthly of birth and death rates. Programmes of suitable relief works were to be revised in every district. It was also realized that 'the best, and often the only, means of securing protection from the extreme effects of famine and drought' were the introduction of proper transportation and irrigation works.[52]

Certain irrigation projects started by the English had earlier initiated by the pre-colonial kings. For example most of the weirs on the Tungabhadra River were constructed by Krishna Dev Raya at the beginning of the 16th century. In 1857 the Madras government proposed a great scheme, known as Tungabhadra project, for the irrigation of the large portions of the Ceded Districts. The Madras Irrigation Company was eventually formed for its prosecution, with a government guarantee. Operations were limited at first to the construction of the part of general scheme known as the Kurnool-Cuddapah Canal. This work was to protect large areas of the Ceded Districts, which were specially liable to severe distress and famine in the years of drought. But it would also require a storage work of enormous capacity on the Tungabhadra and elsewhere in order to obtain a reliable supply for the whole area that could be commanded, while canal channels themselves would be very costly owing to the nature of the soil and the configuration of the area concerned.[53] Several large works which gave little promise of proving directly remunerative were undertaken on the ground of their value as a protection against severe effects of droughts and famines. In 1878, the government made 'dual fiscal provision' to face regular drought conditions by creating a long-term Famine Insurance Fund, money for which was to be raised partly by the imposition of special cesses on land revenue and rent and partly by the levy of a license tax on the commercial and trading classes and artisans.[54]

The government also realized benefits of the railways during the periods of droughts and famines. As the drought conditions were never universal, for when one area was suffering, another was likely to have an abundant harvest, and railways were thought to make possible for the deficiencies of the former to be supplied from the surplus of the latter. In 1865, there were only four railway lines, one from Madras to West Coast, one through Cuddapah district, one through North Arcot to Bangalore and one connecting Nagapatam with Tanjore and Trichnopoly. The Southern Mahratta Railway was begun for protective purposes against famine. In 1883, in consequence of a treaty entered into with the Portuguese government for its connection with the Portuguese Railway and extended up to Bellary.[55]

Though not directly related to the Ceded Districts or for that matter the Madras Presidency, the Order issued by the Lt Governor of Agra in 1868 was certainly a great step towards the management of drought situations. The Order stated that 'every District officer would be held personally responsible that no deaths occurred from starvation which could have been avoided by any exertion or arrangement on his part or that of his subordinates.'[56]

## *Critical Appraisal*

I have evolved my own theory, formula, or parameters for judging the success or otherwise of a ruler or an administration. What I think is that if we know the *objectives, intentions* and *compulsions* of any ruler or administration, it is easy for one to understand the amount of its success or failure, as there is great difference between these three things. It is only these things, which set the priorities of any administrator. Same parameters could be applied to the management of drought situations by the English in the Ceded Districts in particular, and the Madras Presidency and the whole of Indian subcontinent in general.

Briefly speaking, from different reports and action taken by the English government it looks that they were certainly concerned about the droughts and the situations thus created. They wanted to take some steps lest the people or cultivators should think otherwise. Their *objective* was that apparently it should look as if they were doing a lot and rather everything to get the areas rid of the droughts and droughts situations. Their *intention* was to maintain the colonial set up in India under any circumstances as they knew that 'without India there would be no British Empire'. Their first *compulsion* was the industries back home which had to be fed by the raw materials. The second compulsion was the Christian missionaries. The work, existence, and success of both the English rule/government and the Christian missionaries were largely dependent on each other. That is why the drought management during the period under study in the Ceded Districts was not a big success.

It is observed that despite the steps taken by the government, the droughts continued unabated, and lives of many continued to be sacrificed. There were several seasons of prolonged droughts. The result was large numbers of cultivators were classed as laborers.[57] Rural indebtedness continued to haunt the peasants, as there was large scale selling and mortgaging of the land to the moneylenders. The peasant proprietors were virtually reduced to the level of cultivating tenants.[58] In the face of drought, dearth and incipient famine there was a general retreat (though temporary) from cultivation of the commercial crops to the subsistence agriculture.[59] There was subaltern anger, and series of disturbances resulting incidents of looting of grains.[60] All this resulted into the rise in the crime which necessitated the deployment of extra police.[61] The peasants were forced to eat the leaves and roots and the untouchables consumed the flesh of the dead cattle and other animals.[62] There were large scale incidence of sale of cattle and thereafter other possessions like door, windows, utensils, agricultural implements, etc.[63] There were large scale migrations from the villages to the towns and less drought affected districts.[64] Moreover, the relief measures provided by the government were leading to the possible social divide.[65] Above all there was mass conversion especially among the untouchable classes to Christianity.[66]

Lord Curzon once openly declared that 'without India there would be no British Empire'. It means the British government was prepared to go for financial robbery to maintain their colony. Few instances would explain this view point.

The British government spent considerable financial resources on building railways. Since the lines were often built for purely military purposes, they proved unprofitable. It has been computed that by 1900, losses on them had reached 600 million rupees and to cover these tax revenues were used. The construction of railways was of extreme economic importance, especially since no canals were built for transportation purposes. From 1869 to 1879, the colonial administration laid railways at its own expense. From 1879, private companies were involved in this again. Previously, their dividends had been guaranteed, but this time they were given financial assistance and allocated land. But lines were laid from regions where raw- materials were produced to seaports, while the interests of domestic trade were ignored.

The land revenue charged from the cultivators was highest that could be imposed. The essential distinction between the various types of land revenue systems introduced by the East India Company and forms of agrarian relations accruing out of them did not alter the basic fact that the agrarian system and methods of exploiting the peasants developed in one and the same direction through out the country. The British government was encouraging the development of commercial agriculture specializing in the production of specific raw materials or foodstuffs.

The whole of 19th century and even after, India suffered greatly from droughts, famines and epidemics. The British firms were able to exploit hired agriculture labourers and reap monopoly on the world market. The expansion of irrigation system in many cases resulted in bogging up and salination of the soil, the spread of malaria and so on. No doubt economic effects of irrigation were however, significant. But India's agriculture became more specialized and more industrial crops were grown.

The country's agricultural achievements were very modest. The peasants had no access to machinery. Even draft cattle were in short supply, and the land was worked by antiquated methods. The yield was extremely low. Artificial fertilizers were hardly used at all. More raw materials were taken out of the country, which increasingly became an agrarian appendage of Britain. As such, it can be concluded that though the British government took steps to salvage the Ceded Districts from the droughts but their intentions were altogether different.

## References

* Reader Department of History and TTM, Dyal Singh Evening College, (University of Delhi), Lodi Road. New Delhi—110003.

1. Francis. W., *Anantpur District Gazetteer,* Madras, 1912, p. 78. He further writes, "The rain is scanty but it usually falls in light showers, which on a stony soil under tropical sun soon dry up and are insufficient to fill the tanks and wells. Further. It is most capricious and uncertain. The method of dry land cultivation . . . require that to secure good crops the showers shall arrive at certain intervals and any marked irregularity in the rainfalls hampers cultivation in a manner for which showers in subsequent months cannot atone. The absence of rain in June-July will render impossible to sow red land...The prosperity of a year cannot therefore be judged merely by examining the total fall it received. To give good crops the rain must be timely as well as sufficient".

2. In Madras Presidency, the soils most commonly met with would fall either in the "regar" (i.e., black) series or in the "red" series. Alluvial soils were met with in the delta areas of Godavari, Krishna and Kaveri rivers. Arenaceous soils were met with coastal tracts. Calcareous soils were very rare. Ramakrishnan, C.A., Director of Settlements, *Principles of Ryotwari Settlement,* Government Press, Madras, 1952. p. 6.

3. *Census of India,* Vol. XIV, Pt. I, Madras, 1932, p. 48. Also, Satyanarayana, A., *Andhra Peasants Under British Rule: Agrarian Relations and the Rural Economy 1900—1940,* Delhi, 1990. pp. 12-3.

4. *Madras Board of Revenue Consultations 26 Sept. 1805 and Selections from the Old Records of Bellary District 1800-1807,* ASO (D) Vol. 72, Thomas Munro to William Petrie, President of the Board of Revenue, 25 Aug. 1805. However, it is a different matter that what Thomas Munro, like other administrators elsewhere in India, achieved was neither a synthesis of the alien nor that of the indigenous. Instead, distortions took place that, strictly speaking, were not the product of the new institutions, but were alterations in the old structure. Dua, J.C., *Agrarian* System *in South India: Some Aspects,* New Delhi, 1990, p. 54.

5. J.C. Dua, 'Comparative Position of the Village *Patwari/Karnum* during the Early British Rule in the Punjab (up to 1885) and the Madras Presidency (up to 1825)', *Punjab History Conference,* Patiala, 24th session, 1988.

6. Ludden, David, *Peasant History in South India,* OUP, Delhi, 1989, p. 102.

7. Smith, Richard Saumarez, 'Rule-by-records and rule-by-reports: complementary aspects of the British imperial rule of law', *Contributions to Indian Sociology,* 1985, 19, 1, p. 161.

8. Greenway, T., *Farming in India, considered as a pursuit for European settlers of superior class, with plans for the construction of dams, weirs, tanks and sluices,* London, 1864, p. 54; Pogson, Frederick, *A Manual of Agriculture in India,* Calcutta, 1883, p. 98; Shah, Motilal Kashal Chand, *Principles for Agriculture for India,* Ahmedabad, 1988, p. 107. The *Moral and Material Progress Report* for 1907-8 reported that 'thirty years of experience and record gathering since the institution of the Department of Agriculture lead to the recognition that

Government's primary task was to apply European scientific methods to Indian agriculture'. See, Manak, Elizabeth, 'Formation of Agriculture Policy in Imperial India, 1872-1929: a case study of Madras Presidency', Dissertation, University of Hawaii.

9. Benson, C., *A Collection of Telugu Sayings and Proverbs Bearing on Agriculture,* Madras. 1898.
10. *Manual of Administration of the Madras Presidency,* 2 Vols. Madras, 1885.
11. *A Glossary of Judicial and Revenue Terms,* London, 1855.
12. *Hobson-Jobson: A Glossary of Colloquial Anglo-Indian Words and Phrases,* London, 1886.
13. Ludden, David, 'Archaic Formations of Agricultural Knowledge in South India' in Peter Robb (Ed.) *Meanings of Agriculture: Essays in South Asian History and Economics.* OUP, Delhi, 1996, pp.18 & 43.
14. Pal, B.P., 'Foreword', Randhawa, M.S., *A History of Agriculture in India,* ICAI, New Delhi, 1980.
15. *Ibid.*, p. 47.
16. The oldest Neolithic settlement sites known are Ali Kosh, Bus Mordeh phase (7500 B.C.) in Iran, Jericho in Jordan (7000 B.C.), Jarmo in Iraq (6750 B.C.) and Belt Cave below the Caspian (6500 B.C.) in northern Iran. Between them, they more or less embrace the region called the Fertile Crescent, which saw the rise of Neolithic culture. These are mountainous areas where adequate rainfall for non-irrigation agriculture exists. The Ali Kosh villagers harvested their cereals with flint sickles, which were set into hafts by means asphalt. They ground up wheat, barley, and crop weeds on saddle shaped or shallow-basin grinding-slabs using simple discoidal hand stones of pitted limestone. An innovation was the use of stone mortal and pestle. See, Braidwood, R.J., 'The Agricultural Revolution', *Scientific American,* Sept. 1960; Randhawa, M.S., *A History of Agriculture in India: Volume I: Beginning to 12th century,* ICAI, New Delhi, 1980, pp. 101-102.
17. It would not be out of place to mention that there are exhortations to idlers to work rather wasting time in gambling—"Play not with dice; pursue agriculture; delight in wealth so acquired; there, gambler, are cows, there is a wife (to look after)" (R., X. 3.5.13).
18. Appadorai, A., *Economic Conditions in Southern India (1000—1500 A.D.),* vol. I, Madras, 1990, pp. 45-46.
19. *Ibid.*, J.C. Dua, 'Method of Land Measurement and Assessment in Northern Circars during the Pre-British Era as Reflected in the *Chetri Ganitam', IHC,* Dharwar, 1980.
20. *Report of the Irrigation Commission, 1901—03,* Calcutta, p. 5.
21. *Report of the Famine Commission, 1880,* Appendix I, Lt. Gen. R. Strachey, 'Physical Causes of Indian Famine', being a Lecture delivered before the Royal Institute of Great Britain on 18th May 1877.

22. Tamil Nadu State Archives, *Bellary Records (1807) Famine and Scarcity: Relief Work,* 401/311-329, Letter from Thomas Munro to The President and Members of the Board Revenue dated Punganoor 8th January 1807.

23. In UK an official drought occurs when there is a period of 15 consecutive days on each of which there is no more than 0.25 mm/0.1 inch of rain. Permanent drought conditions prevail over approximately one-third of the world's land surface, the sand deserts alone covering a total area more than twice as large as the United States. Recently, however, progress has been made in dry land reclamation by means of new irrigation schemes. Experiments for inducing artificial rainfall through cloud-seeding techniques have also been promising.

24. *Report of the Famine Commission, 1880,* Appendix I, Lt. Gen. R. Strachey, 'Physical Causes of Indian Famine', being a Lecture delivered before the Royal Institute of Great Britain on 18th May 1877.

25. *Report of the Indian Famine Commission, 1880,* Part I, London, 1880, p. 7.

26. Letter from Thomas Munro to The President and Members of the Board Revenue dated Punganoor 8th January 1807.

27. David Arnold, 'Famine in Peasant Consciousness and Peasant Action: Madras 1876-8', in Ranajit Guha (Ed.), *Subaltern Studies III, Writings on South Asian History and Society,* Delhi, 1984, p. 65. Also see, Dando, William A., *The Geography of Famine,* London, 1980, pp. 57-65.

28. Broadly there are four critical periods—(1) as the great power of the tropical sun utterly dries up soil in the hot months that precede the rainy season, the first showers are almost essential to admit the final ploughing, and the sowing may thus be unduly late in unfavourable seasons. (2) Next, the thorough saturation of the soil, and its maintenance in a sufficient state of moisture, are requisite for the germination of the seeds, and this is always one of the most critical periods for every crop. (3) The next critical stage is that of flowering, when a great access of rain may be almost as fatal as want of it, by causing the destruction of the parts of the flower essential for the development of the grain. (4) The period immediately follows in which the grain is fertilized and takes its ultimate form, during which the supply of moisture to the plant is not less essential than in the first stage of its life, and any serious failure of rain is fatal to the harvest.

29. *The Imperial Gazetteer of India: The Indian Empire: Vol. III, Economic,* Oxford, 1907, pp. 475-76.

30. Lt. Gen. R. Strachey, 'Physical Causes of Indian Famine', being a Lecture delivered before the Royal Institute of Great Britain on 18th May 1877.

31. Tamil Nadu State Archives, Chennai, Bellary Records, May 1877, 605, 234-6, V. Venkatachellum Pantulu, Deputy Collector, to Collector, Bellary, 17 April, 1877; also Beck, Brwenda E.F., *Peasant Society in Kongu: A study of Right anti Left Sub castes in South India,* Vancouver, 1972, pp. 52-5.

32. Moses, ST., 'Frog Folk-lore', *Quarterly Journal of the Mythic Society,* 30: I (July 1939), pp. 17-19.

33. For more details in this respect, see O'Flaherty, Wendy Doniger, *The Origin of Evil in Hindu Mythology,* Berkely, 1976, pp. 35-40: 291-5; Cohen, Stephen P. and Raghavulu, C.V., *The Andhra Cyclone of 1977: Individual and Institutional Responses to Mass Death,* New Delhi, 1979, pp. 1-2.

34. Appadoral, A., *Economic conditions in Southern India (1000-1500 A.D.),* University of Madras, reprint, 1990, pp. 748-49.

35. Benson, C., *A Collection of Telugu Sayings and Proverbs Bearing on Agriculture,* (Department of Agriculture: Bulletin no. 22), Madras, 1891, pp. 181-99.

36. Cox, Arthur F., *A Manual of North Arcot District,* Madras, 1881, p. 319.

37. Mahalingam, T.V., *Administration and Social Life Under Vijayanagar: Part II Social Life,* Madras, 1975, p. 175; Appadorai, *op. cit.*, p. 750; Martin, Francois, *Memories de Francois Martin: Fondateur de Pondichery (1665-l694),* Edited by A, Martineau, 3 vols. Paris, 1931-4, II, pp. 497-505.

38. Wheeler, J. Talboys, *Madras in the Olden Times,* 3 vols. Madras, 1861-62, I, pp. 190-3.

39. Mahalingam, *op. cit.*, pp. 175-6; Appadorai, *op. cit.*, pp. 750-1.

40. J.C. Dua, 'Position of Patels and Karnums in the 'Ceded Districts' during the first quarter of the Nineteenth Century', in Bhattacharya, Sabyasachi (Ed.), *Essays on Modern Indian Economic History,* New Delhi, 1987, pp. 25-40; *Report on the Famine Relief Operations in the His Exalted Highness the Nizam's Dominions during 1328, 1329 and Azur 1330 Fasli (1918-1919, 1919-20)* by Mohammad Ali H.C.S., Famine Commissioner, Hyderabad Deccan, Hyderabad, 1923, pp. 1-19, Crisp, B. (Tr.), *The Mysorean Revenue Regulations,* (1792), p. 2.

41. For details in this regard, see, Dua, J.C., *Palegars of South India: Forms and Contents of their Resistance in Ceded Districts,* New Delhi, 1996, pp. 114-185.

42. *Famine in Madras Presidency,* Government Press, Madras, 1934.

43. Tamil Nadu State Archives, *Bellary Records,* (1807) 412/64—68, Letter from Thomas Munro to Frederick Gahagan. Collector of Adwanee dated 10th January 1807 forwarding a copy of the letter from the Board of Revenue: 412/68-70, Letter from Deputy Secretary, FSG to Thomas Munro dated 28th January 1807: 410 / 58-61. Letter from Chief Secretary to Government to the Board of Revenue dated 26th January 1807; 401/311-329, Letter from Chief Secretary to Government to the Board of Revenue dated 9th Feb. 1807.

44. Five classes of irrigation sources were recognized for settlement purposes—(i) *First Classes*—Exceptionally good sources, based on anicuts or reservoirs across perennial rivers supply of water...for practically the whole year; (ii) *Second Class*—Irrigation sources affording a supply for eight months and over; (iii) *Third Class*—Irrigation sources affording a supply for five months and above, but less than eight months; (iv) *Fourth Class*—Irrigation sources affording a supply for three months and above, but less than five months, and (v) *Fifth Class*—All minor sources affording supply for lea than three months. C.A. Ramakrishnan, *Principles of Ryotwari Settlement,* Madras, 1952.

45. Andhra Pradesh State Archives, *Cuddapah District Records,* (1811), 216/44-47. C.R. Ross, Collector, Cuddapah to Board of Revenue, 3rd December 1811.

46. Bipan Chandra, *The Rise and Growth of Economic Nationalism in India: Economic Policies of Indian National Leadership,* 1880-1905, New Delhi, 1982 print, pp. 467-473.

47. Mathew, A. *Christian Missions, Education and Nationalism: From Dominance to Compromise 1870-1930,* New Delhi, 1988, pp. 128-133.

48. *Proceedings of the Board of Revenue,* 277, 30th October 1876,

49. *Report on the Stations in Connection with the South India District Committee of the London Missionary Society, 1876,* Bangalore, 1877, 'Report of the London Mission, Salem, 1877', p. 9.

50. *Report of the Indian Famine Commission of 1880,* p. 9. *The Imperial Gazetteer of India: The Indian Empire: Vol. III, Economic,* Oxford, 1907, pp. 489-90.

51. *The Imperial Gazetteer of India: The Indian Empire:* III, *Economic,* Oxford, 1907, pp. 478-9.

52. *Report of the Indian Famine Commission of 1880,* p. 9.

53. Government of India: *Report of the Royal Commission on Agriculture,* 1928.

54. Strachey, John and Strachey, Richard, *The Finances and Public Works of India from 1869 to 1881,* London, 1882, p. 197; also Bipan Chandra, *The Rise and Growth of Economic Nationalism in India: Economic Policies of Indian National Leadership, 1880-1905,* New-Delhi, 1982 print, p. 516.

55. Bell, Horace, *Railway Policy in India,* 1894, pp. 17-8.

56. Metcalf, Thomas R., *Land, Landlords, and the British Raj: Northern India in the Nineteenth Century,* OUP, Delhi, 1979, p. 316.

57. "*Correspondence between Secretary of State for India and the Government of India on the subject of the Threatened Famine in Western and Southern India,* part 2, London, 1877, 'Memorandum on Kurnool District, p. 34.

58. Benson, C., *An Account of Kurnool District,* Madras, 1889, p. 116.

59. Nicholson, F.A., *Manual of the Coimbatore District,* Madras, 1887, p. 274,

60. Benson, *op. cit.*, p. 34.

61. David Arnold, 'Dacoity and Rural Crime in Madras, 1860-1940', *Journal of Peasant Studies,* 6:2 (Jan. 1979, pp. 145-9; *Report on Criminal Justice and Criminal Judicial Statistics of Madras Presidency, 1879,* Madras, 1880. p. 5.

62. MBRP, 20055, 12 Aug. 1876, C.J. Crosthwaite, Sub Collector, to Collector, Bellary, 5 Aug. 1876.

63. *Madras Revenue Proceedings 55-C, 30th July 1877.* F.A. Nicholson, Head Assistant Collector to Collector, Madurai, 10th July 1877.

64. *Report of the Indian Famine Commission,* Pt. 3, pp. 205-7.

65. *Ibid.*, pp. 147-8.

66. Duncan B. Forrester, 'The Depressed Classes and Conversion to Christianity, 1860-1960, in Geoffrey A. Oddie (ed.), *Religion In South Asia: Studies in Conversion and Revival Movement in Medieval Modern Times,* London, 977, pp. 41-8.

# *Appendix I*

## Physical Causes of Indian Famines

Life, whatever shape it takes, is passed in a continued struggle between the forces that tend to preserve and to destroy it. Among the most active of these forces are the conditions of local climate, and notably those of atmospheric heat and moisture. Speaking broadly, the same conditions stimulate at once the conservative and destructive tendencies by adding to their intensity; so that where the productive powers of nature are the greatest, there also the opposite influences are made commonly the most active. Thus, in the warmer parts of the earth, where the gifts of nature are most profuse, we have to encounter in their extreme form the devastating forces of tempest, drought, flood, and disease; a few weeks, or may be hours; sweep away the results which it has taken years of the labour of man, or the more silent industry of nature to accumulate. The evidence of the truth of this is unhappily too close at hand. You will find it in the drought, which is now laying the iron hand of famine on a large part of southern and western India; in the similar calamity that fell on parts of Bengal three years ago; in the sudden disaster which within the last few months destroyed perhaps 100,000 human beings in two or three hours in the delta of the Ganges by a flood caused by a cyclone; in the ravages of cholera, which sweeps away the survivors of famine or floods and in the long series, of past occurrences of a similar character recorded in the history of India.

The conclusion is painfully forced upon us that practical civilization has gone a very little way when we find that hardly

---

Being a Lecture delivered before the Royal Institution of Great Britain on the 18th May 1877 (slightly corrected), by Lieutenant-General R. Strachey, R.E., F.R.S.

more than a first step has yet been taken in the successful application of our knowledge and material resources to warding off calamities such as these. It is not, however, my intention to dwell on this aspect of the subject, serious though it be. My present task is a much more limited one, that of placing before you, to the best of my ability, an explanation of the physical conditions under which one class of these scourges of India arises, namely, seasons of drought.

Before I enter on the more special matters with which I shall have to deal, I think it desirable to draw attention to certain points bearing on the general subject of Indian droughts and famines, and their consequences, on which it seems to me that erroneous impressions are prevalent.

In the first place, great though the calamity of an Indian famine be; both to the population directly affected by it, and to the general community that has to bear the loss it causes, yet its gravity may easily be exaggerated. There has been not a little declamation to the effect that the frequent recurrence of Indian famines renders the permanent improvement and well being of the country almost hopeless. Let us compare India in this respect with our own country, the prosperity of which cannot be questioned. The two last and severest Indian famines of recent years, that of Bengal, and that under which a large tract now suffers, may be reckoned to have cost the State in all sixteen millions sterling. Of this sum, perhaps, two or three millions may represent loss of revenue, and the remainder the cost of relief. Now the ordinary yearly cost of Poor Law relief in England is about seven millions sterling, while a few years ago it was eight millions. Again, at the present time in India the population in receipt of relief in the British districts is estimated at about one and a quarter millions in all. The number of persons who receive relief in England at the present time may be reckoned at 700,000 for every day of the year, permanently, and a few years ago it was as much as one million.

Further, it is stated on good authority, that of the thirty-three millions of inhabitants of the United Kingdom, eighteen millions are fed by the produce of our islands, and fifteen millions by imported food. It is not possible to form any opinion as to the proportion of food produced locally and that imported for an Indian province suffering from famine; but of the country, as a whole, it may be said with certainty that the food supply easily provides for the entire population under all known circumstances, and that in the late severe Bengal famine the export of grain continued without very great diminution in spite of the local failure of crops.

Much misconception also exists as to the density of the population of India. It is no doubt true that in some districts the population is very great, but this is by no means universal. In the provinces now suffering, the population in the worst districts is only 150 to the square mile; the average of the British Isles being about 260 per square mile. In the Bengal famine the density of population was much greater, being in some districts even 600 or 700 to the square mile. There is no positive evidence that the population of any part of India has rapidly increased of late years. On this subject we have very few facts on which to rely, and the opinion frequently expressed on it are necessarily based on surmise, and are, in my own judgment, more likely to be wrong than right. The first and only census in the province of Bengal was not taken till 1872, and it will show the utter want of value of guesses on such subjects when I mention that the actual enumeration showed that the population was sixty-seven millions, where previous estimates had made it forty-two millions.

I shall now proceed to the main subject of my address.

Let me ask your attention to the map of India before you. On the north, you see the mountainous region of Tibet, the southern border of which is formed by the ranges known as the Himalayas, extending over a length of about 2,000 miles, and rising along the whole line into the region of perpetual snow; few of the passes being at a less altitude than 15,000 or 16,000 feet, peaks yet measured reaching 29,000 feet above the sea level. On the west, this elevated region is connected with the table-land of Afghanistan and Baluchistan, the border of which forms the frontier of India along the Indus. On the east, high mountain spread out from Tibet southward, constituting the western parts of China, and extending to the sea in Burmah, the Malay peninsula, and Cochin-China; the eastern frontier of British India lies along the outer ramifications of these ranges from Assam, by the delta of the Ganges and Brahmaputra, to the districts of Arracan and Burmah.

The northern provinces of British India occupy a great plain, which flanks the Himalaya along its entire length, expanding at both extremities to the sea; on the east over the delta of the Ganges, which is roughly coincident with the province of Bengal, and on the west through the Punjab and Sindh, along the course of the Indus and its great tributaries to the Arabian sea. This plain rises at its highest point between the Sutlej and the Jumna to something less than 1,000 feet above the sea, presenting over its whole extent an almost unbroken surface, which has the appearance of perfect horizontality.

What is commonly spoken of as the Indian peninsula is occupied by a table-land, roughly triangular in shape, having its broadest end immersed, so to speak, in the continent, to the extent of about one-third of the distance from its base to its apex, the immersed portion being surrounded by the great northern plain. The southern half of the western flank of this table-land forms the line of mountains called the Western Ghâts, and the northern half the hills that bound Rajputana on the west, ending at Delhi. The highest points on the Western Ghâts proper hardly exceed 4,000 feet in elevation, though the Nilgheri mountains, near the southern end of the peninsula, rise to 8,000 feet.

The eastern margin of the table-land is less sharply defined than the western, and is less in elevation also, having a varying extent of low-lying land between it and the sea. The northern border is still less strongly developed; it gradually declines in the north-west, where it can hardly be distinguished, the table-land merging into the plain. The average altitude of the plateau is probably about 1,500 feet above the sea, being most in the south, where it rises in some places to 3,000 feet, and generally greater on the west than on the east, so that with two remarkable exceptions all the more important rivers that carry off the drainage, flow off to the eastward.

These exceptions are due to the occurrence of a line of geological disturbance or discontinuity which crosses the table-land from south-west to north-east being marked by the valleys of the Nerbudda river on the west, the first of the exceptional rivers just referred to, and of the Sone on the east, and the lines of elevation that flank them, known as the Vindhya, Satpura, and Kaimor ranges. The Taptee, the second of the exceptional rivers flowing westward, occupies a valley, nearly parallel to, and not far removed from that of the Nerbudda, and no doubt having its origin in the same physical causes.

The table-land of the peninsula, strictly speaking, should be held to terminate at the Nilgiri mountains, immediately south of which a complete interruption of the Western Ghâts takes place. The mountains which extend from this point to the apex of the peninsula at Cape Comorin rise to a considerable elevation at some places, but have no longer any of the characters of a table-land.

The part of India which is at the present time suffering from the effects of drought includes nearly all that which lies on the summit of the table-land, from a line 100 miles south of the Taptee river to the Nilgiris, along a band 200 miles wide, measuring from the Western Ghâts eastward, as well as the low-lying districts on the east coast between the sea and the foot of the eastern slope of table-land south of the Kistna river. The British area affected is about 150,000 square miles with the population of more than thirty millions. You may compare with this the area and population of Spain, which has 200,000 square miles and seventeen millions of inhabitants; and Italy, with 100,000 square miles and twenty-four millions of inhabitants; you can thus judge of the vast magnitude of the task before the Government in dealing with a scarcity spread over such an extent of country.

These same regions are always liable to suffer from deficient rainfall, and the low-lying coast districts not now affected, north of the Kistna, have also on former occasions suffered in an extreme degree. The Bengal drought of 1873 extended over the part of the great northern plain immediately contiguous to the Gangetic delta, and the western border of the delta. It was very exceptional, so far as concerns the portion of the area affected that lay north of the Ganges and in the delta. The portions of the great plain lying south of the Ganges along the northern border of the table-land, from the junction of the Sone with the Ganges as far as the Sutlej, have at intervals suffered from severe drought, proximity to the Himalaya being, as a rule, associated with more favourable rainfall.

The part of the table-land north of the Nerbudda, embracing Rajputana, has suffered very severely within recent times.

The first point to consider in relation to the matter before us will naturally be the ordinary distribution of the rain. This is shown on the map, on which have been drawn lines indicating approximately the average amount of rain over the whole country.

With some exceptions, to which special attention will be necessary, the chief fall of rain in India takes place during the period of the south-west monsoon, that is from May to October, the remainder of the year being comparatively dry. These summer rains prevail over the whole of the coasts of southern Asia which are under the influence of the south-west winds, namely, from Arabia to China; and they are felt in a more or less marked manner to great distances inland, being abundant over India generally, and along the whole of the southern slope of the Himalaya from the Brahmaputra to the Indus.

The rain at this season is very heavy along the coast of the Malay peninsula, through Burmah to Assam and the Himalaya beyond. On the north its progress is in a great degree arrested by the snowy mountains, so that it only just reaches in the slightest, manner the southern borders of Tibet. In the north-west quarter these rains gradually cease in eastern Afghanistan, the city of Kabul being beyond their influence, and generally they do not extend in an important degree beyond the outer ranges of hills that flank the lower course of the Indus.

On the west, or Malabar coast of the peninsula, the summer rainfall is extremely high. On the east, or Coromandel coast, the quantity at this season is, however, comparatively small, the principal fall there taking place in October and November, after the south-west monsoon has ceased. To this apparent anomaly I shall again revert.

Besides the principal season of summer rain, there is clearly developed in the north of India a distinct season of winter rain, which has its maximum nearly corresponding with the period of greatest cold, in January and February. This rain becomes less important as we move southward, being hardly noticeable in Bombay or Calcutta, or farther south; while in Afghanistan, where it is prolonged into the spring; it is the heaviest and most valuable of the whole year.

I need, perhaps, hardly remark that the source from which the summer rains of India are supplied is the continued stream of air highly charged with vapour, which is poured over the land from the Indian Ocean by the winds that blow during the season, known as the south-west monsoon. To apprehend correctly how these winds thus operate some explanation of their cause and mode of occurrence will be requisite.

It is a common but erroneous mode of stating the efficient cause of wind to refer it to difference of temperature of two contiguous areas; namely, that cold air being more dense and heavier, necessarily displaces hot air, which is lighter, the accompanying motion being wind. Indirectly, no doubt, the difference of temperature often operates in this manner; but the true cause of all movements of the atmosphere, which we describe as wind is wholly mechanical, being difference of pressure at neighboring places, and the facts cannot be properly dealt with if this is lost sight of.

The upper strata of the atmosphere press, under the action of gravity on those at the earth's surface, and the effect is indicated by help of the barometer, which measures the pressure of the air at any moment in inches of mercury; 30 inches of mercury over any surface being nearly equal in weight, or producing equal pressure, to that caused by the whole atmosphere over the same surface. The pressure of course diminishes as we ascend there being less and less air above us, and the barometer falls. Moreover, when the atmosphere is at rest, an equal superincumbent mass, accompanied by equal pressure, will be found at all places equally distant from the earth's surface; or, in other words, the planes of equal pressure will be truly horizontal. If, at any time, this is not the case, a result follows like that which takes place in a body of water, the surface of which is not horizontal; namely, the air flows from the higher towards the lower points, which movement continues till the planes of equal pressure are restored to horizontality.

Changes of temperature over any area by causing the expansion or contraction of the superincumbent body of air disturb the levels of the planes of equal pressure in the upper strata of the atmosphere, heat causing them to rise and to separate from one another, and cold bringing them down and closer together; by reason of which the air flows off on all sides, above, *from* a relatively heated area, and flows in on all sides above, *to* a relatively cooled one. The immediate consequence of such movements in the upper strata will be to reduce the pressure of the surface over the hot area from which air has been thrown off, and to increase it over the cold one towards which air has flowed in, and this will be accompanied by a wind at the surface, blowing *from* the cold area *to* the hot one. The movements in the upper and lower parts of the atmosphere are thus the converse one of the other, and tend to restore the equilibrium or horizontality of the planes of pressure disturbed by changes of temperature. But though this is the general law, which regulates such movement, the actual conditions under which the atmosphere is placed, and more particularly the influence of the rotation of the earth, which is imparted by friction to the superincumbent air, and the imperfect fluidity of the air which admits of local accumulations of energy under the action of sudden or irregular changes of temperature, are constantly causing disturbances of what might otherwise, have been comparatively simple movements, so that the resulting directions of the wind as observed are not much more readily connected with the differences of pressures than with the differences of temperatures which lead to them. In our own latitudes, for instance, the direction of the wind is commonly more nearly parallel to the lines of equal pressure at the surface than perpendicular to them, which would clearly be the case if the winds were chiefly regulated by direct differences of pressure.

It is no doubt well known to you that two well-marked seasons of periodical wind recur regularly year by year along the coasts of southern Asia and over the neighboring seas, known as the south-west monsoon of the summer months, and the north-east monsoon of the winter months. The high summer temperature of the great plateaus of Asia causes a dispersion of the air over them, which is marked by a very considerable fall of the barometric pressure over the whole continent, and is accompanied by a less great but perfectly distinct increase of pressure over the adjoining ocean regions south of the equator, which then have their winter season. Under the great difference of pressure thus established the air flows in powerfully towards the continent of Asia from the surrounding seas, the movements becoming well-marked in April with the rapid rise of temperature that then commences, and attaining their maximum in July, soon after the summer solstice. This is the south-west monsoon. When the temperature of Asia falls, which it does in Septemeber, as the sun goes rapidly south, the barometric pressure begins to be restored, and it becomes generally equalized over the southern parts of the continent in October, when this monsoon ceases.

The converse action takes place in the winter. The same causes which led to the great summer heat in Asia, namely, the great extent of dry and barren surface, produce excessive winter cold, which is accompanied by a well-marked increase of barometric pressure, again to be followed by the development of winds from the land towards the sea, which give rise to the north-east monsoon.

As is well known, the winds blowing northward from the equator bring air which has there acquired a high eastward velocity of rotation to places where the velocity of surface rotation is less, and therefore are felt as winds impressed with an eastward movement, and this being combined with their northward movement produces the south-west winds of the summer monsoon. The movements towards the equator in a similar manner lead to the north-east winds of the winter monsoon.

But though this supplies the general key to the great changes in the winds of southern Asia, the local succession of their directions depends on special local influences, which disguise the general law, and may even in a great measure counteract it.

The south-west monsoon begins in the Arabian sea with north-west and westerly winds, which draw round to south-west as the summer advances, and again fall back by west to north in the autumn and winter. In the Bay of Bengal the south-west monsoon blows as a southerly or south-easterly wind, being succeeded by north-easterly winds after October, which in turn give place as the winter months succeed, to winds from north and north-west.

Again, the winds during the south-west monsoon do not generally blow over the land in a south-westerly direction. The current of air flowing in from the sea is gradually diverted towards the area of least pressure, and at the same becomes dissipated and looses much of its original force as it passes from the area of greater pressure and lower temperature to that of reduced pressure and higher temperature. The irregularities of the land surface also operate powerfully in destroying the uniform character, which the winds maintain while passing over the uniform surface of the ocean. The great mountain ranges along the north of India act, moreover, as an effectual barrier to the movements of the wind in that direction. It is from these causes that we find the winds which blow over the Arabian sea from the south-west become southerly winds as they pass up the valley of the Indus; the winds of the Bay of Bengal which have already been diverted to the south, acquire an easterly tendency as they blow over the delta of the Ganges, and pass as south-east winds along the foot of the Himalaya towards the hotter regions in the north-west.

The body of air which is thus carried by the winds of the south-west monsoon from the ocean over India necessarily comes up highly charged with watery vapour; the conditions under which the vapour is released over the land in the form of rain, I next have to explain.

You are all familiar with the fact that water when heated passes into the condition of an invisible vapour, and that vapour when cooled is condensed again into water. Watery vapour, like air, being an elastic fluid, is liable to vary in density and weight, and the greater the density the larger will be the quantity of water held in suspension. But the quantity of water that can thus be kept in the state of vapour depends on the temperature, and therefore when the temperature falls below a certain point some of the vapour is restored to the state of water, and only that part remains in the gaseous form that the particular temperature permits. When air contains as much vapour as is consistent with its temperature it is, said to be saturatead with moisture; the proportion of actual vapour to the greatest possible quantity is termed the proportion of saturation.

The vapour formed by evaporation at the earth's surface, which is much less dense than ordinary air consistently tends to diffuse itself upward, and thus becomes disseminated in the atmosphere. At the same time, since the temperature of the air falls about 1$^{0}$ Fahr. for each 300 feet that we rise from the sea level, the operation of this law leads to such a reduction of the heat in the upper strata, as to cool the ascending vapour, and at length to condense all that is in excess of what the reduced temperature of each successive stratum admits of being retained in the gaseous form.

The supply of vapour passing upwards is therefore being constantly reduced as it ascends, and it thus happens that nine-tenths of the whole quantity of vapour in the entire atmosphere are to be found below an altitude of 20,000 feet. Where the evaporation at the surface is very copious, as it would be in a tropical sea with an air temperature for instance of 80$^{0}$ Fahr., if the vapour spread itself upwards according to the known laws which it obeys, we might commonly find the air near the surface to contain say four-fifths of the quantity required for saturation, and it would therefore be perfectly transparent, and no condensation would occur. But these conditions would at length lead to the quantity of vapour that reached an elevation of 4,000 feet being incompatible with its existence there in a gaseous form, because the air temperature would be only 68$^{0}$, while a temperature of about 70$^{0}$ would be necessary to admit of the vapour retaining its gaseous condition. Condensation would therefore have taken place below 4,000 feet, and a stratum of clouds would have formed, which according to circumstances might either be carried away and dispersed by winds, or discharge downwards the condensed water as rain. There is thus in the atmosphere at all times and places a more or less definite tendency towards the formation of cloud and the fall of rain by reason of the conflicting laws of the diffusion of vapour and of the distribution temperature in the atmosphere; and in strict truth our search might rather be for the causes that intercept or interfere with this action, than for those under which It continues to operate.

There are, however, circumstances which may so greatly add to the intensity of the condensation of vapour in the upper regions of the air as to call for special notice. Where a wind charged with vapour blows over an irregular surface, as from the sea across the face of a mountain, and the whole body of moving air is thus forced upwards, the expansion that follows is accompanied by a fall of temperature analogous to that which is observed in all the higher strata of the atmosphere; and as in this case the whole body of vapour is cooled down, instead of, as in the hypothesis I before made, only the portion that rose by diffusion to the higher level, the condensation is proportionally more copious and sudden and takes the form of heavy clouds that rest on the mountain, or of rain that falls upon its slopes.

The mixture of cold with hot currents of air highly charged with vapour is another possible cause of the condensation of rain; though I think a not frequent one in the countries to which our attention is now specially directed.

We are now in a position to consider somewhat more in detail the phenomena of the Indian periodical rainy seasons. The primary agents are the high summer temperature of the continent, and the consequent influx of a current of air from the south, blowing over a great expanse of tropical ocean, and consequently highly charged with vapour. If at first there appears something anomalous in the chief rainy season occurring at the hottest part of the year, whereas the condensation that causes rain is essentially a result of cold, we have to remember that the requisite cold is relative and not absolute, and that as the water suspended in the air is greater in proportion as the temperature is high, the quantity likely to be released by any disturbances capable of producing condensation will also be greater in a similar proportion. Moreover, the dispersion upwards, over the heated continent, of the air that flows in from the south, conduces to the increase of the quantity of vapour in the upper parts of the atmosphere, and to the maintenance of a state of unstable equilibrium in which moderate local disturbances of temperature are likely to cause condensation and produce rain.

The fall of temperature, which follows the commencement of the rainy season is first, no doubt, an effect of the fall of rain, which brings to the surface of the earth the water condensed in the much coolar higher strata; but the loss of heat is continued afterwards, in consequence of the sun's movement southward, and the disposition to condensation is maintained as long as the southerly winds blow. As the change from the southerly to the northerly monsoon is concurrent with the rapid fall of temperature which begins in northern India about the end of September, the close of the rainy season, like its commencement, is commonly marked by heavy falls of rain; the one caused by the first overthrow of the equilibrium of the vapour unstably suspended in the highly heated air at the solstice, and the other by the direct loss of heat which is experienced after the equinox.

The summer rains make their first appearance on the southern parts of the west coast in April, where the southerly winds have then become established. The region of greatest heat is now to be found at the northern part of the peninsula, the winds at Bombay not yet blowing from a point south of west. By the middle of June, as the area of greatest heat has advanced northward, and the winds have drawn well to the southward in the Indian seas, the rains begin to fall at Bombay, about which time also they become established at Calcutta.

The fall on the west coast is very abundant. The scarp of the table-land, or Western Ghâts, which forms an almost continuous obstacle in the path of the south-west winds, gives rise to great condensation, from causes already explained, the result being excessively heavy falls of rain along the face of the mountains exposed to the sea and all the country between them and the sea, on the more exposed parts of the former the quantity measured reaching more than 250 inches, and or the latter from 100 to 120 inches. To leeward of this line of elevation therein very rapidly diminishes, so that the quantity measured at Poona, 60 miles from the coast is only 25 inches. Manifestly, after any great quantity of rain has been once condensed from the south-west winds, there remains relatively little to supply the districts to leeward; and if, as is here the case, the obstructing range of heights is considerably more elevated than the surface of the table-land, probability of further condensation after the wind passes that range is much reduced. The ridge, however, in fact, is a good deal broken in its outline, and openings occur at intervals through which more or less vapour passes, and aid in supplying rain to the table-land.

The gradual extinction of the very heavy rainfall of the Malabar coast as we approach Cape Comorin, near which we have less than 30 inches, and the corresponding diminution at the northern extremity of the coast, are readily explained by the smaller amount of disturbance caused by the more broken character of the mountain ranges, and by the air being able to pass round the end of the barrier instead of being forced over it. The fact that during this season the rain only extends 40 or 50 miles from the coast out to sea plainly depends on a similar cause.

Following the coast westward, we find that though the south-west winds blow with great force and regularity over the coast, at the mouth of the Indus and in Sindh the fall of rain is very small and irregular. For here this wind meets with no such obstruction as that of the line of Western Ghâts. On the contrary, the air passes from a comparatively cool sea surface, over a very hot surface of low land, and any tendency to condensation that might be caused by the slight rise over the land, is more than compensated by the increased temperature.

The current, therefore, passes on as a southerly wind, carrying with it the uncondensed vapour over Sindh, to be at length precipitated on the outer ranges of the Himalaya in the Punjab, or on the mountains of eastern Afghanistan. There is no room to doubt, that had a range of mountains, such as the Western Ghâts, connected the high land of the Indian peninsula with that of Baluchistan, the whole of the Punjab must have been what the country that lies between it and the sea is, almost entirely deprived of rain.

The importance of the great valleys of the Taptee and Nerbudda, in connection with the rainfall of Central India, will now be apparent. Up these openings to south-west winds pour their vapour-bearing streams, and furnish to a large area in the heart of the peninsula the rain which is precipitated by the atmospheric disturbances that occur around the high lands in the centre of the table-land. This diversion of the vapour-bearing currents aids, no doubt, in producing the diminished fall of rain observed in the northern coast districts around Guzerat, as compared to those near Bombay and farther south, and serves to explain the increased fall of between 40 and 50 inches in Central India, as compared to that, between 20 and 30 inches, in the Deccan.

The south-west winds of the west coast do not properly speaking, extend across the peninsula. On the Madras coast, during the south-west monsoon, the land and sea breezes continue to be strongly marked, whereas on the west coast they disappear and the rainfall between May and September over the southern and eastern portion of the peninsula is relatively small.

On the opposite coast of the Bay of Bengal, and along the Malay peninsula, excessively heavy rain is the rule during this season, the quantity being from 100 to 200 inches. Here, too, a continuous line of mountain follows the coast facing the prevailing winds. On reaching the straits of Malacca, and passing under the lee of the island of Sumatra, the rain diminishes greatly; and at Singapore, at the point of the peninsula, the months between April and September are decidedly the least rainy half of the year, the largest fall taking place in the north-east monsoon, when the winds reach Singapore blowing directly from over the sea.

Phenomena exactly similar to those observed on the Western Ghâts occur on the mountains east of Bengal. At Chira Punji, on the Khasiya hills, which rise abruptly to about 4,000 or 5,000 feet over the delta of the Ganges, the rainfall is believed to exceed that known at any other place on the earth, more than 600 inches being a not unusual annual amount.

The difference between Bengal, with a rainfall of from 60 to 70 inches, and Sindh, with hardly any, is very remarkable. It is sufficiently explained by the distribution of the high land that is contiguous to the former, and, indeed, almost surrounds it. The great mountains on the north communicate with the ranges on the east which separate Bengal from the upper parts of Burmah, and form a serious obstacle to atmospheric movements in that direction. These ranges are all well clothed with forest, and the temperature of the whole areas over which they extend must be considerably lower than that of the country to the west of them. This is accompanied by a higher barometrical pressure, which leads to the development of easterly winds during the summer months blowing from Eastern Bengal to the far hotter regions of north-western India, where the barometric pressure is least. From these causes, the rains begin much earlier in Assam and its neighbourhood than in any other parts of India, *viz.*, in April, soon after the southerly winds are established at the head of the Bay of Bengal; and a tendency towards such early rains is discernible in all the Bengal registers. Thus the conditions are very different from those of Sindh, the free onward progress of the winds being arrested in Bengal by the current set up towards the north-west and the influx of relatively cool air from the east preventing any tendency to a rise of temperature in the air coming up from the Bay of Bengal as it passed over the land, such as would stand in the way of local condensation.

The rainy season rapidly develops itself from Bengal towards the north-west, the fall gradually decreasing in amount as the rain-bearing winds pass on; a fact readily explained by the consideration, that as the condensation of the vapour goes on, less remains to supply the more distant localities.

Concurrently with the reduction of the rainfall in passing from east to west in northern India, we find an increase in the quantity as we approach the Himalaya, and a diminution as we recede from the range, the gradation being distinctly marked, from a distance of 150 or 200 miles to the foot of the mountains. On the outer slopes of the Himalaya the fall is very greatly increased, but it rapidly diminishes again in amount as we penetrate among the mountains.

These results are brought about in a manner that deserves particular attention. At all times of the year winds blow up the valleys of the Himalayas towards the highest parts of the chain, and down them at night; the day winds having their greatest force at the high passes into Tibet, and the night winds at the debouches of the great rivers into the plains. Such winds are well known to be characteristic of all mountain ranges. They are no doubt due to the disturbance of the planes of atmospheric equilibrium, caused by the alterations of temperature in the air over the mountains and low lands. A column of air over the low land, measured from any horizontal plane of equilibrium, being longer, will expand more and contract less. As the day advances, and the heat increases, the planes of equal pressure will all rise over the low land, and the air will flow towards the axis of the elevation; as the night comes on, and the temperature falls, the greater contraction of the longer columns over the low land will bend the planes of equal pressure from the axis of elevation outwards, and the air will move in that direction.

Thus a system of aspiration is established over the mountains, by which the vapour-charged air that comes up from the sea is drawn up from the plains along the valleys and over the outer ranges, and is so brought under the operation of that sort of action which we have already seen to be so efficacious in producing condensation. These movements serve also to explain what seems peculiar in the gradation of the rainfall within and without the mountains. It is, I think, also to the same cause that we may trace the circumstance, that the first heavy falls of rain in upper India take place on the mountains, and that the disturbances are thence developed and extended which lead to a general fall over the plains.

In Northern India the summer rains usually cease before the end of September; in Bengal and along the Arracan coast they are prolonged into October. In western and central India also a little rain falls in October. Over all this area northerly winds are commonly established in October, and the rain that falls at this time must be regarded as the residual condensation under the increasing cold of autumn of the vapour previously brought up by the southerly winds.

With the fall of temperature in September, the region of least pressure is rapidly transferred to the south, and the northerly winds begin first in the north and gradually extend southward; though the southerly winds still continue to blow at the end of the peninsula till November. These changes lead to the establishment of a current of air from the Bay of Bengal, blowing as a north-easterly wind towards the Madras coast, along which there is, in consequence, set up an autumn season of heavy rain lasting from October to December, quite analogous in its efficient causes to the summer rainy season of the western coast. This rain usually extends from about the great bend in the east to Ceylon, though its influence is at times felt as far north as Cuttack; and it is of essential importance to all the eastern border of southern India, which, as was before explained, receives but a scanty supply during the south-west monsoon.

It may here be noticed that the cyclones that originate in the Bay of Bengal in October and November appear to be results of atmospheric movements and condensation developed over an area of low pressure that remains in the bay, after a high pressure area has begun to form rapidly over Eastern Bengal, with the fall of temperature accompanying the close of the year; and that the tendency to the formation of cyclonic movements is to be seen in the north-easterly winds that usually prevail in the north and west of the bay, while south-westerly winds are still blowing in the southern and eastern parts. The cyclones of May and June appear to originate further south, and to depend on some manner still imperfectly explained on the arrival of the winds highly charged with vapour, which begin to blow strongly at that season.

The map which is before you resumes the facts into which I have been entering in some detail. It shows that the part of India east of the 80th meridian has an average yearly rainfall for the most part exceeding 40 inches, and that, excepting the country between the Western Ghâts and the sea, the portion west of that meridian has a smaller rainfall. Further, we see that the quantity is extremely small all over Sindh, and that the tract in which the fall is less than 30 inches includes all the Punjab excepting the mountain districts, a considerable part of the North-Western Provinces extending to half-way between Agra and Allahabad, a large part of Rajpootana and Kattywar. Again, we observe a large area in the peninsula, occupying nearly the whole of the Deccan and Mysore, on which also the rainfall is less than 30 inches.

Of the area in which the rainfall is below 15 or 20 inches, it may be said in general terms that agriculture is not here possible otherwise than with artificial irrigation; and thus it has happened that the population of the districts where the rain is of all others least abundant, have made themselves in a very great degree independent of the local rainfall. On the other hand, it may also be said that where the average rainfall exceeds 40 or 50 inches, the occurrence of such drought as will cause serious scarcity is rare, though when it does occur it may be very severe. It was in a portion of this area that the Bengal famine of 1873 took place, and also that of Orissa in 1866.

The region, the average rainfall of which is between 25 and 35 inches, is probably that which suffers most from droughts. Here, although on the average the supply the rain is sufficient to support an agricultural population, the fluctuations, which reduce the fall below what is essential are so frequent, so to lead to repeated seasons of scarcity of greater or less severity. The north-western part of the North-West Provinces, the north-western part of Rajputana, and the Deccan, with a small part of the Madras districts at the end of the peninsula, fall within this category. The present scarcity affects the whole of the dry region of the peninsula. The drought of 1837-38 was extremely severe in the North-West Provinces as also was that of 1860. In Rajputana a very severe scarcity, followed by great destruction of life, occurred in 1868.

For reasons already suggested, the results of drought have a tendency to be more fatal where the average rainfall is abundant, than where it is scanty. In the latter case, the population is less likely to be dense, and better able by its habits to go in search of subsistence elsewhere, and by its sparseness to succeed in procuring it. A more dense population will be less easily provided for; and in proportion as experience of drought is small, skill in devising means of resisting its effects will be small also, when once present resources are exhausted. Drought also will be more or less fatal, according as it follows a season of bad or good rainfall; and it has commonly happened that severe famines have been caused by a severe drought following one or two years of indifferent rain. The stocks of food become exhausted, and the cattle and the population enfeebles, and thus less able to resist the pressure put on them.

In a country where there is no pasture like India, the feeding of the agricultural cattle is always a difficulty, and their condition is commonly extremely poor, viewed in relation to the standard of temperate countries. The effect of drought in the destruction of the cattle is one of its surest and most pernicious evil consequences.

It will be apparent that the importance of the fall of rain in India, for general purposes of agriculture, will be determined by the requirements of the principal crops, and particularly on those crops on which the food supply of the people depends.

The people of India subsist for the most part on vegetable food, cereal grains, pulses and vegetables, with milk and butter. Other animal food, excepting on the coasts where fish is procurable, is comparatively little eaten, even among the mussulmans, who form about one-tenth of the population. The grain crops, therefore, are of usually great importance. The grains most commonly consumed in three-fourths of India are millets, called in the Hindee dialects, jowar and bajra. Rice is the ordinary food of the people of those regions only where the conditions of climate are suitable for the abundant production of this grain. This would include Bengal, the coast and southern districts of Madras, and the western districts of Bombay, as well as British Burmah. Contrary to what is commonly thought to be the case, the rice-eating population of India is altogether in the minority.

These food-grains, and some others which I need not mention specially, are plants suited to tropical conditions of climate, and they are all raised in the summer or hot half of the year, the crop of which season is known in most parts of India as the khureef. There is, however, a second crop, more particularly characteristic of the parts of India, which have the coldest winter, which is on the ground during the winter months, and is called rubbee.

The kharif is usually sown as soon as the rainfall admits of the ploughing of the land, and it is reaped in September or October. The rice crop varies somewhat in its time of sowing and of ripening according to locality and variety. The chief harvest in Bengal is in December; on the Madras coast, farther south, the later rains lead to a still later harvest, where there is but one; but the more tropical climate of the south admits an almost indefinite succession of crops wherever an artificial water-supply is available to raise them.

It need perhaps hardly be said that most varieties of rice require a large quantity of water to raise them; and aid in some shape or other is given by artificial means in most parts of India to the natural rain-supply, to ensure the safety of this crop. Particularly in the south of India, multitudes of reservoirs have been constructed with this object, in which as large a supply of rain-water is collected as is practicable, to supplement the direct fall. Larger irrigation works have been carried out by the British Government, to divert, with a similar object, the waters of most of the rivers that discharge themselves on the east coast.

The grains, called jowar and bajra, are commonly sown on the higher lands, and left to depend entirely on the natural rainfall. Their requirements in the way of water are very much less than those of rice, and it is very unusual to supply them with artificial irrigation.

The rabi crop is usually sown in October, and ripens in March or April. In the north of India it consists chiefly of wheat and barley, which grains, however, hardly enter into the ordinary food of the agricultural population, being reserved for the better-to-do classes and town population. Certain pulses that are largely used for food also are raised at this season. Excepting on the high lands of Central India and the Deccan, wheat does not thrive much south of the tropic; and in the southern parts of the peninsula the reduction of temperature in the winter months is hardly sufficient to develop any distinctly temperate agriculture, such as forms a very marked feature of northern India.

Great irrigation works exist also in several provinces of northern India. These probably afford more aid to the rabi than to the kharif harvest; and their chief importance in connection with the food supply of the country is without doubt due to the security which they give to the wheat and barley harvests, though their general ability in adding to agricultural produce of all descriptions is very great.

In considering the more special requirements of agriculture in the matter of rain, and the precise manner in which a partial failure is likely to be mischievous or otherwise, the critical time have to be distinguished. First, as the great power of the tropical sun utterly dries up the soil in the hot months that precede the rainy season, the first showers are almost essential to admit of the final ploughing, and the sowing may thus be unduly late in unfavorable seasons. Where artificial irrigation is available, this delay is avoided. Next, the thorough saturation of the soil, and its maintenance in a sufficient state of moisture, are requisite for the germination of the seed, and this is always one of the most critical periods for every crop. In many cases thoroughly favourable rain at this stage will secure a return of some sort, even in an otherwise very bad season; and a bad commencement may often be beyond remedy, however good the subsequent falls may turn out. The next critical stage is that of flowering, when a great access of rain may be almost as fatal as a want of it, by causing the destruction of the parts of the flower essential for the development of the grain. The period immediately follows in which the grain is fertilized and takes its ultimate form, during which the supply of moisture to the plant is not less essential than in the first stage of its life, and any serous failure of rain is fatal to the harvest. Thus, even though the average fall in any year may be fully enough to carry on the ordinary processes of growth, the failure of rain even for a few days at one of the critical periods may lead to a complete loss. The drought of 1873 in northern Bengal arose from the failure of the later rain alone. The troubles of the present time seem to be due to a general failure, both of the south-west monsoon rains on the west coast, and of those of the succeeding north-east monsoon on the east coast; a combination of evil fortune which, it will be seen, necessarily falls with the greatest weight upon the southern districts of Madras.

In attempting to give any general account of the phenomena of Indian rainfall, it has of course been necessary for me to deal with average quantities. But the departures from these averages in separate years are very great; and it is from the fluctuations that thus occur, that the areas of average small and large rainfall may be transformed, without any considerable derangement of the general sequence of phenomena that I have described, into areas of abundance or absolute drought. Thus the well-marked loops that are formed by lines of equal rainfall having their points directed to the eastward, and following generally the line of the Jumna and Ganges from the Punjab to Bengal, indicate the probability, which is supported by actual experience, of areas of drought being formed along this axial line. I apprehend that the Bengal drought of 1873, which affected, though with less intensity, the adjacent districts of the north-west provinces along the Ganges, may be regarded as due to the local exaggeration of the general causes that lead to the peculiar inflexion of the lines of rainfall to which I have alluded.

The great extent of the fluctuations of the rainfall will be shown by the following figures. The Madras average for sixty-four years is 48.5 inches, the greatest excess over the average being 39.9 inches, and the greatest defect below it 30.1 inches. AT Calcutta, for forty-seven years, the average is 65.8 inches, with a maximum excess of

27.5 inches, and a defect of 22.2 inches. At Bombay, for fifty-two years the average between May and October being 76.9 inches, the maximum excess was 42.0 inches, and the defect 41.8 inches. At the three places, the average deviation of a single year from the mean of all is found to be, for Madras 12.4 inches, for Calcutta 9.0 inches, and for Bombay 13.4 inches.

No precise physical connection has hitherto been established between the local rainfall at any place in India, and the temperature or pressure of the surrounding area; and no certain step had yet been made, so far as I know, towards foretelling the character of the seasons. In these respects, however, our knowledge is not less as regards India, than other centuries.

An opinion has, indeed, been quite recently published by Dr. Hunter, to the effect that the rainfall registers at Madras, which extend over sixty-four years, supply evidence of a connection between the quantity of rain and the sun-spot cycles of eleven years or thereabouts. This idea is not novel, having been advanced some years ago by Mr. Meldrum and others, on the alleged basis of facts collected from many different parts of the globe.

So far as Dr. Hunter's views are concerned, I have no hesitation in stating my own conviction, that the facts on which he relies do not support his conclusions. He had inferred, from what must he held to be altogether insufficient numerical data that sure indications of periodicity exist. He arrives, by an arithmetical process at certain figures, which he regards as the probable mean amount of rainfall in the successive years of the eleven-year cycle, and finding a maximum and minimum among them, he infers that this is a proof of a true periodical variation. But such a result alone proves nothing. To test its value it is necessary to compare the calculated quantities of rain for the several years with the quantities actually observed, and then to consider whether the differences are of a character to justify the belief that the calculated quantities afford a reliable approximation to the truth, and what sort of approximation. Dr. Hunter does not seem to have been aware of the necessity for exercising this caution, though the extreme variation of the rainfall from year to year, to which reference has already been made, would appear to have been likely to suggest it. The only conclusion that seems possible, from such an examination of the figures as I have described, is the negative one, that they cannot be accepted as supplying any evidence in support of the views put forward by Dr. Hunter.

Though this argument is mainly negative and goes rather to discredit the alleged proof of Dr. Hunter's conclusion, than the conclusion itself, yet much doubt appears to me to be thrown on the probability of any such direct connection between the rainfall at Madras and the sun-spot period has been spoken off, by a compression of the Madras observations with those made during the same periods at Calcutta and Bombay. It is extremely difficult to conceive, that if such a connection existed at Madras, it should not be apparent at the other two places; yet the same treatment applied to the Calcutta and Bombay figures as that adopted for Madras shows no correspondence in the results. Neither can any persistent relation be seen to exist between the quantities of rainfall at the three places. There is an occasional likeness at one time between one pair, at another between a second, and again between the third, but no uniformity. And this is what might have been expected, from what we know of the general manner in which precipitations of rain take place, and the oscillations of wet and dry weather occur.*

On the whole, our knowledge of the immediate physical causes of rainfall is very rudimentary; and though there be no present appearance of success, in solving the intricate problems that an inquiry into those causes must involve, it can only be by help of a careful examination in detail of all the facts that it can become possible at all. Such a collection of facts as at length been seriously commenced; but what I have already said will indicate the great complexity of the subject, and the many difficulties that will have to be encountered in grasping it in a satisfactory way.

Such being the general position of India in respect to the rainfall necessary for its agriculture and its food supply, and man having no possible means of exercising any control over the atmospheric changes which are effective in adding to or reducing the quantity of rain, and having no present power of foreseeing the changes, it may be asked whether we therefore have to hope of escaping from the terrible consequences of drought. In my opinion there can be no doubt of the possibility of combating successfully its worst results by the progress of civilization; by which the accumulated knowledge and material resources of community are applied in the most effectual way to meet its requirements. The result at, which we aim in India can be brought about by this, and this alone; as this, and this alone, has been able to bring it about in other countries. But as such progress is necessarily slow, we must be content for the present to pass through a condition of periodical suffering of an acute kind, during which the bitter lessons of experience will continue to urge improvement; and thereby intelligence will be stimulated, and ways of escape from these evils will be gradually perfected. These ways of escape are indeed already sufficiently evident, and so far as they have been hitherto applied, have been found to be thoroughly efficacious. They are the provision of artificial irrigation, and of improved means of transport; the first, to give a certain supply of water for the purposes of agriculture, increasing production generally, and supplementing the rainfall so as to prevent calamitous drought and the second to provide facilities for the economic distribution of food and for the operations of commerce by which wealth is increased. Simple as these remedies may appear, the material difficulties in the way of their being furnished to the extent necessary to remove the evils now under consideration, cannot at present be surmounted. They require the application of capital, that is to say, the accumulated results of labour, which, to meet the requirements of the present case, may possibly still have to be prolonged over very many years. For India must perforce supply her own needs from her own material resources. Nowhere, not at any time, has the benevolence of others succeeded in removing the burden imposed on every community of providing for its own existence under pain of extinction. Even if it were possible that external aid could be given on an adequate scale to supply the requisite material appliances, it is certain that the moral qualities would not have been developed, by which alone those appliances could be successfully made use of—self-reliance, and, what this quality makes possible, self-sacrifice.

And if the people of India have on the one hand specially heavy burdens to bear in resisting these and other destructive forces of nature arising from their climate, which will certainly tax their strength to the utmost, yet on the other they find ready to their hands unusual aid in the great reproductive powers of their soil, also due the same cause. Neither can we estimate as of small value to them, the wealth, the knowledge, and the practical skill in all the arts of life, possessed by their British rulers, and so largely employed to their advantage. But that the task will in any case be a very heavy and tedious one to be got through, no one can doubt, who has passed a large part of his life, as I have done, in seeking for the means of extending those essential material allies in the battle of Indian life—irrigation works and railways.

True humanity assuredly demands of all Englishmen their cooperation in what will really conduce to the mitigation of the calamities caused by Indian droughts. But it is certain that there is only one possible mode of escape, namely through *labour*. The fruits of industry in years of plenty must be made to meet the want in years of scarcity; and relief is to be obtained by means of the combined and continued exertions of the localities immediately concerned, and no longer by relying on assistance to be supplied from without. There is no escape from the conclusion that the conditions of their existence impose on the people of India severe suffering and periodic partial destruction, if they submit to these conditions unresisting; severe toil, and persistent intelligent effort, if they are to escape their extreme consequences. The Government and the people must everywhere have this practically enforced upon them, and until it is done the movement will not have fairly set in the right direction. Experience in India leads to exactly the same conclusions as those arrived at elsewhere, that a system of public relief in time of distress not guarded by the sense of specific local financial responsibility, is a source of grievous abuse, misery and demoralization and it is my earnest hope that no temporary impulse of sympathy with present suffering, so selfish (if I may be allowed so to apply the term), no selfish effort to escape at any cost the pain of witnessing it, may be permitted to stand in the way of that real benevolence which is founded on sound principles drawn by dispassionate intelligence from the lessons of experience, principles which I am glad to believe have been adopted by the highest authorities concerned in the government of India.

* See, for further development of the Author's views, his paper in the Proceedings of the Royal Society, pp. 249-261, May 1877.

# *Appendix II*

# Famine

## I. The Cause of Famine

### Famines periodic

From the days of the Buddhist pilgrims from China to the latest Moral and Material Progress Report, famine lies broad written across the pages of Indian history. The accounts of early famines are indeed more meagre. In the chronicles of courts, which cared little for the people, social calamities found but scant record. A few lurid descriptions have come down to us—man feeding on man and even slaying him for food, the violation of all natural ties,[1] conspicuous acts of unavailing charity, depopulation, and the loss of revenue; but of famine history in its wider range there is no trace. We only know that famines were very frequent under Native rule, and frightful when they came.[2] We know also that they have been frequent since the British came to India.

### Dependence of India on agriculture

This frequency of famine is easily explained. Famine is a disease of all agricultural countries. India is, and always has been, mainly agricultural, and agricultural under conditions peculiarly exposed to famine. The soil is parceled out in minute farms. The farmers have no capital and depend on unorganized local credit, which shrinks when harvests fail. Off the land, but dependent on it, are millions of agricultural labourers, the vast majority of whom have only casual employment and are thrown out of work when harvest fail. Thus, the masses of the Indian people depend upon the harvests, and these depend upon a periodic, but by no means regular, rainfall.

**The two monsoons**

The two rain-bearing currents are (1) the south-west monsoon, commonly called *the* monsoon or *the* rains, and (2) the so-called north-east monsoon, the period of which is marked in North-Western India by what are commonly called 'the winter rains'. The agricultural year commences with the former, which is the more important of the two.

**South-west monsoon and the autumn harvest**

For a month or two before the rains the land has rest over the greater part of India. The heat is intense, the soil is baked, ploughing is impossible, and the people sit in their villages literally gasping for rain. The monsoon bursts in June, and dies away at the end of September or beginning of October. After the first heavy shower, ploughing begins, and the autumn harvest (*kharif*), which provides the year's food for the poorer classes, viz. millets and rice, is sown. It occupies the ground for from two to four months, during which period the distribution of the rainfall is even more important agriculturally than its amount. A long break in the rains and hot dry winds cause serious loss; excessive rain produces floods; and continuous rain interrupts work in the fields. On fine days the people are very busy: the autumn harvest requires two or three weedings, and the land reserved for the spring harvest is ploughed many times. Weeding, ploughing, and harvesting employ millions of labourers.

**North-east monsoon and the spring harvest**

In October or November, the spring harvest (*rabi*) is sown, Wheat, barley, pulses, and the more valuable non-food crops[3] are grown in the north; the larger millets predominate in the south of India. The so-called north-east monsoon breaks on the east coast in November or December,[4] while the winter rains fall in the north from Christmas on to February. The spring are less precarious than the autumn crops. But heavy or prolonged rain, accompanied by east winds, causes rust in the wheat and barley; and premature hot west winds shrivel up the swelling grain. Harvesting begins in March and April, and again employs millions of labourers. Intermediate crops, such as sugar-cane and the late cotton, also employ large numbers.

### Cause of famine

Thus, any failure of the rains involves some failure of crops, thereby reducing the supply of food and stopping the demand for labour. But not every failure of the rains causes famine. The people are not generally dependent on the out-turn of a single harvest. The railways have put the whole food-supply of the country into circulation, and what is lost in one part of the country is made good from another. The cultivators have some resources and credit. The spring harvest may be good although the autumn harvest has failed. The agricultural labourers are safe so long as there is a demand for labour, and there are various degrees of crop failure of either harvest will cause distress, especially to the agricultural labourers; but it depends on several conditions, such as the character of preceding harvests, and the degree in which agricultural operations are affected, whether the distress will amount to famine.

## II. The Famine Problem, and Modern Relief

### Removal of former checks on population

Formerly war, rapine, and misrule were direct causes of famine. These have disappeared and in the process a new problem has arisen. Peace has multiplied the people. The custom of the country favours early marriage, while the general security has removed the old checks on population. And as those who have least hope in the world usually bring most children into it, the increase of population has been great among the poorer cultivators and the agricultural labourers. The modern outlets, emigration and industrial development, afford as yet little relief. Large tracts in India still await population, but the inhabitants of congested districts will not move to them, partly from habit, but largely from regard to caste and language. Industries are growing up, but as yet they draw only small numbers off the land, occupation being still prescribed by inheritance and tradition. Pressure, therefore, increases where it is already greatest. Holdings already small are subdivided, or sublet at competition rents, while the supply of agricultural labour outruns the demand for it, and so keeps agricultural wages low.

## Statement of the famine Problem

This is the great famine problem. It is not in the power of man to prevent drought in India, or, so long as the country is mainly agricultural, to prevent drought from causing famine: all he can do is to restrict and mitigate the resultant suffering. Modern famine policy is thus a struggle against nature. As such it has two objects, the one remedial, the other protective. It seeks to relieve distress when droughts come; and it seeks in many ways to fortify the people against drought.[5]

## Modern Relief Policy

Under Native rule there was little thought for, and no effective means of, remedial action. Occasionally a large relief work was started and spasmodic attempts were made to send food to famine-stricken areas. But primitive transport could not enter fodderless and roadless country, and so broke down where most required. The people wandered and died in thousands, the country was desolated and the revenue was not collected. Conditions scarcely changed in the early days of the East India Company, but by degrees a scheme of systematic relief grew up. The modern view of the responsibility of the state was not reached, however, until India had passed under the Crown. In 1868 the famous order was issued[6] that 'every District officer would be held personally responsible that no deaths occurred from starvation which could have been avoided by any exertion or arrangement on his part or that of his subordinates'. And, after some experience of the demoralizing influence of indiscriminate state charity, relief policy assumed its final shape in the declaration made by the Secretary of State in 1877:—

'The Object of saving life is undoubtedly paramount to all other considerations. But it is essential that in pursuing this end you officers should sedulously guard against the danger of inducing the population to rely upon Government aid rather than upon their own industry and thrift. In the interests of the distressed population itself, as well as of the tax-payers generally, you are bound to adopt precautions against indolence or imposition, similar, so far as the circumstances of India will permit, to those with which in this country it has always been found necessary to protect the distribution of public relief from abuse'.

This policy has been accepted by three Famine Commissions—in 1880, 1898, and 1901. It resolves relief administration into the anxious problem of how to hit a happy mean, how to steer between the rock of distress and the whirlpool of demoralization.

**Practical difficulties**

The carrying out of this policy is beset with many and great practical difficulties. India has no poor law. In ordinary times private charity supports the poor; in times of famine this charity dries up, and the recipients of it are thrown upon the state together with large numbers of the agricultural population. In the nineteenth century the largest area simultaneously affected by drought was 475,000 square miles (in 1900), and the largest population so affected was 69,500,000 (in 1897); the largest number relieved at any one time was 6,500,000. Over such large areas, and for such large numbers, the Indian Government may in any year be called to improvise a system of relief without disturbing ordinary public business. Nor do the difficulties end with the numbers. The peoples of India are infinitely various in habits, creed, custom, caste, and language. The language of one part of a Province may not be understood in another part of it. Thousands would die sooner than resort to relief camps or touch food, which they thought was unclean, either in itself or by reason of the agency employed in its preparation. One caste will not feed with another. The shy folk of the hills will not work with the people of the plains. Skilled weavers will not go to ordinary relief works for fear of losing their delicacy of touch. And for dealing with these sensitive, suspicious masses, the Government has to organize and control vast temporary establishments, which are generally untrained and have a low standard of intelligence and integrity. The difficulties would be insuperable if the people were less orderly, or less amenable to discipline. But discipline can be enforced, and corruption and demoralization can be kept down, only if relief is closely supervised by European officers, and it is very hard to find the men.

**A modern plan of campaign**

These difficulties have, however, in great measure been overcome. Under the stern but efficient teaching of experience, an elaborate system of relief has now been worked out. Philanthropists may still mourn that complete success has not been attained; those who are acquainted with Indian conditions will perhaps rather marvel at the progress already made. It may fairly be said that, in spite of inevitable defeats, a modern Indian famine campaign is one of the most remarkable achievements in history of scientific administration.

**Standing preparations**

Standing preparations are made on a large scale. in ordinary times. The Government is kept informed daily of meteorological conditions, weekly of crops and prices, and monthly of birth and death rates. Programmes of suitable relief works are revised annually in every District. The country is mapped out into relief-circles of convenient size. Reserves of tools and plant are stocked, and lists of persons suitable on emergency for famine establishments are annually drawn up. In short, every effort is made so to arrange matters in advance that a telegram from head-quarters can mobilize relief.

**Danger signals**

When the rain fail preliminary inquiries are started; a forecast of the probable crop failure is made; and a careful lookout is kept for the regular danger signals of approaching distress. Prices begin to rise and the people become uneasy. Aimless wandering in search of work takes the place of the seasonal movement of labour, which attends a normal harvest. Private charity in the villages contracts, and the habitual paupers who depend upon it drift to the towns. Petty crimes against property increase; credit becomes more difficult; and grain-dealers make large purchases. During this period of tension the local officers look to their programmes of relief and prepare for action.

**Preliminary action**

As the uneasiness is intensified, the Government makes the necessary financial arrangements and declares it general policy. At this stage great importance attaches to 'moral strategy'. In an Eastern country hope turns quickly to despair, and despair shades off insensibly into a dull resignation. According, meetings are held; policy is explained; non-official gentlemen are encouraged to be active, especially in undertaking local improvements, which will employ labour; committees are appointed to stimulate and organize private charity; village inspection begins, and preliminary lists of helpless persons who may require gratuitous relief are made. All this gives confidence to the people, who are further encouraged by liberal advances of money for wells and work in the field, and by detailed inquiries as to crop failure, which are undertaken at this stage with a view to suspension of revenue. If the number of paupers in the town is great, poorhouses[7] are opened.

**The period of test**

Test works[8] are also started. This is an anxious stage. If the tests are too lenient the state may be led on the unnecessary expenditure; if they are too strict the situation may not be grasped. The condition of those who seek employment on the test works is closely watched, and a look-out is kept by village inspection on the condition of those who stay in their villages. At this, as at every stage, the death-rates are scrutinized.

**The period of general relief**

When the test works, or village inspection, disclose real distress, relief works are opened, the village inspecting staff is increased, the lists of persons entitled to gratuitous relief are revised, and the distribution of gratuitous relief begins. By the end of December in a famine year the numbers on relief are as a rule large. The gathering of an intermediate crop like sugar-cane may reduce them slightly, but generally they continue to rise till the following March. The great spring festival, the Holi, the reaping the of the *mahuâ*, or of the mango, crops usually draw off many relief workers for a time: these mostly return, however, by the end of April. In May distress reaches its maximum, and cholera generally breaks out.

**Cholcra**

An outbreak of cholera is the supreme test of organization. In the Pânch Mahâls District of Gujarât, in 1900, cholera broke out suddenly with extraordinary virulence. In three days the dead numbered thousands and the people fled panic-stricken all over the country, spreading the disease. The native staff and camp attendants deserted in large numbers, and the European officers were left to collect with their own hands and burn some hundreds of corpses. Famine history is lit up by acts of self-sacrifice, and devotion even to death, but it records no nobler work than that performed by the European officers on this occasion.

The power of efficient organization was displayed in the management of a cholera outbreak in Bundelkhand in 1897. The Lieutenant-Governor was prepared, and the relieving staff and the people had been schooled by two years' experience of famine. The country had been divided in advance into circles in which small works were mapped out. On the first outbreak of cholera the people on the large relief works were split up into parties of about 500, and marched with full staff and equipment to the circles in which their villages were. Here they found small works ready for them; the wells had been disinfected; work was commenced at once; there was no panic; and the pestilence was stayed.

**Rains policy; the beginning of the end**

Policy changes somewhat with the advent of the rains. Relief works are generally closed, and there is an extension of local gratuitous relief. In the interests of the country at large, and of the people themselves, it is important that ordinary agricultural conditions should be restored with the least delay, and that as large an area as possible should be sown. For this purpose, the people are moved from the large works to small works near their villages at the end of May, and liberal advances are made to agriculturists for the purchase of plough cattle and seed. When the rains break relief-workers return to their fields in crowds; if any stay on the works they are encouraged to return to their villages as soon as the demand for labor springs up. A few relief works are kept open, in case of need, and every one who cannot work and requires relief receives it gratuitously. The state supports, where necessary, the weakly members of a family, and the able-bodied are able to support themselves.

**Closure of relief**

When the earliest of the principal autumn crops is ripe, the few remaining relief works are closed gradually, and gratuitous relief is discontinued, the recipients being given a valedictory dole, and by the middle of October famine is ordinarily at an end. Quinine is distributed in large quantities during September and October, in anticipation of fever, which generally prevails in the autumn.

### Charitable relief funds

The strictness of Government relief, which must inevitably be confined to the provision of necessaries, is softened and supplemented by private relief funds, to which it may be said that almost the whole world subscribes. These subscriptions are devoted to four principal objects, of which the last absorbs about two-thirds of the whole: (1) providing small comforts of food or clothing to the aged, infirm, sick, children, and others in need of them; (2) helping orphans; (3) relieving the respectable poor in ways acceptable to them; and (4) giving a fresh start in life to those who have lost everything in the struggle. Thousands of desolate homes have been restored by this splendid charity.

### The Indian people's famine trust

In 1900 the Mahârâjâ of Jaipur presented 16 lakhs of Government securities to be held in trust for the relief of the needy in times of famine. This trust has now (1905) 30 lakhs in Government securities, the greater part of which has been contributed by the founder and his family. It is vested in a body of trustees selected from all parts of India, and the income will be devoted, in times of famine, to objects similar to those of the charitable relief fund.

### Improved communications, and greater knowledge, the main Causes of efficiency in famine relief

The greatest administrative achievement of the last twenty years has been the extension of communications. Railways have revolutionized relief. The final horror of famine, an absolute dearth of food, is now unknown. Private trade pours in food wherever it is required.[9] The telegraph has made control efficient; and as the administration has been freed from the primary necessity of finding food, it has been able to grapple successfully with other difficulties, supported, as it now is, by a system of agricultural intelligence, and increased knowledge of the social conditions of India.[10]

### Present elasticity in the relief system

Under these influences the relief system has become increasingly elastic. Relief works are organized with due regard to the feelings of the people. Those who cannot work are relieved, as a rule, in their villages, and special consideration is shown to the respectable poor. The habitual beggars, the waifs and strays of society, are sheltered, clothed, and fed in poorhouses. Children are produced from the rapacity of their parents by being fed in kitchens, a precaution proved by sad experience to be necessary, and milk is given to infants whose mothers cannot nurse them. Weakly persons are specially treated. Deserted children are separately cared for, and returned to their relatives or co-religionists, if they will take them, at the close of the famine. An elaborate scheme for making relief acceptable to forest and hill tribes has been worked out; and weavers and artisans, who formerly suffered on ordinary relief works, are now, as far as possible, relieved in their own trades. Non-official aid and advice are enlisted on the side of Government. In a word, no effort is spared to prevent the loosening of social and moral ties, which is the melancholy accompaniment of an economic cataclysm like famine.

In the following section a sketch will be given of the efforts and experience, the failures and the successes, which have gradually evolved this result.

## III. History of Chief Famines, and of Famine Relief

### Famine during the administration of the East India Company

Sleeman in his *Rambles and Recollections* complains of the ignorance which prevailed in India in regard to the economic aspects of famine; and the fact that Turgot anticipated, in the Limousin famine of 1770, the general principles finally asserted by the Indian Famine Commission of 1880 leads colour to his compliant. But the East India Company really developed a famine policy, although their means of giving effect to it were small. In the Bengal famine of 1770 relief was administered, mainly in the old native way.[11] In the Agra famine of 1838 the beginnings of modern famine policy appear. The period from 1770 to 1838 was generally one of increasing knowledge, experiment, and expenditure, but progress was interrupted by wars, which were themselves one of the causes of famine. All accounts of these early famines are vitiated by guesses which are still a fruitful source of controversy;[12] and there is practically no information for native territory, where famines were most frequent. Only a few general facts stand out of the mass of speculation.

**(1) Prices and food-supply**

Owing to the want of communications, prices in famine areas ran up to a level rarely reached in modern times, when normal prices are probably three times as high as they were a century ago.[13] Government prohibited the export of grain, and tried to import it and fix its price. The attempt was always costly and generally vain. From 1812 onwards the principle of non-interference with trade was adopted, but for many years bounties were given on importation.

**Relief**

Relief works were first opened in Madras in 1792. The obligation to provide work for all who sought it was fully recognized for the first time in the Agra famine of 1838.[14] The relief of the helpless, who crowded into the big towns, was left to the charitable public. The largest direct expenditure on relief was about 23 lakhs in 1838. Remissions of revenue were generally made in the old native way—Government collecting what it could and leaving the rest—and were thus the measure of desolation rather than of relief.

**Mortality**

The depopulation of the country is sufficient proof of terrible mortality, although any estimates of it are practically worthless. A third of the population, or, 10,000,000, are said to have perished in the Bengal famine of 1770; and Colonel Baird-Smith put the death-roll of the Agra famine of 1838 at 800,000 on an estimated population of 15,500,000. Both estimates have been disputed, the former as excessive, the latter as inadequate.

**(2) Famines during the administration of the Crown, before 1880**

A new spirit entered into famine policy when the Government of India passed to the Crown. The famine of 1861 witnessed the first practical demonstration of sympathy by the British public, and was followed by the first famine inquiry. The mortality in Orissa in 1866 deeply stirred the public conscience, and Sir George Campbell's Commission, which followed, effectually called attention to the responsibilities of Government in times of famine. This was the beginning of a more humane policy; but it was not till 1874 that the responsibility of the state for gratuitous relief was fully recognized.

**Famine of 1860-61**

The famine of 1861 struck parts of the Province of Agra and the Punjab, and touched Râjputana and Cutch. The total area affected was 53,500 square miles, with an estimated population of 20,000,000; but famine is said to have been intense only between Agra and Delhi, a tract weakened by two years of irregular harvests and the military operations of the Mutiny. The autumn harvest was lost and very little of the spring harvest was sown. In 1838 remissions of revenue had been liberal, and relief had been given to the able-bodied on ordinary works managed by civil officers. In this famine remissions of revenue were small, but ten large relief works were opened under professional control; moreover the Government doubled the subscriptions of the public for the relief of the helpless. Poorhouses were opened, and the respectable ladies were relieved in their own homes, for the first time, in this famine. Altogether some 33,000,000 units[15] were relieved in British territory, at a cost of about 27 lakhs, of which 9 lakhs was subscribed by the public. The mortality was estimated at 8½ percent of the population in the worst districts.

**Colonel Baird-Smith's inquiry**

An inquiry into this famine was conducted by Colonel Baird-Smith. His report is still of interest, as showing the advance made in general administration, small though it may appear to modern eyes. Stability of tenure and canal irrigation had already increased the staying power of the people. Many modern principles were anticipated, particularly in regard to selection for gratuitous relief. But practice was still crude: the temporary migration of 250,000 people from the Doâb was viewed with satisfaction by this able officer.

**The Orissa Famine of 1865-7**

The next famine fell on the whole eastern coast from Madras upwards reaching far inland. The total area affected was estimated at 180,000 square miles, with a population of 47,500,000; but distress was greatest in Orissa, which was at that time practically isolated from the rest of India. The people depended for food on the winter rice, and the rainfall of 1865 was scanty and ceased prematurely. Food-stocks had been depleted and soon ran short;

but the gravity of the situation was not realized, the Bengal Board of Revenue being misled by defective estimates of the population requiring food and by fictitious price lists. The position was not grasped till the end of May, and then the monsoon had set in. Carriage by sea was extremely difficult, and even when grain reached the coast it could not be conveyed inland. At great cost some 10,000 tons of rice were imported, but this did not reach the people till September. Meanwhile the mortality had been very great. It was estimated that at least a million people, or one-third of the population, died in Orissa alone. The troubles of Orissa did not cease in 1866. The heavy rains of that year caused floods, which destroyed the rice in low-lying lands, and in the following year relief measures were again undertaken. 'Then, as an apparent result of the reaction following the want of foresight and activity in the preceding year, the relief operations were marked by a profusion and absence of check hitherto unexampled. Altogether about 40,000 tons of rice were imported, of which the most lavish use could not dispose of half; and while it cost four times the usual price to procure, the residue had to be sold for almost nothing when the monsoon of 1867, followed by an unusually fine harvest, altogether put an end to the famine in 1868'.[16] In the two years about 35,000,000 units were relieved at a cost of 95 lakhs, two thirds of which was debitable to the expense of importing grain. Adding loss of revenue in all departments, the famine in Orissa is said to have cost the state about 1½ crores.

In Madras, in 1866, about 21,000,000 unites were relieved at a cost of 12 lakhs, and revenue was remitted to the amount of 15 lakhs. Rather more than a lakh was also spent on relief works in Bombay.

The relief arrangements of the first year in Orissa were much criticized by Sir George Campbell's Commission of inquiry, particularly in regard to the poorhouses; but failure was mainly due to the actual dearth of food, which the then imperfect means of information failed to detect until too late, and the then means of communication failed to relieve when detected.

**The Râjputâna famine of 1868-70**

This great famine in the east was shortly followed (1868-70) by a great famine in the west of India, which affected an area of

296,000 square miles, with an estimated population of 44,500,000.[17] The famine centred on the Native States of Râjputâna and the British territory of Ajmer. The rains came late, fell lightly, and practically stopped in August. There was an utter dearth of fodder; and in parts of water; and grain could only be imported on camels. Thus Râjputâna was landlocked in the same way as Orissa. The people emigrated in enormous numbers with their flocks and herds,[18] but were reluctant to go on relief works in British territory, and many wandered till they died. Cholera broke out over the whole country, and there was practically no spring harvest. Large numbers returned to their villages in May, 1869, in the belief that the rains would be early; but the rains held off till the middle of July, and in the interval thousands died. The autumn harvest of 1868 promised well, but swarms of locusts destroyed it. The rains in September and October were heavy, and were followed by a virulent outbreak of fever. A good spring harvest was, however, secured, and the famine ended in March, 1870, after dreadful mortality. In British territory 49 lakhs was spent in direct relief; and in this famine the state spent over 7 lakhs in gratuitous relief.[19] Remissions of revenue amounted to little more than 5 lakhs; but a new departure was taken in making advances to cultivators to the amount of about 21 lakhs. In the Province of Agra 29,000,000 units were relieved at a cost of nearly 30 lakhs; but in spite of the Lieutenant Governor's declaration (referred to on p. 208) as to the responsibility of District officers for saving life, the mortality was great. Immigration from Native States broke down the relief system.

**The Bihâr famine of 1873-4**

The lessons of Orissa and Râjputâna were still fresh, when there followed a partial failure of the rains in Bihâr and in the adjacent parts of Bengal and the United Provinces. The total area affected was only 54,000 square miles, with a dense population of 21,500,000, and the failure of the rainfall was not very serious; but an immense organization was set on foot, and it was decided to save life at any cost. From first to last about 300,000,000 units were relieved (including 20,000,000 in the United Provinces) at a cost of 6¼ crores, of which nearly 4 crores were spent on the importation of grain. Altogether this famine cost the state about 6¾ crores. Financial consideration were thrown to the winds; but life was saved, and a great advance was made in administration. For the first time village inspection, the basis of modern organization, was carried out, and gratuitous relief on a large scale was given by the state. The enormous expenditure on 'a famine of unusual brevity and of no exceptional severity'[20] would probably never have been incurred had any system of agricultural information existed. The want of such a system was shown again in the following year, when, on the premature cessation of the rainfall, the Local Government proposed to renew large relief measures in Bihâr. The Government of India, however, resisted the alarm; and in the result, so far from there being a famine, grain was cheaper than usual in the area of anticipated distress.

**Southern India famine of 1876-8**

The famine which commenced in 1876 afflicted Southern India (Madras, Mysore, Hyderâbâd, Bombay) for two years, and in the second year extended to parts of the Central and United Provinces and to a small tract in the Punjab. The total area affected was 257,000 square miles, with a population of 58,500,000. Embarrassed by the large expenditure on the Bihâr famine, the Government of India insisted on the imposition of proper tests in the interests of both the people themselves and the general taxpayer. In Bombay these tests drove large numbers of relief-workers to strike, and the question arose whether relief should be given to men who could, but would not, work. This was decided by the Government of India as follows: 'We say that human life shall be saved at any cost and effort'; and if it is asked what 'the general principles are by which the District officers should be guided in refusing the aid needed to preserve life, the reply must be that there are no such principles, and that there are no circumstances in which such aid can be refused'. In Madras and Bombay the reduced, or Temple,[21] wage was adopted, but eventually abandoned as insufficient except under favourable circumstances. In the United Provinces little relief was given, and the mortality was very great. Throughout India fever raged in the autumn and winter of 1878. The excess mortality in this famine is said to have been 5,250,000 in British territory alone.

Speaking generally, the administration of relief was as strict on this occasion as it had been lax in Bihar. Prices ranged very high, and owing to the absence of railways private trade was scarcely equal to the demands made on it. Throughout British India about 700,000,000 unites were relieved at a cost of 8 1/3;[22] and charitable contributions from Great Britain and the Colonies amounted to 84 lakhs.

## The Famine Commission of 1878-80

In 1878 the whole question of relief and protection was referred to the first great Famine Commission under the presidency of Sir Richard Strachey. Starting from the principle, laid down in 1877, that the Government should spare no efforts to prevent starvation or an extremity of suffering dangerous to life, but could not attempt to prevent all suffering or to give general relief to the poorer classes of the community, the Famine Commissioner insisted that relief should be so administered as not to check the growth of thrift and self-reliance among the people, or to impair the structure of society which, resting in India upon the moral obligation of mutual assistance, is admirably adapted for common effort against a common misfortune. 'The great object,' they said, 'of saving life and giving protection from extreme suffering may not only be as well secured, but in fact will be far better secured, if proper care be taken to prevent the abuse and demoralization which all experience shows to be the consequence of ill-directed and excessive distribution of charitable relief'. They quoted Turgot to the effect that 'the best and most useful kind of alms consist in providing means of earning them', and laid down the principles (1) that employment should be given on relief works to the able-bodied, at a wage sufficient for support, on the condition of performing a suitable task; and (2) that gratuitous relief should be given, in their villages or in poor houses, to those who, after inquiry into their circumstances, were found to be unable to work. In order to regulate relief, they prescribed constant inspection of the people in their villages. As regards food-supply, they recommended non-interference with trade except in the very rare cases when it might be unequal to the demands on it. Finally, they advised that the landowning classes should be assisted by loans and by general suspensions of revenue in proportion to the general crop failure, it being a condition that proportionate relief should be given by the landowners to tenants and holders of subordinate rights in the land.

**The Provisional Code and the famine wage**

These recommendations were embodied in a Provisional Famine Code. In circulating this in 1883, the Government of India laid down the fundamental principle of the famine wage. That wage is 'the lowest amount sufficient to maintain health under given circumstances. While the duty of Government is to save life, it is not bound to maintain the labouring population at its normal level of comfort. To do so would be unjust to other sections of the community, besides prolonging the period for which the labouring population would cling to the relief works'.

Provincial Codes were then drawn up, and were acted upon in the several scarcities, which followed in different parts of India. These codes were first severely tested by the famine of 1896-7.

**(3) Famines during the administration of the Crown, after 1880.**

**Famine of 1896-7**

The monsoon of 1895 was weak in the Bundelkhand Districts of the Province of Agra, and the winter rains also failed. Famine was declared and relief was commenced, early in 1896. The monsoon of 1896 was generally deficient; and the United Provinces, the Central Provinces, Berâr, parts of Madras, Bombay, Bengal, the Punjab, and Upper Burma, together with portions of Râjputâna, Central India, and Hyderâbâd, were plunged in famine. Altogether 307,000 square miles were affected, with a population of 69,500,000, and the numbers relieved exceeded 4,000,000 at the time of greatest distress.

In the British territory the area and population affected were 225,000 square miles, and 62,500,000, respectively.[23] Famine was intense in the United Provinces, the Central Provinces, Bihâr, and the Hissâr District of the Punjab. From first to last, 821,000,000 units were relieved at a cost of 7¼ crores. In addition, revenue was remitted and loans were given to the extent of about 1¼ and 1¾ crores. The charitable relief fund amounted to nearly 1¾ crores, of which about 1¼ crores were subscribed in the United Kingdom. The famine ended, generally, when the autumn harvest of 1897 was ripe; but it was followed by heavy mortality from fever in the autumn, and by a plague of rats. The actual famine mortality in British Districts may be roughly estimated at about 750,000. This famine will be remembered for the vigorous, efficient, and economical administration in the United Provinces, and for the comparative failure of relief in the Central Provinces. The difficulties in this latter Province were, however, extraordinary great, owing to the reluctance of the wild tribes to accept relief on ordinary terms.

### The Famine Commission of 1898

The incidents of this famine were exhaustively analyzed by a Commission, presided over by Sir James Lyall which passed the following judgment on the administration as a whole: 'We consider that, while the areas over which intense and severe distress prevailed in the famine of 1896-7 were greater than in any previous famines, the success actually attained in the relief of distress and the saving of human life was, if not complete, far greater than any that has yet been recorded in famines that are at all comparable with it in point of extent, severity, or duration; and that this result has been achieved at a cost which, when compared with the expenditure in previous famines, and with other standards which we have had before us, cannot but be regarded as very moderate'.

This Commission also made important recommendations for the future treatment of famines. In regard to the broad principles of relief administration they adhered to the recommendations of the Commission of 1880. But in details they suggested some changes, including a more liberal wage and an extension of gratuitous relief, particularly during the rains. They broke new ground in formulating rules for the relief of weavers in their own trade, for the relief of aboriginal and hill tribes, and for the management of the charitable relief fund; and they laid great stress upon the necessity for liberal remissions of land revenue. The Commissioners seem to have been impressed by events in the Central Provinces, and the general effect of their recommendations was to avoid all risks and to make relief more attractive.

### The Famine of 1899-1900

Before these recommendations had been fully considered, another great famine occurred. Distress began in Ajmer in 1898 and some relief was given. The monsoon of 1899 failed generally over the west and centre of India. In the Central Provinces, Berâr, Bombay, Ajmer, and the Hissâr District of the Punjab, famine was acute;[24] it was intense in Râjputâna, Baroda, Central India, Hyderâbâd, and Kâthiâwar. The total area affected was 475,000 square miles, with a population of 59,500,000. The Meterological Department declared the drought to be unique. 'The mean average rainfall of India is 45 inches. In no previous famine year has it been in greater defect than 5 inches. But in 1899 the defect exceeded 11 inches'. This was for India as a whole; in particular localities there was practically no rainfall. The autumn harvest was a failure, and hardly any spring crops were sown. At the end of July 1900, no fewer than 6,500,000 person were receiving daily relief. The distress was aggravated, and the difficulties of administration were enormously increased, by the failure of the water-supply and fodder.

In British territory[25] 180,000 square miles with a population of 26,000,000 were affected, a smaller area and a much smaller population than in 1897; but the people in most parts had not recovered fully from the famine of two years before. The numbers relieved were far greater than in 1897. At the time of greatest relief—in this famine at the end of July—4,500,000 persons were supported by the state. Altogether about 1,140,000,000 units were relieved at a cost of 10 crores. Cattle died in millions, and the Government helped agriculturists by very large remissions of revenue and by loans, which have since been mostly written off. The total cost to the state has been put at about 15 crores. The charitable relief fund reached 1½ crores, of which nearly a crore was subscribed in the United Kingdom. In addition, loans were made to Native States to the extent of 3½ crores. Although the relief was thus extraordinarily liberal, the mortality was great. The Famine Commission of 1901 thought that about one million deaths might be attributed to famine in British Districts, and that of this total at least one-fifth were caused by cholera. This was largely due to the special conditions of the famine: namely, the extreme rigour of the winter of 1899-1900, the failure and consequent pollution of the water-supply, which led to virulent outbreaks of cholera in the summer of 1900, and the extremely unhealthy autumn in 1900, during which malarial fever attacked the rich as well as the poor. The famine ended, generally, when the autumn harvest of 1900 was ripe; but distress continued in parts of Western India for two years more.

This famine is remarkable for profuse relief in the Central Provinces, great morality in Gujarât, and general emigration from the Native States. In the Central Provinces the reaction from 1896 was complete: the people were all too ready to take relief (even the aboriginal tribes overcame their shyness), and the officers were anxious not to be behind hand in dealing with distress. For some months, over 20 percent of the total population were relieved; and the total cost of direct relief was nearly 4½ crores. In Gujarât the people and the Government were alike unprepared; the former had been softened by a long period of prosperity, and were stunned by the blow. Their wealth was sunk largely in their cattle, and in the vain hope of saving these they clung to their homes until it was too late. Relief of the aboriginal tribes was as difficult in Gujarât and Khândesh as it had been in the Central Provinces in 1897, and the result was much the same. In all Provinces the administration was hampered by crowds of immigrants from Native States, so exhausted by privation in many cases that their lives could not be saved even by the best medical care.

**The Famine Commission of 1901**

A Commission, presided over by Sir Antony MacDonnell, whose own famine relief measures in the United Provinces had been so successful in 1896-7, was appointed to gather up the lessons of this famine. Their judgment on the administration as a whole was as follows: 'In certain districts…people in sore need of relief were denied it in the early stages of the famine, owing to defective administration; but in the main, and taking the famine period as a whole, the relief distributed was excessive. We have no doubt that the excess is to be accounted for by an imperfect enforcement of tests on relief works, by a too ready admission to gratuitous relief, and by a greater readiness on the people's part to accept relief owing to the demoralizing influences of the preceding famine'. Impressed apparently by this demoralization, the Commission clearly restated 'the principles by which alone famine relief on a great scale can be successfully administered'. They recommended a policy of 'prudent boldness', starting from a large and expansive plan of relief, and secured by liberal preparations, constant vigilance, and a full enlistment of non-official help. The wage-scale was revised; the minimum wage was abolished in the case of the able-bodied, payments being made proportionate to the task performed; and provision was made for the exclusion from relief works of those who were in a position to maintain themselves. The relief system was enlarged by proposals for dealing with a fodder famine. Where differing from the Commission of 1898, this Commission reverted as a rule to the recommendations of the Commission of 1880.

**Conclusion**

It will thus be seen that, in the quest of the happy mean, the pendulum has been constantly on the swing; but the arc has become steadily smaller, and the relief system is gradually setting down. The main principles of relief are no longer questioned, and diversity in practice becomes less in each successive famine. The essential difficulty of state relief is deep-rooted. The reluctance of those unaccustomed to famine to accept relief, and the eagerness of those accustomed to famine to seek relief, are likely to perplex the relieving officer in the future as they have done in the past. But as establishments improve, the system will become more elastic and adaptable.

**Famine Mortality**

Although much ground has been gained in the long struggle with nature, and drought has been stripped of its worst horrors, the tale of suffering is still long, and the heart of the civilized world is touched by the mortality of an Indian famine. The Famine Commissions of 1880, 1898 and 1901 agree that 'no imaginable system of relief will completely meet all the various degrees of privation and suffering which a famine produces'. Pestilence is the twin-sister of famine, for the abnormal conditions of drought have from the earliest times lent themselves to disease.[26] Cholera invariably breaks out in the hot weather, and fever almost invariably succeeds in the autumn. Moreover, in every famine many persons refuse relief until it is too late to save them. Nevertheless, the total famine mortality since 1880 has been small compared with what it was before relief was then reduced to system. Moreover, the great majority of deaths in the two recent famines occurred generally among the very old and the very young. There has been since 1880 comparatively little of that morality among healthy adults which was so deplorable a feature of earlier famines, a fact of which the comparatively rapid recovery in the birth rate is at once the result and the proof.

## IV. Protection Against Famine

### Protective Aspect of the Famine Problem

The famine problem is not, however, limited to relief. 'It is of still more essential importance', said the Secretary of State in 1878, 'to ascertain how far it is possible for Government by its action to diminish the severity of famines, or to place the people in a better condition for enduring them'. The Famine Commission of 1880 concluded that much could be done in this direction, particularly by the accumulation of accurate knowledge of the country and its economic conditions, with the ultimate object of stimulating the material prosperity of the people; and much has been done.

### System of Intelligence

Reference has already been made to the elaborate system of agricultural intelligence, but this represents but a part of progressive knowledge. Geological, mineralogical, ethnological, and linguistic surveys have been set on foot, while valuable statistics of trade are annually published and reviewed in the Department of Commerce. Vital statistics are still defective, but each successive Census marks improvement in their registration. The functions of Government have been differentiated, the branches of the administration have been specialized, and action has been taken simultaneously on many lines.

### Productive and Protective Railways and Irrigation Works

Railway and irrigation works—'the best, and often the only, means of securing protection from the extreme effects of famine and drought'[27]—have always been the mainstay in building up material prosperity. From the financial point of view, these works are of two kinds, according as they are, or are not, commercially profitable, the former being called productive, the latter protective.

The cost of the former is met by loans; the latter are debitable to the Famine Insurance Grant.

**The Famine Relief and Insurance Grant**

This grant dates from the famine of 1876. A succession of famines, and a recognition of the duty of the state in regard to them, induced the Government of India to provide a reserve in ordinary years to meet the obligatory and recurrent, but extraordinary, demands of famine relief. This reserve was fixed, on the basis of past expenditure, at 1½ crores annually, and was secured by fresh taxation and economy. Doubts as to the precise objects to which the grant should be devoted arose almost immediately, but were settled in 1881 by a scheme, which, in its general bearings, still obtains. The first charge on the grant is famine relief, the second protective works, and any balance is devoted to the reduction, or rather the avoidance, of debt.

**The Place of Railway and Irrigation Works in Famine Insurance**

Experience in 1866, 1868 and 1878 had shown the imperative need for extending communications, and precedence in the policy of insurance was consequently given to the construction of protective railways, or the guarantee of interest on money borrowed for the purpose. The system of protective railways has been practically completed so far as main lines are concerned, and the Famine Commissions of 1898 and 1901 urged the now greater claims of protective irrigation works.

**Railways and Irrigation Works as they affect Material Progress**

The distinction between productive and protective works is purely financial. It remains to consider the effect of railways and irrigation on material prosperity. The benefits of irrigation have never been disputed; but of late there has been a tendency in some quarters to detract from the advantages of railways. It is contended that, by equalizing prices all over India, railways extend the area of distress beyond the limits of crop failure, and that they have destroyed the habit of storing grain, which formerly served as an insurance against famine. This may be admitted, without really qualifying the overwhelming benefits of improved communications. If railways have somewhat extended the area, they have enormously reduced the intensity, of distress; and if they have discouraged the storage of grain, they have substituted 'the great reserves of the country at large for the petty reserves of individuals'.[28] They have substituted famines which are of money only, for famines in which both food and money were lacking; and by giving access to large markets they have undoubtedly increased the incomes of landowners and cultivators, and enabled them to reap the benefits of high prices.[29] 'It is true', say the Famine Commissioners of 1901, 'that to a certain extent cultivators, who formerly stored grain, because it could be neither sold nor removed, have ceased to do so because they can sell to advantage; and that, owing to their improvidence, the money slips through their fingers. But this change in the habits of the people is a regular attendant of progress: it is merely a transient phase of a great economic movement, which makes for national prosperity'. It has become a proverb in India, as elsewhere, that 'railways make trade'.

**Other Efforts to Increase Material Prosperity**

Much has been done in other departments to promote general prosperity. The land revenue has become progressively moderate in assessment, and increasingly elastic in collection. The rent law of nearly every Province in India has been revised since 1880 in favour of the cultivating classes. Loans are given by the state, at low interest and on easy terms of repayment, for land improvement and for the purchase of seed and bullocks; and attempts are being made, with the active help of the state, to start co-operative credit associations. Experiment in agricultural improvements are continuously carried on. It cannot be said that the agricultural classes have responded very largely to the efforts made to help them or to teach them to help themselves, or that those efforts have always been well devised; but experience is being steadily gained, and the cumulative effect of the action already taken is considerable.

**Steadily increasing recuperative power of the country**

The Famine Commissions of 1880 and 1898 both bore witness to the recuperative power of the country,[30] but the best evidence of the fact is the rapid recovery of cultivation after a famine. The following figures give the cropped area in British Provinces[31] for the years preceding, coincident with, and following the recent famines:—

| Year and Area of Famine | Total Cropped Area is Millions of Acres | | |
|---|---|---|---|
| | Year before famine | Year of famine | Year after famine |
| 1897 (Bengal, United and Central Provinces, Berâr, Madras, Bomaby) | 180 | 167 | 183 |
| 1900 (Central Provinces, Berâr, Bombay, Ajmer) | 49 | 40 | 45 |

As the mortality of cattle was enormous in 1900, and distress continued in Bombay and Ajmer until 1902, these figures show a power of recuperation in the landowning and cultivating classes which would have been thought impossible fifty years ago.

**General progress**

Nor are the evidences of material progress confined to the landowning and cultivating classes. The great increase during the last twenty years in trade and commerce, in the use of the post and the telegraph, in remittances by money orders, and in savings banks deposits; the rise in urban wages, and the expanding revenue under excise, stamps, and income tax, all testify, in different ways and in various degree, to the steady growth of general prosperity. Twenty years is a very short time in an old and conservative country like India.

**The one exception**

One class alone is being left behind in the general progress, and that a large one. Agricultural labourers, as already stated, are multiplying rapidly on the margin of subsistence and beyond the requirements of agriculture, and by so doing are keeping their own wages low, while cash payments for work actually done are superseding, over large parts of India, the old customary payments of grain at each harvest. Agricultural progress will do little to improve their position. Emigration when feasible, will only temporarily postpone the pressure on the soil, unless the growth of population is checked. 'No remedy for present evils', say the

Famine Commissioners of 1880, 'can be complete which does not include the introduction of a diversity of occupations through which the surplus population may be drawn from agricultural pursuits and led to find the means of subsistence in manufactures or some such employments'. In this direction a fair start has been made. The construction of railways and irrigation works employ large numbers; and there is a growing labour market in docks and arsenals, and in the factories and commercial undertakings that are now springing up. But the numbers released from dependence on the land are as yet few in proportion to the normal increase of the rural population. Industrial development is slow, and the growth of population is quick. The country is crying for capital, and native capital is, so far, not forthcoming. 'The natural resources of India are beyond question, as is also the need for their development. In order to develop and reap the benefit of her resources, India requires, and must long continue to require, foreign capital'.[32] The steady application of capital to the organization and development of industry is, indeed, the one thing needful for the gradual solution of the famine problem.

## References

1. 'The flesh of a son was preferred to his love', says one chronicler.
2. 'In 1630,' says Sir W.W. Hunter, 'a calamity fell upon Gujarât which enables us to realize the terrible meaning of the word famine in India under Native rule. Whole cities and districts were left bare of inhabitants. In 1631 a Dutch merchant reported that only eleven of the 260 families at Swally survived. He found the road thence to Surat covered with bodies decaying "on the highway where they died, there being no one to bury them". In Surat, that great and crowded city, he "could hardly see any living persons"; but the corpses "at the corner of the streets lie twenty together, nobody burying them". Thirty thousand had perished in the town alone. Pestilence followed famine... "This, that was in a manner the garden of the world, is turned into a wilderness". The Dutchman estimated that it would take three years before the trade could revive at Surat. Indeed one striking contrast between Native and British rule was the slowness of recovery from famine in the Mughal Empire'.—*History of British India,* vol. ii, p. 59.
3. Opium, tobacco, oilseeds, &c.
4. The rainfall which is so important in Eastern Madras in November and December is really due to the retreat of the south-west monsoon current. The north-east monsoon proper is not established till the end of December.
5. The protective aspect of the problem is discussed in the fourth section of this chapter.

6. By Sir William Muir, the Lieutenant-Governor of what is now the Province of Agra.

7. A poorhouse is a temporary structure, run up in a few days, where paupers are sheltered and given cooked food under conditions of decency and discipline.

8. A test work is an ordinary work employing unskilled labour, usually earth-work. The conditions are strict but not unduly repellent, the object being to ascertain whether the people really need relief.

9. This result seems all the more remarkable when one considers the state of Europe fifty years ago. In the great famine of 1848 in rural Germany 'which decimated the people', we read that 'usury was frightful and bread and potatoes—the ordinary food of the peasantry—were not to be had'. On this occasion Raffeissen organized his first co-operative society, which brought down local prices 50 percent. India has already advanced, in this respect, farther than Europe had gone less than two generations ago.

10. In the Orissa famine, for instance, the Santâls starved in large numbers, because it was not known that they were peculiar in refusing to touch food cooked by Brâhmans; and a new caste, the Chattar-khai or 'kitchen-eaters', dates from that famine.

11. In reality this famine was administered by the Native Government. The East India Company did not assume direct management of Bengal until a few years later.

12. The danger of building conclusions on them is illustrated by the fact that, in spite of the great mortality in the Orissa famine of 1865, the population of the affected districts, as ascertained by the 1871-2 Census, was considerably larger than the estimate made of it by the best authorities prior to the famine.

13. Thus, in 1813, when prices in Râjputâna were 5 seers, in the Agra and Farrukhâbâd District they were never below 21 and 39 seers per rupee, respectively. In 1838, prices in the Province of Agra ranged from 16 to 10 and even 8 seers, while in Mâlwâ they were 50 to 60 seers per rupee. A seer is about 2 lb.

14. This was the first occasion when a fixed famine wage was given. Relief was given on ordinary works without any special arrangement. Relief works under professional control were largely used for the first time in 1854.

15. In famine phraseology a 'unit' means one person relieved for one day; e.g. if 100 persons are relieved daily for a month of thirty-one days, 3,100 units will have been relived.

16. *Report of the Famine Commission of* 1880, Part I, paragraph 51.

17. Gujarât, the North Deccan Districts, the Jubbulpore Division of the Central Provinces, the Agra and Bundelkhand Divisions of the United Provinces, and the Hissâr Division of the Punjab were all affected. These two famines, coming so close together, find their counterpart in the famines of 1897 and 1900 almost exactly a generation later: in each case the centre of distress shifted to the west, and the rains were usually late in the second famine year.

18. Of 1,500,000 inhabitants of Mârwâr, 1,000,000 are said to have emigrated with their cattle.
19. In Native States relief was given on a very small scale, except in Udaipur, where 5 lakhs was spent.
20. *Report of the Famine Commission,* 1880, paragraph 94.
21. So called after Sir Richard Temple, the Famine Commissioner for the Government of India. The wage was 1 lb. of grain *plus* 1 anna for a man, with small reductions for a woman or child.
22. In Hyderâbâd and Mysore about 72,000,000 units were relieved at a cost of 72 lakhs, and revenue was remitted to the amount of 60 lakhs.
23. No complete account of relief in Native States is available.
24. There was also distress in small areas in Bengal, Madras, and Agra.
25. The Native States conducted their own relief under the general advice of the Government of India, which lent them the services of British officers and assisted them with loans. It is impossible to give details. In some States very inadequate relief was given, and in most the mortality was great. But the Commission of 1901 was struck with the advance made by most of the Darbars towards bringing their relief into line with the humane policy of the British Government.
26. It seems worth while to quote an authoritative opinion on famine mortality. 'Dysentery and diarrhoea are peculiarly famine diseases, directly caused by insufficient and unwholesome food, or by reduced powers of digestion and assimilation as the result of continued privation. Again, it is practically impossible to prevent the outbreak of cholera when large masses of men are collected together in the hot weather under famine conditions; but efficient organization and careful sanitary arrangements can stay the spread of the epidemic, and when these precautions are not taken, a considerable share, at any rate, of the resultant mortality must be deemed to have been preventable. Of fevers it can only be said that they often are in origin climatic, but that their fatality is, owing to the reduced power of the people to resist them, largely due to famine',—*Report of the Famine Commission of* 1901.
27. *Report of the Famine Commission of* 1880.
28. *Report of the Famine Commission of* 1901, paragraph 223.
29. It may be noted that, among the reasons adduced by the Board of Revenue in 1812 against a Permanent Settlement in the Upper Provinces, was the fact that 'an exuberant harvest is, in the existing state of society here, almost as detrimental to the landholders as a scanty produce'.
30. 'It is, we believe, demonstrable that the effects produced by the famine of 1876-8 on the general prosperity of the country have been less disastrous than those of former calamities...The famine of 1770 resulted in widespread desolation of the most affected districts, so that we read of depopulation and ruin, the thinness of the inhabitants, many hundreds of villages entirely depopulated, half the ryots credibly reported to have perished, and a complete disorganization among the landed classes which lasted for many years. The famine of 1803

struck such a blow at the prosperity of Khândesh and Abmadnagar that even in 1867 the traces of its ravages were still visible in the ruins of deserted villages, which had not been repopulated. In the famine of 1833 so much land went out of cultivation in the Guntâr District that even in 1850 the land revenue was only three-fourths of what it had been in 1832. In 1837, in the North-western Provinces, the pressure was so great that the ordinary bonds of society seemed to be broken by it. In 1841 the still-deserted lands and abandoned houses in the Etâwah District bore evidence to the devastation and waste of life, and during the next five years the land revenue continued to be less by 12 percent than in the period preceding the famine. Colonel Baird-Smith, from whom the above quotation is made, testified that similar effects were hardly noticeable in 1860-1, and this he attributed to the increased power of resistance and self-support among the landowners following the introduction of long-term settlements, which dated from about 1840. Still more remarkable are the facts recorded in the agricultural statistics of Bombay and Madras for the year 1877-8. In Madras the area occupied exceeded by 50,000 acres that of 1874-5...In Bombay there was an actual increase of 70,000 acres of revenue-paying occupied land in excess of the previous year'.—*Report of the Commission of* 1880, para. 84.

'It may be said of India as a whole that of late years, owing to high prices, there has been a considerable increase in the incomes of the land-holding and cultivating classes, and that their standard of comfort and expenditure had also risen. With a rise in the transfer value of their tenures, their credit has also expanded. During the recent famine these classes, as a rule, have therefore shown greater power of resisting famine, either by in any previous period of scarcity of like severity'.—*Report of the Commission of* 1898, para. 592.

The subject was not referred to, or discussed by, the Famine Commission of 1901.

31. Except in the Punjab, the recorded figures for which are excluded as doubtful.
32. *Report of Sir Henry Fowler's Currency Committee, 1898*, para. 36.

## *Appendix III*

# Irrigation and Navigation

## Irrigation

### Preliminary

Irrigation works, the object of which is the artificial application of water to the land for purposes of agriculture as a means of supplementing the natural rainfall, although almost unknown in Northern Europe, have existed in India, as in most other Eastern countries, from time immemorial. This is a natural result of the conditions of climate. India contain large tracts, such as the deserts of Sind and the South-western Punjab, which are practically rainless, and in which cultivation without irrigation is impossible. There are others, such as the Deccan plateau, where cultivation is exceedingly precarious, owing to the great irregularity of the rainfall and the long intervals during which crops may be exposed to the fierce heat of the sun, and to dry and scorching winds. In such regions there may be an almost complete failure of crops in a year of short or badly distributed rainfall, and a succession of two or more unfavourable seasons might result in famine. In other more favoured tracts, such as the Himâlayan submontane districts, a serious failure of the rainfall is seldom or never known, yet here also irrigation works, which are usually of a simple kind such as can be constructed by the people themselves, are of the greatest value in improving the out-turn of the crops. Lastly, there are districts which ordinarily receive so copious a rainfall that rice is almost the only crop grown; but for this water is required at certain

---

*The Imperial Gazetteer of India: The Indian Empire: Vol. III, Economic,* Oxford, 1907, pp. 326-364

critical periods when there may be a break in the rains, and a full harvest can only be secured by irrigation.[1] In general it may be said that the security of the harvest depends on the existence of some form of irrigation in almost all parts of India, except in tracts such as Eastern Bengal, Assam, or Lower Burma, where the average rainfall does not fall short of 70 inches per annum. As might be expected under these conditions, the simpler forms of irrigation works have been limited in number and capacity only by the resources and engineering skill of the people, by the insecurity of tenure, and by the interruptions caused by invasion or internal dissension. Some of these works were constructed by the former rulers of the country; but it was not until after the establishment of British rule that the larger and more important works, many of which irrigate annually several hundred thousands of acres, were undertaken. As an instance of the magnitude of some of these later works may be mentioned the Chenâb Canal, which irrigates nearly 2,000,000 acres, or about two-fifths of the whole cultivable area of Egypt, with an ordinary discharge of 11,000 cubic feet per second, or about six times that of the Thames at Teddington. 'No similar works in other countries approach in magnitude the irrigation works of India, and no public works of nobler utility have ever been undertaken in the world'.[2]

## Different types of irrigation works

Irrigation works may be conveniently divided into three great types: namely, lift, storage, and river works, which are represented by wells, tanks or reservoirs, and canals. In lift-irrigation the water is raised from a lower level to that which will command the area to be irrigated, the raising being effected either by manual labour or by animal or mechanical power. The source of supply is usually the subsoil water into which wells have been sunk, but lift appliances are often erected on the banks of rivers or pools from which water is raised to the lands to be irrigated. Storage works are reservoirs, formed by the construction of dams across drainage lines, for the purpose of storing the supply, which passes down after every heavy fall of rain for subsequent use during long breaks in the rain or in seasons of drought. River works consist essentially of canals, drawing their supplies from river, which are in continuous flow during the whole or the greater portion of the year. In most cases they include a weir, which is constructed across the bed of the river immediately below the off-take of the canal, for the purpose of holding up water to the full supply level of the canal during low stages in the river. The canals are usually graded with a much lower bed-fall than that of the river from which they take off, and, by a suitable alignment, can often be carried out of the river valley on to high land, or even on to the watershed separating the catchments of the river from that of the drainage line lying next to it. The great canals in Northern India, and in the Orissa and Madras deltas, command nearly the whole of the lands lying between the main rivers in the former and the branches or arms of the deltas in the latter. In the Peninsula proper, conditions are less favourable, and the formation of the country prevents canals being taken far out of the river valleys. It must be remembered, too, that some large rivers, such as the Narbadâ and the Tâpti, are throughout useless for irrigation, by reason of their deep and often rocky channels.

**Overlapping of types**

Although these three types are in themselves as distinct as the sources of supply on which they depend, they sometimes overlap. Lifting appliances are often required to raise water from canals to ground on a higher level, and the cultivation under some tanks and canals can only be matured by the use of supplemental wells. Large storage works are incomplete without a network of distributing channels; and canals taking off from rivers in which the supply is uncertain and intermittent require storage works, which may be constructed either at some distance up-stream from the head-works, in the valley of the main river or of a tributary, or as 'tail tanks' at suitable points on the line of the canal itself. But although in particular cases all three classes may be found in combination, each is so distinct from the others that it deserves separate consideration.

**Area irrigated from wells**

An important point in connexion with pure lift-irrigation works is that they have been constructed by private enterprise on the part of the owners or cultivators of the soil. The works are all of a petty character, and irrigate an area, which may be as low as one acre and seldom exceeds twenty. Such works cannot conveniently be owned or maintained by the state, which can do no more than encourage their construction by agricultural loans and by liberal rules in the matter of land-revenue assessment. But although these works are small and have cost the state nothing, their importance in the aggregate is very great. Taking the average area annually irrigated from works of all classes in British India at 44,000,000 acres, it is found that nearly 13,000,000 acres, or about 30 percent, are irrigated from wells. Well-cultivation is moreover of the highest order; and it may be safely estimated that the produce annually raised from pure lift-irrigation is, in value, considerably more than a third of the out-turn from irrigation works of all kinds. The most favourable conditions for well-irrigation are found in the alluvial plains of Northern India, the subsoil of which contains an inexhaustible supply of water. Out of the 13,000,000 acres thus irrigated more than 9,500,000 are in the United Provinces and the Punjab, and about 2,750,000 in the Madras and Bombay presidencies. In other Provinces well-cultivation is inconsiderable, being confined to garden or other special crops.

**Permanent and temporary wells**

When the spring level is near the natural surface and that soil is fairly stiff, a well may consist of nothing more than a hole in the ground over which the appropriate lifting appliances are erected. These well, which usually fall in or are abandoned after one or two years' working, are called 'temporary' wells, to distinguish them from 'permanent' or masonary-lined wells, which if solidly built, may last for an indefinite period. In some parts there is an intermediate type, in which the well is lined with a wooden cylinder or with the brushwood or wicker-work. In the United Provinces less than one-fourth of the total number of wells are permanent; and both here and in the Punjab the number of temporary wells fluctuates greatly from year to year according to the season, being greatest in years of drought. The cost of a well varies from a few rupees for a temporary, to over Rs. 1,000 for a deep and permanent structure, but the average cost of a permanent well is between Rs. 300 and Rs. 600 according to size and depth. In the Punjab, where the wells are mainly permanent, the average area irrigated per well is 12 acres; but in the United Provinces, where so large a proportion of the wells are temporary, irrigating only 1 or 2 acres, the average area per well is not more than 4 acres. In Southern India the average area is between 2 and 3 acres; but here well-irrigation is, as a rule, applied only to the most valuable class of crops, which require frequent waterings.

**Lifting appliances**

The well now in use throughout India, and the lifting appliances employed, do not differ materially from those in use in former times. The water is almost invariably raised either by manual labour or by bullocks. For the former the favorite contrivance is the well-known *picottah*, in which the water is drawn up by means of a bucket suspended by a rope to the end of a long pole, which is pivoted near the other end to a post so as to revolve through a vertical plane. The shorter end is weighted, so as nearly to counterbalance the weight of the longer arm and the full bucket. The bucket is lowered by the man in charge, who draws the long end of the lever by a pull at the rope, or in some cases, as in Southern India, by running up and down the pole. This contrivance is seldom used for lifts of more than 15 feet, and for very small lifts (of 4 or 5 feet) other simple appliances are used. For lifts of over 15 feet bullock-power is almost invariably employed, and is often used even for lower lifts. The most common contrivance, which is to be found all over India except in some parts of the Punjab, is the *mot*, which consists of a large leather bag, holding from 30 to 40 gallons of water, fastened to one end of a rope which passed over a pulley overhanging the well. When the bag has been lowered the other end of the rope is attached to a pair of bullocks, who then walk down a ramp of a length approximately equal to the depth of the well. When the bullocks arrive at the end of the ramp the bag has been drawn up to the top of the well, and its contents are emptied into a trough or sump, generally by a man who stands by, but sometimes by a self-acting mechanical arrangement. The rope is then detached from the bullocks, the bag is lowered, and the bullocks return without a load to the top of the ramp, when the operation is repeated. In some parts the rope is not detached and the bullocks walk backwards up the ramp, as the empty bag descends. The alternative to the *mot* is the Persian wheel, which is used extensively in the Punjab. This consists of an endless chain of waterpots passing over a vertical wheel erected over the top of the well, and rotated by means of rough wooden gearing which is worked by a pair of bullocks walking round a circular track. When bullock-power is used water is sometimes lifted for purposes of irrigation as much as 60 feet, but ordinarily the lift seldom exceeds 40. The use of any form of purely mechanical motive power is practically unknown in India. A few isolated attempts have been recently made by private owners to use oil engines, and a project is under consideration to irrigate about 50,000 acres from the Kistna river in Madras by similar means. But even if these should prove successful the practice is not likely to be extensively followed by small cultivators.

**Means of promoting the extension of well-irrigation**

Wells play such an important part in the agricultural system of India, and are of such great protective value, that the extension of this form of irrigation must be regarded as highly desirable. There are, however, obvious limits to such extension, even in tracts where conditions of soil, climate, and spring level are favourable. The first cost of a well is only one of the factors to be considered, for its subsequent working requires a considerable amount of capital and very careful husbandry. The extension of well-cultivation must, therefore, always be gradual, and although it may be effectively encouraged it cannot be forced. The encouragement hitherto afforded by the state for the construction of wells and other works of agricultural improvement has been of two kinds—a system of agricultural advances known as *takâvi,* and a permanent of temporary exemption of the lands depending on the well from any enhancement of land revenue as a consequence of the improvements. *Takâvi* advances are made freely to approved applicants, the general rate of interest being 6¼ percent, except in Madras and Bombay, where it is only 5 percent. Recovery is made by installments extending over periods varying from seven to thirty years. During the ten years ending 1900-1, as much as 625 lakhs was thus advanced by Government, 348 lakhs as agricultural loans, and 277 lakhs for the specific purpose of land improvement. In the Madras and Bombay Presidencies, ryots who construct wells or other works of agricultural improvement are exempted from any future enhancement of land-revenue assessment on the ground of the increase in the agricultural value of their land due to the improvements. In other Provinces the exemption lasts for specific periods, the term being generally long enough for the owner to recoup the capital outlay incurred in the construction of the work.

**Extension of well-irrigation during recent years**

It is for many reasons very difficult to compare the area irrigated from wells at the present day (1904) with that irrigated as recently as twenty-five years ago. The Irrigation Commission of 1901-3 reported that in the four Provinces in which well-irrigation is most extensively practiced—namely, the United Provinces, the Punjab, Bombay, and Madras—the increase in the number of permanent wells during the decade ending 1900 amounted to 11, 25, 33 and 44 percent respectively; but it seems certain that the increase in the total area irrigated from wells, in the Northern Provinces at any rate, has not been in any way proportional to these figures. This may be due partly to the imperfection of the earlier statistics, partly to a reduction in the areas irrigated from old wells in tracts where canal-irrigation has been introduced. The Famine Commission of 1880 estimated the area irrigated from wells in 1876-7 at 5,794,000 acres in the United Provinces, and 3,176,000 acres in the Punjab. The Irrigation Commission of 1901-3 found that during the years 1900-2 the area irrigated from wells in the former Province varies from 4,544,000 to 6,122,000 acres, and in the latter from 3,018,000 to 4,155,000 acres. The Famine Commission of 1880 gave no details of well-irrigation in Bombay; but stated that the number of private wells in ryotwâri lands in Madras was believed to be about 375,000, and, on the assumption that the average area to each well would be about 5 acres, estimated the total area served at 1,800,000 acres. This assumption was probably much too high, for the Irrigation Commission of 1901-3 reported that the number of permanent wells in 1900-1 (excluding mere supplemental wells used on tank-irrigated lands) amounted to 522,300, irrigating about 1,680,000 acres, or not more than 3.2 acres to each well. In this Presidency there appears to have been a material increase not only in the number of wells, but also in the well irrigated area.

**Storage works**

Tanks or storage works are of all sizes, ranging from the great lakes formed by the construction of high dams across the beds of large but irregularly flowing rivers, such as Lakes Fife and Whiting in the Bombay Deccan, and the Periyâr lake in Travancore, in which are impounded from 4,000,000,000 to 6,500,000,000 cubic feet of water, to the small village tanks to be found throughout Southern India, many of which irrigate less than 10 acres. Any general extension of large works of this description is of course limited by the cost of construction and the loss of supply by evaporation. The idea of forming reservoirs in the beds or valley of streams which are in flow only for a few weeks or months in the year, must have presented itself to the rulers of the country or to the occupiers of the soil at a very early stage in Indian civilization, at any rate in those parts of the country where the conditions were most favourable; and in such tracts tanks of great activity bear witness to the readiness of former rulers to encourage the constructions of works of this kind. Some of these works, such as the Chembrambâkam and Cumbum tanks in Madras, are of the great size, holding from 3,000,000,000 to 4,000,000,000 cubic feet, and with water-spreads of over nine square miles. There are remains of other works of even greater size, such as the Madag tank in the Dhâwâr District of Bombay, which have failed or been abandoned. The inscriptions on two large tanks in the Chingleput District of Madras, which still irrigate from 2,000 to 4,000 acres, are said to be more than 1,100 years old. In Upper Burma there are many tanks constructed centuries ago of which that at Meiktila is the most important. The celebrated lake at Udaipur (Râjputâna), which is said to be the largest in India, is not utilized for irrigation; but of the many old tanks in Râjputâna and Central India some are still so used, although the majority have been abandoned, or no longer hold water. In the Native States of Mysore and Hyderâbâd, tank-irrigation has been very highly developed. The area irrigated from large tanks is, however, small in proportion to that dependent on smaller works, most of which were probably constructed originally by the owners or occupies of the lands protected, with but little assistance from their rulers. The most notable example of these is to be found in the smaller irrigation works in Madras. It is estimated that there are no less than 40,000 of these works in the ryotwâri tracts of that Presidency, of which less than 3,500 irrigate more than 200 acres, while many serve less than 10 acres. The former are cared for by the Public Works Department; more than 31,000 Minor works are in charge of revenue officers; and about 5,000 are small private works. The average area irrigated from the works controlled by Government amounts to more than 3,000,000 acres, or about as much as the entire area irrigated from all the great canals and larger irrigation works in the Province. These petty works include a certain number of small canals, but are mainly tanks or storage works. Tanks abound also in the zamindâri estates of this Presidency, in which it is estimated that about 2,500,000 acres are irrigated, of which 2,000,000 are dependent on storage works, and the balance on wells and river channels. No approach to these figures is made in other Provinces; but, excluding well areas, nearly two-thirds of the irrigation in the Gujarât, Deccan and Carnatic Districts of Bombay depends upon small storage works, and there are 50,000 small private tanks in the Central Provinces, which are said to be capable of irrigating from 150,000 to 650,000 acres, according to the season, being almost the only form of irrigation in that Province, as the area under wells is there inconsiderable. Tank-irrigation is practically unknown in the Punjab and in Sind, but is to be found in some form or other in all other Provinces, including Burma. The *jhils* or natural depressions scattered at intervals over the flat alluvial plains of the United Provinces, most of which are privately owned, irrigate about 2,000,000 acres.

**Method of construction**

Storage works consist eventually of four parts. The dam, which may vary in height from 15 to 160 feet, may be constructed of earth, concrete, or masonry, but earthwork is seldom relied on for greater heights than 80 feet. When concrete or masonry is used, sound rock foundations are essential, and many sites otherwise eligible must be rejected when this cannot be found. The submerged area may, when full, have a water surface of many square miles, and here again sites otherwise eligible must be rejected on account of the large areas of cultivable land, which would be thrown out of cultivation or the high compensation that would have to be paid.

The outlet and distributing channels, through which water is drawn off from the reservoir and carried to the lands to be irrigated, often form a very expensive item. Lastly, there is the waste-weir or escape, through which flood-waters must be passed at times of abnormally heavy rainfall in such a way as not to imperil the safety of the work. The total cost of a storage work varies enormously according to the site. The two largest works executed by Government, the Nira Canal and the Periyâr Project, have each cost about Rs. 1,300 per 1,000,000 cubic feet in a full lake. Although these and many other large storage works have been constructed by the British Government, tank-irrigation is essentially a product of native rule, and almost the whole of the tank-irrigated area is from old native works, the maintenance of which is now undertaken in whole or in part by the state. These works are mainly confined to the crystalline and sand-stone formations, which occupy the whole of the Indian Peninsula between the Deccan trap area and the narrow strip of alluvium on the coast. The formation of the country in this area favours the construction of tanks, which form the principal means of irrigation The area comprises the greater part of the Madras Presidency, nearly the whole of Mysore, half of Hyderâbâd, nearly two-thirds of the Central Provinces, the Baghelkhand States of Central India, the eastern half of Râjputâna, and portions of the United Provinces and of the Orissa and Chotâ Nâgpur Divisions in Bengal.

**Storage works maintained or controlled by the state**

It has already been stated that wells are constructed and maintained solely by private enterprise. This is also true of the smaller forms of tank, the petty works which serve a single holding or irrigate little more than 10 acres; but the largest works, which impound several thousand million cubic feet of water and submerge many square miles of country, could only have been constructed by the rulers of the country, and have always been maintained as state irrigation works. Between these extremes are the moderately sized tanks, capable of irrigating from 10 to 300 or 400 acres annually. Many of them appear to have been originally constructed by private or communal enterprise, but the state is so interested in the land revenue dependent on them that it has gradually undertaken their control or management and contributes largely to their improvement and up-keep. Thus it happens that in the ryotwâri tracts of Madras and Bombay all but he smallest tanks are controlled by Government. In the Central Provinces, on the other hand, the Government has no concern in the management of the *mâlguzâr's* tanks; and in the United Provinces, where the greater part of the irrigation recorded as from tanks is effected from the *jhils* above been mentioned, it maintains only the large tanks which have always recognized as state works. In Ajmer-Merwâra and in Upper Burma most of the tanks are kept up by Government.

**Area irrigated by tanks**

The average area recorded as irrigated from tanks in British India is about 8,000,000 acres, but the supply to many of the works is very precious, and is apt to fail in years of extreme drought. This figure does not include the large areas over which rain-water is held up for some time after every fall by means of field embankments, such as are to be found under different names in Bengal, Bundelkhand, the Central Provinces, Gujarât, and the Bombay Deccan. The agricultural value of these temporary storage works is considerable, but the areas protected by them are not usually recorded or regarded as tank-irrigation.

**Small private canals**

The third and most important class of irrigation works, viz. river works or canals, are generally of such magnitude, and affect so many different interests, that they could only have been constructed, and can only be efficiently maintained, by the state. There are, however, a certain number of petty works of this class, which have been constructed and are still maintained by private enterprise, with occasional assistance in some Districts from Local funds. In the Punjab nearly 1,000,000 acres are irrigated annually from works of this class, of which more than 100,000 acres are dependent on inundation canals made by the people, but now under the control of the District Boards. Nearly 100,000 acres are irrigated from canals of the same kind belonging to private landowners, and about 800,000 acres receive irrigation from hill streams, or from *jhils* from which water is diverted by means of simple works and small channels that have been constructed by communal effort. In the United Provinces about 750,000 acres are irrigated from private canals, of which the most important are the works constructed in the Basti and Gorakhpur Districts by two English landowners, which irrigate areas of 40,000 and 15,000 acres of rice and *rabi* crops within their respective estates. In the permanently settled Districts of Bengal, and especially in Bihâr, there are a great number of small canals, called *pains,* by which water is diverted from the innumerable streams, which traverse the country and is conducted directly into the rice-fields or stored in small reservoirs (*ahars*) which have been formed by field embankments, for use during breaks in the rains. The total area protected in Bengal by means of these *pains* and *ahars* is estimated at nearly 5,000,000 acres. In Madras about 336,000 acres are irrigated annually from private canals, including the spring channels which are made in the beds of streams during the dry season, of which nearly nine-tenth are in *zamindâri* estates. The Minor works under Government control in this Province also include many small river channels. In the Bombay Deccan and in Gujarât there are many works of the same kind, most of which are under Government management. It is difficult to state with accuracy the areas irrigated throughout India from these small canals, as in the Provincial returns some are included under the head 'Canals', others under 'Tanks' (which are often associated with them), and others, as in Bengal and the United Provinces, under 'Other sources'; but the total area protected by private canals is probably between 7,000,000 and 8,000,000 acres. Many of these works are, however, apt to fail in years of prolonged or severe drought.

**Perennial and inundation canals**

We now proceed to consider the great canals which have been constructed and are maintained by the state, most of which extend over very wide areas, irrigate many thousand acres, and comprise hundreds or thousands of miles of distributary channels. These works may be divided into two classes, perennial and inundation canals. Strictly speaking, a perennial canal is one which has an assured supply of water all the year round; but this generally involves the construction of a weir or 'anicut' across the bed of the river, to hold up the low supplies and divert the whole, or as much as may be needed, into the canal. This is not, indeed, always necessary, for the head-works of the Swât River Canal in Peshâwar District (Frontier Province) are so favourably situated that a perennial supply can be obtained without the assistance of a weir; which is also considered unnecessary for the Tribeni Canal now under construction in the Champâran District of Bengal. On the other hand, the river supply may fail in a river across which a weir has been constructed. As a general rule, however, a canal which takes off from above a properly constructed weir is assured of a fairly continuous supply during the season when water is required, and it is at any rate possible to utilize every drop of water that comes down, however low the state of the river. The term 'perennial' is therefore generally applied to a canal which can draw off a constant supply without the assistance of a weir, or which is provided with a weir which will render the supply to the canal dependent only on the quantity of water in the river and not on its surface level; while if the supply is not sufficiently continuous for the purposes required, it can generally be rendered so by the construction of storage works. Inundation canals are simple channels taking off from the banks of a river at a level, which is generally considerably higher than the ordinary low-water level of the stream. Water flows into these cuts during the flood season, and they remain in flow until the river falls below the level of their beds, which is generally 2 or 3 feet higher at the end than at the beginning of the season, owing to silt deposits, which have to be cleared during the low-river season. The most important inundation canals are to be found in the Punjab and Sind, i.e. in the valley of the Indus and its tributaries. They are in flow, generally, from the beginning of May until the end of September, although the supplies fluctuate greatly during this period with the surface levels in the river. Cultivation, which is practically impossible without irrigation in the rainless tracts they serve, has adapted itself to these conditions. The average area irrigated from the inundation canals under Government amounts to about 3,500,000 acres, of which 2,500,000 are in Sind. In addition, about 1,000,000 acres are irrigated by the Bahâwalpur State Canals and by the District and private canals in the Punjab, 75 percent of this area being in the Native State of Bahâwalpur.

**Canals made by former rulers of the country**

Although the present system of large irrigation works has been almost entirely constructed by the British Government, examples are not wanting of old river works undertaken by former rulers of the country. Irrigation was carried out on a large scale in the Cauvery delta, the supply being maintained by means of a weir, known as the Grand Anicut, which is said to have been constructed over 1,500 years ago. This is the work which Sir Arthur Cotton strengthened and improved in 1835-6, and the success of which encouraged him to propose the great Godâvari works which he afterwards constructed. Most of the weirs on the Tungabhadra, above which the present Tungabhadra channels draw their supplies, were constructed by the Hindu monarch, Krishna Râya, at the beginning of the sixteenth century. In Northern India the Muhammadans appear to have made frequent attempts to utilize the water of the river Jumna. In the middle of the fourteenth century Firoz Shâh Tughlak, constructed a canal on the right bank of the river, 150 miles in length, for the irrigation of his domains in Hissâr. This canal, which had silted up, was reopened in Akbar's reign, and a branch was made to Delhi in the reign of Shâh Jahân; but during the decline of the Mughal dynasty both canals gradually silted up. A canal was also made on the eastern bank of the Jumna at the beginning of the eighteenth century, but appears to have likewise been abandoned, although it is said to have carried water to below Sahâranpur. These canals were subsequently cleared and reopened by the British Government, have since been realigned, extended, and improved, and are now first-class irrigation works known as the Western and Eastern Jumna Canals. In the Punjab the small Hasli Canal had been made by former rulers, for the purpose of carrying water from the river Râvi to Lahore and Amritsar, on very much the same alignment as the present Bâri Doâb Canal. The simple system of irrigation by inundation canals appears to have been practiced from time immemorial in Sind and the Punjab; and many of the existing canals of this class in Multân, Muzaffargarh, and Dera Ghâzi Khân were brought to a fair state of efficiency under the more energetic Pathân and Sikh governors of these Districts, and were in operation at the time of annexation, but have since been considerably developed.

### Attempts to construct large irrigation works by private enterprise

Although the earliest results attained by direct Government agency on the Cauvery, Godâvari, and Jumna works were sufficiently encouraging, the East India Company was reluctant to commit itself to any extensive scheme of state irrigation works. Funds for such works as were sanctioned were provided out of revenue, and the policy of a productive public works loan had not then been inaugurated. It was at first thought that the construction of large irrigation works, like that of railways, could be most advantageously entrusted to private enterprise. In 1857 the Court of Directors asked for proposals for new irrigation works in Madras, to be constructed by this means. The Madras Government, under the advice of Sir Arthur Cotton, proposed a great scheme, known as the Tungabhadra project, for the irrigation of large portions of the Bellary, Kurnool, Cuddapah, and Nellore Districts; and the Madras Irrigation Company was eventually formed for its prosecution, with a Government guarantee. Operations were limited at first to the construction of that part of the general scheme known as the Kurnool-Cuddapah Canal, which was completed by the company; but the capital cost had greatly exceeded the original estimates, the financial prospects of the project were very unfavourable, and the company was in such difficulties that the Government was compelled to take over the work in 1882.

In pursuance of the same policy the East India Irrigation and Canal Company was formed in 1860 for the purpose of carrying out the Orissa Canal Project, also proposed by Sir Arthur Cotton. Here, again, it was found that the capital cost of the works had been greatly under-estimated, while a very exaggerated estimate had been formed of the revenue, which would be derivable from the work. The company was unable to raise the necessary funds for completing the undertaking, and in 1869 Government purchased the works and the company ceased to exist.

### Construction of new irrigation works by the state. Productive and protective

### Major works

The selection of these two projects for execution by private companies was unfortunate, for experience has since shown that neither of them is ever likely to prove a directly remunerative undertaking. But it was soon recognized that, even in more favourable circumstances, the construction and control of irrigation works of this class could not conveniently be entrusted to private enterprise; and, under the viceroyalty of Lord Lawrence, a new policy was initiated under which irrigation works that gave a fair promise of proving directly remunerative were to be constructed by the state from loan funds, as 'productive' public works. From that time the construction and extension of works of this class by means of borrowed money has been actively and systematically proceeded with, the total capital outlay recorded to the end of 1902-3 on works classed as 'productive' amounting to about 38 crores of rupees. State expenditure has not, however, been confined to works which were considered likely to prove remunerative at the time they were undertaken, although loan funds have hitherto been applied only to works of this class. In accordance with the recommendation of the Famine Commission of 1880, several large works, which gave little promise of proving directly remunerative have been undertaken on the ground of their value as a protection against famine. The capital cost of these undertakings, which are called 'protective' works, has been met from the Famine Insurance Grant,[3] the total expenditure thereon recorded to the end of 1902-3 amounting to more than 2½ crores of rupees. These two classes of works, productive and protective together, make up what are known in irrigation accounts as Major works. They are works which have been wholly constructed or reconstructed by the British Government, and for which regular capital, revenue, and interest accounts are kept, which exhibit the financial results attained as fully as is usual in other commercial undertakings.

It should be added that Major works do not consist entirely of river works or canals. The irrigation works in the Punjab, Sind, the United Provinces, and Bengal are all of this type; but those in Madras and the Bombay Deccan include some purely storage works, and some canals, such as the Periyâr Project and the Nira Canal, with large storage works are combined.

**Minor works for which capital accounts have been opened**

Considerable expenditure has also been incurred by the British Government on works which do not fall under the Major category.

Reference has already been made to those old or indigenous irrigation works the maintenance of which, as Minor works, is undertaken by Government. The more important of these have, however, been not only maintained, but extended and improved, at the cost of the state. The cost of such improvements has been recorded as capital expenditure, although the funds have been provided from general revenues. There are also a few new works, generally of small size, the cost of which has been met in the same way. Both kinds of works are classified as 'Minor works for which capital accounts are kept'.

**Total outlay on irrigation and results**

The total capital expenditure on works of this class to the end of 1902-3 amounted to 329 lakhs of rupees, while the area irrigated from them is nearly 2,000,000 acres. The aggregate capital outlay to the end of 1902-3 on Major and Minor works together amounted to nearly 43 crores, and the area irrigated from them in that year was about 14,000,000 acres. The annual value of the crops raised by the works for which capital accounts are kept is estimated at 40 crores, or about 88 percent of the capital outlay thereon.

**Detailed statement of Major works**

Details for each Major work, and, as a whole, for the Minor works for which capital accounts are kept, are given in the table on pp. 251-53 for each Province. The figures are given for the year 1902-3, and may be regarded as fairly normal in the present stage of development of the irrigation system.

It will be seen that, although many individual works, especially those in Bengal and Bombay, show an insignificant return on the capital outlay, the Major works as a whole have proved a very profitable investment, the net revenue yielding a return of nearly 7 percent, while the Minor works have been hardly less profitable. A brief description will now be given of the principal state irrigation works in each Province.

**Punjab and Frontier Province: Major Works**

No Province presents greater facilities for irrigation than the Punjab with its snow-fed rivers and level plains. The restoration of Firoz Shâh's Canal on the west bank of the Jumna was commenced during the administration of the Marquis of Hastings (1814-23), and the canal was gradually brought into such a state of efficiency that it was capable of irrigating over 500,000 acres in the year 1870. By reason, however, of its original faulty alignment, this canal, although a very profitable work, caused great injury to the country by water-logging, and could not be extended owing to the insecurity of the supply. In 1870 it was decided that the canal should be wholly remodeled; and the greater part of it has since been re-aligned and reconstructed, while new branches have been made, so that in the famine year 1897-8 it irrigated 764,000 acres.

| Province | Name of Work | Capital outlay to end of 1902-3 in lakhs of rupees | Area irrigated during 1902-3 in acres | Percentage of net revenue for 1902-3 to capital outlay |
|---|---|---|---|---|
| **Punjab** | *Major Works* | | | |
| | Western Jumna Canal (including Patiâla section)... | 1,84 | 595,229 | 7.7 |
| | Bâri Doâb Canal... | 1,96 | 893,862 | 12.9 |
| | Sirhind Canal (including Native States) | 3,87 | 1,112,425 | 4.4 |
| | Upper Sutlej (including Lower Sohâg and Pâra Canal) | 17 | 233,887 | 6.3 |
| | Chenâb Canal | 2,75 | 1,829,169 | 21.3 |
| | Sidhnai Canal | 13 | 60,791 | 3.9 |
| | Jhelum Canal | 1,15 | 138,911 | -1.0 |
| | **Total Major Works** | **11,87** | **4,864,274** | **9.7** |
| | **3 Minor Works** | **13** | **235,087** | **8.0** |
| | **Total** | **12,00** | **5,099,361** | .. |
| **North-West Frontier Province** | Swât River Canal (Major Work) | 42 | 173,772 | 10.6 |
| | 1. Minor Work... | 5 | .. | 23.0 |
| | Total | 47 | 173,772 | .. |
| **Sind** | *Major Works* | | | |

| | | | | |
|---|---|---|---|---|
| | Desert Canal... | 26 | 187,061 | 3.7 |
| | Unar Wah Canal... | 6 | 64,350 | 11.6 |
| | Begâri Canal... | 17 | 225,612 | 15.8 |
| | Eastern Nâra Works... | 64 | 256,938 | 6.8 |
| | Jâmrao Canal... | 83 | 269,358 | 3.8 |
| | Dad Canal... | 21 | 60,256 | -1.2 |
| | Mahi Wah Project... | 10 | 8,426 | -2.0 |
| | **Total Major Works** | **2,27** | **1,072,001** | **5.0** |
| | **8 Minor Works** | **42** | **794,530** | **20.5** |
| | **Total** | **2,69** | **1,866,531** | .. |
| **Bombay (Deccan & Gujarât)** | *Major Works* | | | |
| | Hâthmathi Canal... | 5 | 287 | -1.2 |
| | Lower Pânjhra River Works... | 5 | 2,503 | 1.5 |
| | Kâdva River Works... | 8 | 2,775 | 0.2 |
| | Lâkh Canal... | 4 | 1,206 | -0.3 |
| | Muthâ Canals... | 68 | 8,101 | 2.4 |
| | Ekruk Tank... | 13 | 2,030 | 0.5 |
| | Kistna Canal... | 8 | 5,963 | 3.7 |
| | Mhasvâd Tank... | 21 | 4,075 | 0.02 |
| | Nira Canal... | 57 | 35,102 | 3.1 |
| | Shetphal Tank... | 7 | 216 | 0.02 |
| | **Total Major Works** | **1,96** | **62,258** | **1.9** |
| | **26 Minor Works** | **76** | **38,237** | **0.4** |
| | **Total** | **2,72** | **100,495** | .. |
| **Madras** | *Major Works* | | | |
| | Godâvari Delta System... | 1,34 | 810,634 | 18.4 |
| | Kistna Delta System... | 1,44 | 627,850 | 15.8 |
| | Penner River Canals... | 63 | 163,641 | 5.0 |
| | Cauvery Delta System... | 31 | 982,356 | 28.5 |
| | Srivailkuntam Anicut System.. | 15 | 44,526 | 6.1 |
| | Kunool-Cuddapah Canal... | 2,17 | 60,154 | 0.5 |
| | Barur Tank... | 4 | 5,325 | 1.4 |
| | Periyâr Project... | 90 | 154,068 | 3.6 |
| | Rushikulya Project... | 49 | 92,399 | 0.6 |
| | **Total Major Works** | **7,47** | **2,940,953** | **8.7** |
| | **28 Minor Works** | **1,05** | **584,081** | **7.0** |
| | **Total** | **8,52** | **3,525,034** | .. |

| | | | | |
|---|---|---|---|---|
| **Bengal** | ***Major Works*** | | | |
| | Orissa Project... | 2,65 | 224,779 | 0.05 |
| | Midnapore Canal... | 85 | 87,464 | 0.8 |
| | Son Project | 2,67 | 483,567 | 3.3 |
| | **Total Major Works** | **6,17** | **795,810** | **1.6** |
| | **1 Minor Work** | **7** | **..** | **-0.4** |
| | **Total** | **6,24** | **795,810** | **..** |
| **United Provinces** | ***Major Works*** | | | |
| | Ganges Canal... | 3,04 | 871,862 | 10.5 |
| | Lower Ganges Canal (including Fatehpur Branch)... | 3,98 | 849,061 | 3.8 |
| | Agra Canal... | 99 | 236,721 | 6.2 |
| | Eastern Jumna Canal... | 43 | 284,079 | 25.0 |
| | Betwâ Canal... | 45 | 64,457 | -0.5 |
| | **Total Major Works** | **8,89** | **2,306,180** | **7.0** |
| | **4 Minor Works** | **31** | **137,375** | **2.8** |
| | **Total** | **9,20** | **2,443,555** | **..** |
| **Ajmer-Merwâra** | Minor Works in 3 subdivisions... | 31 | 26,199 | 1.2 |
| **Baluchistân Burma** | 2 Minor Works... | 17 | 2,939 | -0.6 |
| **Burma** | Mandalay Canal (Major Work) | 47 | 7,223 | -0.2 |
| | **GRAND TOTAL MAJOR WORKS** | **39,52** | **12,222,471** | **6.9** |
| | **GRAND TOTAL MAJOR WORKS (WITH CAPITAL ACCOUNTS)** | **3,27** | **1,818,448** | **6.0** |
| | **GRAND TOTAL MAJOR AND MINOR WORKS** | **42,70** | **14,040,919** | **..** |

The Bâri Doâb Canal, which takes off from the right bank of the Râvi at the point where it debouches from the hills, and irrigates large portions of the Gurdâspur, Amritsar, and Lahore Districts, was undertaken almost immediately after the annexation of the Province, and was opened for irrigation in 1860-1, but it has since been greatly enlarged and extended. The Sirhind Canal which taps the Sutlej at Rupar, as it emerges from the Siwâlik hills, was originally proposed by Sir William Baker in 1841, but the first estimate was only sanctioned in 1870, and the canal was opened by Lord Ripon in 1882. More than one-third of the cost of this canal has been contributed by the three Phulkiân States—Patiâla, Nâbha, and Jind, which are entitled to a corresponding share of the supply. The canal irrigates large areas in these States, and also in the Faridkot State and in the British Districts of Ludhiâna and Ferozepore. The Swât River Canal, in the Peshâwar District of what is now the Frontier Province, is said to have been suggested by Sir Henry Lawrence soon after the annexation of the Punjab, but was first definitely proposed by Sir Henry Durand in December, 1870, and was opened for irrigation in February, 1885.

The Sidhnai, Lower Sohâg and Pâra, and Chenâb Canals were commenced in 1884. The first of these is a small canal for the irrigation of a portion of Multân District, which takes off from a weir constructed on the Râvi at a short distance above its confluence with the Chenâb. The Lower Sohâg and Pâra is an inundation canal from the right bank of the Sutlej, and has no weir; it irrigates a portion of Motgomery District, and has recently been grouped with the Upper Sutlej inundation canal, formerly a Minor work. The Chenâb Canal was also originally designed as a small inundation canal, and opened as such in 1887, but in 1889 it was decided to convert it into a perennial canal of the first magnitude. A weir and head-works across the Chenâb river at Khanki, about 8 miles below Wazirâbâd, were completed in 1892. The canal has since been enlarged and extended so as to command the greater portion of the Rechna Doâb, the tract lying between the Chenâb and Râvi rivers in the Gujrânwâla, Jhang, and Montgomery Districts. Great part of the area commanded by the Sidhnai, Lower Sohâg and Pâra, and Chenâb Canals was uninhabited crown waste, so that the success of the works depended on the introduction of settlers or colonists who would take up and cultivate the land. The first efforts were made on the two smaller canals with encouraging results, and the experience gained was of the utmost value in subsequently carrying out the great scheme for the colonization of the Rechna Doâb. The magnitude of this scheme and the success, which has attended it are shown by the fact that up to the end of 1902-3 the area, which had been sold or leased to cultivators amounted to 1,750,000 acres; while the population of the colonized tract, which in 1891 was practically non-existent, was returned at 792,000 in the Census of 1901. The colonists were drawn from the agricultural classes in the congested districts of the Province, and are now a thriving and prosperous peasantry. The total area irrigated by the canal in 1902-3 amounted to 1,829,000 acres. The Jhelum Canal was opened in October 1901. It was commenced in November 1898, and is at present estimated to cost 144 lakhs and to irrigate annually more than 600,000 acres. It takes off from the right bank of the Jhelum near Rasul, the site of the battle-field of Chiliânwâla, and will irrigate a portion of Shâhpur District. Here also there is a large area of crown waste into which colonists must be introduced; but there is no reason to doubt that the canal will prove a successful and highly remunerative work.

**Punjab inundation canals**

The Minor Punjab works entered in the table include two systems of inundation canals, the Shâhpur and the Dera Ghâzi Khân Canals, for each of which a capital account has been opened.[4] There are, moreover, three other large systems of old inundation canals—the Lower Sutlej, the Lower Chenâb, and the Muzaffargarh Canals—which were constructed under native rulers, but are now maintained as Minor works by Government, although capital accounts are not kept for them, and which together irrigated 815,690 acres in 1902-2. The total area irrigated annually from state works in the Punjab and the Frontier Province is about 6,000,000 acres.

**Scope for extension of irrigation in the Punjab**

Although so much has been done to extend irrigation in the Punjab, the field is by no means exhausted. Apart from all extensions of existing works and many small schemes that may be adopted, two large tracts remain to be brought under irrigation. One of them is known as the Bâri Doâb, including nearly 1,600,000 acres in the Montgomery and Multân Districts, of which about half is crown waste. A detailed project for the irrigation of this tract, by means of a canal taking off from the right bank of the

Sutlej immediately below the confluence of the Beâs, has been prepared, but has been set aside in favour of an alternative proposal for irrigating the same tract by means of new canals from the Chenâb river, the cold-weather supply of which would be augmented by a feeder from the Jhelum. This canal will command and protect a much larger area than the Sutlej project, and will have the advantage of leaving the supply in the Sutlej available for further extensions of irrigation on the left bank, in British or Bahâwalpur territory. The second tract is the great Sind Sâgar Doâb, which comprises an area of over 5,000,000 acres lying to the south of the Salt Range and bounded by the Indus river on the west, and by the Jhelum and Chenâb on the east. The whole of this country could be commanded by a great canal taking off from the Indus at Kâlâbâgh; but the work would be very costly, and a great part of the area is so covered with sand-hills that it would be unsuitable for irrigation. It is possible that this scheme, or a modification of it, may be carried out eventually, but it cannot be considered as urgent or as a very promising financial investment. Almost all the Districts of the Punjab contain stretches of inferior soils, impregnated with salt or *reh;* and although it is beyond doubt that some extension, or further deterioration, of these areas has been the result of excessive water-supply, there is also evidence that such lands are not always unsuitable for irrigation, and that they have in some cases been improved or reclaimed by it. Moreover, these stretches are not so numerous or extensive as to render it unprofitable to carry canals through them for the improvement of better soils around or beyond them.

**Sind**

Agriculture in Sind, which is an almost rainless tract, is wholly dependent on artificial irrigation, and population is to be found only where the means of irrigation have been provided. Here, as in the Punjab, irrigation has completely altered the face of the country, and has converted barren wastes into fertile fields of wheat and rice. The works in Sind consist almost entirely of inundation canals from the Indus. The Desert, Unar Wah, and Begâri Canals all take off from the right bank, above Sukkur, and have been practically constructed by the British Government. The Eastern Nâra is a branch from the Indus, which takes off from the left bank, immediately above Sukkur, and discharges into the Rann of Cutch. This branch has been depended at the head and brought under control, so that it provides a perennial supply to the canals, which take off from it. Among these is the recently constructed Jâmrao Canal, which takes off from the Nâra at the lower boundary of the Khairpur State and commands a large area of waste land. Colonists are being introduced on the system, which has been so successfully followed in the Punjab, and the prospects are promising. The canal was opened in November 1899, and irrigated more than 269,000 acres in 1902-3. In addition to these Major works, Sind contains several large inundation canals, which are Minor works with capital accounts. Among these the largest and most important is the Fuleli Canal in Hyderâbâd District, which is navigable and generally in flow all the year round, and is capable of irrigating over 400,000 acres. There are also, as in the Punjab, a number of smaller canals, which are maintained by Government as Minor works, for which no capital accounts are kept, and which together irrigate about 900,000 acres.

In addition to the works mentioned, four small productive works are under construction on the left side of the Indus, and many extensions of existing canals have been proposed. It is estimated that when all these have been completed the total area annually irrigated, which may be taken as averaging about 2,700,000 acres, will be increased by about 20 percent. The irrigated area fluctuates greatly according to the state of the river, the difference between a very favourable and an unfavourable season being as much as 800,000 acres. In spite of these fluctuations the canals never wholly fail, and are remarkably cheap and profitable works. It has been suggested that the area under irrigation might be greatly extended, and the efficiency of many of the existing canals increased, by constructing a weir across the Indus at Sukkur, and that this will be rendered necessary sooner or later by the continued abstraction of the water in the Upper Indus and its tributaries by the new Punjab canals. The cost and engineering difficulties of such a work would be very great, and no opinion can be pronounced on its feasibility until it has been more fully considered; but a great deal can be done in the meanwhile to improve and extend existing canals and the system of distribution.

**Bombay (Deccan and Gujarât)**

It will be seen from the table already give that, although nearly every irrigation work in Sind is highly remunerative, those in the Bombay Deccan and Gujarât are financially failures. Many of them do not pay their working expenses, and the best does not yield a return of much more than 3½ percent on its capital cost. The main reason for this is the great cost of storage works and the precarious and unreliable nature of the water supply. A second cause is the inconsistancy of the demand in districts where in ordinary years excellent crops can be grown without the aid of irrigation, which is taken regularly only for the more valuable class of crops. For these high rates are paid; but the areas are small, and the total area irrigated by all the works shown in the table, on which a capital expenditure of 272 lakhs had been incurred up to March 1903, does not on the average exceed 100,000 acres. The Major works and the Minor works with capital accounts are all of the same class and may be considered together. Of the whole thirty-six only two small works are situated in Gujarât, the remainder being scattered over the Deccan Districts. The most important are the Muthâ and the Nira Canals, in connexion with which two fine Ghât-fed storage works, known as Lake Fife (Kharakvâsla) and Lake Whiting, have been constructed, which are capable of impounding 3,833,000,000 and 5,312,000,000 cubic feet respectively. The area irrigated from the Muthâ Canal may appear remarkably small as compared with its capital cost; but one of the main objects of the work is the supply of water to the cantonment and municipality of Poona and to Kirkee, and the whole cost of the waterworks has been debited against the project. The supply available for irrigation is therefore but a portion of the whole; and it is taken mainly for the highest class of sugar-cane, which is grown in the vicinity of Poona, and which requires frequent and heavy waterings and pays very high rates. The Nira Canal has been constructed solely as a protective irrigation work, and, although hitherto not directly remunerative, it proved of the greatest value during the severe famines of 1896-7 and 1900-1.

In Bombay, as in several other Provinces, the area irrigated from petty works which are maintained by Government as Minor works for which capital accounts are not kept, exceeds that irrigated from the Major and Minor works on which capital expenditure has been incurred. There are 387 of these petty works in Gujarât, which irrigate about 32,000 acres, of which more than two-thirds is in Surat District. The Deccan and Carnatic Districts contain 1,019 of these works, which irrigate on an average about 111,000 acres.

**Scope for new works in the Deccan**

Irrigation works in Bombay (excluding Sind) having proved unremunerative, no new works of any importance have been sanctioned in recent years. But the Deccan Districs are so liable to famine that there is no part of India in which the protection which irrigation works can afford is more urgently required. The rainfall in the Western Ghâts provides an unfailing supply of water; but the cost of storing and utilizing it would be so great, and the demand for irrigation in ordinary years is so small, that there is little prospect of any work, which can be constructed proving directly remunerative. Nevertheless, it is mainly by the multiplication of works of the Nira Canal type that substantial protection from famine can be obtained, and the value of this may justify the state in incurring the permanent liabilities, which the construction of such works must entail.

**Madras Major Works**

The most important among the nine Major works of the Madras Presidency are the three deltaic systems of the Godâvari, the Kistna, and the Cauvery, which together irrigate more than 2,400,000 acres. In these deltas the conditions are as favourable for irrigation as in the tracts served by the great perennial canals of the Punjab. It has already been stated that irrigation had been extensively developed in the Cauvery delta under native rule, but that the works were added to, strengthened, and improved by Sir Arthur Cotton in 1835-6. The irrigation is here effected not from artificial canals, but from the numerous natural channels into which the river divides after entering the delta. The works consist therefore almost entirely of weirs, escapes, and regulators, constructed for the purpose of controlling the distribution of the supply. After these works had been completed, Sir Arthur Cotton turned his attention to the Godâvari and constructed the canal system on that river between 1847 and 1850. He subsequently planned, but did not himself carry out, the Kistna project. The remaining Major works are of a wholly different character from these three deltaic systems, as they depend more or less on storage works or are carried out in more difficult country. The Kurnool-Cuddapah Canal, as already explained, is part of the great Tungabhadra scheme originally projected by Sir Arthur Cotton, the construction of which was entrusted to the Madras Irrigation Company. This work has for various reasons never proved a financial success, and even at the present time the gross revenue does not much more than cover the working expenses. The Periyâr Project is one of the most interesting works in the Presidency. It consists of a large storage work in Travancore territory, on the western side of the Ghâts, formed by the construction of a concrete dam 156 feet in height across the Periyâr river, the natural course of which is towards the Arabian Sea. The impounded water is, however, diverted by means of a long tunnel into one of the tributaries of the Vaigai river, which discharges into the Bay of Bengal below Madura. Many old irrigation works exist on this river, and new works have been constructed for the full utilization of the supplementary supply. The work was opened in 1896; and although the net revenue as yet only covers the charges for interest; it may be expected to improve before long, when irrigation is more fully developed. The only other Major works in Madras, which have not proved remunerative are the small Barur tank in Salem District, and the Rushikulya Project in Ganjâm; but the latter was originally constructed as a protective work witout any expectation that it would be directly remunerative.

**Minor works in Madras**

The twenty-eight Minor works on which capital outlay has been incurred do not call for special remark. They consist either of anicut systems or storage works, or of a combination of these; and they may, on the whole, be regarded as directly remunerative, for the net revenue attributable to them in 1902-3 was equivalent to return of 7 percent on the capital cost. But, as has already been shown, half of the total area in Madras irrigated from works under Government control is dependent on 35,000 petty works, which are maintained by the state as works for which no capital accounts are kept. The revenue derived from these small works exceeds 80 lakhs a year, and about 20 lakhs is devoted annually to their maintenance or up-keep.

**Scope for extension**

There is no Province in which irrigation is more appreciated or has been longer established than Madras. Many of the works are of great antiquity, and they are to be found in large numbers in almost every District. Except in the deltas, the conditions are less favourable than in the Punjab or Sind for large canals unaided by storage; but, on the other hand, the country is better adapted for the small storage works which form such an important feature in the agricultural economy of the Presidency. There is still a wide scope for the extension of the irrigated area, but few extensions are possible without storage. The supplies of even the great Kistna and Cauvery rivers are often insufficient for the irrigation at present dependent on them, or for the second crop, which might be grown, and proposals have been made to form large storage works on both these rivers. From a protective point of view the most important undertaking, which can be proposed is the completion of the Tungabhadra Project on the scale originally suggested by Sir Arthur Cotton. This work would protect very large areas in the Districts of Bellary, Anatapur, Kurnool, Cuddapah, and Nellore, all of which are specially liable to severe distress and famine in years of drought. But storage works of enormous capacity would be required on the Tungabhadra and elsewhere in order to obtain a reliable supply for the whole area that could be commanded, while the canal channels themselves would be very costly owing to the nature of the soil and the configuration of the country. As much of the area that would be served consists of black cotton soil, upon which in ordinary years, 'dry' crops can be raised, the demand for water would be much less constant than in the rice-growing tracts; and such a work is not, therefore, likely to prove directly remunerative. There is no doubt, however, that an unfailing supply of water is available, and that, if it can be stored and utilized at an expense which will not be prohibitive, a large area in these districts could be securely protected from famine. The question is now (1905) being investigated in detail. Numerous other works of a less ambitious character are possible in almost all districts, but practically all will involve the construction of storage works. Such works are likely, however, to be less costly and unremunerative than in the Bombay Deccan, and it seems probable that many schemes can be proposed which will not involve a greater permanent burden on the finances of the state than would be justified by their protective value.

**Bengal**

State irrigation works have never hitherto proved remunerative in Bengal. The ordinary rainfall is so great that water is not in constant or regular demand, although there may be a great rush for it during long breaks in the rains, or at critical periods of the rice crop. The three Major works, which have been constructed are all unremunerative. The Orissa Canals, to which reference has already been made, do not pay their working expenses, and the Son Canals in Southern Bihâr, which are the most successful, do not on the average yield more than 3 percent on their capital cost. A small canal, the Tribeni, is now under construction in the north of Champâran District as a protective work. There is scope for extension of irrigation in Bengal, especially in the Bihâr Districts, which are densely populated and the most liable to famine; but until higher rates for water can be obtained from the people, such works are never likely to be remunerative. In Eastern Bengal the rainfall is so abundant that there is no demand for irrigation.

**United Provinces**

It has already been shown how the canal constructed by Firoz Shâh on the west bank of the Jumna was reopened in the early part of the nineteenth century, when it was within the Province of Agra. The small canal on the eastern bank was reopened and extended soon afterwards, and now irrigated portions of the District of Sahâranpur, Muzaffarnagar, and Meerut. The knowledge and experience gained on these works were subsequently applied by Sir Proby Cautley in the design and construction of the Ganges Canal, which was the first original irrigation work of any magnitude constructed in Northern India, and is even now second to none in the boldness of its conception, and to few in its utility and financial success. It was the pioneer of all the large canals subsequently constructed in the United Provinces and the Punjab. The canal, which was opened in 1854, takes off from the right bank of the

Ganges immediately below the sacred *ghâts* at Hardwâr, and after being carried over the Solâbi river by the celebrated Solâni aqueduct, irrigates portions of nine Districts in the Jumna-Ganges Doâb. Seven Districts in the lower part of the Doâb receive irrigation from the Lower Ganges Canal, which also takes off from the right bank of the Ganges at Naraura, about 130 miles below Hardwâr, and was first opened for irrigation in 1878. The Agra Canal, opened in 1874, is a smaller work which takes off from the right bank of the Jumna at Okhla, 11 miles below Delhi, and irrigates portions of the Districts of Gurgaon, Muttra, and Agra. All these canals have proved remunerative; but this cannot be said of the remaining Major work, the Betwâ canal, which takes off from the left bank of the Betwa, a tributary of the Jumna, about 12 miles north of Jhânsi, and irrigates portions of the Jâlaun and Hamirpur Districts in Bundelkhand. This canal, which was opened in 1885, has not a perennial supply, and the demand for irrigation during the period that the river is in flow is very slack, except in dry seasons, so that it does not pay its working expenses. A certain amount of storage (2,700,000,000 cubic feet) has been provided above the weir, where the river is impounded to a height of 56 feet above the lowest point of its bed; but this is sufficient. The canal was sanctioned as a protective work and was not expected to be remunerative, but it proved of great value during the severe famine of 1896-7, when it irrigated more than 87,000 acres.

The four Minor works for which capital accounts are kept include three small systems of canals—the Dun, the Rohilkhand, and the Bijnor, which are all profitable works; and the Bundelkhand lakes, which irrigate 3,000 acres and just pay their working expenses. There are no other Minor works.

It must be added that the canals in the United Provinces have not always conferred unmixed benefit upon the land, which they command. In many places their introduction led to a gradual but steady rise in the level of the subsoil water, and resulted eventually in the water-logging of the soil, the increase of malaria, and the further deterioration of *usar* or *reh*-covered tracts. To remedy these evils, and to prevent further injury, it was found necessary to incur a large outlay on the re-alignment of some of the older canals, and on the construction of a large system of drainage channels, the aggregate length of which now exceeds 3,000 miles. These measures have proved successful.

**Scope for extension of irrigation**

The field of extension of canal irrigation in the United Provinces is not large. A project for a great canal, to take off from the right bank of the Sârdâ river for the irrigation of the Oudh Districts, was prepared in detail more than thirty years ago, but was not sanctioned owing to the doubts expressed as to the necessity for such a work and the opposition of the owners of the lands which would be affected. The project has been several times reviewed and modified, but has found few advocated among landowners or revenue officers, while it is strongly opposed by many. A smaller scheme has been suggested which would protect the only portions of this tract which have in the past been liable to famine; but there are doubts and difficulties attending this also, and it will not, in any case be taken up at present. Additional protection from famine is most urgently required in the districts, which lie to that south of the river Jumna; but canals in this tract would have to take off from tributaries of the Jumna, the supplies in which, as in the case of the Betwâ, can be relied on only form a few months in a year. The most important scheme recently sanctioned as a protective work is a canal from the river Ken, to protect a large portion of Bândâ District which suffered severely in the famine of 1896-97; but however valuable works of this kind may be in this tract in seasons of drought, there appears to be little hope of their proving directly remunerative.

**Ajmer-Merwâra**

The irrigation works in Ajmer-Merwâra consist entirely of tanks, which were either made or restored about 1850, under Colonels Hall and Dixon. There are no natural rivers on which reliance can be placed for irrigation, and the rainfall is so irregular, and often so inadequate, that wells are apt to run dry. In such tracts tanks are of the greatest value, not only on account of the irrigation directly effected from them, but as a means of maintaining the spring level in the wells in their vicinity. Tanks have been constructed in almost every available catchment basin, and every effort has been made to utilize to the utmost the scanty rainfall, so that there is little room for the extension of irrigation in this small territory. In favourable years the tanks are capable of irrigating nearly 40,000 acres, but in a dry year not more than one-third of this can be protected. In ordinary years the works yield a net revenue equivalent to about 3 percent on their capital cost, but in dry years working expenses are sometimes not covered. Apart from the tanks the only means of irrigation is from wells, the area under which varies from 44,000 to 108,000 acres according to the season.

**Baluchistân**

Two small works have been constructed by the British Government in the Quetta-Pishin District of Baluchistân, which irrigate between them from 4,000 to 8,000 acres, according to the season, but at present they do not quite pay their working expenses. Other small works have been proposed recently, but all permanent supplies of water are now so fully utilized that there is little scope for new state irrigation works. Private irrigation works, utilizing the waters of perennial streams and to a certain extent the flood-waters of hill torrents, are numerous; but the distinctive private irrigation works of Baluchistân are the *kârez*, or underground tunnels, which tap the subsoil supply of water on high ground and lead it on to the surface of lower country. The people display much skill in the construction of these works, for which the country is well adapted.

**Upper Burma**

Irrigation is not required in Lower Burma, where the rainfall is so regular and abundant that rice, the staple crop of the country, can be grown without it. Up to 1901 there were no Major irrigation works in operation in Upper Burma; but two projects—the Mandalay and the Shwebo Canals—were then under construction. The former was opened in 1902-3 and irrigated upwards of 7,000 acres in that year; the latter was opened in 1906. These two works are estimated to cost 95 lakhs, and to irrigate together about 230,000 acres, and there is reason to believe that both will prove remunerative. Another scheme, known as the Mon Canals, of about the same scope as each of these works, has also been sanctioned, and is now (1905) under construction. There are about 200 Minor works, for which capital accounts are not kept, but which are now administered and maintained by the state. Most of these existed before the annexation, but many had fallen into disuse. About 50 lakhs has since been spent on restoring or repairing them, and in 1902-2 they irrigated about 400,000 acres.

Private irrigation works are also numerous in Upper Burma, especially in the Magwe District, or on the tributaries of the Irrawaddy. The area irrigated by these is estimated at 475,000 acres, of which 300,000 acres are from small canals, and the balance from tanks and other sources.

**Central Provinces and Berâr; Assam and Coorg**

There are at present no state irrigation works in the Central Provinces, although, as already shown, certain rice-growing districts possess no less than 50,000 small private tanks, capable of protecting from 150,000 to 650,000 acres according to the season. The necessity for protective irrigation does not appear to have been recognized until recently, as the pressure of population was light. Moreover, until 1896 a complete failure of the rains was hardly known, and in many parts of the Province the cultivation is said to have suffered more frequently and severely from excessive rainfall than from drought. Under such conditions the people are never likely to pay as much for irrigation as it will cost to provide it, but the Province has suffered so severely from famine during the last five or six years that the construction of suitable state irrigation works is contemplated as a protective measure. In Berâr there are practically no irrigation works of any kind, state or private, except wells. Here, too, the necessity for irrigation works has not often been felt, but the Province was seriously affected by the failure of the later rains in 1896, and severe famine occurred in 1899. Storage works may be possible in the hilly tracts in the north and south known as the Melghât and Bâlâghât, but tanks in the latter tract would not be secure from failure in years of severe drought.

Irrigation works are not required in Assam, where the rainfall is heavy and unfailing; nor in any part of Coorg, except in a narrow strip on the eastern border, in which failure of the rains occasionally occurs and where a few petty works have been constructed.

**Total area irrigated in British India from all sources**

The Irrigation Commission of 1901-3 estimated the total area ordinarily irrigated in British India from all sources as below, the total cultivated area being taken in 226,000,000 acres:—

| Sources of Irrigation | State Works | Private Works | Total |
|---|---|---|---|
| | Acres | Acres | Acres |
| Wells | ... | 12,895,000 | 12,895,000 |
| Canals | 15,644,000 | 1,235,000 | 16,879,000 |
| Tanks | 2,944,000 | 5,194,000 | 8,138,000 |
| Other Sources | ... | 6,186,000 | 6,186,000 |
| **G. TOTAL** | 18,588,000 | 25,510,000 | 44,098,000 |

It should be noted that the figures given in this table do not include the large areas directly watered by river floods, nor the many thousand acres which, though not directly irrigated in the ordinary sense, are artificially saturated by rain-water held up within field embankments.

It is difficult to determine the increase of area under private works since 1878. As regards wells, the question has been already referred to, and it may be doubted if there has been a greater increase under private works of other kinds than under wells. With regard to state works there is no difficulty, and it may be safely said that between 1878 and 1903 the area under irrigation increased from 10,500,000 to 18,500,000 acres; of this increase nearly 7,000,000 acres are due to Major works.

**Distribution of total irrigated area among Provinces**

The distribution of the total irrigated area among Provinces is shown in the table on the next page.

The actual area for each Province in any one year may differ considerably from that shown in the penultimate column. In a very dry year tanks are liable to fail and the area irrigated by them falls very short. On the other hand there is an unusually strong demand for water in such years, and the greatest inducement to economy in its use, so that maximum areas are often then irrigated by perennial canals or from wells in which the supply is maintained.

| Province | Population (1901) | Average area annually cultivated Acres | Area ordinarily irrigated from all sources Acres | % of irrigation on area cultivated |
|---|---|---|---|---|
| Punjab and North West Frontier Province | 22,357,000 | 28,207,000 | 10,430,000 | 37,0 |
| Sind | 3,211,000 | 3,323,000 | 2,923,000 | 88.0 |
| Bombay Proper | 15,305,000 | 24,327,000 | 1,077,000 | 4.4 |
| Madras | 38,209,000 | 36,574,000 | 10,532,000 | 28.8 |
| Bengal | 74,745,000 | 63,664,000 | 6,349,000 | 10.0 |
| United Provinces | 47,692,000 | 41,086,000 | 11,055, 000 | 26.9 |
| Ajmer-Merwâra | 477,000 | 388,000 | 142,000 | 36.6 |
| Baluchistân | 308,000 | (?) | 5,000 | ... |
| Upper Burma | 3,847,000 | 4,666,000 | 828,000 | 17.7 |
| Central Provinces | 9,877,000 | 16,814,000 | 700,00 | 4.2 |
| Berâr | 2,754,000 | 6,820,000 | 56,000 | 0.8 |
| Coorg | 181,000 | 195,000 | 1,000 | 0.5 |
| **TOTAL** | 218,963,000 | 226,064,000 | 44,098,000 | 19.5 |

**Irrigation in Native States**

A few remarks may be made about irrigation in Native States. The Irrigation Commission of 1901-3 obtained statistics from all the more important States in which irrigation is practiced, excepting those in Burma and Baluchistân. These statistics covered an area of 438,000 square miles, the population in which amounts to 51,326,000. The average area cultivated is estimated at 71,076,000 acres, of which 7,763,000 acres, or 10.9 percent, are irrigated in an ordinary year. After making some allowance for areas not included in the returns, the Commission estimated the total area annually irrigated in the Indian Empire, excluding the Native States in Burma and Baluchistân for which no particulars can be given, at 53,000,000 acres, of which 19,000,000 are irrigated from canals, 16,000,000 from wells, 10,000,000 from tanks, and 8,000,000 from other sources.

**Mysore**

Among individual States the first place may be given to Mysore, where there are said to be abut 39,000 tanks, or four to every three square miles. Almost every valley contains a chain of such tanks, the first overflowing into the second, and so on until the terminal tank is filled. The largest existing tank has a capacity of 3,118,000,000 cubic feet; but there are only ten tanks with a capacity of over 270,000,000 cubic feet, and not more than 2,300 are capable of irrigation in 80 acres or more. The average area irrigated annually by all tanks is about 540,000 acres. There are also about 1,000 miles of canals or river channels, which irrigate about 100,000 acres. The well area is about 70,000 acres. The State is now constructing two very large storage works, the Bora Kanave and Mâri Kanave reservoirs, which are to have storage capacities of 2,354,000,000 and 30,000,000,000 cubic feet respectively. The latter work, which is being constructed on the Vedâvati or Hagari river, a tributary of the Tungabhadra, in Chitaldroog District, will have a masonry dam 142 feet high, and a waterspread when the lake is full of over 40 square miles. It will then have a capacity very nearly equal to that of the Nile reservoir at Assuân, but the lake will only fill during years of extraordinary rainfall, or perhaps not more than once in thirty years. In a year of average rainfall the tank will not impound more than 10,000,000,000 cubic feet, but it has been proved more economical to build the dam to the height proposed than to provide the necessary escape at a lower level.

**Hyderâbâd**

In the Hyderâbâd State an area of about 773,000 acres is said to be irrigated in years of normal rainfall, but in a dry year, such as 1899-1900, this area is reduced to less than half. Most of this irrigation is from tanks, of which there are said to be 18,000, but the capacity of the largest of these does not exceed 300,000,000 cubic feet. Some of these tanks are of great antiquity, but the majority of them were until recently breached and ineffective. A great deal has, however, been done to repair them since 1893: more than 7,000 have been restored, while many projects have been prepared for the restoration of others or the construction of new works. There are also some small canals which take off from the left bank of the Tungabhara river, and irrigate nearly 4,000 acres, and a new work of this kind has been recently sanctioned which is estimated to irrigate 10,000 acres.

**Other States**

In the Native States under the Madras Government, 625,000 acres, or more than 57 percent of the average area cultivated, are said to be irrigated. In Bombay the area irrigated in Native States, including Baroda, in years of normal rainfall is estimated at 1,147,000 acres, but his is less than 5 percent of the area cultivated. In the Râjputâna Agency, where the need for irrigation is very great, about 1,172,000 acres, or 18 percent of the area cultivated, are irrigated from wells and tanks in years of good rainfall, but the irrigation is very precious. The States best protected are Jaipur, Bharatpur, Shâhpura, Kishangarh, Alwar and Kotah. The Jaipur State has done a great deal during the last thirty years, under the advice of Colonel Sir Swinton Jacob, in constructing irrigation tanks and in advancing money for the construction of wells; and in Bharatpur a sum of 10 lakhs has been spent since 1897, principally in constructing embankments for impounding and distributing spill waters from the Bângangâ and other rivers, which has resulted in an increase of 50,000 acres in the irrigated area. There is scope for extension of irrigation in some of the Râjputâna States, but the rainfall is so uncertain that sites for reliable storage works are not easy to find, and the question is complicated by territorial difficulties. Râjputâna is, however, in such urgent need of protection that investigations are now (1905) being made with the object of drawing up projects for utilizing to the best advantage all available sources of water supply. In the Central India States irrigation is not very extensively practiced, and the total area irrigated from all sources does not amount to 6 per cent, of the average area cultivated; but many tracts are liable to severe drought. In the Native States of the Punjab nearly

2,000,000 acres are irrigated in ordinary years, of which about 750,000 acres represent irrigation from the Sirhind and Western Jumna Canals in the States of Patiâla, Nâbha, Jind, Faridkot, and Kalsia, while an equal area is irrigated in the Bahâwalpur State by means of the Bahâwalpur inundation canals which take off from the left bank of the Sutlej.

**Irrigation revenue**

The revenue receipts from Government irrigation works are derived almost entirely from the charges made for water or for water advantages; and these charges depend throughout India not on the volume of water supplied, the amount of which may vary largely according to the character or the season and other considerations, but on the kind of crops cultivated and the areas actually or ordinarily irrigated. In former days, when land revenue was taken in kind, the state's share of the produce increased with the introduction of irrigation; and it was in anticipation of such an increase that rulers or farmers of land revenue constructed, or contributed towards the cost of constructing, irrigation works.

**Consolidated with land revenue**

When, under British rule, the system of cash payments succeeded, and assessments were made with reference to average produce, lands which were assured of irrigation were naturally assessed at higher rates than similar land which did not enjoy this advantage. The difference between this 'wet' rate and the ordinary 'dry' rate leviable on unirrigated land of the same class represented the true revenue earned by or due to the works. In Madras almost all the new works included a considerable area of old irrigation, dependent on works which were superseded by or incorporated in the new works. In the case of lands newly brought under irrigation, power was taken to impose a water-rate which might be levied on the whole area for which water had been applied (or in some cases on the areas actually irrigated) in addition to the 'dry' rate' but in course of time the two rates were consolidated at revision of settlement, the consolidated rate representing the land revenue assessed on the land entitled to irrigation, in consideration, among other things, of its water advantages. The system is still followed throughout the Madras Presidency, in Sind, on a number of old irrigation works in Bombay, and in the Burma Districts which have undergone settlement. It has many advantages where, as in Southern India, over 90 percent of the irrigated area is under rice cultivation and water is delivered to the same fields year after year, and when the practice is in accordance with immemorial usage. In Northern India, however, where the new perennial canals were carried into tracts where irrigation had been before unknown, and water was applied to a number of different kinds of crops, and to different fields in different seasons (for the area actually irrigated in a single year is often not more than a third or fourth of the area under command), it was found that this system was inapplicable, the demand from particular lands being less constant, and the irrigation much more widely diffused.

**Or levied by separate rates**

In the Punjab and the United Provinces, and also in Bengal (where the land is under Permanent Settlement), the charge for water is distinct from the independent of the land-revenue assessment, and is levied in the form of a water-rate on the occupier. The occupier's rate varies according to the crop grown, and in the first two Provinces is chargeable only in respect of fields for which water has actually been taken. In Bengal it has been found convenient to introduce a system of long water leases (five or seven years) for blocks of land comprising many holdings, and each occupier is charged according to the area of his holding within the block, whether he has actually taken water or not. The occupier's rate is subject to periodical revision, and remissions are freely given in case of failure of crops, even when this is not due to the irregularity or insufficiency of the supply. It has been found, however, that the occupier's rate does not prevent a rise in rents due to water advantages. In the Punjab and the United Provinces, where the land revenue has not been permanently settled, the Government can take a share of this increase at revisions of settlement; and under the Northern India Canal and Drainage Act, 1873 (which does not apply to Bengal), it may, during the currency of a settlement, impose, in addition to the occupier's rate, an 'owner's rate' on lands which have been brought under irrigation after the settlement was made, provided that such rate does not exceed half the increase in the rental value of the land due to irrigation. The rate, like the occupier's rate, is leviable only on lands which have actually received irrigation during the year.

On the inundation canals in the Punjab which were taken over at annexation, the land revenue was until recently fixed with reference to water advantages, in accordance with ancient custom, and no other charges were made for irrigation. But in accordance with the same custom the people were also required to carry out, or to contribute to the cost of, the annual canal clearances. On the Multân and Muzaffargarh Canals this obligation was enforced by means of the now moribund *chher* system, under which each owner was required to send to the canal clearances a number of labourers proportionate to the extent of his holding which had been irrigated during the previous season. On the Dera Ghâzi Khân Canals a fixed 'clearance-rate' equal to half the estimated average cost of the clearances was levied rateably on all owners. The supply in inundation canals is liable to such fluctuation that a fixed land revenue was open to many objections, and the people no longer desired the continuance of the *chher* system. At the last resettlements of these districts it was therefore decided to impose an occupier's rate in addition to an assessment at 'dry' rates, Government undertaking the clearance by hired or contract labour in the ordinary way. The change is being introduced gradually, and the practice of *chher* clearances (which has sometimes been incorrectly regarded as forced labour) is still followed on some of the canals, but will in a few years cease to exist.

Occupiers' rates are also levied on all the Major, and on several Minor, works in the Bombay Deccan. In Sind, where almost all cultivated land is irrigated, the charge for water forms part of the land-revenue assessment; but the latter varies with the method of irrigation applied (flow or lift), with the area under cultivation, and, to a certain extent, according to the crop sown. Nine-tenths of the revenue assessed on irrigated lands is regarded as irrigation revenue, for which the canals are entitled to credit.

**Average charges for irrigation**

The charges for irrigation, whether taken in the form of enhanced land revenue of occupiers' and owners' rates, vary very much depending on the kind of crop, the quantity of water ordinarily required for it and the time when it is required, the quality of the soil, the intensity or the constancy of the demand, and the value of irrigation in increasing the out-turn. In the immediate vicinity of Poona a rate of Rs. 50 per acre is paid for sugar-cane. This is a quite exceptional rate, and obtains only over a limited area. On other parts of the Munthâ Canal the rate varies from Rs. 40 to Rs. 12, and on other canals in the Bombay Deccan from Rs. 25 to Rs. 10 per acre. In Madras the maximum rate for sugar cane is Rs. 10, and in the Punjab it does not exceed Rs. 8-8. The rate charged for rice varies in Madras from Rs. 5 to Rs. 2, and in Bengal from Rs. 2-8 to Rs. 1-8 per acre. In both these Provinces irrigation is practically confined to rice; in the Punjab, where this crop is not extensively grown, the rate varies from Rs. 7 to Rs. 3-4 per acre. The ordinary rate in the Punjab for wheat, which is the principal crop, varies from Rs. 4-4 to Rs. 3-12, and for fodder crops from Rs. 3 to Rs. 2-8, per acre. The average rate realized on Major works from irrigation of all kinds is about Rs. 3-8 per acre, the Provincial averages being Rs. 1-9 in Sind and Bengal; Rs. 3-4 in the Punjab; and Rs. 4-8 in Madras, the United Provinces, and the Bombay Deccan. The working expenses per acre vary from 8 annas in sind to Rs. 2-8 in the Bombay Deccan, the average for all Provinces being about Rs. 1-1. The charges for irrigation may be taken as varying from 10 to 12 percent of the value of the crop, except in Bengal and the Bombay Deccan, where the average is little more than 6 percent.

**The Irrigation Commission of 1901-3**

During the famines that occurred in nearly every Province of British India, and in most of the Native States, between 1896 and 1901, the protective value of irrigation was very plainly shown, in spite of failures of some of the smaller storage works; and the question naturally arose whether this protection might not be extended to those tracts in which the most severe distress had occurred, and in which means of irrigation had not been provided or were inadequate. In 1901 the Government of India referred this question to a Commission which was directed to report (*inter alia*) on the extent to which irrigation had been provided by works constructed by the state, and on the results—productive, protective, and financial—which had been attained; to determine the scope which existed for further extensions of state irrigation works, and the probable net cost of carrying them out; and to consider the extent to which local capacities for irrigation had already been utilized by private individuals, and the manner in which it might be possible to stimulate the extension of private irrigation works. Sir Colin Scott Moncrieff was appointed President of the Commission, which completed its report (from which many of the statements and figures in this chapter have been quoted) in April 1903.

**Recommendations of the Commission**

The Commission reported that the Major irrigation works constructed by the state have been, on the whole, so profitable that the surplus revenue, after meeting all interest charges on the capital outlay, now exceeds a crore of rupees a year; but they found that the field for the construction of new works of any magnitude on which the net revenue would exceed the interest charges was very limited, being restricted to the Punjab, Sind, and parts of Madras, and that the tracts in which most of such works could be constructed were not liable to famine. They recommended that such works of this class as were feasible should be constructed as soon as possible, as they would not only be profitable investments, but would have a protective value in increasing the food supplies of the country. They recognized that irrigation was most urgently required, such as the Deccan Districts of Bombay and Madras, the Central Provinces, and Bundelkhand; but they were of opinion that such works might be undertaken in these tracts as would tend to reduce the cost and mitigate the intensity of future famines, although they would not pay much more than their working expenses. For the protection of the Bomaby Deccan they recommended the construction of storage works, like Lakes Fife and Whiting, in the Western Ghâts, where the rainfall has never failed even in the driest years. For Madras they recommended a detailed investigation of the old Tungabhadra project, or some modification thereof, and of a scheme for a storage work on the

Kistna, on the understanding that it was not essential that either scheme should fulfil the conditions of a productive work, provided that it would afford, at a reasonable cost, reliable protection from famine to the districts which are now most liable to it. They also proposed that Government should undertake the construction of protective works in the rice-growing districts of the Central Provinces, and recommended the Ken Canal project in Bundelkhand and the examination of the rivers which traverse that territory for sites for storage works. The investigations which have been undertaken in the Râjputâna States were also started on the recommendation of the Commission, who proposed that they should be extended to the Central India and Kâthiâwâr States. The Commission further sketches out a rough programme of new Major works to be constructed in different parts of India, which would cost not less than 44 crores of rupees, and would result in an increase of 6,500,000 acres in the irrigated area. It was estimated that the construction of these works would impose a permanent yearly burden of nearly 74 lakhs on the state, through the excess of interest charges on capital cost over the net revenue due to the works. Against this would have to be set, however, the reduction in the cost of future famines resulting from the construction of the works, which, the Commission thought, could not be estimated as likely to average less than 31 lakhs per annum. The balance of 43 lakhs would represent the net annual cost of the works to the state, or the price to be paid for the protection from famine which the works would afford, and for all other indirect advantages that might be attributed to them. The Commission also called attention to the fact that the area actually protected by private irrigation was greater than that which is dependent on all the works constructed or maintained by the state; and considered that a great deal might be done to encourage the extension of such works by a more liberal and elastic system of Government loans, by grants-in-aid in famine tracts, and by other means. The Commission were, however, of opinion that, although much could be done by irrigation to restrict the area and to mitigate the cost and distress of famine, India could not be entirely protected from famine by means of irrigation alone. They estimated also that, if all the works which they proposed could be constructed, they would not intercept for purposes of irrigation more than 2¼ percent of the volume of water which now, unused, flows onward to the sea. The practical application of these proposals is under consideration; and the annual allotment from revenue for expenditure on irrigation projects, which stood at one crore between 1900-1 and 1903-4, has now (1904-5) been raised to 1¼ crores.

**Comparative merits of irrigation works and railways as a means of famine protection**

The relative merits of railways and irrigation works as a means of preventing famine have often been the subject of discussion, but the claims which may be made on behalf of either are not conflicting, for the means of production and distribution must be regarded as mutually supplementary. Railways do not, like canals, increase the food-supply of the country, but they render possible the transfer of surplus supplies to parts which require them. They are the only means of ensuring a food-supply in times of famine to many tracts where irrigation is impossible or could only be supplied at a prohibitive cost. Again, the protective value of many of the most important irrigation works, such as those which have converted into unfailing granaries the unpopulated and uncultivated wastes of the Punjab and Sind, depends on the existence of railways by which the surplus produce may be readily and cheaply distributed. It may be that the construction of a particular railway might well have been held in abeyance in favour of an irrigation work, or vice verse; but improvement in the means of production and of distribution must nevertheless proceed concurrently. The smallness in the difference of prices in all parts of the country during the famines which have occurred since 1896 is the best justification of the policy of railway extension as an alleviation of famine. Irrigation works can do much, but they cannot by themselves give as complete or universal protection as is required.

## Navigation

**Connexion of irrigation with navigation**

Inland navigation and irrigation are closely connected, for each depends for its fullest development in India on the construction of canals. If the natural waterways of the country are to be utilized to the utmost for the purpose of communications, it is as necessary to connect them by navigable channels as it is to tap their waters by canals for purposes of irrigation. At first sight it may appear that the same channels might be made to serve both purposes, and that when the great cost of constructing a large irrigation canal has been undertaken, there should be no hesitation in incurring the extra expenditure required to render it navigable. Even if the revenue to be anticipated from navigation dues should be insufficient to yield an adequate return on the additional capital outlay involved, it may be admitted that unremunerative expenditure of this kind would be justified if there were a certainty that the canal would be extensively used for navigátion, that a new line of communication would be established, and that a material saving would be effected in the cost of transport. Apart, however, from all questions of cost, it has been found that the exigencies of irrigation and navigation are not always compatible, and that traffic is not attracted to a navigable canal which does not pass through large cities or important trade centres, or which is not in uninterrupted connexion either with the seaboard or with the waterways which form the most convenient outlet for the produce of the tract which the canal traverses. Hence it happens that irrigation canals are not always suitable for navigation, and, on the other hand, that many canals have been constructed for purposes of navigation only and do not irrigate a single acre. It will be convenient to consider in the first place the sytem of irrigation canals which are also navigable.

**Godâvari and Kistna Canals**

The two two most important navigable systems of irrigation works are the Godâvari and Kistna Canals in the Madras Presidency. The total length of the main canals and branches of these systems is 506 and 372 miles respectively, of which 493 and 332 miles are navigable. There were strong reasons for applying these canals to navigation. During many months in the year they carry away all, or nealry all, the river supply, and so cut off the upper waters of the rivers from the seaboard. They traverse flat and fully cultivated deltas, in which there are no great falls to be overcome, and which are ill provided with roads or other means of communication, while the people on the coast are accustomed to the use of boats. The navigable canals which have been made rediate from the head-works at Dowlaishweram and Bezwâda towards the sea, which connects their lower ends, while the head of each system is connected with the other, with the upper waters of the Godâvari and Kistna, with the Buckingham Canal, and with the railway system of the country. The total number of boats entering the two systems annually is about 80,000, with a tonnage estimated as varying from 700,000 to 800,000 tons, and there is also a small amount of raft traffic. The facilities for navigation are undoubtedly a great boon to the cultivators and tend materially to reduce the cost of transport; but although great use is made of them, it cannot be said that navigation even here is directly remunerative. The navigation receipts, which have been materially affected by the opening of direct rail communication along the east coast, average only 1½ lakhs per annum, and do not as a rule exceed the working expenses, so that there is little direct return on the expenditure incurred in rendering the canals navigable. On the other hand, the assessment on the irrigated lands would no doubt have to be considerably lower if the people did not enjoy their present advantages of cheap transport.

### Kurnool-Cuddapah Canal

The only other irrigation work in Madras which has been adapted for navigation is the Kurnool-Cuddapah Canal, but here the conditions are very unfavourable. The canal is navigable throughout its entire length of 190 miles, in which there are no less than forty locks. It has, however, no water connexion with the seaboard, although it is connected with two railways, at its 109th mile and at its tail (Nandyâl and Cuddapah). The traffic is practically *nil,* although no navigation dues are levied, while the navigation charges exceed Rs. 10,000 a year. The advantages of navigation would probably have been more appreciated if the complete Tungabhadra project as originally conceived had been carried out, if a navigable connexion with the seaboard through Nellore District had been provided, and if large storage works had been constructed on the Tungabhadra so as to ensure at all seasons an adequate supply for purposes of navigation. However this may be, there is little prospect of navigation ever being successfully developed on the existing canal.

**Navigable irrigation canals in Bengal**

The three Major irrigation works in Bengal have all been adapted for navigation. The Orissa Canals comprise 280 miles of main canals and branches, of which 205 are navigable, as is the whole length of the Midnapore Canals (72 miles). It was originally proposed to connect these two systems by a high-level canal, which would afford a continuous water communication between Cuttack and Midnapore and thence to Calcutta; but this was only carried as far as Bhadrakh on the Salandî river. In the absence of such a connecting link, the boats on the Orissa Canals proceeded to Calcutta via Chândbâli and the Bay of Bengal. But in order to provide inland communication for small craft, the Orissa Coast and Hijilî Canals, which are purely navigation canals, were subsequently constructed; and there is now free and uninterrupted water communication at all seasons between Cuttack at the head of the Orissa delta and Geonkhâli, near the confluence of the Rupnârâyan and Hooghly rivers a few miles above Diamond Harbour. The construction of these two navigation canals has not resulted in such an increase in traffic onthe Orissa system as was anticipated. During the year 1902-3 the combind navigation receipts of the three canals were less than Rs. 1,40,000, and the net revenue did not amount to Rs. 23,000, although the capital expenditure incurred on account of navigation alone cannot be estimated at less than a crore of rupees. Even less favourable results may be anticipated in future, as the traffic is affected by the recently constructed extensions of the Bengal-Nâgpur Railway. The Midnapore Canal has been more successful as a navigation work, but here also the traffic is likely to be affected by the railway.

The three main canals of the Son system, with an aggregate length of 218 miles, are all navigable and tail into the Ganges at Buxar, Arrah, and Dinapore. The traffic has always been very moderate, and the tolls do not cover the working expenses due to navigation. During the last two years the receipts have suffered serious diminution in consequence of the opening of the Mughalsarai-Gayâ Railway, in 1902-3 they did not amount to Rs. 19,000, which is about a quarter of the average for the three years ending March, 1899.

## Navigation in the United Provinces

In the United Provinces the main lines of the Upper and Lower Ganges Canals (275 miles) and of the Agra Canal (100 miles) are navigable throughout. The Ganges systems are connected with the Ganges river at Cawnpore, and the Agra Canal has a channel leading into the Jumna river near Agra, while it is connected at its head, by means of the Okhla navigation channel, with the Western Jumna Canal in the Punjab.[1] It might have been expected, therefore, that a considerable through traffic to Calcutta would be developed, but as a matter of fact the traffic is purely local and of inconsiderable volume. The average number of boats plying monthly on the canals in the United Provinces is less than 250, and the traffic receipts do not average more than Rs. 15,000 per annum, which is about half the amount of navigation working expenses.

## Punjab

In the Punjab the only navigable canals are portions of the Western Jumna and Sirhind systems. The former is navigable from its head to Delhi, and is then, as already stated, connected with the Agra Canal and the Jumna. A portion of the Hânsi branch is also navigable, the total length of navigable channels being 207 miles. The Sirhind Canal is navigable for 180 miles, or from its head at Rupar to Ferozepore, where the canal connects with the river Sutlej, and there is a continuous waterway onwards to Karâchi. The boat traffic on these canals is so insignificant that the details are not recorded, and the boat-tolls on both together amount to less than Rs. 5,000 per annum. There is, however, a considerable raft traffic, particularly on the Western Jumna Canal, where the rafting dues average about Rs. 40,000 per annum. The rafts consist principally of timber, sleepers, scantling, and bamboos, which are floated down from the hills to the canal heads, and are then passed into the canals. These rafts used to pass down the rivers before the canals were constructed, but the abstraction of the whole of the cold-weather supply has rendered the canal route necessary. The effect of constructing the canals has therefore been to divert rather than to create traffic.

## Sind

Inundation canals are not adapted to navigation, with the single exeption of the great Fuleli Canal in Sind, which enjoys an alomost perennial supply and is so situated that it has been possible to render it navigable at a very moderate cost. The Eastern Nâra, which takes off from the left bank of the Indus above Sukkur, is also navigable all the year round.

## Navigation works which are not also irrigation works

## Madras

Besides the state irrigation works which are also navigable canals, Madras and Bengal possess other canals which have been constructed solely for purposes of navigation. In the former the most important work is the Buckingham Canal, which is connected with one of the branches of the Kistna system and then, proceeding almost due south, skirts the Coromandel coast for a distance of 262 miles, and passes through Madras city. It is a tidal canal, and costly locks have been required at each of the numerous river-crossings, so that the capital cost of the work amounts to nearly 90 lakhs of rupees. There is a moderate traffic on this canal, on which more than 200,000 tons of goods are carried annually; but this also has been affected by the extension of rail communication along the east coast, and the navigation receipts do not fully cover the working expenses. Nevertheless the work must be regarded as one of considerable public utility. There is also a navigation coast canal in Tanjore District, known as the Vedâranniyam Canal, and a small canal connected with the Chilka Lake in Ganjâm District. Madras possesses no other navigable canals, but has many miles of natural waterways formed by river backwaters, especially on the west coast, and on these there is a very considerable traffic. Mention may also be made of the works on the first rocky barrier on the Godâvari, at Dummagudem, 120 miles above the head of the Godâvari Canals at Dowlaishweram, which render that river navigable for boats to the foot of the second barrier, a distnce of 188 miles.

**Bengal**

Reference has already been made to the Orissa Coast and Hijilî Tidal Canals in Bengal. There are two other important works in the Province, the Calcutta and Eastern Canals, and the Nadiâ Rivers. The former consist of short lengths of locked canals and open channels which have been made for the purpose of connecting many of the natural river-channels in the deltas of the Ganges and the Brahmaputra, so as to provide a continuous interior line of communication between Calcutta and the Sundarbans, Eastern Bengal, and Assam, for the benefit of steamers, flats, and small craft constructed for inland waters. These works are of great importance, for they comprise a length of 735 miles of navigable canals ad river channels. There is a great deal of traffic, the average tonnage of cargo and passenger-boats amounting to over 1,000,000 tons a year. The works are more nearly self-supporting than any other navigation works in India. The capital expenditure has been about 68 lakhs, the average annual receipts amount to 4¼ lakhs, and the net revenue exceeds 1½ lakhs. The Nadiâ rivers comprise the Bhâgîrathi, the Jalangî, and the Mâtâbhânga, which constitute the upper waters of the Hooghly. These rivers have not been canalized, nor has any capital expenditure been incurred on navigation works. Steamers can navigate them from July to October, but in very dry years they are not open even to small craft throughout the remaining months. Some expenditure is incurred annually in keeping open the channels, which have an aggregate length of 472 miles. The aggregate capacity of the boats using them amounts to about 500,000 tons per annum, and the tolls to 1 lakh, the average working expenses being about Rs. 1,20,000.

**Burma**

In Burma, which abounds in natural waterways, there are only two important navigable canals, the Pegu-Sittang and the Sittang-Kyaikto. These are maintained by Government, but no capital expenditure on them has been recorded. The recepits on the former amount to about Rs. 1,40,000 per annum, but do not cover the working expenses. On the latter no revenue is realized, but about half a lakh is spent annually on maintence. Some expenditure is also incurred on the conservancy of navigable rivers, so as to facilitate navigation.

**General results attained on navigation works**

From the foregoing description of the navigable canals in British India it will be seen that not one of them, whether intended primarily for irrigation or constructed solely as a navigation work, is directly remunerative, and that in many cases the navigation receipts do not cover the working expenses. The extension of navigation works must therefore depend for its justification on the benefits which the country will derive from a reduction in the cost of transport. This reduction will be real and material only in those tracts where the public can be trusted to avail themselves freely of the advantages offered by water communications. There is no Province in which facilities for navigation are so likely to be appreciated as in Eastern Bengal, with its dense population, its thriving industries, and its innumerable river channels. There is great scope for further extensions of inland navigation in this tract; and if the works will not prove directly remunerative, they are not likely to impose a heavy permanent charge on the state, while they will be of great value in increasing the wealth of the community. Navigation advantages have also been fairly appreciated in the deltas of Orissa and Madras, and have certainly proved of great value to the cultivators. Elsewhere, as on the Kurnool-Cuddapah and Son Canals, or the great perennial canals in Northern India, navigation may be regarded as a failure. Not only have the works required in connexion with it been very costly, but the people have evinced no desire to avail themselves of the means of navigation afforded. There is, moreover, another objection to the combination of navigation with irrigation on perennial canals which deserves notice. Navigation is not only costly, but cannot be maintained during seasons of short supply without detriment to the efficiency of the canal as an irrigating work. In general it may be said that, outside the deltaic tracts in Bengal, Orissa, Madras, and Sind, navigable canals will never be of much use or value as a means of inland communication.

## Navigable rivers

We have hitherto referred only to navigation works by which the natural waterways of the country have been artificially connected. It remains to consider briefly the value of these waterways themselves as a means of inland communication. Some of large rivers of India, such as the Narbadâ and the Tâpti, are unfortunately, by reason of their rocky beds and swift floods, practically useless for navigation except at their mouths. The Indus, the Ganges, and the Brahmaputra are navigable by steamers all the year round, or for the greater part of the year, for hundreds of miles above their mouths, or above the heads of the navigable canals traversing their deltas. The Indus is thus constantly navigable as high as Dera Ismail Khân in the North-West Frontier Province, 800 miles inland and 250 miles beyond the Sind border. Its tributaries, the Chenâb and the Sutlej, are open to small craft all the year round, but there is little traffic above Chiniot on the former and Ferozepore on the latter. The Fuleli Canal and the Eastern Nâra may be regarded as navigable branches of the Indus. The Ganges is navigable as high as Cawnpore, and steamers also pass up the Gogra as far as Fyzâbâd. Steam navigation on the Indus and the Upper Ganges has, however, been greatly reduced by the development of rail traffic, though on the Bengal portion of the Ganges it is still active. The Brahmaputra is navigable by steamers as high as Dibrugarh, and there is steam navigation on its tributary the Surmâ as far inland as Sylhet and Câchâr. The Hooghly is navigable all the year round up to Nadiâ, and steamers can pass up the Nadiâ rivers above this point from July to October. The great rivers on the east coast of the Peninsula—the Mahânadî, the Godâvari, and the Kistna—are all navigable for some distance above the heads of their deltas, but the traffic on them is not very considerable. Many tributaries or branches of these rivers are also navigable during the monsoon months, and several are open to small craft all the year round. There are, in effect, all round the coast innumerable small rivers, creeks, and backwaters affording facilities for water transport which are fully utilized by small native craft; but outside the zone of such operations inland navigation is practically confined to the deltas and to the valleys of the great rivers which form the natural waterways of the country.

As to Burma, there is no Province in which the natural waterways afford greater facilities for inland navigation, or in which it is more extensively practised. In the Arakan Division the Mayu and Kaladan rivers are navigable by steamers during a great part of the year for distances of 50 and 90 miles respectively above Akyab. Many of the other rivers which fall into the Bay of Bengal are similarly navigable for some miles above the seaboard, and native craft can of course proceed much farther inland. Farther east the great Irrawaddy river, which traverses nearly the whole length of Upper and Lower Burma (excluding Tenasserim), is navigable by steamers at all seasons of the year as high as Bhamo, or more than 500 miles from its mouth, and steam launches and country boats can proceed much higher, or for some distance to the north of Myitkyinâ. The numerous deltaic channels which fall into the Bay of Bengal from the Irrawaddy form waterways connected with the main river and with the sea, which are for the most part navigable throughout the year, while higher up many of the tributaries of this river are navigable for some distance above their confluences. Of these the two most important are the Chindwin and Myitnge rivers, the former of which is navigable by steamers during the monsoon as high as Homalin in the twenty-fifth parallel of latitude, and by smaller craft as far as Kyaukse. Farther east again are the Sittang and the Salween rivers, both of which discharge into the Gulf of Martaban. The former of these is navigable by small steamers during the monsoon as far as Toungoo, and for small craft as far as Pyinmanâ in Upper Burma. All these rivers have numerous navigable affluents, and branches or mouths which spread fanlike over their deltas and are in navigable communication with each other. There are also, all round the Burma coast, innumerable creeks and backwaters open to steamers or smaller craft.

**Navigation dues**

The tolls charged for navigation vary very much on different works, and cannot be easily compared. In the United Provinces and the Punjab monthly or quarterly charges are made according to the size of the boat, which is then free of the canal during the period for which the pass is given. On the Fuleli Canal in Sind the same system is adopted. In Bengal the charge depends on the maundage, which is taken roughly as half the displacement measured in cubic feet. There are fixed rates per 100 maunds for different reaches, which vary with the length and other circumstances. In Madras the Bengal system of distance-tolls on all vessels plying between certain stations was originally in force; but has been replaced by a system of annual and short-term (6 weeks) licences, for which moderate fees are charged, and which leave the holders free to navigate all parts of the connected waterway systems. In Burma navigation tolls are levied only on the Pegu-Sittang Canal, where they are charged on the carrying capacity of the boats expressed in baskets of paddy ('unhusked rice'), and on the Shwetachaung Canal in Mandalay District, which is navigable for about 13 miles. Conservancy or registration fees are sometimes charged on vessels navigating the large rivers. On the Indus the charge is at the rate of Rs. 4 per annum per maund of registered burden for native craft, while steamers which pay no port dues are charged three times this amount.

**Navigable canals compared with railways**

The comparative merits of railways and navigable canals as means of communication have sometimes been discussed. The principal argument in favour of the latter is that the cost of haulage or transport is less. On the other hand, canal routes are more devious; cross-communications or connexions between different systems are more difficult; feeder canals cannot be taken into new areas of supply with the same facility as feeder railways; the time occupied in transport on canals is much greater; and, lastly, there are many tracts in which canal navigation cannot be maintained, even at great expense, without the diversion and absorption of a large volume of water which might be more advantageously used for irrigation. The comparison of these advantages and disadvantages is, however, only of academical interest. The commercial, the administrative, the military, and even the agricultural needs of India could never have been met by means of navigable canals alone; and the real question is not of the comparative merits of canals and railways, but whether in particular cases navigation canals may not suffice for immediate requirements, or may not serve as useful supplements to railway facilities already provided. Individual cases of this kind must be considered on their merits, but it is noteworthy that there is hardly a single tract in which navigable canals have been made by Government in which a railway has not been subsequently constructed. There may be now, or eventually, room for both, but the fact that the construction of a railway causes a very serious diminution in the volume of previous canal traffic indicates that the lower cost of haulage on canals cannot in many cases be set against the other advantages which may be claimed for railways. It may be said that during the severest stress of recent famines railways have sometimes failed for a time to cope fully with the situation, but this has been generally due to the want of a reserve of rolling stock, and navigation canals would be equally liable to failure from insufficiency of cargo boats. It is, indeed, difficult to conceive any practicable system of navigable canals by which the exigencies of famine-distressed districts could have been met as effiectively as by the existing network of railways. Lastly, it may be said that, whatever the comparative capital cost of navigable canals and railways may be, the former have never proved directly remunerative, whereas the latter yield on the whole a net revenue which is more than sufficient to cover all the interest charges on their capital cost. Much can, no doubt, still be done for the improvement of communications in the deltas of Eastern Bengal and similar areas by improving the open waterways of the country and connecting them by navigable cuts, but outside these tracts the field for the extension of inland navigation cannot be regarded as either wide or promising.

## References

1. The Agra Canal was closed to navigation in June, 1904.

## Bibliography

A. Deakin—*Irrigated India* (1893).

R. B. Buckley—*Irrigation Works in India and Egypt* (1893).

J. and R. Strachey—*Finances and Public Works of India* (1882).

Report of the Irrigation Commission, 1903.

Reports of the Famine Commissions of 1878-80, 1898, and 1901.

Annual Irrigation Reviews of Government of India and Local Governments. 'Completion Reports' are also published, under the authority of the Govenment of India, for each Major irrigaiton work when completed.

# 5

# Nature of The Poligar Revolts in the Ceded Districts During the First Half of the Nineteenth Century: A Case Study

There has been a continuous resistance against the British rule in India from its very inception. The resistance might be traditional in character, but during the course of time it had taken the form of armed resistance on the part of the chief's as well as the *in'amdars* and other retainers. The persons who took the leadership were mainly the deposed chieftains or their descendants and relations, *zamindars*, poligars,[1] *in'amdars,* ex-soldiers, officials and other retainers of the Indian States. The majority of the persons who joined and formed the backbone of these revolts were petty village officials holding small *in'am* lands, peasantry and artisans.

In south India broadly during the last decade of the 18th century and first half of the 19th century the revolts were prominantly led by the poligars, their descendants and relations. The poligars of Tamil Nadu revolted during the 1790's, Malabar and Dindigal in 1800-01, Parlakimedi from 1813 to 1834. In Andhra the poligars of the coastal areas and the 'Ceded Districts'[2] revolted from 1801-05 and then in 1846.[3] But the nature of the revolt of 1846 marks a distinct change from that of earlier revolts in the Ceded Districts. The earlier revolts on the part of the chiefs were mostly political in character whereas the latter revolt comprised much larger canvas where the economic interests of the higher and lower classes of *in'amdars* were at stake.

---

Paper read at *Indian History Congres*, 25th Session, Jadavpur, 1974 and published in the *Proceedings*, pp. 235-245.

At the time of the cession of the Ceded Districts by the Nizam of Hyderabad to the East India Company (1800) there were, as many as 80 poligars, haying under their exclusive command about 30,000 armed retainers.[4] All 'these poligars, were originally either public servants of government or renters of districts, who revolted in times of disturbance. Some of the poligars like that of Owke had initially received their villages in *in'am* in lieu of their rank, while others like the poligars of Rayadurg and Harpanahalli owned through usurpation. Some of them like the poligars of Chitweyl were renters and held villages as personal *jagir* for the maintenance of the contingent comprising horsemen and footmen. There are cases like the poligars of Nossum and Mullel who did not hold any *jagir* but as renters paid cash money after having been absolved from military service. After having held those districts for a number of years during the turbulent period they got the term *peshkash* substituted for that of rent. A few landed intermediaries like that of Kallibundah as renters used to be assessed at full revenues *(Kamil)*[5] but owing to the political disturbances, they as well assumed the role of poligars.[6] Many *patels* (village headmen) like that of Gurrumkondah also took the advantage of the weakness of the government and having held the revenue also became the poligars.[7] This shows that it was the title of the poligar that was important and all the poligars had to pay, at least in theory, a fixed *peshkash* to the ruler. As such, they could be easily compared with the *muqarrari peshkashi* zamindars found in some other parts of the country.[8]

The first and the most important task that the British administrators had before them was the 'immediate and vigorous assertion of the Company's authority'[9] in the Ceded Districts. In order to achieve this, Thomas Munro, the first Principal Collector of the Ceded Districts adopted a very calculated policy. In order to assert the Company's authority in the Ceded Districts and to introduce proper administrative system it was very necessary to completely finish the political and economic power of the poligars. It was both administrative and agrarian necessity. Without law and order efficient running of administration was not possible. Moreover, like feudal lords, they exercised a considerable influence on the agrarian life of the villages.

In the beginning Thomas Munro adopted peaceful but diplomatic attitude towards them. All the poligars were allowed to remain as they were but at the same time he raised the magnitude of the revenue assessment so high as to render it impossible for them to maintain any troops except by withholding their revenue payments. The idea behind this was to change the fixed *peshkash* into a land rent, assessed at nearly the same rate as that on the government land. This policy, on the one hand, changed the nature of the relations of the poligars, *vis-a-vis,* the government and on the other hand, the most dangerous poligars with the greatest number of followers would either have to submit or else provide Thomas Munro with an excuse for acting against them.[10] The result was that he could, to a great extent, successfully deal with this problem and within a period of one year he was able to place the Ceded Districts in high degree of security.

Narasimha Reddy was the third and the youngest son of Malla Reddy, the poligar of Ooyalewada in the Koilkuntla taluq, Cuddapah district. From his mother's side he was the grandson of Jayaram Reddy, the poligar of an extensive *polliam* Nossum also situated in Koilkuntle taluq, Cuddapah district.[11] After the death of Jayaram Reddy in 1795, his son, Narasimha Reddy (known as Nossum Reddy) became the poligar of Nossum. At the time of the cession of the district (1800), the Ooyalewada and Nossum *polliams* yielded an annual revenue of Rs. 30,480-8-5 and Rs. 83,230-0-0[12] respectively. The poligars of both these *polliams* refused to accept the *cowle* (*Jama*) fixed by Thomas Munro. Nossum Reddy was apprehended by General Campbell in 1801 and was confined in the fort on the Gooty hill in the Bellary district. Pedda Malla Reddy, poligar of Ooyalewada, brother-in-law of Nossum Reddy, left his *polliam* with his younger brother, Chinna Malla Reddy and took refuge in the Hyderabad territory, where he remained for nearly 8 years. The *polliam* was resumed and an allowance of Rs. 88-9-0 per mensum was granted to their mother, who did not live for long. Nossum Reddy was released from confinement in 1802 while his *polliam* was resumed and he was granted a pension of Rs. 8,323-10-5[13] per annum. Pedda Malla Reddy returned from Hyderabad in 1808 and along with Chinna

Malla Reddy appeared before Chaplin, the then collector and solicited a pension. Chaplin granted them a pension of Rs. 70/- p.m., i.e., Rs. 35/- p.m. each. But Pedda Malla Reddy, being the brother-in-law of Nossum Reddy could get some financial assistance from the latter as well. This pecuniary assistance was available to Pedda Malla Reddy and after his death to his three sons Kamaru Malla Reddy, Varda Reddy and Narasimha Reddy for a pretty long time. The Nossum *Polliam* after the death of Nossum Reddy passed on to his step-mother Seetamah and thereafter to his widow Siddamma. But after the death of Siddamma the pension was reverted to the government. Now all the three sons of Pedda Malla Reddy advanced their claims for the continuance to them of the Nossum pension on the plea of their relationship with the original grantee. But the government was not prepared to accept the claims. The result was that three brothers were left with a meagre pension of Rs. 35 p.m.[13] Due to some dissensions in the families of three brothers, Narasimha Reddy separated himself with his share of pension amounting to Rs. 11-10-8 p.m.[14] At the same time he had also to support a very large family,[15] with such reduced financial resources.[16]

The first information regarding the revolt of the Poligar Narasimha Reddy came during the first week of July, 1846 when J.M. Cochrane the acting collector of Cuddapah reported the matter to the higher authorities and requested for assistance. The revolt was so sudden that the collector of Cuddapah was taken by surprise.[17] In spite of the stern efforts of the British government, they were unable to apprehend him and as such there was lot of excitement in the British Camp.[18] Narasimha Reddy and his followers kept them on toes for nearly three months. Even though the areas affected by the revolt were broadly speaking the taluks of Koilkuntla, Dhoor and Jammalamadugu, the British Government had got so much panicky that they could never make any correct assessment about the number of followers that the Poligar had.[19] They even went to the extent of declaring an award of Rs. 1000/- for the apprehension of the Poligar.[20] The task for the Britishers had become all the more difficult due to the active support of the heads of the villages, *kattubadis*[21] Brahmin *bhatta-vritti*[22] *in'am* holders and the *raiyats* in general.[23] It was only in October 1846[24] that the poligar could be captured and then was publically hanged in February 1847.[25]

There are as many as three full-length reports dealing with the causes of revolt and two observations made by the Board of Revenue. The first and the most important report comes from W.A.D. Inglis, Special Commissioner appointed[26] to try the prisoners engaged in the revolt and report about the causes of the revolt.[27] The second report was given by J.H. Cochran, Ag. Magistrate and Collector, Cuddapah, when he was asked[28] to submit his views of the causes of the outbreak and opinion on the Special Commissioner's report.[29] The third report on the outbreaks in Cuddaph and opinion on the Special Commissioner's report were submitted by S. Scott, Agent to the Governor in Cuddaph.[30] On the basis of the above three reports the Board of Revenue made its own observations[31] and thereafter the opinions were expressed and recorded in the Minutes of Consultations.[32]

Of all the three reports, the report given by the Special Commissioner seems to be more exhaustive, informative and objective, whereas, the other two reports are contradictory and defensive in nature, agreeing, of course, though with some reservations, on all the basic issues. One point on which all the reports agree was that the Poligar Narasimha Reddy had got the active support of the *kattubadis,* the village headmen, *raiyats* in general and the moral support of the upper classes like the Brahmins. Narasimha Reddy may be having his own reasons of discontentment, but the way he was supported by the above mentioned classes shows that the discontentment was not only confined to the Poligar but was general. Other classes found a proper opportunity of showing their discontentment when Narasimha Reddy rose against the British Government. The excitement, alarm and discontentment had been prevailing in the district because of the British policy towards the *bhatta-vritti* and *kattubadi in'ams* initiated a few months before the outbreak. No doubt it was the resumption of certain *kattubadi in'ams,* which had immediately led to the insurrection, the measures adopted towards the *bhatta-vritti in'ams* had made the upper classes also very much dissatisfied.[33]

The *bhatta-vritti in'ams* were in existence since the cession of the districts. Thomas Munro in his instructions to the surveyors had directed them that all sundry *in'ams* having no specific designation, under which they could be classed, should be entered, if belonging to the Hindus as *"Bhatta-vritti"*, and if belonging to the Mohammadans, as *"Khairati"*[34] In the abstract list in the court classifying *in'ams, khairati* and *bhatta-vritti* were bracketed together as *Dharmadayam* or secular, as distinguished from *Devadayam* or religious grants.[35] Before being appointed as Special Commissioner, Inglis was a Civil Judge in the Sadar Adawalat and as such had more intimate knowledge. However, both Cochrane and Scott differ from Inglis on this point and are not prepared to call those *in'ams* as secular ones.[36]

The *bhatta-vritti in'ams* were quite extensive, rent free land tenures. All the *in'ams* under this head, and that of *khairati* were comprised of the *in'ams* of less than a village in the district. They were not the service lands nor were granted on a specific account. The *khairati in'ams* were comparatively less in number and value whereas *bhatta-vritti in'ams,* according to the survey assessment, bore a value of more than Rupees Six lakhs per annum. Such *in'amdars* had held their holdings as a private property, having perfect liberty to alienate them by gift or sale. Munro had given the understanding that the government would maintain *status quo* with them though no new such grants would be made.[37] But in 1845, the Board of Revenue declared the *bhatta-vritti in'ams* as the *Devadayam* or the religious grants or the charitable allowance[38] and enforced the clause 2, Regulation IV of 1831.[39] Accordingly the transfer of such *in'ams* by gift or sale was prohibited and the jurisdiction of the courts over these *in'ams* was finished. In case of the death of any incumbent the collector was to report the matter to the government for their instructions about successor of the *in'ams.* The result was after the death of an *in'amdar,* his land were attached immediately, and his family, even if he had left sons, was kept in a state of anxiety and suspense for months together. Even after the orders of the Government arrived (if the decision was positive) the heir would receive the ancestral estate not as his hereditary right, but as the government land, and for his life only. Though the regulations had been enforced, they had not been given proper publicity and the *in'amdars* came to know about them when the hammer started falling on their heads. The result was that they lost the confidence in the government and became hostile towards it.[40]

Another important factor, which helped in making the revolt more extensive was the British policy towards the *kattubadi in'ams.* The *kattubadis* were generally of two classes—(i) relations of the Poligars and their chief retainers who had received larger hereditary grants for their support; (ii) the lower class of retainers, who held only very small hereditary *in'ams,* which was a sort of retaining fee to secure their services whenever required." Of course, the *in'ams* of both the classes of *kattubadis* were subject to a quit rent. Apart from their attachment with the Poligars, the *kattubadis,* though they had never formed the part of the village police and were only a sort of militia, were called out occasionally to assist the village police:[42]

The *kattubadis* had received a special guarantee from Thomas Munro on the part of government that their hereditary *in'ams* would be continued during good behaviour on the condition of their yielding to the British government the same services they had been formerly rendering to the Poligars.[43] There are numerous letters showing the hereditary nature of *kattubadi in'ams.* Even as late as 1821, the Secretary to the Government wrote to the Board of Revenue that "...the *kattubadi in'ams* in the Ceded Districts have always been hereditary, and that the succession to them ought to be regulated by the usage of the country...you will make such communication...to the collectors of Cuddapah and Bellary desiring them not to disturb the *kattubadi* peons in the possession of their *in'ams.*"[44] Thomas Munro, by adopting such policy towards the *kattubadis,* was successful to the highest degree in his object of establishing peace and safety in the region.[45]

In December 1845 a plan was prepared according to which the government was to retain in a village only a required number of *kattubadis.* The excess *kattubadis* in a village, in case they were 'willing', were to be removed to other village in the same *taluq* where there were less than the required number. Their existing *in'am* lands were to be resumed and they were to be granted the fresh grant of waste lands according to a minimum standard of remuneration in the villages of their appointments. These appointments and the land grants were not to be hereditary and would be subject to re-adjustments after the death of a *kattubadi.* All the remaining *kattubadi in'ams* were to be resumed on the death of the existing incumbents.[46]

According to this plan the *in'ams* of as many as 1396 *kattubadis,* rated according to the survey assessment at Rs. 27, 767-4-7, were to be resumed on the death of the present possessors; 239 *kattubadis* were to be removed to other villages, of course with their own consent; and the *in'ams* of 1695 *kattubadis,* bearing a survey assessment of Rs. 74,895-15-10 were to be reduced to Rs. 29,623-12-5.[47]

In early 1846 as many as 239 *kattubadis,* with their consent[48] according to the tahsildars, were removed from their villages. According to the plan, referred above, Cochrane, Acting Collector, acting on the further instructions of the Board of Revenue of May 1845[49] resumed the *in'ams* of 23 *kattubadis* in June 1846 after the death of their possessors.[50] All the affected *kattubadis,* excepting two, had left male heirs entitled to succeed their lands. It will be interesting to note that except four cases, all the lapses and resumptions took place either in the Koilkuntla *taluq* or in the adjoining *taluqs,* and on the immediate borders of it. It is also worthy of remark that the *kattubadis* of mainly these areas took the most active part in revolt[51] which occurred in the very next month *i.e.,* July 1846.

*Kattubadis* and their friends initiated the insurrection and the resumption of their *in'ams* was the immediate cause of the revolt. No doubt the revolt took place in Koilkuntla and the surrounding *taluqs,* the feeling of discontent and disposition, as has been reported by the Special Commissioner, prevailed universally throughout the Cuddapah district amongst the *kattubadis.* Narasimha Reddy admitted before the Special Commissioner that he had to remain with the *kattubadis* on the latters insistence. Even otherwise most of the principal *kattubadis* were related to Narasimha Reddy and as they belonged to the cultivating class, they were also related to many of the heads of the villages and principal *raiyats.* Moreover, he had some hereditary influence on the *kattubadis* because they had received their land grants from his ancestors. This shows that they had made a common cause and revolted against the British government. The *kattubadis,* as stated by the then *tahsildar* of Koilkuntla, declared that "if successful, they will not only retain their present *in'ams*, which the sircar were bent on taking from them, but would obtain increased grants from Narasimha Reddy."[52] Narasimha Reddy had accepted to be their leader as he also wanted to improve his position and was of the view that the insurrection might result into a compromise with the British government which may grant him more pension.[53]

Thus, in spite of the traditional loyalties that Narasimha Reddy enjoyed from the *kattubadis,* the latter made common cause with the former not merely because they owed traditional loyalty to him, as has been stated by Cochrane[54] and Scott[55] but also because their own personal interests were adversely affected by the policy of the British Government towards their *in'am* lands. Both Cochrane and Scott do accept that the British policy towards the *kattubadi in'ams* had created lot of disaffection among them and as many as three-fourth of the village *kattubadis* had sided with the Poligar.[56] At the same time the British policy towards the *bhatta-vritti in'ams* had already made the upper class of the society very much hostile towards them. Because of their influence in the society the Brahmins created better atmosphere for the revolt, which helped in keeping the British intelligence at bay and consequently the Britishers would never get correct report about the whereabouts of the insurgents from the people. This shows that this revolt was not aimed to gain any political power, as was the case with the Poligar revolts during the late 18th and early 19th century but was essentially a socio-economic rising.

## References

1. For the further details about the Poligars, see, J.C. Dua, "Poligars: Their rise in the Ceded Districts", *I.H.C.,* XXXIII, 1972, pp. 467-477.
2. The Ceded Districts comprised the present districts of Cuddapah, Kurnool, Anantapur (in Andhra Pradesh), Bellary (in Karnatka) and two *taluqs* of Chittoor District (A.P.)—Madanpalle and Vayalpad.
3. The revolt of the Poligar Narasimha Reddy under discussion.
4. Tamil Nadu State Archives (TNSA), *Madras Board of Revenue Consultations,* 31 Aug. 1801; also *Col. Munro's Report regarding Poligars in the Ceded Districts with*

*a Memorandum of Poligars, 1801-1802,* RSO (D) 66 (21), Munro to the Board of Revenue, 12 August, 1801.

5. *i.e.,* full survey assessment.

6. TNSA, *Col. Munro's Report regarding the Poligars in the Ceded Districts with a memorandum of Poligars, 1801-1802,* RSO (D) 62 (21), Letter from Thomas Munro to William Petrie, President and Members of the Board of Revenue, 20 March 1802; (hereafter *Thomas Munro's Report regarding the Poligars,* dated 20th March 1802); *William Thackeray's Report on Malabar, Canara and the Ceded Districts,* 8 Sept. 1807. ASO (D) 66; also see, J.C. Dua, "Poligars; Their Rise in the Ceded Districts", *I.H.C.,* XXXIII (1972) pp. 467-77.

7. *Ibid.;* also see, J.C. Dua, "The position of the *Patels* and *Karnums* in the Ceded Districts during the first quarter of the 19th century," *I.H.C.,* XXXLV, (1973).

8. For further details about the *Peshcushi Zamindars* see—B.R. Grover: Evolution of *Zamindari* and *Taaluqdari* System in Bengal *(1576*-1765 AD.). *Bangladesh Itihas Parishad, Proceedings of Third History Congress, Dacca, 1973.*

9. *Thomas Munro's Report regarding the Poligars,* dated 20 March 1802, Para 4-5.

10. TNSA, *Selections from the Old Records of the Bellary District, 1800-1807.* ASO (D) 72, Thomas Munro to the Board of Revenue, 27 March, 1801; also *Thomas Munro's Report regarding the Poligars,* 20 March 1802.

11. TNSA, *Official Report of a Revolt by Poligar Narasimha Reddy in Koilkuntla Taluq (which formed part of Cuddapah District)* in 1846, Vol. II, *(hereafter Official Report of a Revolt)* ASO (D) 112, Letter from W.A.D. Inglis Esq., Special Commissioner at Cuddapah to Sir H.C. Montgomery Bart, officiating Secretary to Government, Judicial Department, dated, Cuddapah, 19th Jan. 1847.

12. This amount has been wrongly stated as Rs. 21,840-8-0 in the letter from J.H. Cochrane, Ag. Collector to H.C. Montgomery Offg-Secy. to Govt. dated 15th Aug. 1847 c.f. *Selection of Papers relating to the revolt of Poligar Narasimha Reddy of Koilkuntla (1846)* (hereafter *Papers relating the Revolt)* Vol. 1, ASO (D) Vol. III) because the earlier evidence shows that Thomas Munro, the then Principal Collector of Ceded Districts, fixed the pension of the Poligar of Nossum at Rs. 8323, *i.e.,* 10 per cent of the total revenue (c.f. *Thomas Munro's Report regarding the Poligars,* dated 20 March 1802; also See *Fifth Report,* Vol. III (1812), Madras 1883, p. 508).

13. W.A.D. Inglis has wrongly stated it as Rs. 1,000/- P.M. (c.f. *Official Report of a Revolt.* Vol. II). It has been shown at f.n. No. 2.

14. Other share of Rs. 35/- granted to Chinna Mulla Reddy being still enjoyed by his widow, Doddummah.

15. His family consisted of

    (a) 1st wife's son-Butches Mulliah aged 16 years.

    (b) 2nd wife's daughter.

    (c) 3rd wife Wabalummah.

    (d) Two sons—(i) Mulliah and *(ii)* Soobiah.

(e) Mother—Neelummah.

(f) Father-in-law Narain Reddy.

(g) Mother-in-law.

16. TNSA, *Papers relating to the Revolt* ASO (D) Vol. III, letter from J. H. Cochrane, Acting Collector to H.C. Montgomery, Offg. Secy. to Govt. dated 15 April, 1847; Letter from J.H. Cochrane to E.P. Thompson, Secy. to Govt., Judicial Deptt. dated 15 Sept. 1846; also see, *op. cit.,* f.n. 1.

17. TNSA, *Official Report of the Revolt* Vol. IV, ASO (D) Vol. 114, Letter from J.H. Cochrane to the Agent to the Governor of Fort St. George at Kurnool, dated 6 July 1846; also *Selection of Papers Regarding the Revolt,* Vol. I, ASO (D) Vol. III, J.H. Cochrane to the Secretary to Government (Judicial Department) dated 12 July 1846.

18. TNSA, *Selection of Papers Regarding the Revolt,* Vol. 1, ASO (D) Vol. III, Cochrane to the Secretary to Government dated, 10th August 1846.

19. Cochrane in his letters to the Agent to the Governor dated 11 July 1846 to the Secretary to the Govt. dated 12 July 1846 has put the figures at 9000. In his letter to Secretary to Government and to the Magistrate of Guntur both dated 20 July 1846, he has put the figures at 3000. But in his letter to Montgomery dated 15 April 1847 he says that the number of followers never increased 200. Com. Detch. 19th Regt. in his letter to OC Field Marshal, 29 July 1846 has put the figures at 4000.

20. TNSA, *Selection of Papers Regarding the Revolt,* Vol. 1, Cochrane to the Secretary to Government, 20 July 1846; also Minutes of consultation, 27 July 1846.

21. Holders of the Lands granted by the Poligar to militiamen on condition of military service. The mains were subject to a quit rent.

22. Holders of rent free grants, mainly Brahmins.

23. TNSA, *Selection of Papers regarding the Revolt,* Vol. I Cochrane to the Agent to the Government at Kurnool dated 25th July 1846; Cochrane to the Secretary to Government dated 28th July 1846 and dated 10 August 1846.

24. TNSA, *Selection of Papers regarding the Revolt,* Vol. 1 Cochrane to the Secretary to Government, dated 7 October 1846.

25. TNSA, *Selection of Papers regarding the Revolt,* Vol. I Vol. III Recommended to be hanged by Special Commissioner vide *Proceedings of the Special Commissioner's Court,* dated 8 December 1846; Approval of the Court, *vide* Proceedings of the Faujdarres Adawlwat dated 5 January 1847; Approval of the Governor in Council vide Minutes of Consultations dated 6 Feb. 1847; Conveying of the decision to hang Narasimha Reddy on 22 Feb. 1847 with full publicity vide letter from J.H. Cochrane to the Magistrate of Bellary, dated 18 February 1847; to be hanged at 7 A.M. on 22 Feb. 1847 vide Cochrane to the Acting Sub-Criminal Judge of Cuddapah, dated 21 Feb. 1847; Informing the Faujdari Adawlwat about the execution, witnessed by more than 2000 persons, vide Cochrane to Ag. Sub-Criminal Judge of Cuddaph, dated 22 Feb. 1847.

26. TNSA, *Minutes of Consultations,* dated 9 Oct. 1846.

27. TNSA, *Official Report of a Revolt* Vol. II W.A.D. Inglis, Special Commissioner at Cuddaph to Sir M.C. Montgomery Bart, Offg. Secretary to Government, Judicial Department, dated 19th January 1847.
28. TNSA, *Minutes of Consultations,* dated 2 March 1847.
29. TNSA, *Selection of Papers Regarding the Revolt,* Vol. 1 Letter from J.H. Cochrane to M.C. Montgomery, Offg. Secy. to Government dated 15 April 1847.
30. TNSA, *Selection of Papers Regarding the Revolt,* Vol. III, Letter from S. Scott, Agent to the Governor to the Chief Secretary to Government, Fort St. George, dated 11 May 1847.
31. TNSA, *Proceedings of the Board of Revenue,* dated 10 August 1848.
32. TNSA, *Minutes of Consultation,* Judicial dated 4 June, 1852.
33. *Op. cit.,* f.n. 26, para 5.
34. TNSA, *Col. Munro's Correspondence regarding the survey and Rayatwari Settlement of the Ceded Districts, 1802-1827*, ASO (D) 79, Munro to his subordinate collectors regarding the modes of conducting the Rayatwari Settlement, 30 Sep. 1802.
35. *Op. cit.,* f.n. 26, para 8.
36. *Op. cit.,* f.n. 28. para 50 and f.n. 29, para 12.
37. *Op. cit.,* f.n. 26, Paras 6-7.
38. No doubt the *Khairati in'ams* could be of the religious or charitable nature as these grants were mainly connected with the preservation and care of Mohammadan tombs.
39. *A Collection of Papers relating to the main Settlement in the Madras Presidency, I, Madras,* 1958, pp. 312-313.
40. *Op. cit.,* f.n. 26 para 8.
41. Later on these *in'amdars* were required to perform ordinary police and revenue duties. They were divided into *"Grama Kattubadis"* and *"Jangi Kattubadis"*. The formers were strictly village servants or peons, and were required to perform service throughout the year. The latter were only called out for service on emergent occasions.
42. Inglis Report Para 19, 29.
43. TNSA, *Selection from the Old Records of the Bellary District, 1800-1807,* ASO (D) 72, Thomas Munro to the Chief Secretary to Government, dated 30 September 1801.
44. Andhra Pradesh State Archives, *Cuddapah Records (F. 1231)* 419/348, Letter from D. Hill, Secretary to Government to the President and Members of the Board of Revenue, dated 18 September 1821.
45. *Op. cit.,* f.n. 6 and f.n. 26, para 31.
46. *Op. cit.,* f.n. 26, para 17.
47. *Ibid.,* para 18.

48. Inglis is not sure whether their consent was obtained through a normal course or by a threat of the total resumption of their *in'ams.*
49. Proceedings of the Board of Revenue dated 28 May 1846. also *op. cit.,* f.n. 38.
50. In case their heirs wanted to retain those lands they could do so but on the payment of the full revenue according to the survey assessment.
51. *Op. cit.,* f.n. 26. para 18 & 13.
52. *Op. cit.,* f.n. 26. para 38
53. *Op. cit.,* f.n. 28. para 5
54. *Op. cit.,* f.n. 28
55. *Op. cit.,* f.n. 29.
56. TNSA, *Papers Regarding the Revolt,* vol. 1, Cochrane to the Government, dated 28 July 1846.

# 6

# Landed Elites in Upheaval—Forms and Contents of Resistance by the Palegars—1800-1846

## Lecture 1

## The Palegars

Respected Professor R. Balasubramanian, Distinguished Scholars, Ladies and Gentlemen:

I am extremely indebted to the Department of Politics and Public Administration, Madras University for inviting me to deliver the prestigious Dr. Kalaignar Thiru M. Karunanidhi Endowment Lectures, thus, giving me an opportunity to share with you my ides and thoughts on some aspects of the history of South India. I am fully conscious of my limitations for delivering lectures before this august forum, which has had the privilege of having most eminent scholars in the past. It is only long association with the history of South India and the affection of my colleagues over here, which has given me this honour and privilege.

The choice of the subject, 'Landed Elites in Upheaval—Forms and Contents of Resistance by the Palegars' looks rather ambitious. It is a study of an important institution, the Palegars, and two different phases of their resistance in South India especially the Ceded Districts, an important part of the erstwhile Madras Presidency, during the period 1800-1847.

While discussing the palegar institution, it has been emphasized that it cannot or rather should not be looked into in isolation. An

Dr. Kalaignar Thiru M. Karunanidhi Enodwment Lectures, Madras University, Madras, 7th, 10th, 11th April, 1995.

attempt has been made to draw parallels between the different categories of the zamindars of the Mughal empire and the palegars. The first phase of their resistance was part of the chain of such spontaneous resistance against the English, which had continued almost right since the very inception of the English as a political power in India. It was mainly aimed at seeking greater share in the power over, and thus in the revenue of, their region. The latter resistance, though part of the same chain, was the first against the British policy towards one of the most sensitive and traditionally adorable institutions, the *in'am* lands. Their seeming intention to subvert the traditional social order aroused the hostility of the conservative element, the general people, the *in'amdars,* the country people and villagers of different social status and, as such, gave strength to the already disgruntled elements, the palegars.

It is a technical and difficult subject and any reliance on fragmentary source material would be unsystematic and easily liable to misinterpretation. The important source material consulted includes—the relevant records, both manuscript and printed, contemporary and near-contemporary, preserved in the Tamil Nadu State Archives, Madras; OML, Madras; Andhra Pradesh State Archives, Hyderabad; Karnataka Secretariat Library, Vidhan Sauda, Bangalore; National Archives of India, New Delhi; and in Collectorate/Deputy Commissioner Offices and Tehsildar Offices of the Cuddapah, Kurnool, Anantapur and Bellary. It is notwithstanding the fact that extremely valuable contributions made by different scholars to the study of the palegars have been an immense inspiration and guiding force to me.

I propose to entitle my three lectures as **'The Palegars': Two Phases of the Palegar Resistance and British Policy': and 'Comparative Study of the Nature of Palegar Resistance'.**

"It is absurd to say that we must never extend our dominions though we see a state falling to pieces, and every surrounding one seizing a portion of its territory," wrote Thomas Munro to his father.[1] It is a very apt comment on the period of political turmoil and turbulation through which India had been passing during the eighteenth century and the intentions of the English East India Company which wanted to take fullest advantage of the prevailing situations. In order to achieve their objectives, as the history shows, the Governor Generals like Warren Hastings, Cornwallis, John Shore Wellesley etc. would not pay any heed to the directives from the home government. It is quite well known that the Act of 1784 had Stated that 'the pursuit of schemes of conquest was repugnant to the honour and policy of the British nation', yet the unsettled state of India was a sufficient excuse for them to go to war.[2] It cannot however, be completely ruled out that perhaps both the home government and the East India Company were hands in glove.

In contrast to the mid-eighteenth century, during the second half of the same century, as both empire and commerce grew, imperical interests in Indian affairs became valuable, politically and financially, both for the Company and the British nation. The history, particularly of the last quarter of the eighteenth and first quarter of the nineteenth centuries, shows that though the meaning of imperialism depended on the goals, intellect, and intensity of interest among individuals and groups involved in India, they had a unanimity on their elemental conviction that British power must be maintained in India.[3]

The East India Company certainly bad a very active imperial interest in India as its very survival as a commercial corporation depended on the preservation of the Indian empire. The imperial attitudes of the Company were directly derived from their political and economic stakes in India. The Governors and officials in India, besides reflecting the imperial sentiment of aristocratic Britain and the mercantile interests of the Company, had a personal stake in the permanence of British power in India. As such, there was a general agreement that British power must be preserved in India.[4]

The acquisition of Bengal, Bihar and Orissa may be considered 'in a great measure accidental,'[5] but after this success the diplomacy and the military force of the English East India Company had given them 'such a superiority over the ever-changing, tottering governments of the native Princes' that 'by watching times and opportunities, and making a prudent and vigorous use' of their resources had extended their dominion without much danger and expense.[6]

It was the same diplomacy and the military force, which accounts for their acquisition of the areas known as the 'Ceded Districts' and their policy towards the palegars.

All the English reports pertaining to the early nineteenth century have written about the existence of as many as 80 palegars and their about 30,000 armed retainers in the Ceded Districts at the time of their cession to the East India Company in 1800.[7] The palegars in the Ceded Districts were semi-independent revenue collectors and, of smaller pretensions, police-in-aid of the revenue collector. They held possession of an extent of territory, maintained an armed establishment and headed the administration. During the course of the time the palegars had started assuming the role of petty sovereigns and claimed hereditary proprietary rights over their estates called *palaiyam*. However, they could not legally and properly be called landlords. As a matter of fact, only a few of them, who were really men of local weight and standing, could claim to have become landlords, and held the *sanad-i-milkiyat-i-istimrar* or title deed of perpetual ownership.[8] They did not buy or sell land, or dispose it of by gift, as it was an *in'am* and resumable at will. The grants bestowed on the palegars were given for a specific purpose and entitled them the share of the produce payable as rent, though in theory they got 'complete ownership of the soil', including, according to the mode of expression, all its property both above and below ground. The grant given away in this manner could be a piece of land, a village or villages, and sometime *taluk* or *taluks*. Since all grants were resumable at pleasure, and as all persons were every moment liable to be deprived of their estates, technically they could never be considered as landlords. Their primary duty was to render military service and pay *peshkash* for the land, they possessed, to the sovereign.[9] The concentration of these two important duties, together with the rights arising therefrom, accounted not only for the vast influence of the palegars but also both politically and economically, a potential danger in the Ceded Districts. As such, it had become quite imperative for the Company's officials to go deep in the background of the palegars and to come out with the ways and means to check their growing power if the English had to establish an effective political power and introduce administrative measures in the Ceded Districts.

Different writers, chroniclers, travellers, English records, and archaeological survey reports pertaining to various parts of South India, have commented on the palegars and the *palaiyam* system, their origin, nature and working as an institution.

The origin of the *palaiyam* and palegar system have been by and large, unanimously attributed to Vishvanatha Nayaka of Madura (A.D. 1529-1564) and his *dalavay*[10] and *pradhani*[11] Ariyanatha. Some of the sources, however, do point out that the system did exist even prior to the Nayakship of Vishvanatha and accepting the prevalent system he improved upon it, thereby making it basis for his effective administration. In this regard the *Mackenzie Manuscripts*[12] are of considerable importance for not only the above viewpoint but also for understanding the origin and history of the palegars and the *palaiyams.*

The numerous manuscripts make it amply clear that the *palaiyam* system was in existence much before the rule of the Nayaks of Madura.[13] C.S. Srinivasachari has also opined that the elements of the system were in existence even before the spread of Vijayanagar sway into the Tamil country.[14] However, it is quite possible that before their rule the system was perhaps in a rudimentary shape and the Nayaks sufficiently systematized and organized it on a rational basis.

It is also amply clear from the *Mackenzie Manuscripts* that the prominent palegars holding *palaiyams* with hereditary rights were *boyas, gollas* and dominant peasants like *kapus* and *reddis.*[15] It is also borne out by the 14th Century inscriptions that the *boyas* of this region, referred to as *boyaviharadesha* (the land where *boyas* roam) and *boyavidu* (the land of *boyas*), were already powerful in early medieval times.[16] With their economic prosperity and rise in social hierarchy some of the *boyas,* from around 12th century A.D., also made gifts of cattle, money and land to the temples. Subsequently they began to give up the suffix 'Boya' and adopted the ones like 'Nayak', 'Reddi', Nayudi', 'Nedu' and Raju'.[17] The *gollas* too emerged as palegars and legitimized themselves as Yadavas like those of Kunkanur, Dudikonda and Maddikera. For instance, palegar Madapa Naidu, great-grandson of palegar Mallikarjuna Naidu received (A.D. 1570-72) from Tirumal Naidu of Aravidu dynasty 29 villages as *jagirs*, as was also bestowed with regal insignia. Palegar Madapa Naidu belonged to the *karisena golla* lineage but in his genealogical records he claimed descent from the *yadavas*, and the *chandravamsha* (moon born).[18]

The *Mackenzie Manuscripts* speak of the creation of seventy-two *palaiyams* by the new rulers of Madura, each under a palegar who was responsible for its defence. It is hard to believe that the number of the *palaiyams* created in the beginning remained the same or this system remained confined to Madura alone. Considering the clamant demands of Vishvanatha's multitudious followers, and the arduous nature of the improvements to be effected in the region, the number must have started increasing immediately after the inception of this institution. The later references show that the system had even travelled to other parts of south India also.[19]

In the *palaiyam* system the possession of land, though on military tenure, not only provided a palegar dignified status but was also the basis of the system. However, it is notwithstanding the fact that in due course of time the position and the grant, legally and illegally, had become hereditary. The palegars were given complete powers of police and judicial administration. In return for the assignments of lands and other administrative powers, a palegar was required to fulfil certain obligations to the imperial house. The obligations included the payment of annual *peshkash* or tribte (in theory one-third of their income from land), maintenance of a standing army (again in theory, with another third part of his income), which his master would require in case of war and, attendance at the Imperial Court on important and ceremonial occasions. In practice, however, they would enjoy more than one-third of their revenues. At the same time, for loyal and public services remissions in the tribute were also given, sometimes even to the extent of whole amount. My research shows, it was not always necessary that a palegar would be given a land grant for the maintenance of the army. He could meet this expenditure partly from the land grant and partly from the cash payment made by the government or wholly by the cash payment made by the government. Sometimes part of the land grant was converted into a *in'am* land or the *vice versa.* In some cases if the land grant was not sufficient to meet the requirement, he was appointed *kavalgar* (police incharge for the protection of the villages) of some neighbouring villages and *kaveli russom* (protection money) thus collected would meet the requirement of the army and *peshkash.* At times, the number of soldiers to be maintained was increased or decreased resulting into corresponding decrease or increase in the tribute. The tribute was sometimes increased or decreased even without decreasing or increasing the number of soldiers to be maintained. The service could be completely remitted and the tribute was increased or was supposed to pay the land revenue as per the assessment. Above all, in case of disloyalty or habitual non-payment of the tribute, a palegar could even be expelled. There is at least one reference, which shows that the grant given on military tenure would lapse if it was mortgaged to a *sahukar* against a loan taken from him.[20]

The institution as such and administrative, judicial and police rights of the palegars had close links with another old institution, also current during the Vijayanagar period and even after i.e., *kavalgars.* Whereas in the centrally administrated areas in the Vijayanagar empire, there existed three types of police (i) maintained by the state, (ii) maintained by the people, and (iii) special police at the capital, the provinces under the *Nayaks* and *Kavalgars* were remunerated by assignments of land for their maintenance. They themselves appointed *talaiyaris* (village police functionaries) for the village under them (usually one *talaiyari* for each village) who, in return for their services rendered, were paid both in kind and in cash, besides being granted land free of rent. In some places the villages sold the right of policing (called *padikaval*) to the *kavalgars.* In many an instance some local chieftains, especially the palegars, were assigned *padikaval* duties. Sometimes the grant of *kaval* rights was made to certain people as a reward for their services.[22] The protection money was also paid by the merchants, artisans, shepherds, fishermen, washermen and others.[23] As stated above, many palegars were assigned the duties of *kavalgars* and in many places the *kavalgars* also grew into palegars. T.V. Mahalingam has opined that the authority of the Palegars was derived from *padikaval,* a right to income in return for the provision of protection over a village, or in some cases over a locality during the Vijayanagar period.[24] In due course of time, especially after 1564, not only many other categories of persons, Brahman immigrants, many Telugus, and other favoured agents in the new regime received official titles and the perquisites attached, but institutions of *kavalgar* had also started becoming hereditary.[25]

The *palaiyam* system was indigenous in origin and design and it would be wrong to align it with feudalism in medival Europe. The terminology of that peculiar socio-political system which arose in the Middle-ages in Europe has been very vaguely and carelessly applied to Indian institutions by many a writer. Some western or even Indian writers persist in calling as 'fiefs' even the assignments which were made to their officers by the different rulers of India, and the word feud is quite as freely and indiscriminately used. Some scholars, like Moreland, for instance, wrote that the use of feudal terminology of Europe to denote any institutions of India which might have a superficial or even partial resemblance with the former is highly inappropriate and misleading.[26]

The palegars were bound by the ties of military to the above chief or the king and held lands on *amaram* tenure i.e., military tenure.[27] They had no proprietary right over the land nor could they count on the cultivators as their serfs. They were to pay dues from their lands to this superior chief and were responsible for the supply of the stipulated number of foot and horse soldiers. In case the stipulated service was not rendered, the *amarams* were resumed by the grantor.[28]

Indeed, several incidents of the *palaiyam* system and feudalism look so akin that they seem to have a common origin. For instance, the palegars also held the lands immediately or mediately of the suzerain in return for a fixed annual *peshkash* and the maintenance of stipulated military contingent. They also gave their lands to their subordinates on similar terms. It was these rather striking resemblances and common incidents, which have misled some writers into drawing an exact analogy between the two systems.

The *palaiyam* system was the result of the deliberate policy of the rulers in assigning territories on *amaran* tenure in return for military service and fixed financial contribution. This system linked together only a section of the population and its gradual expansion did not reach a high degree of perfection in Vijayanagar nor afterwards. Though in due course of time the office and the land grant had become hereditary yet they were still in theory as well as in practice under the suzerain power and could be expelled and their grants resumed. Moreover, the comparative independence they enjoyed within their territories provided them opportunities for waging wars against each other. At the same time, they would go even to the extent of defying the central authority if the rulers were inefficient.

In the aftermath of the victory at the battle of Talikota, the frontier of Golconda extended to the south below the Krishna river which included the major portion of the Ceded Districts. For the maintenance of order as well as collection of taxes in the newly acquired territories the services of most of the palegars cum *kavalgars* or palegars and *kavalgars* were recognized. This was with or without changing their service conditions.[29] At the same time, apart from creating new palegars/*kavalgars,* some who were already in service in different capacity were appointed as palegars/*kavalgars.* The research shows, as many as twenty three old ones were retained, sixteen were fresh appointments and six were those who had earlier served in different capacity.[30] The Golconda sultans, in brief, tried to obtain, at a minimal cost, the consolidating and continuing protection of the newly acquired southern frontier. It was, merely, a policy of compromises and accommodations. The conquerors, in fact, 'formed a political elite in a complex society of pre-existing social and political institutions'.[31]

The battle of Talikota provided Bijapur rulers also ample scope for expansion in the Karnatak and some of the areas namely, Adoni, Penukonda, Harpanahalli, Jenimulla, Bellary, Doodikonda, Dewankonda, Anantapur, Raydroog etc., which later on formed the parts of the Ceded Districts.[32] They, however, had to face resistance from the palegars and other chiefs of the region. These chiefs were temporarily prevailed upon to pay annual tribute. Being equally determined to preserve their newly achieved independence, these chiefs/palegars would yield and pay tribute only when pressed hard by the Bijapur army. The result was that the Bijapur army had to conqueror again and again the same territory.[33]

Apart from the resistance provided by the chiefs/palegars to both Golconda and Bijapur, the artificial league between the Muslim powers also could not last long and broke almost immediately after their victory over the Vijayanagar empire. The internecine quarrels were resumed with greater fury than ever before and had rather provided additional ground for hostilities. The inability to establish effective political ascendancy and central authority upon the erstwhile Vijayanagar areas on the part of the Muslim sultans resulted into unchecked rise of the local chiefs and the palegars. These chieftains who, in fact, exercised sovereign rights within their jurisdiction, were never adequately dealt with during this period.[34]

During the Mughal campaigns in the Deccan from 1685 onwards these chiefs/palegars constituted a body of officers available for military and administrative service, and were politically and economically dominant in different parts of Golconda and the areas under study. Many of them were discharged or their service remitted or reduced; amount of *peshkash* was increased; land grants were reduced or resumed; and some were replaced by Muslim officers. Some of those who were retained were employed as auxiliaries hired by the Mughals in the Maratha war in the Karnatak.[35] Some of the redundant chiefs turned to banditry. There were widespread turbulences as well as plundering by the local chiefs. Moreover, as is evident from almost every contemporary source, the distress in the region from famine and epidemic had also resulted into political troubles. A large number of disturbances were due to high prices and food shortages as *zamindars* and bandits looted stocks of grain and money from the merchants and other wealthy persons.[36] As such, it is scarcely surprising that public opinion in these areas continued to exhibit a dislike of the new regime. These circumstances gave sufficient impetus to the palegars to defy the central authority and their status attained permànancy. William Thackeray in his *Report* has rightly emphasised that the palegars found in the Ceded Districts at the time of their cession were generally those who rose between 1565 and the time of Aurangzeb.[37]

During the eighteenth century the areas under study were the scene of fierce struggle for power between the Cuddapah Nawabs,

Marathas, Nizam, Haider Ali and later Tipu Sultan. All these powers tried to establish their suzerainty over different chiefs/palegars and tried to collect *peshkash/chauth* from them. The palegars paid the tribute not according to any fixed principles, but according to the power of the government to enforce it. The management and administration of their *palaiyam,* and the control of their subjects, were left entirely to the palegars. They were constantly at war either with each other for the extension of their respective power or against the sovereign power.

It can safely be argued that the rise of the palegars and turning of the Ceded Districts into a state of deterioration and anarchy, was, by and large, because of the succession of inefficient governments and rapacity and weakness of the persons who were entrusted with their management.[38]

The palegar institution in the Ceded Districts, or for that matter in several other parts of South India, cannot or rather should not be looked into in isolation. It is necessary to see whether this type of institution existed only in this part of India or in other parts of contemporary India also, though with a different nomenclature. For that matter a peep into the period specially from Akbar down to the end of the 18$^{th}$ century, including the rise of the Sikh sardars in parts of the *subahs* of Delhi and Punjab, cannot be avoided and certain parallels can be drawn between the different categories of *zamindars* of the Mughal empire and the palegars. In this regard reference may be made to the scholarly contributions made and the conclusions drawn by B.R. Grover,[39] S. Nurul Hasan[40] and Irfan Habib,[41] the pioneers on the Mughal economic history. The above writings highlight that despite a clash of interests, the Mughal empire was fundamentally dependent on the cooperation and support of the each of the broadly three categories of the *zamindars,* namely the chieftains, the intermediary and the primary *zamindars.* Even though there were important regional differences, the nature of land rights in most parts of the country was basically similar.[42] The first category of the *zamindars,* namely the chieftains, were hereditary autonomous rulers of their territories. The Mughals in order to obtain from these chieftains the recognition of their overlordship, imposed on them the obligation to pay regular tribute/*peshkash* and render military assistance whenever called upon, and at the same time absorbed many of them in the imperial hierarchy and administrative machinery. They were also responsible for the maintenance of the law and order and the freedom of transit. Depending upon the circumstances and the number of soldiers to be maintained, apart from the hereditary dominions, called *watan jagirs,* they were also assigned *jagirs* in other area. The amount of *peshkash* was fixed on the basis of the actual production, data regarding the area under cultivation, the crop pattern, and the revenue realized. Moreover, they were also entitled to a share in the plunder while conducting compaigns on behalf of the empire. A chieftain, however, depended for his position on the goodwill of the emperor rather than on his inherent rights. The hereditary succession as well as his remunerations/*jagir* were both conditional upon the performance of the services to the state.[43] All this shows hardly and difference between the reasons and circumstances under which the institution of palegars came into existence and the position enjoyed by them.

The intermediary *zamindars* were those who collected the revenue from the primary *zamindars* and paid it to the imperial treasury, or to the *jagirdars,* or to the chieftains or in certain cases kept it themselves. This right was of intermediary nature and not a proprietary right, rather a right of service and a service obligation. They were also responsible for the maintenance of law and order. As remunerations they enjoyed various types of perquisites, like commissions, deductions, revenue free lands, cesses etc. Though usually the *zamindars* possessed hereditary rights, in a few cases they held their position on short-term contracts as well. In this category, apart from the class of *zamindars* who contracted with the state to realize the revenue of a given territory, *deshmukhs, desais, deshpandes* and *muqaddams* etc. were included. Despite being hereditary an intermediary *zamindar* could not only be dismissed or transferred, the state reserved the right to interfere with his succession also.[44]

The primary *zamindars* for all practical purposes held proprietary rights over agricultural as well as habitational lands and carried on cultivation themselves, or with the help of hired labour. Those who would bring forest and waste under cultivation were also bestowed with the *zamindari* rights. A primary *zamindar* could be a *zamindar* of some area, a village or even several villages. The rights held by them were hereditary and alienable.[45]

It has to be clearly borne in mind that the above divisions of the *zamindars* during the Mughal period is a very broad one. There could be numerous divisions of the *zamindars* within these three broad categories. The main idea behind giving the position in the Mughal period is to pin-point similarities between the areas under discussion and the contemporary north India. In both the regions the existence of the various types of landed interests had been the result of long process of evolution spread over several centuries.

If the above broad division of the *zamindars* is applied in case of the palegars that existed in the Ceded Districts at the time of their cession to the English it could be argued that out of eighty palegars the ancestors of as many as thirty nine belonged to the category of chief *zamindars*/palegars right since the beginning of their career. They were assigned lands, supposed to maintain a contingent (big or small) and/or paid *peshkash*.[46] As many as twenty nine got their positions during the period of Vijayanagar empire; two during the period of Raja of Annagundi; six during the Golconda period, one during the Bijapur period; and one during the Cuddapah Nawab's period.[47] The ancestors of eight palegars could be put in the category of intermediary *zamindars*. Two of them were initially *diwans* and two were *patels* while one had a few villages in *jagir* during the Vijayanagar period. One of them came into existence during the Golconda period and two during Aurangzeb's period. Three of them were recognised as chief *zamindars*/palegars during the Golconda period, one during Bijapur period; one during Aurangzeb's period; while three of them came to be recognized so by the time Marathas dominated the areas.[48] Two palegars were originally *dalavays* and one a *daffedar* during the Vijayanagar period, and one each got the recognition as chief *zamindar*/palegar during Bijapur, Golconda and Aurangzeb's period.[49] Out of fourteen originally primary *zamindars*, four became so during Vijayanagar, nine during Golconda and one during Aurangzeb's period. Two of them were recognized as chief *zamindars*/palegars during Golconda, four during Aurangzeb's period and one during Cuddapah Nawab's period, and while five tried to assume that role during Haider's period but were subdued and one remained practically satisfied with his positiion.[50] Eleven of the palegars were originally *kavalgars,* so appointed, seven during Vijayanagar, two during Golconda, one during Aurangzeb and one during Cuddapah Nawab's period. Four palegars were initially *taliarys,* and one was either a *taliary* or *kavalgar,* all the five appointed during the Vijayanagar empire. Out of these sixteen, six got the recognition as chief *zamindar*/palegar during Golconda, one during Bijapur, and three during Aurangzeb's period, while two assumed such role during Haider's and one during Tipu's period. Three of them were very petty or insignificant palegars.[51] The Table given below will make the position still clearer.

**Table**

| S.No. | Palegar of | Original Appointment/ Recognition | Period | Period in which recognized As Palegar/ Chief Zamindar |
|---|---|---|---|---|
| 1 | 2 | 3 | 4 | 5 |
| A. | | | | |
| 1. | Raja of Annagundy | Raja | Vijayanagar | - |
| 2. | Jenimulla | Palegar/Chief Zamindar | -do- | - |
| 3. | Busvapur | -do- | -do- | - |
| 4. | Pulalcherru | -do- | -do- | - |
| 5. | Bollapally | -do- | -do- | - |
| 6. | Neelagutla | -do- | -do- | - |
| 7. | Niddamaddoddi | -do- | -do- | - |
| 8. | Nosum | -do- | -do- | - |
| 9. | Chitveyal | -do- | -do- | - |
| 10. | Singapattan | -do- | -do- | - |
| 11. | Bodyemenoor | -do- | -do- | - |
| 12. | Talmurlah | -do- | -do- | - |

| | | | |
|---|---|---|---|
| 13. Pyapalli | -do- | -do- | - |
| 14. Sampilli | -do- | -do- | - |
| 15. Yerragunta Palaiyam | -do- | -do- | - |
| 16. Madanpalli | -do- | -do- | - |
| 17. Papypilli | -do- | -do- | - |
| 18. Rampicherlah | -do- | -do- | - |
| 19. Mullel | -do- | -do- | - |
| 20. Dudipalli | -do- | -do- | - |
| 21. Maddancherru | -do- | -do- | - |
| 22. Kokimti | -do- | -do- | - |
| 23. Millacherroo | -do- | -do- | - |
| 24. Wudiamunhi | -do- | -do- | - |
| 25. Yagawamarapahgunta | -do- | -do- | - |
| 26. Digawamarapahgunta | -do- | -do- | - |
| 27. Sanyapanyni | -do- | -do- | - |
| 28. Vimlah | -do- | -do- | - |
| 29. Rattangery | -do- | -do- | - |
| **B.** | | | |
| 1. Oapalur | Palegar/Chief Zamindar | Golconda | - |
| 2. Marsellah | -do- | -do- | - |
| 3. Talpool | -do- | -do- | - |
| 4. Chintalguntah | -do- | -do- | - |
| 5. Motguntlah | -do- | -do- | - |
| 6. Jallalmundah | -do- | -do- | - |
| **C.** | | | |
| 1. Dewankonda | -do- | Bijapur | - |
| **D.** | | | |
| 1. Ghuttim | -do- | Raja of Annagundy | - |
| 2. Butlapur | -do- | -do- | - |

| | | | |
|---|---|---|---|
| E. | | | |
| 1. Nangangunta | Plegar/Chief Zamindar | Nawab of Cuddapah | |
| F. | | | |
| 1. Bellary | Diwan/ Intermediary Zamindar | Vijayanagar | Bijapur |
| 2. Hundi Anantapur | -do- | -do- | Aurangzeb |
| 3. Narsapur | Patel/ Intermediary Zamindar | -do- | Golconda |
| 4. Whurpur | -do- | -do- | -do- |
| 5. Muddikerah Mulla | Intermediary Zamindar | -do- | -do- |
| G. | | | |
| 1. Kalupalli | -do- | Golconda | Marathas |
| H. | | | |
| 1. Talpool Taluq | Intermediary Zamindar | Aurangzeb | -do- |
| 2. Kadiri | -do- | -do- | -do- |
| I. | | | |
| 1. Rayadroog | Dalvovy | Vijayanagar | Bijapura |
| 2. Tutt | -do- | -do- | Golconda |
| 3. Madicheroo | Daffedar | -do- | Aurangzeb |
| J. | | | |
| 1. Owk | Primary Zamindar | -do- | Golconda |
| 2. Tipradipalli | -do- | -do- | -do- |
| 3. Tumalgundi | -do- | -do- | Cuddapah |
| 4. Yellutlah | -do- | -do- | Haider Ali |
| K. | | | |
| 1. Chuppalmurragu | Primary | Golconda | Aurangzeb |

| | | | |
|---|---|---|---|
| | Zamindar | | |
| 2. Vencatadry | -do- | -do- | -do- |
| 3. Woorlaguntah | -do- | -do- | -do- |
| 4. Kullipundah | -do- | -do- | Cuddapah |
| 5. Bvanmullah | -do- | -do- | Haider Ali |
| 6. Rangangar *Palaiyam* | -do- | -do- | Aurangzeb |
| 7. Yedamuneyn *Palaiyam* | -do- | -do- | Haider Ali |
| 8. Nellamune *Palaiyam* | -do- | -do- | -do- |
| 9. Moodiampaur | -do- | -do- | -do- |
| L. | | | |
| 1. Rawoor | -do- | Aurangzeb | Cuddapah |
| M. | | | |
| 1. Doodikonda | Kavalgar | Vijayanagar | Golconda |
| 2. Pundikonda | -do- | -do- | -do- |
| 3. Mutialpur | -do- | -do- | -do- |
| 4. Shilliwar *Palaiyam* | -do- | -do- | -do- |
| 5. Ganguichentlah | -do- | -do- | Aurangzeb |
| 6. Noputnutlah | -do- | -do- | Petty Palegar |
| 7. Momutnutlah | -do- | -do- | -do- |
| N. | | | |
| 1. Kotapalaiyam | -do- | Golconda | Haider Ali |
| 2. Madaneyn *Palaiyam* | -do- | -do- | Tipu Sultan |
| O. | | | |
| 1. Yellamundah | -do- | Aurangzeb | Haider Ali |
| P. | | | |
| 1. Kapugunapalli | Kavalgar | Cuddapah | Petty Palegar |
| Q. | | | |
| 1. Harpanahalli | Taliary | Vijayanagar | Bijapur |

| | | | |
|---|---|---|---|
| 2. Kodikonda | -do- | -do- | Aurangzeb |
| 3. Kapitral | -do- | -do- | -do- |
| 4. Yerrawar *Palaiyam* | -do- | -do- | Golconda |
| **R.** | | | |
| 1. Kamlapur | Kavalgar or Taliary | -do- | -do- |

Another common features amongst the different categories of the *zamindars,* in different parts of India during the medieval period, was that they were constantly struggling to enhance their position and tried to go up the ladder. In this attempt they frequently came into clash either with the state or the superior category of the *zamindar*. The chief *zamindar*/palegars would hardly miss an opportunity of taking advantage of the difficulties faced by the empire. In such circumstances they attempted to convert their *amaram* lands or the *jagirs* assigned outside their ancestral territories into hereditary ones, and would on occasion even assume independence. In case the state was unable to maintain its military pressure on the chiefs, the revolts became more frequent, as was the case in those parts of the Ceded Districts which came under the Nizam in 1792 and 1799.[52]

The different categories of the intermediary *zamindars* tried to improve their position in two ways. They would try to reduce the primary *zamindars* to the status of tenant-farmers or would try to go a step higher and become chieftains. They struggled and strived to appropriate a greater share of the revenue if not the whole of it, so that they could spend more on their armed contingents. Tipu Sultan must have faced similar difficulties from the *patels* that is why *Hukam Nama-i-Tipu Sultan* mentions about the strict instructions given to them.[53] There are unnumerable references pertaining to the palegars and the *zamindars* in Mughal empire who would not pay the revenues unless demanded forcibly. Such *zamindars*/palegars could be put under the well-known category of the *zamindaran-i-zor-talab.* In order to achieve objective they frequently rose in rebellion either on their own, or along with their fellow brethren, or even joined hands with some of the chieftains who were already in revolt against the state.[54]

In the quest for a higher status, the primary *zamindars* were also not lagging behind and thus struggled to become intermediaries and then chiefs. In this process they frequently came into conflict with the superior *zamindars* and the state on the one hand and the peasantry on the other.

Some of the erstwhile high state officials, *kavalgars* and *taliaries,* taking advantage of the weak government and their military/police powers, also rose and were successful in getting the status of palegars.

The question for higher economic and political status and struggle for achieving that was also true, among others, in case of the Maratha chiefs and the Sikh sardars during 17th/18th centuries.[55]

## References


1. Letter from Thomas Munro to his father, dated Trichangoor, 21 September 1798, Gleig, G.R., *The Life of Maj. Gen. Sir Thomas Munro, Bart and K.C.B Late Governor of Madras* (London, 1830), Vol. I, p. 203.
2. Carrington, C.E., *The British Overseas, Expolits of a Nation of Shopkeeprs: Part I (Making of the Empire),* (Cambridge—at the University Press, 2nd Edn., 1968), p. 181.
3. *Parliamentary Debates from the Year 1803...Forming a Continuation of the work entitled 'The Parliamentary History of England From the Earliest Period to the Year 1803'*—Published under the superintendance of T.C. Hansard, 22 November, 1803-28 February 1830, 41 vols., London, XXIV, p. 412, 23 January, 1784 (Hereafter, *Hansard*).
4. Bearce, George D., *British Attitudes Towards India 1784-1858* (Oxford University Press, 1961), pp. 34-37. *East India Company, Debates at the East India House in the General Court of the Proprietors of East India Stocks* (8 vols., London, 1813-44), ii, pp. 17-50. David Scott, *Correspondence,* 2 Vols., (London, 1951), ii, p. 39.
5. 'Result of Lord Wellesley's Administration', Col. George Chesney, *Indian Polity,* Ist Edn., 1868, p. 32, quoted in Owen, Sidney J. (ed.), *A Selection From the Despatches, Treaties and Other Papers of Marquess Wellesley, During His Government of India* (Oxford, 1877), p. 812.
6. Letters from Thomas Munro to his father, dated 21 September 1798, *op. cit.*, p. 203.
7. TNSA, *Poligars: Col. Munro's Report Regarding the Poligars in the Ceded Districts, with a Memorandum of Poligars 1801-1802;* ASO (D) Vol. 62 (21), Letter from Thomas Munro to William Petrie, President and Members of the Board of Revenue, 20 March, 1802; Letters from Thomas Munro to the Board of Revenue, 12 August 1801, *Selections from the Old Records of Bellary District 1800-1807,*

ASO (D) Vol. 72, Letter from Thomas Munro to Josiah Webbe, Chief Secretary to Government, 12 July 1807. *Selections from the Records of Bellary District—Political, Revenue and Agricultural Matters 1800-1857,* ASO (D) Vol. 73, Letter from Thomas Munro to William Patrie, 22 July, 1801. Mahalingam, T.V. (ed.), *Mackenzie Manuscripts, Summaries of the Historical Manuscripts in the Mackenzie Collection,* ii, (Madras, 1976), Different Manuscripts, *Fifth Report,* pp. 499-530.

8. Baden-Powell, B.H., *The Land Systems of British India,* 3 Vols. (Oxford, 1892, Reprint, Delhi, 1974), III, pp. 15, 19.

9. TNSA, ASO (D), Vol. 72, *Selections from the Old Records of the Bellary District 1800-1807,* Letter from Thomas Munro to William Petrie, President of the Board of Revenue, dated Anantapur, 25 August, 1805.

10. *Dalavay* was the principal officer of the Vijayanagar empire, combining in himself the control of all civil and military adminstration. It was, as a matter of fact, the fusion of the functions of a *mantri* i.e., chief minister and a *senapati* i.e., Commander-in-chief. The Jesuit letters have indicated his great power under Queen-Regent Mangammal (1689-1706 A.D.). He was entrusted with the entire administration, of which he was absolute master. He was thought to be greatest master that ever governed Madura. 'Letter of Father Peter Martin to Father Le Gobien, Aoor, in the kingdom of Madura, 11 December 1700'. John Lockman, *Travels of the Jesuits,* being translations from the *Letters edifiantes etc. curieuses, ecrites des Missions etrangers, par les Missionaires de la Compagnies de Jesus* (20 March 1762), 2 Vols., I, p. 461, reproduced in Aiyar, R. Sathyanatha, *History of the Nayaks of Madura,* edited by S, Krishnaswami Aiyangar (Oxford University Press, 1924), (hereafter *Nayaks of Madura*), pp. 235-36, 308. J.H. Nelson in his *The Madura Country: A Manual* (Madras: Asylum Press, 1868), p. 145, does not give much importance to this official and has described his functions as 'merely advisory'.

11. *Pradhani* was technically the finance minister, principally engaged in directing the collection of revenue and its expenditure. However, it seems that in the absence of *Dalavay* from the capital he acted as 'the governor or rather the despot of the whole kingdom.' *Nayaks of Madura*, p. 237.

12. Mahalingam, T.V. (ed.), *Mackenzie Manuscripts: Summaries of the Historical Manuscripts in the Mackenzie Collection,* 2 Vols. (Madras University, Vol. I, 1972 and Vol. II, 1976), (hereafter *Mackenzie Manuscripts*).

13. *Ibid.* I, Manuscript No. 1, section 3, pp. 6-7, 'Genealogical Account of the Poligar of Naduvakuricci in the Cola Country.

Manuscript No.2, section 6, pp. 21-23, 'Genealogical Account of Kulappa Nayaka Poligar of Nallakata (Nilakkuttai) in the Dindigul District'.
Manuscript No.3, section 2, p. 27, 'Account of the Poligar of Kakkuvadi in Kongunadu'.

Manuscript No.3, section 5, p. 29, 'Account of Vanava Rayagauda Poligar (Vanaraya Kaundan Poligar) of the Samattur Palaiyappattu'.

Manuscript No. 3, section 6, pp. 29-30, 'Account of Debnik Poligar of Pullaksi (Deva Nayaka Poligar of Pollachi) in the Dharmapura District.'

14. Srinivasachari, C.S., 'The Polegar System—Its Development and Decay', *Journal of Madras University,* Vol. III, 1955, p. 272.
15. *Mackenzie Manuscripts,* Maddikera kaifiyat, Manuscript 168, No. 1201; Aspari Kaifiyat, Manuscript, 168, No. 1201; aspari Kaifiyat, 123, No. 923; Nandyal Kaifiyat, Manuscript 110, No. 793; Rollamadugu Kaifiyat, Manuscript, 108, No. 738.
16. For details see, B.S.L. Hanumantha Rao, 'The Boyas in Andhra History', Journal of *Andhra Historical Research Society,* 38, 1983-84, pp. 77-91.
17. M.L.K. Murthy, 'Environment, Royal Policy and Social Formation in the Eastern Ghats South India, A.D. 1000-1500', Presidential Address, Historical Archaeology, Epigraphy and Numismatics Section, *Indian History Congress,* 53rd session, Warangal, 1992-93, pp. 615-631.
18. *Mackenzie Manuscript,* Kunkanur Kaifiyat, Manuscript, 123, No. 928; Dundikonda Kaifiyat, Manuscript, 146, No. 1149; Maddikera Kaifiyat, Manuscript, 116, No. 855.
19. *Mackenzie Manuscript,* I, Manuscript No. 2, Section 6, 7, No. 36; II, No. 105-136. *Nayaks of Madura,* pp. 58-59.
20. *Mackenzie Manuscript,* I, Introduction, pp. xxxi-xxxii; II, Manuscript No. 118, p. 128. Mahalingam, T.V., *Administration and Social Life Under Vijayanagar,* 2nd edn. Part I (Madras, 1969), p. 138. Taylor W. (ed.), *Oriental Historical Manuscripts,* 2 Vols. (Madras, 1862), II, pp. 160-68. Venkatasubramanian, T.K., *op. cit.,* pp. 10-11; *Nayaks of Madura,* p. 59. *Narrative of Domingo Paes,* the Portuguese Traveller (written, probably, A.D. 1535-37) reproduced in Sewell, Robert, *A Forgotten Empire: Vijayanagar* (New Delhi: Publication Division, 1962), pp. 228-78 and 279-376.
21. About the functions of the police, see The Persian Ambassador, Abdur Razzak's account in Elliot, H.M. and Dowson, J., *The History of India, As Told by Its Own Historians,* 8 Vols. (London, 1866-1877), IV, p. 112. Fernao Nuniz's account in Sewell, Robert, *op. cit.,* p. 361.
22. *Annual Report on Epigraphy* (South India) for the years 1887-1944/45 (Madras, 1887-1955), para 240 of 1912 and para 368 of 1914. *Inscriptions in the Pudukkottai State* (tr.) English by K.R. Srinivasa Iyer. Parts I and II (1941, 1946), II, para 751.
23. Ludden, David, *Peasant History in South India* (Oxford University Press, 1989), p. 73. M.L.K. Murthy, *op. cit.,* p. 625.
24. Mahalingam, T.V., *South Indian Policy* (Madras: Madras University, 1967), pp. 247-49.
25. Ludden, David, *op. cit.,* p. 72. Mahalingam, T.V., *Administration and Social Life Under Vijayanagar,* I, *op. cit.,* p. 139.
26. Moreland, W.H., 'Feudalism (?) in the Moslem Kingdom of Delhi', *Journal of Indian History,* Vol. VII, Part I, 1938, Saran, P., *Studies in Medieval Indian History.*

27. *Amaram* means land or revenue granted by a chief to his retainers for military service (*Tamil Lexicon, op. cit.*, I, p. 102). McClean, C.D. defines an *amaram* grant as a grant of land to the prince or poligar on condition of service generally military or police (*Manual of the Administration of Madras Presidency*, III, (Madras, 1885), pp. 24, 352.

28. *Inscriptions in the Pudukkottai State, op. cit.*, para 743. 'Narrative of Domingos Paes' and 'Chronicle of Fernao Nuninz', Sewell, Robert, *op. cit.*, pp. 269-70 and p. 354 respectively. Barbose, Duarte, *An Account of the Countries Bordering on the Indian Ocean and Their Inhabitants Written by Duarte Barbose and Completed About 1518,* tr. With notes etc. by Longworth Dames, 2 Vols. (London, 1918), I, p. 209.

29. *Mackenzie Manuscripts,* esp. no. 109, section 1-13.

30. Sherwani, H.K., 'The Region of Abdul'l Qutab Shah (1626-1672): Economic Aspects I', *Journal of Indian History,* XLII (August 1964), pp. 443-70; II, XLV (December 1967), pp. 115-60. *Fifth Report,* pp. 499-530.

31. Richards, J.F., *Mughal Administration in Golconda* (Oxford, 1975), pp. 30-34.

32. *Mackenzie Manuscripts,* No. 105, Section 6 and No. 209, Section 1-3. *Tarikh-i-Farishtah* by Muhammad Qasim, Hindu Shah, Farishtah, English translation, Briggs, John, *History of the Rise of the Mohamedan Power in India,* 4 vols. (Calcutta, 1910), II, pp. 40-46.

33. *Tarikh-i-Farishtah, op. cit.*, II, pp. 47, 56-57; Verma, D.C., *History of Bijapur, op. cit.*, pp. 126-36.

34. *Tarikh-i-Sultan Muhammad Qutb Shahi,* account of Golconda inserted in, Briggs, John, *op. cit.*, III, pp. 416-17. Brackenbury, C.P., *Madras District Gazetteer—Cuddapah* (Madras, 1917), p. 38.

35. Sarkar, Jadunath, *History of Aurangzeb*, 5 Vols. (Calcutta, 1912-30), IV, pp. 350-352. Richards, J.F., 'The Hyderabad Karnatik, 1687-1707', in *Modern Asian Studies*, IX, (1975), pp. 241-60. Ali, M. Athar, *The Mughal Nobility Under Aurangzeb* (Aligarh, 1966), pp. 216-71. *Fifth Report*, pp. 499-530.

36. TNSA, *Records of Fort St. George: Diary and Consultation Books*, Diary of 1687. *Record of Fort St. George: Despatches to England*, Different letters from and letters to Fort St. George pertaining to years 1687-1688. Raychaudhuri, Tapan, *Jan Company in Coromandel: 1605-1690.* Verhandelingen van het Koninklijk Institut voor Taal-Land-en Volkenkunde, Vol. XXXVIII (The Hague, 1962), pp. 68-74. *Mackenzie Manuscripts*, No. 144, pp. 224-28.

37. TNSA, ASO (D), Vol. 66, *Report of William Thackerary*, dated 8 September 1807.

38. TNSA, *Selections From the Records of Bellary District, Political, Revenue and Agricultural Matters*, ASO (D), Vol. 73, Munto to Josiah Webbe, dated 18 March 1801; Letter from George Garrow to Munro, dated 8 December 1801.

39. Grover, B.R., 'Nature of Land Rights in Mughal India', *The Indian Economic and Social History Review*, Vol. I, No. I, 1963, pp. 1-23. 'Nature of *Dehat-i-*

*Taaluqa* (zamindari villages) and the Evolution of the *Taaluqdari* System During Mughal Age', *The Indian Economic and Social History Review*, Vol. II, No. 2, 1965, pp. 166-77 and II, No. 3, 1965, pp. 259-288. 'Elements of Continuity and Change in Land Ownership and Rights from the Mughal Age to the Early British Administration in India', Presidential Address, Medieval Indian Section, *Indian History Congress*, 37th session, Calicut, 1976. 'The Position of *Desai* in the *Pargana* Administration of Subah Gujarat under the Mughals', *Indian History Congress*, 1961, pp. 150-55.

40. S. Nurul Hasan, 'The Position of the Zamindars in the Mughal Empire', *IESHR*, IV, pp. 107-19, also in Frykenberg, Robert Eric (ed.), *Land Control and Social Structure in Indian History* (New Delhi, 1979), pp. 17-31 (under the title 'Zamindars under the Mughals'); 'Three Studies of the Zamindari System', *Medieval India: A Miscellany* (Bombay, 1968), pp. 233-39; 'Aspects of Zamindari System in Deccan', *IHC*, 1969, pp. 262-66; *Thoughts on Agrarian Relations in Mughal India* (New Delhi, 1973, rpt. 1983).
41. Habib, Irfan, *Agrarian System of Mughal India* (Bombay, 1963).
42. For a discussion on various types of land rights see, Grover, B.R. 'Nature of Land Rights', *op. cit.*
43. S. Nurul Hasan, *Thoughts in Agrarian Relations…, op. cit.*, p. 28; 'Position of the Zamindars…', *op. cit.*, Grover, B.R., 'Nature of *Dehat-i-Taaluqa…, op. cit.*, Khan, A.R., *Chieftains in the Mughal Empire During the Reign of Akbar* (Simla, 1977), p. 6-7.
44. S. Nurul Hasan, *Thoughts on Agrarian Relations, op. cit.*, pp. 29-33; 'Position of the Zamindars', *op. cit.*, Grover, B.R., 'Nature of *Dehat-i-Talluqa', op. cit.*, Position of Desai', *op. cit.*, Dua, J.C., 'Comparative Position of the Village Headmen During the Early British Rule in the Punjab and the Madras Presidency', *Punjab History Conference*, Patiala, 23rd Session, 1987; also in Dua, J.C., *Agrarian System in South India (Some Aspects)*, (Delhi, 1990), pp. 123-36.
45. S. Nurul Hasan, 'Position of the Zamindars', *op. cit.*
46. In this regard see Grover, B.R., 'Elements of Continuity and Change…', *op. cit.*
47. See Table.
48. *Ibid.*
49. *Ibid.*
50. *Ibid.*
51. *Ibid.*
52. TNSA, Munro to William Petrie, dated 20 March 1802, *op. cit.*, ASO (D), Vol. 72, Thomas Munro to the Secretary of the Committee of Police, dated 10 September 1806. Report of William Thackeray, dated 8 September 1807, *op. cit.*, Munro to Josiah Webbe, dated 18 March 1801, *op. cit.*, S. Nurul Hasan, 'Zamindar Under the Mughals', *op. cit.*, Grover, B.R., 'Nature of Dehat-i-Talluqa…', *op. cit.*
53. APSA, *Hukamnana-i-Tipu Sultan* (Persian), dated 1206 *Fasli*, Clause No. 11 (I am grateful to Professor B.R. Grover for deciphering and interpreting relevant

portions for me). Dua, J.C., 'The Position and Role of the Village Headman in the Village Administration of the Ceded Districts During the First Quarterly of the 19th Century', in Dua, J.C., *Agrarian System in South India, op. cit.*, pp. 83-106.

54. *Supplementary Report of the Special Committee, op. cit.*, p. 39, Raju, A. Sarada, *Economic Conditions in the Madras Presidency, 1800-1850,* (University of Madras, 1941), p. 45. S. Nurul Hasan, 'Zamindars Under the Mughals', *op. cit.*

55. Dua, J.C., *British Historigraphy: Eighteen Century Punjab* (New Delhi, 1992), pp. 95-96, 214n. Grover, B.R., 'An Analysis of the Contemporary Revenue Documents and Correspondence Pertaining to Patiala Chieftainship (*Zamindari*) during the later half of the 18th Century', *Punjab Past and Present,* XXIV-I, April 1990, pp. 196-233.

## *Lecture II*

# Two Phases of Palegar Resistance and British Policy

### First Phase

Thomas Munro, the Principal Collector of the Ceded Districts (1800-1807), on entering the districts, found a general rebellion of the palegars. Every one of these palegars, howsoever, petty his territory, kept up a mimic court and a small standing army of permanently appointed soldiers aided by a militia of relative of these soldiers. As already explained in the previous lecture, these palegars had attained their position in a number of ways. Some of these had originally been servants of government, or renters of districts or had received their villages at first in *in'am* as personal allowance for the support of their rank, and had revolted in times of disturbances. Some of these palegars had received their villages at the usual revenue, both as a personal *jagir*, and for the service of a body of horse and foot soldiers. Some were commanders of body of soldiers, paid in cash not by *jagir*, then after being absolved from military service became renters of some villages, and finally by holding those areas for a number of years during the times of confusion, came at last to be denominated as *zamindars*/palegars substituting the term *peshkash* for that of revenue. Some were merely renters assessed to the full *kamil* (*i.e.*, full assessment of land), and ultimately grew into palegars. In some parts of the Ceded Districts, almost every head of a village, favoured by the natural strength of the area became a palegar. All these people took advantage of the weakness of the government, withheld the revenue to support the troops, and enjoyed all the forms of a prince of an extensive territory.[1] Almost every village was exposed to their ravages and the Ceded Districts were nothing more than a nest of 'robbers'. Here it may be pointed out that describing the palegars as 'robbers' 'maraudars', 'predatory bands' and their activities as 'depredations', 'pillaging', 'highway robbery' is a concept usually used from the imperialist viewpoint. Whenever the revolting *zamindars* or chiefs realized the revenue of a particular area after occupation, from the imperialist angle it was described as plunder, loot, pillage etc. Same is true about the Mughal description about the Marathas, and the British description, amongst the other chiefs, about the palegars in the South India and the Sikh sardars in the Punjab during the eighteenth century.[2]

The palegars maintained large bodies of armed followers (called 'peons' in the English reports) for the performance of their police duties in addition to those who acted as their armies. These armed followers could be compared with those maintained by the chief *zamindars* in north India and the Northern Circars. They consisted of (i) those paid entirely in cash, had no other means of living, and they were the least numerous; (ii) those who enjoyed service lands, but who, being composed of *rayats* who rented other lands, regarded their *in'ams*, only a secondary object; and (iii) who confined themselves to the cultivation of their *in'ams*. However, each one of them received *bhatta*, when called out beyond the limits of their villages. The usual allowance of land, as revealed by the survey and investigations conducted by Thomas Munro, to a common armed follower, in the Ceded Districts, appears to have been a field valued at six pagodas annual rent. The village headmen, who used to maintain armed followers, were allowed a piece of land from 9 to 24 pagodas rent for parties of 10, 50 or 100 as the case might be. It is also learnt that the palegars in general kept up 6 persons for every 100 Star Pagodas of gross revenue in their respective *palaiyams*. Since every one of them had relations able to bear arms and was required to bring them into the field in cases of emergency, the palegars were enabled, whenever necessary, to assemble a much larger force than their fixed establishment amounted to.[3]

The armed followers maintained by the palegars were also known by the term *kattubadis*. Functionally speaking, the *kattubadis* were of two types—*grama kattubadis* and *jangi kattubadis*. The former were purely village servants and were required to perform service throughout the year. The latter were called out for service on emergent occasions. The lands granted to them came under the title *kattubadi in'ams* and were subject to quit rent.[4]

The contemporary records show that though practically whole of the areas under the Ceded Districts were directly or indirectly affected by the activities of the palegars, their menace was not identical in all the areas. For instance, in Cuddapah, despite the fact, that the palegars did not hold great proportion of the lands, were greater in number, were very powerful and had on the account produced great resistance. The palegars, especially, of Chitvel, Nossam, Narasapur, Vimla and Talpoor, had been repeatedly in resistance particularly during a decade before and after the cession of the areas and were considered to be most powerful in the Ceded Districts. In Gurramkonda, the palegars had even defied the authority of Tipu Sultan, and, though expelled, had been collecting large annual contributions from their old possessions. The palegars of Rayadrug and Harpanahalli, who, during the course of time, had acquired considerable territory, and that of Owke, Chitvel and Anantapur whose ancestors had held high positions during the Vijayanagar period, were regarded by the different powers, who ruled over the areas under study, as holding an independent authority. However, the degree of their resistance was not always the same. Contrary to the palegars of other portions of the Ceded Districts, especially the Cuddapah area, as already referred to, where all those who had survived all the changes of government which had followed so quickly upon one another's heels frequently required regular troops to reduce them to order, in the Anantapur area none of the chieftains were formidable enough. Of the four palegars, except the one of Kamalapur who was obstreperous, those of Anantapur, Nadimidoddi and Talmurlah were not at all troublesome.[5] However, in Adoni, not far from Anantapur, the position was quite alarming.

The disturbed political condition and proper land revenue collections would not normally coexist. The case of Ceded Districts was in no way different and the palegars' activities had their bearing on the income of the government from the then greatest source of earning. The first attempt of the Company to collect the revenue from this newly acquired territory provoked a general resistance of the palegars.

"War, famine and bad management", remarked William Thackeray, "all appear to have combined to reduce the Ceded Districts, but the rebellions of the Polligars seem to have been the major cause of the decline of the revenue."[6] Moreover, in the areas which, either wholly or partly, composed of the palegars' possessions, the government was bound to appoint extra manpower, and receive less revenue than in those which were 'properly Sirkars'.[7]

The authorities in Madras and Bengal were in favour of divesting the palegars of their military and political powers and wanted them to be treated as *zamindars* under the principles of the Permanent Settlement of Bengal. Different reports and incidents are eloquent to the fact that the Company's position with regard to the palegars had already become set even before Thomas Munro assumed control of the Ceded Districts. During the second half of the eighteenth century when palegars were considered as a formidable obstacle to the consolidation of its authority in the far south, the Company was engaged in a high cost long series of compaigns against them, which had culminated in the widespread uprising of 1800-01.[8] This must have produced some circumspection within the Madras government by the time Munro took over. The Governor General, Lord Wellesley, the Court of Directors and the Madras Board of Revenue all had come to favour more leniency and 'progressive approach to the improvement of the administration of Poligar affairs'. In addition to this sagacious and discreet reconsideration of policy, the Madras Government was also instructed that the Bengal regulations were to be established in Madras and in 'poligar countries', and they (palegars) were 'to receive the permanent possession of their lands on zamindary tenure'.[9]

However, there were not many voices in the Madras Presidency that had any good to say of palegars, and the persons who had closely watched their activities and had to actually deal with them, e.g. Thomas Munro, Thackeray and even Madras Board of Revenue were hardly enthusiastic about Wellesley's instructions that these chiefs were to be vested with permanent rights in their lands.

Thomas Munro, however, had a different way of looking at the things and the claims made by the palegars, backed, of course, by the authorities in Madras and Bengal. His understanding of the nature of landownership and rights of the *zamindars* in India in general and Madras Presidency in particular was perhaps much better than his contemporaries and near contemporaries. The people usually termed *zamindars*, he opined, were not more land owners than the *in'amdars*. The appellation of *zamindars* among the natives of India, he felt, comprehended every person who held land and discharged the duties of a civil officer down to the village *taliary* and also all palegars and rajas.[10]

Thomas Munro was not in favour of using force right away. If the palegars were wise enough to submit, they could be permitted to retain their estates in which they collected rent, part of which was to be passed on the government as land revenue. Another condition that he wanted to impose was that they must give up their power of justice, their armed retainers, and all the tattered shreds of sovereignty they had pulled around themselves.

In order to put the onus of action by the government on the palegars themselves and avoid any risk of mass reaction by them, Munro issued a Public Notification on 15 April 1801. This Notification banned garrisoning of any fort by the palegars, *jagirdars, zamindars, patels* or even *rayats*. They were asked to desist from maintaining the body of armed men and extorting money from the inhabitants either in the shape of *kaveli russom* or under any other pretence. Major-General Dugald Campbell, who had been appointed to command the troops in the Ceded Districts and to assist Thomas Munro to restore peace, was empowered to trial, and punish with death any person convicted of any of the above crimes.

Munro also proposed to raise the level of *peshkash* to the highest previously ever demanded by the Nawabs of Cuddapah or Haider Ali or by the Nizam's regime. At this high pitch of demand, Munro reasoned to Webbe, palegars would not be in a position to pay their troops, and maintain their military capacity and also pay the tribute to the Company. They could, however, maintain the troops only by withholding their payments to the Company. When, as he expected, they defaulted on the payments, they could be deposed and expelled legally. He concluded his proposal with the remarks, in a letter to Webbe, 'I am convinced that it is possible to expell them all and to hang the great part of them. The idea was also to change the *peshkash,* or customary tribute, into a land rent assessed at nearly the same rate as that on the sarkar land.[11] This would not only change the very character of the palegar institution and the nature of the palegars' relations with the government, but would also revert back to the original positions those palegars who had earlier changed their revenues to *peshkash*. Since this measure would considerably deprive the palegars of their hitherto enjoyed, power and position, opposition was bound to be there, but Munro was confident of overcoming that by perseverance.

As regards the troops employed by the palegars, government had several options before it. Their services could be dispensed with; even while being out of service they could be allowed to retain their *in'ams* by granting them *sanad* in the name of the Company; or their services could be transferred to the government.

It may be pointed out that identical policy in regard to all the three types of armed personnels,[12] referred earlier, was not approved/allowed by the government, All those who were paid cash remunerations were straight away recommended to be enlisted in the government battalions. The other two categories who were paid in the form of *in'am* lands were permitted to hold their lands on easy terms or on the payment of a stipulated quit rent, and were to be considered militia in times of necessity.

A Proclamation (1801) was issued directing the palegars and others to surrender the said arms within a period of three months from the time of issuing the proclamation. The palegars were, however, authorised to retain a certain number of pikesmen (number to be determined by the Governor in Council upon the representation of the palegars) for the purpose of maintaining their pomp and state. The pikesmen, thus allowed, were to be registered in the *kach'hari* of the collector, and the pikes to be stamped by the collector.

The practical aspect of different ideas and the policies proposed showed that Thomas Munro, in the first instance, maintained a *status quo* in regard to the lands held by the palegars. As planned, he raised the *peshkash* too high to render it impossible for them to pay and at the same time maintain their troops. He knew it fully well that even if they consented to pay, that would be without any serious intention of doing so.[13]

The experience of a few months proved Munro's hunch correct that the palegars would not pay the requisite amount and that little was to be got from them without compulsion. Most of them even refused to come to the *kach'hari* unless they were allowed to settle the amount of their *peshkash* in their own way.[14] Obviously, most of them had large amount of balances against their names. It was against Munro's policy to act leniently with the defaulters and wanted 'to insist upon their becoming answerable for the whole assessment' of their *palaiyams.*[15] The result was that some of the most powerful and several inferior chiefs who fell into the arrears, resisted, refused to come to the *kach'hari*, and/or took up arms, forces were sent against them and were captured, imprisoned, expelled, and/or were pensioned off. There is a long list of palegars who showed resistance against the government.[16]

The action taken against the above palegars did not mean that their power had been completely finished. Not only many more of them had not still been apprehended, even those who had apparently accepted the terms dictated by the English were likely to endeavour to recover their lost power.

Major General Campbell, who had been appointed the commanding officer to try and punish all rebels and all others opposing the English establishment in the Ceded Districts, was, meanwhile, given additional powers to try and award capital punishment on conviction to all such palegars.[17]

Encouraged by the success of the early steps taken to curb the power of the palegars in an attempt to establish Company's authority throughout the Ceded Districts completely and not to leave a set of turbulent chiefs in a condition to oppose it, Thomas Munro applied/got approved a set of new measures which were both more effective and economical. Acting on the suggestion of the Chief Secretary, communicated to him through General Campbell, he appreciated the expediency of inducing the Nizam to consent to allow part of the subsidiary force stationed at Raichur to move to Bellary.[18] He further suggested that the local militia should be chiefly stationed in the palegar areas. The appointment of the local militia was regularized and the subordinate collectors were asked to appoint the Companies as per the requirements of different areas.[19]

Despite making sufficiently elaborate arrangements to deal with the palegars, a stiff opposition from them could not be ruled out. All these chieftains had, by then, emerged to be quite defiant by nature. Even earlier, as already discussed, though 'bound certainly to pay to the ruling power tribute and military contingent, for most part, had generally managed not only to evade these payments, but in many instances to exact tribute from other smaller chiefs.' The earlier wars had, of course, impoverished them and reduced their power but they had escaped annihilation by yielding allegiance to each new master. They, as a matter of fact, had seen so many successive governments that they did not expect the British rule to be a permanent one. They, therefore, endeavoured 'as much as possible to evade its demands.' It was, however, difficult to escape from the 'clutches' of the 'new master', 'who would not be content with mere professions of allegiance, unless at the same time he received the practical proof of it in the shape of regularly- paid rent'.[20]

Thomas Munro dealt with several other palegars,[21] during his tenure as Principal Collector of the Ceded Districts, but the intention is to give only a few samples rather than giving the details about each and every palegar. In nutshell, it may be mentioned that in 1807, when Munro left, the palegars had been thus disposed off:[22]

| | | |
|---|---|---|
| i) | Pensioned | 2 |
| ii) | Holding a *jagir* | 1 |
| iii) | Residing on their estates but deprived of authority | 23 |
| iv) | Managing their own estates | 40 |
| v) | Expelled by force | 6 |
| vi) | In confinement | 8 |
| | Total | 80 |

None of the above categories had been given a free hand in his *palaiyam*. All those who were residing on or managing their estates were entitled only to a portion of the revenues as pensions or remunerations. The families of those expelled or in confinement were also given some pensions.

The policy of Munro's military action and the seizure of different palegars led to a great controversy and protracted correspondence involving the Principal Collectors, Madras Government and the Court of Directors. The Court of Directors were not convinced by the reasons given by Munro for the proceedings taken against different palegars. They felt that the only principle upon which Munro had based his action was that it was 'absolutely necessary to the establishment of anything like a regular authority in the Ceded Districts that no opportunity should be lost of expelling the Polligars.' They even directed that Thomas Munro 'be removed from his situation of collectors in those Districts (Ceded Districts), and that he be not employed in any Revenue Post in future, which the violent and mistaken principles of his conduct seem to render him unqualified to fill in a way that would be satisfactory to our feelings.[23]

It seems there was either a lack of proper coordination between the English authorities in Madras and the Court of Directors or the former did not care much about the orders and instructions from England, or were more enthusiastic about the establishment of the Company's authority in India.

Thomas Munro, in his defence, argued with the Board of Revenue (in a letter to be forwarded to the Court of Directors)[24] that for carrying into effect the government's instructions to establish their authority and in view of the state of the Ceded Districts in 1801,[25] the reduction of the palegars had become essential. However, it seems that the Board of Revenue 'quietly pocketed the increased revenues, which were the result of Munro's (as he was charged) "disingenuous and ill-considered policy", and to have made up their minds to say nothing about it. In 1807 when Munro resigned his post of Principal Collector and proceeded home on leave, he received a handsome acknowledgement by the Madras Government.

A careful study of the pension register maintained in the *taluq* office indicates that the columns 'Hereditary' and 'Not Hereditary' were left blank. It seems that either Munro wanted to play safe and did not want to commit whether the pension was hereditary or otherwise, or the government wanted to grant pensions to different palegars on different conditions. As far as the second contention is concerned, it is found, for example, that the Ghattum palegar and the Nossum palegars were sanctioned the pensions on the condition that 'the pension should depend entirely upon poligars continuing to reside at such place as the Collector may direct.'[26] Similarly, Baswapur palegar would get pension 'during good behaviour.'[27] The Register prepared by Robert Charles Ross Collector of Cuddapah, in 1814 mentioned an additional remark on the subject. He wrote, "in the column of hereditary added—during good behaviour to lineal descendents only". This matter became a subject of discussion in 1822 when the Chitvel family petitioned for the continuation of the pension after the demise of the then incumbent. The Board of Revenue expressly stated, on the authority of Collector Ross, that the pensions were hereditary.[28] This matter once again became a topic of discussion in 1830. Incidentally, it again pertained to the Chitvel palegar, of course, linked with another thirty-six cases of the same type. The Board of Revenue asked Robertson, Collector of Bellary and Dalzall, Collector of Cuddapah about the nature of the land grants or pensions granted to the palegars. The Collector of Bellary observed that he could not discover that any actual pledge had any time been given to the parties that these allowances were to be hereditary. However, he quoted the example of Nossum palegar, whose mother, after the death of the incumbent, had been allowed by Thomas Munro to draw full allowances during her life. It was done on the plea that if decided otherwise, 'it would naturally exert a distrust among the Poligars that their lands or pensions would not descent to their children'. The Collector of Cuddapah simply narrated the above quoted example of Ross. The Board recommended the pensions to be hereditary but decided that any share of the pension, if given to the sister of deceased, would lapse on her death.[29] As such, it can be safely accepted that the pensions granted were to be enjoyed by the grantee and his heirs both in the male and female lines during good behaviour, and were liable to resumption on the family becoming extinct.[30] It was also clarified that the continuance of the pension depended on the pleasure of government and could not be claimed as a matter of right. In case of a lapse by death, the pension would be resumed *protempore* and the case reported for the orders of government.[31] In 1843 a suggestion to pay some money in lump sum in lieu of regular pension was turned down by the Governor General in Council on the plea that 'the payment of money, by way of redemption would soon be forgotten', while the abolition of pension 'would be remembered forever.'[32]

The descendants of the palegars continued to receive small allowances as pensions from the Government of India. In 1928, there were only ten such cases who received pensions in Bellary district.[33] On a visit to Cuddapah *tehsildar* office in 1969, it was found that some representatives were still receiving pensions.

The post Munro scenario of the Ceded Districts was comparatively much more peaceful and had only a few incidents of general interest. The only incident which could be termed as an incident of palegar resistance, took place in 1816 when a descendent of the dispossessed palegars of Koilkuntla and Nossum attempted to excite a general resistance.

**Second Phase**

The palegar resistance in the Ceded Districts was practically non-existent for nearly four decades after Thomas Munro's departure in 1807. It was in the year 1846 that the areas under study once again witnessed a major resistance from the palegars which incidently had much larger mass base covering different sections of the society, It is, however, by no means the intention to suggest that the palegars had suddenly turned into a happy lot and had no grouse against the East India Company during the intermittent years.

The successors of the palegars with whom Thomas Munro had made settlements had been, because the enormous divisions in the pensions and allowances, reduced to comparatively indigent circumstances. The loss of rank, influence and power coupled with meagre monetary allowance had made them a discontented lot. They would even draw a comparison between the rank and affluence of their ancestors and their own impoverished circumstances and unexalted condition in life. That is a different matter that perhaps the paucity of resources and manpower deterred them from revolting against the English.

This period of nearly four decades, especially the post-1813 period, was also full of active steps, on the part of the East India Company, taken towards the transformation of Indian society and culture. The more conservatives amongst the English administrators maintained that Indian civilization was different from European civilization. Opposing any programme of rapid modernization, they favoured the introduction of reforms very cautiously and gradually lest it should produce a violent reaction in the country. The things started taking a radical change due to the influence of Mill, Munro, Malcolm, Elphinston, Metcalf, Bentinck and above all with the coming of reforming Whigs in power in England after 1830. Despite their influence, the English policy continued to be imperialistic and exploitative favouring only those reformist measures which came within the framework of easier and more thoroughgoing exploitation of India's resources, One of the things that came into their accepted framework was the attempt to discontinue/fully tax the revenue free or favourably taxed grants, known as *in'am* lands in south, which had been, in some form or the other, in existence since the ancient times$_0$ Even persons like Raja Rammohan Roy, who was in league with the introduction of many a social and religious reform and was against priestly domination in the society had protested against the attempts to impose taxes on such grants.[34] However, the Regulation XXXI of 1802, the orders of 1825, the Regulation IV of 1831 extended by the Acts XXXI of 1836 and XXXIII of 1838, and the Minute of Consulation, 26 April 1845 clearly indicate the British intentions and policy towards one of the most important aspects of economic/ agrarian administration, the *in'am* lands.[35]

Without going into a detailed exposition on the origin and nature of the *in'am*, it could be roughly defined as a gift or benefaction conferred by a superior to an inferior person or institution. It was the custom to grant assignments of land revenue or at favourable revenue for all kinds of purposes like payment to troops, civil officers, maintenance and support of temples/mosques etc. and their servants, charitable institutions and reward for public services.[36]

In order to get familiarized with the *in'am* lands, it becomes essential to give a brief resume of such holdings. 'A descriptive list of the *in'am* tenures of the Madras Presidency' submitted to the Government on 30 October 1869, contained more than 400 separate categories of *in'am*.[37] Most of these *in'ams* were defined or described as land holdings either wholly free or partially taxed.

The East India Company's administrators alleged that a new phenomenon had started emerging in the grant of *in'am* lands during the period of anarchy, which preceded the English rule. They wrote, "the power of granting *in'ams* was assumed by various petty chiefs, officers of Government, and others, who alienated the revenues to a considerable extent. There is good reason to suppose that a large extent of land was granted as a *in'am* during this period by the parties who had not even the shadow of authority to make such alienation."[38] It seems to be too generalized a statement as the categories of the persons mentioned above had, though qualified, rights to bestow *in'ams* especially when they had assumed the role of a prince and the period was politically disturbed. The study of the pre-British system, in brief, shows that the *zamindars* and other assignees, both Hindus and Muslims, enjoyed transferable rights and could grant even hereditary revenue free grants. At the same time it may be pointed out, "The *malkiyat* rights of the assignees for the revenues and the land ownership rights of the self-cultivating riaya co-existed. In case an assignee tried to interfere with the latter's rights, his assignment was liable to be transferred."[39] As such, if there was deviation, it was not in the assignment of *in'am* lands by the *zamindars*/palegars etc., it was in the interference of the *riaya's* ownership rights. The English had their own interpretations and tried to act accordingly.

Instituting an inquiry at a very early date of their administration, the Company passed the Regulation XXXI of 1802 'to try the validity of the titles of the persons holding, or claiming to hold, lands exempted from the payment of revenue under grants not being *Badshahi* or royal grants.'[40] Despite a proposal put forward by the government that the *in'ams* be 'resumed and money payments substituted' the general result was that exempted lands were not only interfered with during the early surveys, the government of the day, following the custom of the country, also 'adopted the practice of rewarding meritorious services by grants of *jagirs,* and thus many villages were alienated either in perpetuity or for a stated number of lives'.[41] The practice of remunerating the village *patels* and *karnams* by land grants was also continued, though on new conditions.[42]

The practice of granting *jagirs* gradually fell into disuse after the orders from the Court of Directors, dated respectively 2 July 1822 and 27 May 1829. However, nothing was done in regard to the investigation of *in'am* tenures. Meanwhile, in 1825 orders were issued and a special establishment was sanctioned for that purpose in Bellary, but these measures were not put into practice. By Regulation IV of 1831, afterwards extended by Acts XXXI of 1836 and XXXIII of 1838 the *adalats* were prohibited from taking cognizance of claims the personal or hereditary grants of money or of land revenue whether conferred by the English government or made earlier by 'Native Governments' and confirmed or continued by the Company, except with the special permission of government.

Notwithstanding these legislative measures, neither the transfer nor lapses of *in'ams* were subjected to scrutiny as they occurred. In fact, no active measures were taken to vindicate the law until 1845, when the government issued orders strictly prohibiting local officers from continuing *in'ams* on the occurrence of lapses, and directing that each case should be reported for their orders through the Board of Revenue. This was followed in the next year (16 March 1846) by a proclamation notifying that adoptions involving inheritance to *in'am* lands should not be recognized unless reported at least six months before the death of the party making adoption.[43]

The policy initiated as an aftermath of the proclamation (16 March 1846) had the worst impact on two of the heretofore, discussed categories of the *in'ams*. These were *kattubadi in'ams* and the *bhatta-vritti in'ams*. It not only involved serious disputes but also proved to be the immediate cause of resistance against the East India Company in 1846.[44]

The *bhatta-vritti* and *Khairati* (if belonging to Muslims) *in'ams* had been in existence since the cession of the Ceded Districts to the Company. Thomas Munro had directed his surveyors that all sundry *in'ams* having no specific designation, under which they could be classed, should be entered, if belonging to Hindus, as '*Bhatta-vritti*', and if to the Muslims, as *Khairati*.[45] These *in'ams* were in the beginning bracketed together as *Dharmadayam* or secular, as distinguished from *Devadayam* or religious grants.[46]

The *bhatta-vritti in'ams* in the Ceded District were quite extensive, revenue-free landed tenures, held by different classes, but generally by Brahmins, as is implied by the term, which means 'For the support of Brahmins.' The *khairati in'ams* were of less than a whole village and were not service lands or granted on some specific account. The value of *bhatta-vritti in'ams* was much more than the *khairati* and were valued approximately at six lakhs rupees as per the survey assessment. The real annual value was, however, much less, as the lands were not all cultivated, and those cultivated were usually taken by the 'Circar' *rayats* on terms lower than the assessment. It was in reality a great assistance to the *rayats*, and in consequence a source of general prosperity to the area.[47]

The *bhatta-vritti in'amdars* were a large body of native gentry, many of them possessing considerable estates, comprising lands in many different villages, while others had but small holdings. Some of them were in the public service, others were engaged in commerce; but a great number lived on their properties, and subsisted on the production and rents of them, They had held their estates since the cession of the areas as private property, having perfect liberty to alienate them by gift or sale. They had confidence in the good faith of the British Government. They were sure that though no new grants would be made, no changes would be made in regard to old tenures.[48]

In 1845, the Board of Revenue declared the *bhatta-vritti in'ams* to be of the nature of charitable allowances mentioned in clause 2,

Regulation IV of 1831. The Board prohibited any transfer of them by gift, or sale. These instructions were strictly acted upon, Accordingly, when an *in'amdar* died, his lands were attached immediately, and his family even when he left sons, were kept in a state of anxiety for months, When the order for continuing the *in'am* arrived, (if such was the order), the heir was informed that he would receive the estate of his ancestors not as his hereditary right, but as the bounty of government, and for his life only. The people were generally ignorant about the Regulations enacted by the government, and learnt its intentions only from the enforcement of orders by the local officers, They lost confidence in the permanency of anything, and would commonly say, "in what can we now trust" and, "in what respect is the Company's Government better than former Governments".

The *kattubadis* had received a special guarantee from Thomas Munro on behalf of the government that their *in'ams* would be continued to them hereditary during good behaviour and on condition of their yielding to the Company's government same services, which they had formerly been giving to the certain palegars.[49] Certain political motives, however, could not be denied behind the continuation of their hereditary *in'ams* and allowances as that was done to buy peace and to keep them quiet. Thomas Munro, vide his letter dated 10 April 1806, had agreed to maintain *status-quo* in the *in'ams* enjoyed by the *kattubadis* to save the Ceded Districts, especially the Cuddapah district, from the state of anarchy.[50] These measures were entirely successful in accomplishing the desired object. There are numerous documents to prove the hereditary nature of the *kattubadi imams*.[51]

The comparative change in the political scene between 1800 and 1845-46 cannot be denied. With the lapse of more than four decades the English had acquired vast administrative experience, political authority and military power. They had attained better position to suppress the armed and recalcitrant elements, if present, rather more easily and effectively. Besides, they would not hesitate in deviating from the position and policy adopted not only by the former Indian rulers but even by the earlier English administrators, in a bigger way.[52] What else could explain the policy initiated by the English government in December 1845? The policy was to retain only such number of *kattubadis* as was required in the village; to remove the rest, if they were willing (?), to other villages in the same *taluk* where there were few or none; to resume their *in'am* lands and to give fresh grants of waste land, according to the minimum standard of remuneration, in the villages of their posting; their appointments as well as the land grants were not to be hereditary and were subject to readjustments after their death; and all the remaining *kattubadi in'ams* were to be resumed on the death of the existing incumbents. However, their heirs could retain the lands if they chose to pay the full assessment.[53]

Accordingly, in Cuddapah alone the *in'ams* of 1396 *kattubadis* were to be resumed on the death of then possessors; 239 *kattubadis* were to be removed to other villages with their own consent (?); and the *in'ams* of 1695 *kattubadis* worth, as per the survey assessment, Rs. 74,895-15-10 were to be reduced. Incidently, excepting two, all the deceased *kattubadis* had left sons, brothers, or nephews, male heirs, entitled to succeed to their land. These incidents were directly connected with the insurrections that took place soon in the most adversely affected areas.[54]

The *bhatta-vritti* and *kattubadi in'amdars*, though agitated, could not give vent to their feelings unless they had an acceptable leadership who could unite them under his banner. The leadership was provided by another discontented youngman, Narasimha Reddy, a scion of two prominent and extensive erstwhile palegars of Oyelwada and Nossum *palaiyams* (both in Koilkuntla taluk then in Cuddapah and now in Kurnool district A. P.). Narasimha Reddy was the grandson in the male line to Oyelwada *palaiyam* and on his mother's side to Nossum *palaiyam*. Pedda Mulla Reddy (father of Narasimha Reddy) and his brother Chinna Mulla Reddy resisted the English authority and took refuge in Hyderabad territory where they remained for nearly 8 years. When they presented themselves before Chaplin, the Collector of Cuddapah, and solicited a pension, they were granted a monthly allowance of Rs. 70/-, i.e., Rs. 35/- to each. This amount of pension was quite inadequate to support them in a suitable manner and altogether very trifling in comparison with the revenues of their *palaiyam*, lately resumed.

Meanwhile both Pedda Mulla Reddy and Chinna Mulla Reddy had also died. Whereas the latter's pension of Rs. 35/- p.m. was continued to his widow, the former's pension was divided amongst his three sons — Kumara Mulla Reddy, Vurda Reddy and Narasinha Reddy. The three brothers advanced their claims for the continuance to them of the Nossum pension on the plea of their relationship to the original grantee, which was, however, rejected (1831).[55]

While his two elder brothers acquiesced in the decision given by the English government and uniformly manifested their submission to authorities, Narasimha Reddy was unable to reconcile himself to his straitened circumstances. The consequent poverty and indigence of his mature years, compared with the state and affluence of his childhood, had no doubt rankled in his mind. The different reasons given by various English reports for his ultimate armed resistance, the consensus is that he had both heard of and seen 'insurrections when protracted for some time ending in a compromise.'[56] He even thought of proceeding to Cuddapah and make a representation to the Collector regarding his circumstances and motives,' but was persuaded by the *kattubadis* to the extreme step.[57] Incidently most of the resumptions of *in'ams* had taken place in different villages of Koilkuntla taluk.

The sources indicate two prominent reasons as to why the *kattubadis* looked towards Narasimha Reddy as their leader. One, most of the *kattubadis* who ultimately joined him in the armed resistance, indiscriminately all were the descendants of the dependents and retainers of Naraimha Reddy's ancestors from whom they had derived their *in'ams.*[58] W.A.D. Inglis pointed out that many of the *kattubadis* had admitted indirectly in their depositions that all that class was engaged in a common cause.[59]

The second reason of their close connections was the caste factor. Not only Narasimha Reddy and many of the principal *kattubadis* but even many heads of the villages and principal *rayats* belonged to *Kapu* community.

It is, therefore, quite probable that Narasimha Reddy's relations, friends, the principal *kattubadis* and even *patels*, being alarmed at the threatened loss or curtailing of their *in'ams* and having consulted and complained to their leader, and at the same time the idea of bettering their lot, led them to an armed resistance against the English. Moreover, the people of the Ceded Districts in general and that of Cuddapah in particular, as indicated in the Inglis' report, had always felt confident that the settlement of landed tenures made nearly half a century ago, was to be permanent, and would not be altered in any way to their disadvantage. It was, therefore, to be expected that the serious changes attempted by the government would produce discontentment amongst the people in general.[60]

W.A.D. Inglis, Special Commissioner investigating the causes of resistance had attributed the remote cause of outbreak "to the frequent changes in the office of Collector in this District (Cuddapah)".[61] His observations about the people of and conditions in Cuddapah were absolutely correct. After all, he himself had been the acting Collector there for about six months, and as Special Commissioner he must have investigated all possible causes of resistance quite deeply.

The evidence shows that Narasimha Reddy had been preparing himself for a long drawn struggle against the English than a mere insurrection. It could be ascertained from the statements made before the magistrate by his close associates that he had in his possession a *sanad* (J.H. Cochrane thought it to have been a forged one) 'bearing the impression of a large seal in Persian Character' which he carried about with him stating that it had been sent to him by the Nawab of Golconda. The purport of the *sanad*, it was told, was an injunction to all the palegars in the Ceded Districts, who were formerly attached to the Nizam's territory, to assist him (Narasimha Reddy) in the object he had in view. With this *sanad* he also visited all the villages, which formerly comprised the *palaiyams* of his ancestors and obtained the goodwill and promised assistance. Initially he had the company of about 30 *kattubadis*, but gradually the number went on increasing, who all accompanied him from village to village. Narasimha Reddy confessed that he had shown the same *sanad* to the persons of influence in the Ceded Districts as well as in Hyderabad and not only obtained their support but also of others through them.[62] The prominent areas from where he could muster sufficient support were the palegars/chiefs of Hyderabad, Kurnool, Owk, Banganapally and even Annegundy. These areas not only provided him with material support but could also easily use them as escape routes as well as hideouts—in case of emergency. However, the largest support that he got was from Koilkuntla, which incidently was his main centre of activities. His influence in Koilkuntla was so great that apart from the *kattubadis*, the people, including Brahmins, and the heads of the villages were at his back. It could not be denied that in this regard both the factors, the genuine support and fear, were working. In any case, it had made things so difficult for the English government, before and during the course of resistance, that it was almost impossible for them to get any correct intelligence about his activities and whereabouts.[63] Which *patel* or *kattubadi* was with the English or against them, was not easy to judge. Several letters written by J.H. Cochrane have given a detailed account of the events of the resistance.

It may be mentioned here that apart of his known associates in the campaign, Narasimha Reddy was duly assisted by the geographical conditions of the area. The government had got so much panicked that they could never make any correct assessment about the number of followers that the palegar had and their guess ranged from 200 to 9,000.[64] They even went to the extent of declaring an award of Rs. 1,000/- for the apprehension of Narasimha Reddy.[65] The task of the English had become all the more difficult and had become almost impossible for them to get any intelligence about the whereabouts, plans and activities of the palegar due to the active support that he was getting from the *patels*, *kattubadis*, *bhatta-vritti in'am* holders and the *rayats* in general.[66] It was only on 6 October 1846 that Narasimha Reddy could be captured.[67] After a trial lasting nearly 3 months, the Court of Faujdari Adalat delivered their judgment on 9 January 1847 and was hanged on 22 February 1847.

The resistance led by Narasimha Reddy and the report on its causes submitted by the Special Commissioner, W.A.D. Inglis (19 January 1847) had far reaching impact on the British policy towards the *in'am* lands. Both the things had forced the Court of

Directors to give a second thought on the future course of action in regard to such grants, which 'have always been treated as hereditary.'[68] Howsoever, they might call this incident as 'insignificant in its political bearing'[69] or 'disaffection was local',[70] the very acceptance by the Court of Directors that the incident was 'connected with the course of treatment latterly pursued towards *in'ams*',[71] proves that their socio-economic policies lacked proper understanding of the priorities especially of the then conservative society. By simply quoting the 'insurrection of Narasimha Reddy', ascribed by the Court of Directors 'to a course of measures in violation at once of the stipulated and prescriptive rights of property in the district', as a cause of fresh 'discussion regarding the policy of disturbing long-existing rights of property in *in'am* lands',[72] gave added importance to that resistance.

The government issued a series of instructions upon which were founded the rules for the treatment of lapsed *in'ams*. The new rules declared that all *in'ams* held on grant at the date of the British assumption, and held by the same family at the time of the passing of Regulation XXXI of 1802, should be continued to the next heir on the same terms.[73] In those cases where the *in'am* had passed out of the original family, or had been fraudulently obtained or irregularly inherited; where it was claimed on invalid grounds, as through the female line, or by a collateral branch, in virtue of an illegal or suspicious adoption; or generally where there were any circumstances affecting the prior transmission of the *in'am* or the title of the existing claimant, the collector was required to report to the Board of Revenue and ultimately to the government. The immediate attachment of *in'ams* on the occurrences of lapses, which was a source of great distress, was prohibited.[74]

They accordingly announced certain principles, which were incorporated in the Minute of Sir Charles Trevelyan, the Governor of Madras (13 May 1859). The Governor in the same Minute also propounded certain rules on which the main Commission based his investigations. It was announced that if a land had for fifty years been in the possession of a person, or if those through whom he claimed, without the payment of land-tax, such length of possession should be held to be a good title to that land of *in'am*, whatever might have been the origin of the possession (whether held under any *sanad* or not).[75]

The *bhatta-vritti* and *khairatti in'ams* held respectively by the Brahmins and Muslims were enfranchised under the rules and were granted title-deeds. The *kattubadi in'ams*, irrespective of their origin, were also enfranchised, but the issue of title-deeds was suspended pending the completion of the new police arrangements. However, the whole extent of *in'am* lands was enfranchised on a quit-rent of five-eighths of the assessment. As regards the amount of quit-rent, it may be pointed out, as the study of the records preserved in the offices of the different Collectors/Deputy Commissioners shows that there were cases when the amount of quit-rent could be less than 5/8 and could be equal to the total survey assessment of the land.[76]

## References

1. In this regard see for instance the palegars of Owk, Rayadrug, Harpanahalli, Chitvel, Nossam, Mullel, Kallibundah and different palegars of Gurramkonda district. *APSA, Cuddapah District Records (1802)*, 647/574; TNSA, *Madras Board of Revenue Proceedings,* 1 November 1802; *Col. Munro's Report Regarding the Ceded Districts* (1801-1802), ASO (D) Vol. 21 (67), Thomas Munro to the President and Members of the Board of Revenue dated 20 March 1802 (Hereafter, *Munro's Report Regarding the Poligars, 20 March, 1802*). ASO (D), Vol. 66, *Report of William Thackeray,* dated 8 September 1807. Dua, J.C., 'Poligars: Their rise in the Ceded Districts', *I.H.C.*, 1972, pp. 467-74. Sastri, K.N. Venkatasubba, *The Munro System of British Statesmanship in India* (Mysore, 1930), p. xiii.
2. Dua, J.C., *British Historiography: Eighteenth Century Punjab* (New Delhi, 1992), pp. 101, 108, 115.
3. TNSA, *Madras Board of Revenue Consultations*, 31 August 1801; *Col. Munro's Report Regarding the Poligars in the Ceded Districts with a Memorandum of Poligars, 1801-1802*, RSO (D), Vol. 66 (21), Letter from Thomas Munro to the President and Members of the Board Revenue, dated 12 August 1801. *Fifth Report*, pp. 88-89. *Munro's Report Regarding the Poligars*, 20 March 1802. Dua, J.C., 'Position of Patels and Karnams in the Ceded Districts during the first quarter of the nineteenth century', *I.H.C.,* Chandigarh, 1973.
4. APSA, *Cuddapah District Records* (1813), 655/246, Letter from Robert Ross, Collector to the Board of Revenue, 22 November 1813. *Report of the Madras Estates Land Act Committee* (Madras, 1938), 'Appendix', pp. 409-17. *Selections From the Records of the Madras Government,* New (Revenue) Series, No. 1, *A Collection of Papers Relating to the In'am Settlement in the Madras Presidency*

(Madras, 1948), p. 347. Baden-Powell, B.H. *The Land-System of British India* (rpt. Delhi, 1974), 3 Vols., III, p. 82. Dua, J.C., 'Nature of the Poligar Revolts in the Ceded Districts During the First Half of the Nineteenth Century', *IHC* (Jadavpur) 1974, pp. 235-45.

5. *Munro's Report Regarding the Poligars*, 20 March 1802. Thomas Munro to the President and Members of the Board of Revenue, dated 12 August 1801, *op. cit.* TNSA, *Bellary Records* (1801), 396/453; *Selections From the Records of Bellary Districts-Political, Revenue and Agriculture Matters 1800-1857*, ASO (D), Vol. 73, Letter from Munro to William Patrie, President and Members of the Board Revenue, dated 22 June 1801. Francis, W., *Madras District Gazetteers: Anatapur* (Madras, 1905), p. 24.

6. *William Thackeray's Report*, dated 8 September 1807.

7. TNSA, *Bellary Records* (1801), 396/181, Letter from Munro to Wiliam Patrie, President and Members of the Board of Revenue, dated 30 July, 1801.

8. For further details about the widespread revolt of the palegars, see, TNSA, *Secret Despatches to England*, Vol. 2, pp. 66-70. Despatch of Edward Clive, 18 March 1801; *Secret Consultations*, Vol. 12, p. 118. Mornington to Edward Clive, 23 August 1800; *Military Despatches to England*, Vol. 31, pp. 136-37, Despatch of Edward Clive, 15 October 1801; *Military Consultations*, Vol. 283, pp. 3554-58, Madras Council, 22 May 1801. *Fifth Report, op. cit.*, pp. 547-61. 'Report From Special Commission to the Governor in Council', Fort St. George, 5 April 1803. Ṛajayyan, K., *South Indian Rebellion: The First War of Independence 1800-1801* (Mysore, 1971), pp. 35-42, 123-213.

9. *Fifth Report, op. cit.*, pp. 614-41. 'Memoir of Mr. Hodgson, On Advantages of a Permanent Zamindari Settlement, 1806; pp. 547-61. 'Report from Special Commission to the Governor in Council, Fort St. George', 5 April 1803; pp. 317-35, 'Instructions issued to Collectors under the Presidency of Fort St. George, AS to Permanently Settling the Lands', 15 October 1799.

10. TNSA, *Madras Board of Revenue Consultations, 26 September 1805; Selections From the Old Records of Bellary District, 1800-1807*, ASO (D), Vol. 72, Thomas Munro to William Patrie, President and Members of the Board of Revenue, 25 August 1805. Dua, J.C., *Agrarian System*, p. 36. For a detailed discussion on the pre-British land ownership and rights of the *zamindars*, see, for example, Grover, B.R., 'Nature of Land-Rights in Mughal India', paper read at the Indian Economic History Seminar, Delhi, April 1961 and published in *Indian Economic and Social History Review*, Vol. I, 1963, pp. 1-23; 'Elements of Continuity and Change in Land Ownership and Rights from the Mughal Age to the Early British Administration in India', Presidential Address, Medieval India Section, *Indian History Congress*, 37th session, Calicut, 1976.

11. TNSA, *Madras Political Consultations/Proceedings*, 3 April 1801; *Selections ... 1800-1856*, ASO (D), Vol. 73, Munro to Josiah Webbe, Chief Secretary to Government of Fort St. George, 27 March 1801; *Papers regarding the Revenue Settlement 1801-1823*, ASO (D), Vol. 76, Letter from William Patrie etc. members to Edward Lord Clive, Governor in Council, 2 October 1801. *Munro's*

*Report Regarding the Poligars,* 20 March, 1802. Also, Beaglehole, T.H., *Thomas Munro and the Development of Adminstrative Policy in Madras, 1792-1818, The Origin of 'The Munro System',* Cambrige University Press, 1966. p. 62; Stein, Burton, *Peasant State and Society in Medieval South India,* New Delhi, OUP, 1980, p. 88, Chaudhuri, Shashi Bhusan, *Civil Disturbances During the British Rule in India, 1765-1857* (Calcutta, 1955), p. 129; Brackenbury, C.F., *Gazetteer of the Cuddapah District* (Madras, 1915), p. 48; Francis, W., *Gazetteer of the Bellary District* (Madras, 1904), pp. 46-40. It may be pointed out that in a few instances the rent was kept lower than the ordinary rents of the *sarkar* villages where the palegars produced the *sanads* of Lord Cornwallis and Sir Charles Oakley promising them reinstatement, or where raising it any further might have driven them into rebellion (Munro to Webbe, 27 March 1801).

12. They were: (i) those who were paid in money for their services, and were least numerous; (ii) those who were paid in land but were, notwithstanding farmers and regarded their service *in'ams* as a secondary object; and (iii) those who depended entirely upon their *in'am* lands for their subsistence and were more numerous than the first two categories.
13. *Munro's Report Regarding the Poligars,* 20 March 1802; also, Munro to Joshiah Webbe, Chief Secretary to Government of Fort St. George, 27 March 1801, *op. cit.*
14. *Ibid.*
15. Munro believed 'had they (the defaulters) met with any indulgence they would have continued to keep up the same number of peons next years, whereas by pressing rigidly the recovery of the defalcations, the more poor and timid will disband their followers—and the more powerful will feel themselves compelled to reduce the number of those which they retained'.
16. These palegars included four powerful ones, as mentioned earlier, that of Talpool, Vimlah, Chitvel and Nossam. The inferior ones included the palegars of Dasmuru, Ganjikota, Kalva, Kamalapuram, Kapotra, Mullel, Cumbun, Gurramkonda, Gudikota, Oopalur, Rarvah, Telpula, Tippreddipalle, Adoni, Baswapur, Bellary, Devankonda, Ghattu. Regarding the different types of the actions taken against the above palegars, see TNSA, *Bellary Records* (1801), 351/158; 396/106, 466, 374/92; 389/134; 376/137; 396/118; 396/480; 387/132; 396/463; 270; 396/4, 21, 26; 374/36, 39; 374/65; 66; 374/102, 103; 396/210, 472, 480; 351/158; (1800), 396/449; 452. APSA, *Cuddapah District Records* (1802), 647/572; 647/357; (1801), 647/560; (1802), 648/60; (1801), 647/551; 647/551; 647/59, 536.
17. TNSA, *Bellary Records*, (1802), 396/510, Order No. 275, 16 May 1802.
18. Letter from Thomas Munro to Lt. General Stuart, C-in-C. Madras, 11 November 1802, Gleig, *op. cit.,* I, pp. 335-39.
19. For Example, Harpanahalli was to have 2 Companies, Adoni 4 and Cumbum 3. TNSA, *Bellary Records* (1803), 404/236, Circular datd 21 May 1803 issued by Munro for the Collectors of Ceded Districts. Other things of note contained in the circular were:

(a) The salaries of the Sardar and Jamadar were fixed at Star Pagodas 6/- and 3/- respectively.

(b) Same writer could be appointed for upto 3 companies and would get salary from all.

(c) As there were no Jamadars before the regulations were passed, the collectors could nominate deserving Daffadars and fill up the Daffadars from Peons.

(d) Those who were disabled by wounds and the widows of every man killed on service were entitled to half the pay as pension.

(e) Contrary to the earlier practice, the peons were to desist from paying any *russom* to their Sardar.

20. Gribble, J.D.B., *A Manual of the District of Cuddapah* (Madras, 1875), pp. 104-07.

21. They were, for instance, the palegars of Chittoor, Dudikonda, Ghattu, Konakondla, Gudikota, Nileswaram, Punganuru, Hudgupa, Kullur etc., and also the attempts were foiled. See, TNSA, *Bellary Records* (1804), 375/132; 399/47, 101, 402/222, 381/170, 397/9, 398/232, 399/9; (1805), 315/190; (1806), 399/222, 364; (1804), 398/214, 222, 230, 399/26; (1806), 381/162, 410/176; (1802), 396/330, 650/8, 38; (1805), 632/146, 650/159, 225; (1806), 652/35; (1804), 650/71; (1805), 650/148.

22. Maclean, C.D., *Standing Information Regarding the Official Administration of the Madras Presidency in Each Department in Illustration of the Yearly Administration Reports* (Madras, 1879), 2nd edn., p. 90.

23. TNSA, *Revenue Despatch to Fort St. George*, 10 April 1804; APSA, *Cuddapah District Records* (1804), 633/48, Extract from a general letter from the Hon'ble Court of Directors, 10 April 1804.

24. TNSA, *Madras Board of Revenue Consultations/Proceedings,* 4 March, 1805; *Selections … 1800-1856,* ASO (D), Vol. 73, Thomas Munro to the Board of Revenue, 22 February 805 (It was a very rare case that this letter was transmitted to Court of Directors without any comment by the Madras Government, TNSA, *Revenue Letter from Madras to England,* 8 March 1805, paras 178-79.

25. In this case a reference may be made to a 'Munro's Report of 1801'. He, 'for example, wrote: The economy of the Ceded Districts tracts became almost entirely depopulated. Hunnumuntgoond rated at 15,000 Cantaroy Pagodas in the Treaty Schedule produced Cantaroy Pagodas 4,000 only and Narsapoor rated at more than Cantaroy Pagodas 8,000 did not yield even 500 when they came under the Company'. See, TNSA, *Board's Consultations,* Vol. 296, p. 10592, Munro's Report, 20 August 1801.

26. APSA, *Cuddapah District Records* (1813), 640/26, Letter from Deputy Secretary, Fort St. George to the Collector of Cuddapah, 13 September 1813; Extract of a letter to the Chief Secretary to Government, 18 June 1813; Extract of a letter from the Secretary to Government in the Revenue Department, 10 September 1813; (1813), 640/39, Letter from P. Bruce, Magistrate, Zillah Court of Bellary to D. Hill, Secretary to Government, 6 September 1813, sent to the Collector

of Cuddapah by D. Hill on 14 September 1813; (1813), 640/87. D. Hill to the Collector in Cuddapah, 28 September 1813.

27. APSA, *Cuddapah District Records* (1811), 637/183, Letter from W. Oliver, Secretary to the Collector in Cuddapah, 4 February 1811.

28. NAI, *Home Department—Land Revenue,* 17 May, 1845, Letter from Secretary, Board of Revenue, Fort St. George to Acting Chief Secretary to Government, 26 April 1830.

29. *Ibid.*

30. NAI, *Home Department—Land Revenue,* 24 April 1847 (4-9), Letter from Sir Montgomery Bart, Offg. Secretary to Government of Fort St. George, 10 March 1847; Letter from G.A. Bushley, Secretary to the Government of India to Montgomery, 24 April 1847.

31. NAI, *Home Department—Land Revenue,* 19 August, 1843 (4-10), Letter from J.D. Bourdillon, Secretary, Board of Revenue to Arbuthnot, Acting Principal Collector Cuddapah, 30 June 1843.

32. NAI, *Home Department—Land Revenue,* 19 August, 1843 (4-10), Letter to J.H. Thomas, Secretary to Government, Fort St. George, 19 August 1843.

33. *Madras District Gazetteers, Bellary District,* Vol. II (Madras, 1930), p. 63.

34. Carpenter, Mary, *Last Days of Raja Ram Mohun Roy in England* (Calcutta, 1915), p. 113. Roy, Raja Rammohan, *Exposition of the Practical Operation of the Judicial and Revenue Systems of India* (London, 1832), pp. 69-77.

35. For the application of these Regulations/Acts See, 'Report by Mr. W.T. Blair on the entire operations of the In'am Commission', 30 October 1869, *Selections from the Records of the Madras Government New* (Revenue) *Series No. 1, A Collection of Papers relating to the In'am Settlement in the Madras Presidency* (Madras 1948), pp. 311-326. (Hereafter, *the In'am Settlement Papers*). For details about the Regulations see, *The Regulations of the Government of Fort St. George in Madras, 1801-34.*

36. Frykenberg, Robert Eric, 'The Silent Settlement in South India, 1793-1853: An analysis of the Role of Inams in the Rise of the Indian Imperial System', in Frykenberg, Robert Eric (ed.), *Land Tenure and Peasant in South Asia* (New Delhi, 1984), pp. 37-53, p. 39. Krishnaswami, S.Y., *Rural Problems in Madras: Monograph* (Madras, 1947), p. 58. Apart from the known ways of giving land grants, a recent research/book has given new dimensions to the subject. It has come to light that "Early medieval India also witnessed a parallel custom of putting the actual sale of landed property in the form of a sacred donation. Sometimes the sale of property was openly recorded and donation was proclaimed as the purpose of the sale. In such cases the vendor is the state and the donor is the individual who has purchased the land and requested the government to make it a rent-free holding. But sometimes the king himself is the donor and yet he happens to have actually sold out the property to the person on whose request the grant had been made. Without reading between the lines it is not possible to detect the real character of these characters which have been

intentionally given the patent look of a land grant." The author has quoted such cases from Rajasthan, Uttar Pradesh, Bihar, Bengal, Gujarat, Madhya Pradesh, Maharashtra, Goa, Orissa, Andhra Pradesh, Karnataka and Tamil Nadu. Om Prakash, *Early Indian Land Grants and State Economy* (Allahabad, 1988), pp. 85-182.

37. *The In'am Settlement Papers,* pp. 342-54. Moreover, the *In'am Fair Registers* preserved in the collectorates (I have personally checked these registers in the Anantapur Collectorate) give a detailed description of the number, character, value, and nature of *in'ans* in every village of that district.

38. *The Inam Settlement Papers,* p. 311. 'Report by Mr. W.T. Blair on the entire operations of the *In'am* Commissioner', 30 October 1869, p. 211. TNSA, *Papers Regarding the Revenue Settlement 1801-1823,* ASO (D), Vol. 76, Thomas Munto to the Board of Revenue, 1 July 1801. *Correspondence between the Collector, the B/Rev. and the Government regarding the Settlement of Fuslies 1230 and 1245 (1820-1835).* ASO (D), Vol. 78, Letter from the Secretary to Government to the Board of Revenue, 12 July 1825.

39. See for example, Grover, B.R., 'Elements of Continuity and Change in the Land Ownership and Rights from the Mughal Age to the Early British Administration in India', Presidential Address, Medieval India Section, *Indian History Congress* (Calicut, 1976).

40. 'Report of Mr. W.T. Blair....', 30 October 1969, *op. cit.,* p. 312.

41. *Ibid.,* Also, APSA, *Cuddapah District Records* (1808), 635/48, Letter from Secretary Fort St. George to the Collector of Cuddapah, 21 March 1800.

42. TNSA, *Bellary Records,* 384/54; and *Selecttions from the Old Records of the Bellary District, 1800-1807,* ASO, Vol. 72, Circular issuedby Thomas Munro, 14 April 1807. J.C. Dua, 'Positions of the Patels and Karunums ...', *op. cit.*

43. TNSA, *Revenue Department, Minute of Consultation,* No. 533, 26 April 1845. Also *Ibid.,* pp. 312-313. A letter from Home Department (Revenue) to the Secretary to Government Fort St. George (22 August 1846) reveals that some *in'amdars* produced *sanads* even 150 years old granting them the *in'ams,* Collector of Cuddapah advocated to the Board of Revenue for the continuation of the *in'ams*; and the Government did not have any objection to that. See, NAI, *Home Land Revenue* (22 August 1846), pp. 11-15, 'Cuddapah', instructions re. Certain *in'ams* in'.

44. TNSA, *Official Report of a Revolt by Polegar Narasimha Reddy in Koilcuntla Taluk in 1846,* ASO (D), Vol. 113 (Vol. III), Letter from S. Scott, Agent to the Governor to the Chief Secretary to Government, Fort St. George, 11 May 1847. *Selection of Papers relating to the Revolt of the Poligar Narasimha Reddi of Koilkuntla* (1846), ASO (D), vol. III, (Vol. I), Letter from J.K. Cochrane, Ag. Magistrate to H.C. Montgomery, Offg. Secretary to Government, 15 April 1847. (Hereafter, *Official Report of a Revolt,* Vol. III and *Papers Relating to Revolt,* Vol. I respectively).

45. TNSA, Col. *Munro's Correspondence regarding the Survey and Ryotwari Settlement of the Ceded Districts, 1802-1827,* ASO (D), Vol. 79, Munro to his subordinate

collectors regarding the modes of conducting the Ryotwari Settlement, 30 Settlement 1802.

46. TNSA, *Mintues of Consultation,* Judicial, 9 October 1846.

47. *Ibid.,* Also *Official Report of a Revolt by PalegarNarasimha Reddy in Koilkuntla Taluk in 1846,* (ASO (D), Vol. 112 (Vol. II), (hereafter *Official Report of a Revolt,* Vol. II), Letter from W.A.D. Inglis, Special Commissioner at Cuddapah to Sir H.C. Montgomery Bart Offg. Secretary to Government, Judicial Department, 19 Januray 1847.

48. *Ibid.*

49. TNSA, *Selections from the Old Records of the Bellary District,1800-1807,* ASO (S), Vol. 72, Letter from Thomas Munro to the Chief Secretary to Government, 30 September 1801, Also, *Thomas Munro's Report Regarding the Poligars,* 20 March 1802.

50. TNSA, *Selection from the Old Records of the Bellary District, 1800-1807,* ASO (D), Vol. 72, Thomas Munro to the Secretary of Police, 10 April 1806.

51. APSA, *Cuddapah District Recrods* (f. 1231), 419/348, Letter from D. Hill, Secretary to Government to the President and Members of the Board of Revenue, 18 September 1821. Also quoted in the letter from W.A.D. Inglis, 19 January 1847, *op. cit.*

52. In this regard, see the observations made in Dua, J.C., 'Comparative Position of the Village Headmen During the Early British Rule in the Punjab and the Madras Presidency', *Punjab History Conference,* Patiala, 23rd session, 1987. Also in, Dua, J.C, *Agrarian System, op. cit.,* p. 124.

53. Letter from W.A.D. Inglis, 19 January 1847, *op. cit.*

54. *Ibid.,* It is quite strange that there is some discrepancy in the reports submitted by W.A.D. Inglis and J.H. Cochrane. As against the information regarding *Kattubadi in'ams* provided by Inglis, according to Cochrane the position was: There were a total number of 8985 *kattubadis* in the Cuddapah District. According to the latest regulatoins each *kattubadi* would get an *in'am* of worth survey assessment Rs. 23-10-0, for one life and thereafter was to be remunerated in cash. The implications of the Regulation was that *in'ams* of 1557 *kattubadis* were to be resumed on the occurrences of lapses. The *in'ams* 1396 *kattubadis* which were in excess of the amount fixed were proposed to be reduced on their demise to the required standard (and were to be for one life only). The emoluments of remaining 6032 *kattubadis* were to be raised to the minimum standards. (Letter of J.H. Cochrane, 11 September 1847, *op. cit.*).

55. TNSA, *Proceedings of the Board of Revenue,* 10 August, 1848; *Minutes of Consultation,* Judicial, 27 May 1847, 4 Januray 1848 and 8 February 1848. *Papers relating to Revolt,* Vol. I, Letter from J.H. Cochrane, Ag. Magistrate to H.C. Montgomery, Offg. Secretary to Government, 15 April 1847, (Letter from W.A.D. Inglis, 19 January 1847, *op. cit.,* NAI, *Home, Land Revenue,* 17 May 1845 (10-12), Letter from Secretary, Board of Revenue, Fort St. George to Acting Chief Secretary to Government, 26 April 1830.

56. Letter from W.A.D. Inglis, 19 January 1847, *op. cit.*
57. Letter from W.A.D. Inglis, 19 January 1847, *op. cit.*
58. Letter from W.A.D. Inglis, 15 September 1847, *op. cit.*
59. Letter from W.A.D. Inglis, 19 January 1847, *op. cit.*
60. *Ibid.*
61. *Ibid.*
62. Letter from Cochrane, J.H., 15 September 1847, *op. cit., Papers Relating to Revolt,* Vol. I. Letter from Cochrane, J.H., Acting Collector to the Secretary to Government (Judicial Department), 12 July 1846. Two things could be learnt from these letters: (1) the important persons he met including Panpa Khan of Kurnool, Latchman Royadu, palegar of Jutapolur and Rama Krishna Reddy, palegar of Wunpurty, both in Hyderabad and Palegar of Owk, and (2) he asked the Owk palegar to request Pumpaputy Raju, Palegar of Annaugundy to write to other palegars in the Bellary district.
63. In this regard see, for example, *Papers Relating to Revolt,* Vol. I, Letter from Cochrane, J.H., to the Secretary to Government, 10 August 1846; 7 September 1846, 16 November 1846.
64. Cochrane, J.H., in his letters to the Officer Commanding, Ceded Districts, 11 July 1846, and to the Agent to the Governor, 12 July 1846 (*Official Report of a Revolt,* Vol. IV), and to the Secretary to Government (Judicial Department), 12 July 1846 (*Papers Relating to Revolt,* Vol. ) put the figures at 9000. Cochrane in his letter to the Magistrate of Guntur, 20 July 1846 (*Offcial Report of a Revolt,* Vol. IV) put the figures at 3,000. But in his letter to H.C. Montgomery, Offg. Secretary to Government, 15 Aprl 1847 (*Papers Relating to Revolt,* Vol. I) stated that the number of followers never increased more than 200. Commander Detachment 19th Regiment in his letter to the Officer Commanding Field Detachment 19th Regiment, 29 July 1846 (*Official Report of a Revolt,* Vol. III) put the figures at 4,000.
65. *Papers Relating to Revolt,* Vol. I, Cochrane to the Secretary to Government, 10 August 1846. TNSA, *Minutes of Consultation, Judicial Department,* No. 441, 27 July 1846.
66. See for example, *Official Report of a Revolt,* Vol. IV, Cochrane, J.H., to the Agent to the Governor at Kurnool, 25 July 1846. *Papers Relating to Revolt,* Vol. I, Cochrane to the Secretary to Government, 28 July 1846 and 10 August 1846.
67. *Papers Relating to Revolt,* Vol. , Letter from Cochrane to the Secretary to Government, 7 October 1846.
68. TNSA, *Revenue Despatch to the Honourable Court of Directors,* 2 November 1846, No. 49.
69. Report of Blair, W.T., 30 October 1869, *op. cit.*
70. *Official Report Regarding the Revolt,* Vol. V, Extracts Minutes of Consultations, 2 March 1847.
71. TNSA, *Judicial Despatch from the Court of Directors,* 13 October 1847, No. 19.

72. *Ibid.*

73. The instructions issued were through—*Minutes of Consultation,* 9 May 1848; *Minutes of Consultation,* 11 May 1848; *Proceedings of the Board of Revenue,* 19 June 1848; *Minutes of Consultation,* 4 July 1848 and *Board's Circular Order,* 27 July 1848. For details see, *The In'am Settlement Papers,* G.O. No. 677, Revenue, 22 March 1861, pp. 183-93; G.O. No. 2330, Revenue, 7 December 1860, pp. 193-202; and Report by W.T. Blair, *op. cit.*

74. *Ibid*

75. Quoted in the Report of W.T. Blair, *op. cit.,* pp. 314-15.

76. The study of, for instance, the *In'am Fair Registers* in the Collector Office, Anantapur shows that one Duar Chola Terimungala Rao Maharah, Paddinonikalva Village, Rayachoti Taluk was confirmed an *in'am* on 1/8th quit rent but in 1935 he was fully assessed. There are cases where ½ and in some ¼ quit-rent was charged. Then there were *in'ams* which were confirmed only for one-two lives. Amongst various other registers, one known as *Statement showing the Village Service In'ams Fully Assessed in the Taluk of—in the District of*—itself means that the *in'amdars* incorporated in that were not holding *in'ams* on concessional rates. While in *Quit Rent Register of Personal In'ams in the Taluk of —in the District of*—to quote one example, Kadavella Devappa, who had acres 46.58 in dry and 17.01 in wet land and whose survey assessment was Rs. 89-14-9, was paying same amount as quit-rent.

## *Lecture III*

# Comparative Study of the Nature of the Two Phases of Palegars Resistance

The palegar resistance, though apparently looks like a challenge to the English system of law, revenue, production and property relations and thus offers the most intelligible clue to proper understanding and a rational evolution to its nature, could easily be bracketed together with the spontaneous resistance against the English East India Company which continued in India for nearly hundred years preceding the revolt of 1857. A close examination of the history of India as a whole shows that this process had started right since the early eighteenth century, the period which witnessed the emergence of rebel *zamindars* of different categories and the palegars. Their main aim was to seek greater share in the power over, and thus in the revenues of, their region. These revolts were sometimes directed against the state, and sometimes against the nobles in the respective regions who, with the emerging political situation had begun to dictate state actions. However, during the course of the period, the scuffle between different *zamindars*/palegars was also not uncommon. In certain areas, including the ones under study, the *zamindars* acted as 'local despots', and were in an uncompromising conflict with the state authorities. They allied with the state rulers only due to two broad reasons, (i) in the face of the fear, and (ii) with an objective of promoting and protecting their self-interests *vis-a-vis* the others within the region. Whenever they found themselves strong enough, they would be up in arms. However, as their interests were invariably narrow and parochial, they could not effectively incorporate the interests of other fellow *zamindars*/palegars. They relied mainly on the support from peasants, smaller *zamindars* and the local officials, but that support was forthcoming again because of fear or for promoting individual interests. In these conditions of unfattered political and military adventurism, it is noteworthy that none of the adventurer *zamindars*/palegars was either strong enough to be able to win the allegiance of others or in a position to replace the state power. They would struggle separately for their individual fortunes and thereby threatened each other's position and achievements. In the event of success in the establishment of dominance by some over the others, the former would, however, definitely seek to institutionalize validation of their spoils which necessitated the need of a centre to legitimize their acquisitions.[1]

The second half of the eighteenth century witnessed the beginning of the process of the British Conquest of India and the consolidation of the English rule was accompanied by serious discontent and resentment among the people. The popular discontent took the form of armed resistance led, amongst others, by the palegars of the Ceded Districts.[2] Since the military contingents were maintained by the palegars out of the revenues assigned to them, the tendency on the part of the state was to set the revenue demand at the highest rate possible so as to secure the greatest military strength for the state and to keep as little as possible with the palegar so that his military and political designs were kept in check. Whereas the palegar would try to collect the maximum, legally or even otherwise, to enhance his social and military status and to keep his political hopes alive. As such, the main point of conflict between the state and the palegars was the size of latters share in the revenues. The dilemma faced by the palegars was that it was difficult for them to collect the revenues, pay that or *peshkash* or both to the authorities without harming their own interests. The geographical conditions of the Ceded Districts had also contributed to make the situations there still worse. It is well known that usually, the areas, which were protected in some measures by ravines or forests or hills, were more likely to defy the authorities than those in the open plains. During the Mughal period these areas were known as *mawâs* and *zor-talab,* as opposed to the revenue paying villages, called *ra'iyati.* Refusal to pay the revenue or *peshkash* or both, as the case might be, on the part of the palegars, and attempts, on the part of the Company, to force them not only to pay the same but also curb their military and political power, led the former to show resistance. It frequently turned into armed conflict and became an important feature of the political situation of the time,[3]

The Company aimed at the liquidation of the landed elite and favoured corporate village groups or the individual *rayat* rather than the palegars, making them (the *rayats*) responsible to Government for revenue. Barrington Moore, Jr., for example, writes, "A paternal attitude toward the peasantry, a romantic and self-serving notion that the strong and simple folk could and should be the source and justification of their power, constituted a powerful theme in British policy throughout the occupation, even if peasant benefit therefrom are dubious.[4] It can, as such, be safely argued that the palegar resistance was part of the, to use the term used by Kathleen Gough, 'Restorative Movements'. It was either against the conquest itself and the imposition of heavy revenue or *peshkash* on the palegars, or retaliatory attempts to drive out the British after they had dispossessed a palegar or a raja for failing to pay the revenues/*peshkash* and had replaced him with some other claimant to the *palaiyam* or with direct company's administration. Their aim was, to quote Kathleen Gough again, "complete annihilation or expulsion of the British and reversion to the previous government and agrarian relations".[5]

The nature of the palegar resistance during the early nineteenth century has been dealt in great detail by Professor K. Rajayyan.[6] Though concentrating mainly on the areas other than the ones presently under discussion, general remarks on the palegar institution and the resistance have been discussed in great length. An analysis of the above painstaking work shows that if the British were at one extreme and called the palegars as 'robbers, freebooters, marauders and the like', Professor Rajayyan is on the other extreme, calling the palegar resistance as 'The First War of Independence' and 'the most widespread of all the liberation wars of the pre-Congress epoch and the first and the last violent popular struggle of any formidable dimensions in the annals of British India.' However, as has been discussed earlier, the palegars were subjected to, at least at the time of the inception of this institution, set and well defined rules, duties and responsibilities. It may or may not be true about the earlier period, but it is quite evident from the contemporary records of Haider and Tipu that during 'the last decades of the eighteenth century' a new phenomenon could be traced in the working of the palegar institution.

The Company took severe action against the palegars when the *peshkash*, fixed and demanded, was refused. That is notwithstanding the fact that palegars were up in arms immediately after the districts were ceded to the Company. Technically speaking the English were following the policy already adopted earlier by Haider Ali and Tipu Sultan as far as the fixation of the land revenue and the amount of *peshkash* were concerned. That is a different matter that they (palegars) could evade complete extinction or annihilation earlier either due to the then political situations or by using the tactic of yielding allegiance to each new master and had not only managed to reassert their authority but had appeared even stronger.

It is true that large sections of peasants and artisans as well as locally recruited 'peons' joined the palegar resistance and formed its backbone. It, however, does not mean that they had whole-hearted sympathy for the palegars. They had joined it because of their own grievances and hardships.[7] In the Ceded Districts where the *rayatwari* system of land revenue 'predominated the peasant holding land on the rights of the *rayat'* was equally exploitative as was the case in its counterpart in the *zamindari* regions, where big landed proprietorship predominated. As a matter of fact, the essential distinctions between the various types of revenue systems introduced by the East India Company and the forms of agrarian relations accruing out of them did not alter the basic fact that the agrarian system and methods of exploiting the peasants developed in one and the same direction throughout the country. The land revenue policy of the British authorities pursued the aim of obtaining highest possible revenues and maintaining them at the achieved level. Under earlier regimes the revenue demand was usually adjusted according to the results of the harvest. Furthermore, the peasant could cultivate more or less land in keeping with the availability of family labour and other things.

These elements of flexibility had disappeared under the English rule. As such, it can safely be presumed that the peasants were not blind loyalists.[8]

As regards those who formed the militia of the palegars, their loyalty to the latter was as doubtful as that of the palegars themselves towards their suzerain. If the palegars were more interested in the advancement of the power of their own *palaiyams*, their military personnels were more concerned about their own service *in'ams*, known as *kattubadi in'ams*. When they were offered employment and the grant of fresh *sanads* in the name of the Company, especially when the palegars were officially relieved from all military services their loyalty towards the palegars became extremely shaky. Once they were convinced that there was no intention of resuming their *in'ams*, and thinking that it was much more likely that the palegars would be driven out, they considered their own tenure under the Company more sure than under the palegars.[9]

The institution of caste also does not seem to have helped in making the palegar resistance as a popular movement. This institution, of course, provided a way of organizing the local community in such a way as to make the state authority something superfluous rather than something to be changed when things went wrong. As a matter of fact, it was practically from the beginning of the twentieth century when 'The imperial system had...created a new political arena within which to compete for rights, precedence, and resources in the public domain', that the caste political associations 'became a recognized institutional means for voicing demands in the media and in the urban context of government decision making'.[10]

It, as such, can be maintained that the partisans of the theories like the 'national awakening', or 'The First War of Independence' in regard to the palegar resistance have relied more on present sentiment than on contemporary evidence. The reader may judge their case as presented in their own writings. Our main concern is with what late eighteenth and the early nineteenth century sources/ authorities have to say, It will be seen that they, at any rate, put the greatest store by the political, economic and administrative causes of the resistance and know little of national consciousness. Right since the disintegration of the Vijayanagar empire, except when they were forced especially by the rulers like Haider Ali and Tipu Sultan, the palegars had followed the practice of the evasion of the payment of taxes/revenue/*peshkash*. They had once again got a free hand when the areas came under the Nizam. All this had not only resulted into the increase of their territorial possessions but had also enhanced their economic and military power. It, however, goes without saying that they were landed *zamindars*, having set economic and military duties to perform for which they had been assigned lands. It was obligatory on their part to pay the revenues or *peshkash* or both, as the case might be. Their practically continuous success in evading to perform their obligations was tantamounted of their independence.

So long as there was more than one centre of political power the palegars continued to have divided loyalties. When one area was transferred from Vijayanagar to the Golconda or Bijapur or the Mughals, the Marathas and so on, the palegars of that area were slow to transfer their loyalties to their new masters. Similar was the situation when the areas came under the East India Company. The palegars often supported their deposed or earlier chief, either because of their loyalties or for their self interests, against the Company as long as there was the slightest hope of his restorations.[11] Gribble has rightly pointed that the palegars had 'seen so many successive governments that it can be understood they did not expect the British rule would be a permanent one'.

If the palegar resistance in the Ceded Districts is not judged in isolation and if an attempt is made to draw parallels with other such incidents, especially the events of 1857, the question of non-acknowledgement of the English suzerainty on the part of the palegars may also appear as one of the important factors of their resistance.

The British occupation in India was looked upon as nothing short of the usurpation of the authority by them. They could in no way be less 'usurper' than was Haider Ali or for that matter palegars were considered by them. The source of the establishment of English control over the Ceded Districts was either in sword or the political intrigues that Nizam was unable to understand. There may not be any evidence to prove it but hypothetically it could be observed that it might be a matter of non-recognition of the English as the suzerain power by the palegars, which led the latter to resist the English authority. In any case, whether usurper or legitimate, the restrictions imposed by the Company's government upon the palegars were bound to invite resistance from them.

It may, thus, be observed that this phase of the palegar resistance was based on the traditional links and qualified loyalties between the peasants and the palegars or the petty chieftains. This resistance was wholly local and isolated in character lacking required mass appeal. Its main objective was the restoration of the political, administrative and economic powers lately or heretofore enjoyed by the palegars. It was, like other contemporary, 'Restorative revolts', backward looking and in no way attracted any modern feeling of nationalism. Nor did it have any 'modern understanding of the nature and character of colonialism or the building of a new society on the basis of new social relationships.' The palegar resistance was represented by a leadership, which was, like the nature of opposition offered, pure and simple, traditional in character. The leaders were also absolutely ignorant about the changing world around them. Despite the fact that the English power had to, at times, deploy large armies to suppress the resistance, the palegars could not pose a real challenge to the Company. However, the palegars could not be denied the credit of the great contribution made by them in a long history of resistance against the foreign rule. Their resistance as well as other such revolts in India laid the foundations of valuable local traditions of struggle against the British rule.[12]

**Phase II**

"A strict observance of our treaties," spoke Benjamin Disraeli in the House of Commons on 27 July 1857, "the rigid maintenance of laws and customs of the people, and, above all, a faithful respect for our guarantees of their land...these were the sources of our strength, and upon these our great Indian statesmen always insisted. But, Sir, of late years a new principle appears to have been adopted in the Government of India...Everything in India has been changed. Laws and manners, customs and usages, political organizations, the tenure of property...everything in India has either been changed, or there is a suspicion among the population that a desire for change exists on the part of our Government".[13] In brief, for Disraeli, the primary mistake of British rule in India was its increasing tendency to interfere with the established rules and customs. It is true that the above observations were made while tracing the causes of the revolt of 1857, but they as well hold good for the resistance of 1846-47. Narasimha Reddi's resistance had taken place just about a decade before the revolt of a great magnitude like that of 1857. It was the first against the English policy towards the *in'am* lands at least in south India. In this regard, they completely neglected the value of the indigenous institutions as a means of giving social happiness and material well-being to the people.[14] They paid no attention, or, it seems, tried to test the then universal belief that the Indians generally did not care who ruled them as long they were left free to follow their immemorial customs. The result was that along with the other disgruntled elements, like the palegars, the English had also aroused the hostility of conservative elements generally by their seeming intention to subvert the traditional social order.

The first instructions pertaining to the *in'am* lands issued by Thomas Munro, were that all *in'ams* which had been granted under the *sanad* of Haider Ali, or Tipu Sultan, or some of the more ancient princes or their ministers were not to be resumed.[15] In case of the areas under Cuddapah Collectorate, Munro directed Alexander Stodart, the Collector, that 'the *in'ams*, though granted originally by Amildars or inferior revenue officers may be continued', provided that they had been held since the extinction of the Nawab's power and commencement of Haider's Government, without interruption. His interpretation about such *in'ams* being that such long possession constituted 'a kind of prescriptive right'.[16]

It is important to note that a considerable number of old *in'ams*, which had been suppressed due to various reasons by the different *karnams* of Ceded Districts were also restored.[17] As a matter of fact, Munro was neither in favour of the resumption of the *in'ams* nor wanted that they should be replaced by cash salary or pension. According to him, a pension could never be considered as a compensation for the loss of landed property. "It is neither so honourable nor so secure," he argued. He also reasoned, "The amount of their Enam lands in the Ceded Districts is so inconsiderable that Government might, with hardly any perceptible loss of revenue, continue them as they are, until they should gradually revert by the failure of the different families by which they are at present enjoyed".[18] It would not be wrong to conclude that his land settlement as well as *in'am* policy laid the true foundation of peace in the turmoil stricken Ceded Districts. In addition to the reasons mentioned above, he continued *in'ams* on the ground that it was as 'difficult for the *In'amdar* to verify his title as for the Sirkar to disprove it,'[19] and permitted the holding of service lands by village officials (like *patels, karnams* etc.) upto 10 percent of their village revenue, with a view to facilitate the rapid creation of private property in land.[20] He did not resume any of the lands of religious and charitable institutions, but, however, exercised control against misappropriation.[21]

As regards the *kattubadi in'ams*, Thomas Munro in 1801 observed that the loss to the revenue by the continuation of those *in'ams*, 'would not be so great as it may at first sight appear'.[22] As late as 1841, A. Mellor, Collector of Bellary, while commenting 'on the propriety of making a direct payment in money...in lieu of assignments of land sanctioned' in *kattubadi* tenure, pointed out that those *in'ams* had been 'considered from time immemorial, (though in fact service *in'ams*), as a kind of *meeras*, little differing from simple hereditary property'. He warned, "To disturb this arrangement would produce a feeling of insecurity and discontent among the whole body of *in'amdars*".[23] Quoting Chaplin's views on the same subject with approval Mellar further explained that since they were accustomed to the possession of *in'am* land, and to transmit that possession from father to son, 'they naturally feel strong attachment to their hereditary property and would not willingly relinquish it for any pay, however, high'. By giving detailed figures, though about Bellary district, he tried to stress that *in'ams* were more economical than paying *kattubadis* cash salaries.

The correspondence pertaining to the year 1843 shows that even in that year *in'ams* in the Ceded Districts were 'confirmed and continued in perpetuity' on the recommendation of the Collector, the Board of Revenue, the Governor of Fort St. George and authorization by the Governor General.[24]

Right since the formation of the Ceded Districts in 1800, there had been a continuous desire and demand on the part of the English administrators to conduct a survey and inquiry into the nature and extent of the *in'am* lands. The inquiry conducted by Thomas Munro in the initial stages was described by the authorities in the Madras Presidency as 'superficial' and inadequate.

It could not ascertain the extent of 'Sirkar land surreptitiously held as Enam'. Stating that they had 'long wished that an enquiry should be instituted respecting them (*in'ams*)', the Board of Revenue asked William Chaplin (1809) to 'institute a general enquiry into Enam Lands, or at all events threat to do so'.[25] The Board of Revenue through their Minute (9 May 1811) simply asserted that the Government had a right to dispossess the *in'amdars* if they renounced their service upon which they held their lands.[26] Chaplin, in the same year reiterated that though the *in'ams*, under the rules, were 'resumable at the pleasure of the ruling authority', and 'however strictly the scrutiny into them may be carried on', the object could 'hardly be accomplished without instituting new rules for investigating the validity of titles'.[27]

By the above discussion, an attempt has been made to stress upon the fact that if the Government had reason to believe that many of the *in'ams* were held upon forged documents, it was no more than their duty, and perfectly consonant to justice, to investigate such cases, and resume the lands proved to be so held. In any case, they should have borne in mind that the investigations and decisions were ought to be speedy, final, and good. Had there been a proper provision for that purpose, there would have been little to complain of. Even in 1842, as is evident from Lord Elphinstone's Minute of the same year, the position of investigation was no better than what it was in 1801.

The inordinate delay on the part of the English Government in conducting a proper investigation into the *in'am* lands, and even grant of fresh *in'ams*, despite periodic orders for an enquiry, had given hopes to *in'amdars* about the continuation of their land grants in perpetuity. In India every situation held for a long while has a tendency to become hereditary (e.g. *patel, karnam, qazi, in'amdar* etc.) and the natives of all classes are peculiary ready in advancing claims".[28]

History and common sense alike show that an armed resistance or a rebellion can never take place without provocation. The question is, had the English Government given such provocation? The palegar Narasimha Reddi along with some of his breathren and the *bhatta-vritti* and *kattubadi in'amdars* saw their power, their privileges, and their perquisites crumbling away from them, and they tried to gird themselves up to arrest the devastation.

The conversion of hereditary pensions/*in'ams* into personal annuities was, to quote Disraeli, "confiscation by a new means, but on most extensive, startling and shocking scale".[29] The palegars were reduced to utmost humiliation and almost to absolute beggary. The government had practically disturbed the settlement of property by their conduct with regard to the resumption of *in'ams*, by abolishing the principle of heredity, and by changing the *in'ams* into annuities.

It was the responsibility of the government to protect the society and the social order, and, as far as possible, 'every member of the society from the injustice or oppression of every other member of it', and 'establishing an exact administration of justice'.[30] Before promulgating a legislative enactment, the government should have, through local enquiry and research, looked into the traditions of the society.[31] "Whether the state should interfere at all; on what principle; with what limitations; what property, if any, should be . . . inalienable; what means of protection, temporary or permanent, the state should create or allow to be created; are all questions to which", remarked Mr. Justice West, "clear answers, appropriate to the people and their circumstances, should be obtained by a Government anxious to deal beneficiently and consistently with the problems connected with the occupancy of the soil in this country".[32]

Thomas Munro was quite critical of the activities of the civil and military officers who by acting precipitately, often upon wrong information, involved government in hostilities.[31] He not only blamed their misconduct for the insurrection of petty chiefs, but also cautioned his government "not to be led away by fanciful theories founded on European models, which will inevitably end in disappointment".[34]

The opinion expressed by Thomas Munro was in no way less than a warning to the future English administrators also that nothing disgusted the natives of this country more than the resumption of traditionally revenue free lands, and their resumption would set the whole people against the English. Though initially only *bhatt-vritti* and *kattubadi in'ams* were being resumed or their nature was being changed, it could rightly be contemplated that the other category of *in'ams*, as was indicated by different Regulations, could no longer be safe either. Apart from the brahmins and the *kattubadis*, the *patels*, *karnams* and even weavers, carpenters, smiths, barbers, washermen, potters or for that matter every artisan and labour were primarily paid by an allotment of *in'am* land. Their *in'ams* were 'adequate to keep a family in comfort as tropical needs go, though not in luxury'.[35] In case of any danger to their *in'ams*, the resentment was obvious. The English government could hardly expect tenderness from those, whose *in'ams* had been resumed, or their hereditary nature scrapped, or those whose *in'ams* could be adversely affected in the foreseeable future.

The tradition of the *in'am* lands had been so deep-rooted in the Indian social order that not only in the Ceded Districts but in other parts of India also, when the subject of their resumption came, it became a topic of lengthy discussions, difference of opinions amongst the English administrators, and even led to the cases before the Privy Council. In Punjab (1849-53), for example, there was difference of opinion between the two Lawrences, Henry and John, whether the grants assigned for the services no longer wanted, or could not be maintained, were to be continued. Whereas Henry held that 'grants ought to be continued, although the obligation of service might be remitted,' John wanted that 'these grants must at once be curtailed, and provision made for their cessation on the demise of present incumbents.'[36]

The case of Khurda (Orissa), which was incidentally also under the *rayatwari* system, was not only interesting but also almost similar to that of the Ceded Districts. Khurda also witnessed resistance (1838 onwards) due to the resumption and assessment of certain revenue-free tenures. The agitation spread from a small and influential class to the whole estate. H.A.D. Phillips, criticising the English policy, pointed out, 'To say the least, it is an unwise policy to interfere with customary rights.' The ruling given by the Privy Council in this regard, as stated by Phillips, pointed out:

> The distinction between the grant of an estate burdened with certain service, and the grant of an office, the performance of whose duties are remunerated by the use of certain lands, and have ruled that a tenure of the former description cannot be resumed merely on the ground that the service is no longer required . . The *Sanad* did not state that the tenure was to cease, if the services ceased. The Privy Council held that the grant had been made *proservitiis impensis et imendendis*—partly as a reward for past, part an inducement for future services. . they may be liable to forfeit the tenure if they willfully fail in the performance of . . duty, are not liable to have their land resumed, because there is no longer any occasion for the performance of . . particular service.[37]

The case of *bhatta-vritti* and *kattubadi in'ams* in the Ceded Districts was in no way different to that of the *in'ams* in Khurda. Despite suggestions, warnings and cautions, the Company initiated the policy of the resumption of the *in'am* lands. The hereditary palegars backed by a proud ancestry, and the *in'amdars*, with a long possession of lands for generations, had undoubtedly momentous consequence in the continuous continuation of the mainstream of life, and so alike in a political and social view the extinction of these classes was fraught with serious repercussions. Lord Macaulay aptly remarked in 1844 that "of all forms of tyranny the worst is that of a nation over a nation."[38]

As far as Narasimha Reddy was concerned, undoubtedly, he had his own reasons of discontentment. He was the successor of one of those chiefs who had already, willingly or unwillingly, submitted to the English. The submission of a particular chief or a palegar of a *palaiyam* did not necessarily guarantee the loyalty and fidelity of his successors. The terms accepted by a palegar might not be acceptable to his successor, and the paramount power had to win over the loyalty of the new palegar afresh, which might not be so easily forthcoming. Moreover, the prerogative exercised by the paramount power in matters of succession to a *palaiyam* and the right to recognize or de-recognize a palegar greatly helped in sowing the seeds of resistance, especially in case of Narasimha Reddy. He took full advantage of the situations created by the English policy towards the *in'am* lands and found a favorable opportunity to give vent to his own grievances. However, in any case the resistance was not for getting freedom but to force the government to take corrective measures.

The noteworthy aspect of this resistance was the co-operation of the general people, the *kattubadis*, brahmins, some of the fellow palegars, the country people and the villagers of the different social status including the *patels*. The brahmins, who had become hostile to the English because of the latters, policy towards the *bhatta-vritti in'ams*, used their influence in the society and created better atmosphere for the resistance. It helped, to a great extent, in keeping the British intelligence at bay and people would never give correct report about the whereabouts of Narasimha Reddy and his associates. E.J. Hobsbawn has classified the resistance of Narasinha Reddy and his followers as 'social banditry.'[39] Wherever such activities called forth the support of large bodies of common people, as distinct from personal retainers or mercenaries, wherever some initiative in the struggle passed to inhabitants of the affected area, one cannot in fairness deny the existence of a resistance movement.[40]

This shows that this phase of resistance was not aimed to gain any political power, as was the case with the palegar resistance of late 18th and early 19th centuries, but was essentially a socio-economic one in which a considerable section of the people felt, however dimly, the stirring of a common impulse.

## References


1. Dua, J.C., *British Historiography: Eighteenth Century Punjab* (New Delhi, 1992), 'Preface' and 'Introduction'. Dua, J.C., 'Review Article' on K. Rajayyan, *South Indian Rebellion: The First War of Independence 1800-1801* (Mysore, 1971), in *The Indian Historical Review*, Vol. II, No. 2, January 1976, pp. 490-92. (Hereafter, 'Review Article'). Alam, Muzaffar, *The Crisis of Empire in Mughal North India: Awadh and the Punjab, 1707-48* (Delhi, 1986), pp. 13-17.
2. The armed resistance was in a large proportion led by Hindu and Muslim petty rulers, former revenue agents under the Mughals, tribal chiefs in hill regions, *zamindars* and the palegars. The most important leaders and the regions of the resistance were Raja Chait Singh and other Hindu and Muslim *zamindars* of Awadh in 1778-81; the subsequent revolt of Vizier Ali, the deposed Nawab of Awadh, in Banaras, Gorakhpur and surrounding areas in 1799, the resistance of the palegars and their peasants in Tinnevelly, North Arcot, and the Ceded Districts in 1800-05; the uprising of the Chuar tribesmen of Midnapore in 1799; the revolt of the Pazhassi Raja of Malabar in 1796-1805; and almost immediately afterwards, an insurrection further south in Travancore and Cochin by Velu Thampi. For further details in this regard see, Chaudhuri, S.B., *Civil Rebellion During the British Rule in India (1765-1857)*, (Calcutta, 1955), pp. 56-58, 74-76 and 125-32. Ghosh, Benoy, 'Prepolitical Rebellions in Bengal', *Frontier*, Calcutta, Vol. V, Nos. 27-29, 14 October 1972, pp. 9-14. Gough, Kathleen, 'Indian Peasant Uprisings', *Economic and Political Weekly*, Vol. IX, Nos. 32-34, Special Number, August 1974, pp. 1391-1412, also in Desai, A.R. (ed.), *Peasant Struggles in India* (Delhi, 1982), pp. 85-126. Chandra, Bipin, Tripathi, Amalesh, De Barun, *Freedom Struggle* (New Delhi, 1980), pp. 41-42, Dua, J.C., 'Review Article', *op. cit.*
3. For the geographical conditions of the Ceded Districts, see for example, TNSA. *Extract from Mr. William Thackeray's Report, 8 September 1807*, ASO (D), Vol. 66. Hamilton, Walter, *A Geographical, Statistical and Historical Description of Hindustan and the Adjacent Countries* (London, 1820, reprint, Madras 1990), II, pp. 323-27. For similarities of political situations during pre-British period see, Habib, Irfan, *The Agrarian System of Mughal India (1556-1707)*, (Bombay, 1963), pp. 318-51.
4. Moore, Jr. Barrington, *Social Origins of Dictatorship and Democracy: Lord and Peasant in the Making of the Modern World* (Penguin Books, 1969), pp. 348-49. Also see, Baden-Powell, B.H., *The Land-Systems of British India* (Oxford, 1892, reprint Delhi, 1974), II, pp. 20-21. Komarov, Erik, 'Content and Principal Forms of the Evolution of Agrarian Relations in India in the 19th Century', *New India Studies by Soviet Scholars—"Social Sciences Today"*, No. 33, 1976, pp. 34-47.
5. Gough, Kathleen, *op. cit.*
6. Rajayyan, K., *South Indian Rebellion: The First War of Independence 1800-1801* (Mysore, 1971).
7. Dua, J.C., 'Review Article', *op. cit.*

8. Dua, J.C., *Agrarian System in South India: Some Aspects* (New Delhi, 1990), p. 54. Komarov, Erik, *op. cit.* Rothermund, Dietmar, *The IndianEconomy Under British Rule and Other Essays* (New Delhi, 1983), pp. 4, 31. *East India Sugar: an Enquiry* (London, 1824), p. 8. 'The Land Revenue in Madras', *The Calcutta Review*, 1852, No. 34, p. 322.

9. TNSA, *Bellary Records* (1801), 391/34, Letter from George Garrow to Thomas Munro, 8 December 1801. *Col. Munro's Report Regarding the Poligars in the Ceded Districts with a Memorandum of Poligars (1801-1802)*, RSO (D), Vol. 62 (21), Letters from Thomas Munro to the President and Members of the Board of Revenue, 12 August 1801. *Selections from the Old Records of the Bellary District 1800-1807*, ASO (D), Vol. 72, Letter from Thomas Munro to the Secretary of the Committee of Police, 10 April 1806.

10. Ludden, David, *op. cit.*, pp. 195-96.

11. For such type of Parallels during the Mughal period see, Khan, Ahsan Raza, *Chieftains in the Mughal Empire During the Reign of Akbar* (Simla, 1977), pp. 219-20.

12. Dua, J.C., 'Review Article', *op. cit.*, 'Nature of the Palegar Revolts in the Ceded Districts During the First Half of the Nineteenth Century: A Case Study', *Indian History Congress Proceedings* (Jadavpur, 1974), pp. 235-45. Gough, Kathleen, *op. cit.*, Bipan Chandra, Amales Tripathi and Barun De, *op. cit.*

13. *Parliamentary Debates*, 3rd Series, Vol. 147, 27 July 1857, pp. 440-472; Speech by Benjamin Disraeli, excerpts given in the form of an article, 'Military mutiny or National Revolt', in Embree, Ainslie T. (ed.) *India in 1857: The Revolt Against Foreign Rule* (Reprint Delhi, 1987), pp. 9-21, especially 10-11.

14. Chaudhuri, S.B., *Civil Disturbances During the British Rule in India 1765-1857* (Calcutta, 1955), p. 207.

15. TNSA, *Selections From the Old Records of the Bellary District 1800-1807*, ASO (D), Vol. 72, 'Instructions issued by Col. Munro, Principal Collector to Mr. Cochrane, Collector of Bellary, 31 December 1800.

16. *Ibid.*, 'Instructions for Alexander Stodart'.

17. Thomas Munro to Board of Revenue, 13 May 1805, *op. cit.* Regarding the various reasons and circumstances under which the *karnams* used to suppress the information, also see, Dua, J.C., 'Position of the Patels and Karnams in the Ceded Districts during the First Quarter of the Nineteenth Century', in Bhattacharya, Sabyasachi (ed.), *Essays in Modern Economic History* (New Delhi, 1987), pp. 23-40.

18. Letter from Munro to the Board of Revenue, 13 May 1805, *op. cit.*

19. TNSA, *Selections from the Records of Bellary District—Political, Revenue and Agriculture Matters*, ASO (D), Vol. 73, Letter from William Chaplin to the Board of Revenue, 24 April 1814. Also, Sastri, K.N. Venkatasubba, *The Munro System of British Statesmanship in India* (Mysore, 1930), p. XIV.

20. *Ibid., Selections...*, ASO (D), Vol. 72, Thomas Munro to the Board of Revenue, 23 June 1801.

21. TNSA, *Revenue Despatch of the Court of Directors,* 30 August 1809, para 169.
22. TNSA, *Col. Munro's Report Regarding the Poligars in the Ceded Districts with a Memorandum of Poligars 1801-1802,* RSO (D), Vol. 62 (21), Letter from Thomas Munro to the Board of Revenue, 12 August 1801.
23. TNSA, *Correspondence regarding the Grants of Land Instead of Money Allowance to the Police Establishments and the Revision of Assessment 1841-1850,* ASO (D), Vol. 28 (75), Letter from A. Mellor, Collector Bellary to the Secretary and Board of Revenue, 13 March 1841.
24. NAI, *Home Department Land Revenue,* 7 October, 1843, 9-14 (b) Letter from A. Mellor, Collector of Bellary to C. Lovell, Acting Secretary to the Board of Revenue, Fort St. George, 10 May 1843; Same to same, 25 July 1843; Home Department, Revenue to the Chief Secretary to the Government, Fort St. George, 7 October 1843 (dispatched on 13 October 1843).
25. For the difficulties faced by the collector in making the settlement, see, TNSA, *Bellary Records* (F. 1219), 417/348, Letter from Chaplin, Collector to the Board of Revenue, 2 November 1809'; and for the remedy suggested see 417/462, Letter from Secretary, Fort St. George to the collector of Bellary, 13 November 1809.
26. TNSA, *The Proceedings of the Board of Revenue on the Introduction of Village Lease in the Ceded Districts—1811,* ASO (D), Vol. 31 and 32, Minute of the Board, 9 May 1811.
27. APSA, *Cuddapah Records* (1811), 637/352, Letter from William Chaplin to the Board of Revenue, 10 June 1811.
28. TNSA, *Minutes of Consultations,* 9 October 1846, para. 8.
29. Speech by Benjamin Disraeli, *op. cit.*
30. 'Adam Smith on government responsibility', in *Readings in Economic and Social History,* Selected and Edited by M.W. Flin (London, First Edition 1964, Reprint 1965), p. 178-79.
31. Kurnool Collectorate Library, *Papers Relating to Reform of Police in India,* 1861, J/154, Minute by the Hon. Mr. Fullerton, 27 April 1816.
32. Kurnool Collectorate Library, *Selection from Papers on Indebtedness and Land Transfer,* J/276, Mr. Justice West's "The Land and the Law in India", 1872.
33. Thomas Munro to the R. Hon, C.B. Bathurst, 28 September 1821, Gleig, II, pp. 50-60.
34. Thomas Munro's Minute, 31 December 1824, *op. cit.*
35. Venkataramani, K.S., *The Indian Village: A Ten Year Plan* (Svetaranya Ashrama, Mylapore, Madras, 1936), pp. 6-7.
36. Temple, Sir Richard, *Lord Lawrence* (Macmillan, 1936), pp. 61-62.
37. Phillips, H.A.D., *Our Administration of India* (London, 1886), pp. 31-33.
38. Cited in Rao, M. Ramachandra, *The Development of Indian Polity* (Madras 1917), p. 61
39. Hobsbawn, E.J., 'Social Bandits: Reply (to Blok)', in *Comparative Studies in Society and History,* Vol. 14, No. 4, September 1972, p. 504.
40. For this type of opinion, also see, Chaudhuri, S.B., *op. cit.*, p. 261.

# *Index*

J